HAMMER OF ROME

www.penguin.co.uk

HAMMER OF ROME

Douglas Jackson

BANTAM PRESS

LONDON · NEW YORK · TORONTO · SYDNEY · AUCKLAND

TRANSWORLD PUBLISHERS
61–63 Uxbridge Road, London W5 5SA
www.penguin.co.uk

Transworld is part of the Penguin Random House group of companies
whose addresses can be found at global.penguinrandomhouse.com

First published in Great Britain in 2018 by Bantam Press
an imprint of Transworld Publishers

A CIP catalogue record for this book
is available from the British Library.

ISBNs 9780593076170 (cased)
9780593076187 (tpb)

Typeset in 11.5/15.25pt Electra by Jouve (UK), Milton Keynes
Printed and bound in Great Britain by Clays Ltd, Elcograf S.p.A.

Penguin Random House is committed to a sustainable
future for our business, our readers and our planet. This book
is made from Forest Stewardship Council® certified paper.

1 3 5 7 9 10 8 6 4 2

Hammer of Rome is dedicated to all of my loyal readers who've enjoyed the Valerius adventures, and without whose support they would never have been written. Thank you!

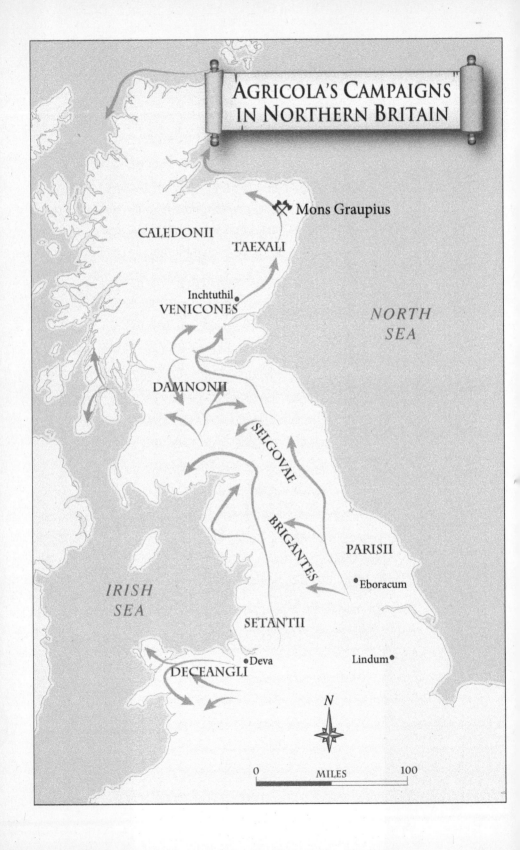

AGRICOLA'S CAMPAIGNS
IN NORTHERN BRITAIN

Mons Graupius

CALEDONII

TAEXALI

Inchtuthil
VENICONES

DAMNONII

SELGOVAE

BRIGANTES

PARISII

Eboracum

NORTH
SEA

IRISH
SEA

SETANTII

DECEANGLI

Deva

Lindum

N

0   MILES   100

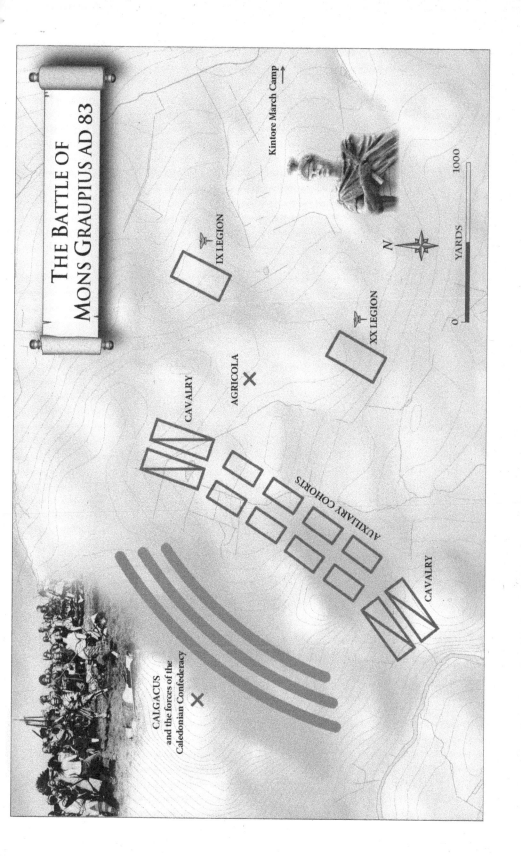

THE BATTLE OF MONS GRAUPIUS AD 83

Kintore March Camp

IX LEGION

XX LEGION

AGRICOLA

CAVALRY

AUXILIARY COHORTS

CAVALRY

CALGACUS
and the forces of the
Caledonian Confederacy

N

YARDS

0   1000

Cast of Characters

Gaius Valerius Verrens: Legate of the Ninth legion Hispana and a Hero of Rome

Titus Flavius Vespasian: Emperor of Rome

Titus Flavius Vespasian (Titus): The Emperor's elder son and his heir

Titus Flavius Domitianus (Domitian): The Emperor's younger son and Valerius's deadly enemy

Domitia (later Augusta): Domitian's wife and Valerius's former lover

Gnaeus Julius Agricola: Governor of Britannia

Domitia Decidiana: Agricola's wife

Tabitha: Valerius's wife and a princess of Emesa, mother of Lucius and Olivia

Gaius Rufus: Roman scout, midget, survivor of the Temple of Claudius

Quintus Naso: *Praefectus castrorum* of the Ninth, Valerius's second in command

Cornelius Felix: Commander of Valerius's escort, rank of decurion

Shabolz: Member of Valerius's escort, former Pannonian auxiliary

Hilario: Member of Valerius's escort

Rufius Florus: Member of Valerius's escort and Lucius's personal bodyguard

Ceris: Tabitha's maid/companion, a native Briton, Florus's lover

Cathal (known to the Romans as Calgacus): King of the Selgovae

Olwyn: Cathal's wife, mother of Dugald and Berta

Gwlym: A blind druid, fugitive from Mona, sometimes adviser to Cathal

Emrys: Cathal's sword brother and leader of his bodyguard

Colm: Cathal's bodyguard

Ranal: Cathal's bodyguard

The Argento Rìgh: King of the Venicones

Donacha: Venicones lord

Oenghus: Venicones druid

Crinan: King of the Caledonians

Rurid: Caledonian war chief

Bruda: A petty Caledonian chief

Vodenos: Leader of the Brigante contingent that fights beside Cathal

Metilius Aprilis: Agricola's aide and Valerius's enemy

Herenius Polio: Legate, Second legion Adiutrix

Tiberius Julius Ursus: Legate, Twentieth legion Valeria Victrix

Aulus Atticus: Prefect of the Ala Petriana, a cavalry wing of Gaulish auxiliaries

The enemy suddenly changed their plan, and with their whole force attacked by night the Ninth Legion, as being the weakest, and cutting down the sentries they broke into the camp.

Cornelius Tacitus, *Life of Julius Agricola*

I

Rome, AD 79

Titus Flavius Vespasian smiled at his friend across the glittering gold surface of the table, the flickering oil lamps creating shadows and planes on the other man's face that made him appear much older than his forty-five years.

'It was kind of you to invite me.' Aulus Caecina Alienus's voice echoed in the great chamber of the dining room. 'It is many years since I dined on the Palatine.'

'Of course,' Titus agreed blandly. 'Vitellius favoured the Domus Aurea, did he not? He found the palaces on the hill draughty and uncomfortable, I remember.' He took the sting from the words with a laugh. Caecina didn't like to be reminded of his service to the short-lived Emperor Vitellius and the rumours of plots, conspiracies and downright betrayal it involved. And not just rumours.

When the tide shifted and Vespasian's generals marched on Rome from the east, Caecina might have turned the campaign irrevocably in Vitellius's favour, but inexplicably – or perhaps not – offered to turn himself and his legions over to the Flavians. A misjudgement, it turned out. He'd misread the mood of his centurions, who promptly threw him in a cell to await execution. Only Vespasian's swift triumph saved him from the axe. Somehow, he'd also persuaded the new emperor to spare his life when his fellow generals were losing theirs. What was it they said of him? Yes, that was it. *Aulus Caecina Alienus could sell a wooden leg to a four-legged dog.* Titus laughed again and Caecina gazed at him with something like reverence.

A rogue, but an amusing one, charming with an endless supply of stories and anecdotes. Men instinctively liked him and women were attracted to him for reasons they could never explain. Once regarded as the most handsome man in Rome, his fine-boned features were puffy with excess and the dark eyes red-rimmed from the wine of the previous evening.

'What gossip do you have for me, Aulus?' Titus demanded as the *gustatio* of eggs and intricately carved vegetable dishes was placed on the table by a stream of slaves. Hidden away, but somewhere nearby, another slave played a pleasing melody on a lyre.

'You must hear all the interesting news,' Caecina said with a sly sideways look. 'Being the Praetorian prefect with access to all those ears at all those doors.' He grinned and took a long pull from the gold cup in front of him. An Opimian, by the gods; old Titus was doing him proud tonight. His voice dropped into a stage whisper. 'But I hear Julius, manager of the Greens, is to be brought up before the authorities for race fixing.'

'Never,' Titus gasped, knowing it wasn't true.

The courses came and went, with Caecina becoming increasingly voluble and Titus saying less and less. Eventually Caecina ran out of words and they sat together as the silence lengthened. Something had changed. Silence. Yes, that was it. Silence. The music had ended.

'Tell me about Marcellus, Aulus.' Caecina was puzzled for a moment. When the true import of the words struck he froze and stared at Titus as a mouse is transfixed by a snake. 'What gossip do you have about him?' Titus continued relentlessly. 'I heard a whisper that Diogenes and Heras were back, flapping their tongues.'

Caecina somehow forced a smile. 'I hear Flavinius . . .'

'I don't want to know about Flavinius, Aulus.' The voice contained a hint of iron that hadn't been apparent earlier. 'It's Marcellus I want to hear about. Marcellus and all your other friends. The ones who meet behind those closed doors when they think I am not listening.'

Caecina stared down at the table.

'Lost your tongue, Aulus?' Titus shook his head with genuine sorrow. 'I was so good to you all. Paid off Marcellus's gambling debts when Sabinus wanted to hire the Society to break his legs. Looked the other way the first time he brought those crooked lie-mongers to the city and I had to have them whipped from the Porta Salaria. And you, Aulus? How many husbands have I had warned off when they were waiting in some dark alley with their cudgels? How much do you still owe me from the loan for the house on the Esquiline?'

'Please, Titus, I'll pay. Just give me a chance.'

It was as if he hadn't spoken.

'But how can I forgive this? You have plotted against my father, the man who saved your life and treated you as a son. Colluded with the worst elements in the Senate and the military. No, don't deny it.'

How could he not have heard them? Rough hands took Caecina by the shoulders and forced him down so his face slammed on the table. He struggled, but there were too many of them and they were too strong. 'Please, Titus.' The words were incomprehensible because his broken lips were forced against the sheeted gold.

'I know what you've been saying to them, you and Marcellus and the others. My father is too old, or too sick, no longer up to the challenges of being Emperor. He must step down, or . . . well, we know what the alternative is, don't we, Aulus?' Caecina was weeping now. The metallic taste of blood from his nose and his smashed lips filled his mouth. 'And Titus?' the Emperor's son continued. 'Titus forfeited his right to be Emperor when he consorted with the Eastern bitch. That's what you called Berenice, wasn't it, Aulus, you of all people, who stalked her like a dog in heat? The Eastern bitch. Titus has none of his father's talents and all of his father's weaknesses. He's too trusting. Not ruthless enough . . .'

Caecina waited for more. Hoped for more. Prayed for the opportunity to talk himself out of this. He could, if only . . . He screamed as a hand wrapped itself in the thick dark hair he was so proud of and hauled his head back, exposing his neck. 'No, plea—' An almost innocuous sting across his throat and his vision turned black as a terrible prolonged gurgle punctuated the vain plea for a mercy that had never been on offer.

Above them, two men watched from a darkened balcony that stretched the length of the room.

'Let your brother's bearing be a lesson for you,' Titus Flavius Vespasianus Caesar Augustus told his younger son. 'If we are to survive as a family and our name is to endure as a dynasty we must act with strength, but compassion.'

Titus Flavius Domitianus, known as Domitian, looked from his father, bowed and rheumy-eyed with age, his hands shaking with some ague, to the man still sitting at the table as the dark stain spread wider and wider across the beaten gold. He understood this was not the only lesson he was supposed to learn from this exhibition. Caecina's murder was, in a way, a gift to him. Oh, Caecina was guilty enough, but put to the hot irons and the gouging hooks, he would have implicated not just Marcellus, but Priscus and the others. They in turn would have led the inquisitors to Mucianus, long dead, but still dangerous, because his circle contained others who would scream a name that could not be allowed to fall from any man's lips. His eyes never left his brother. 'You have my word on it.'

As he walked away, Vespasian's frail body was racked by a hacking cough that seemed to go on for ever. The Emperor put a cloth to his mouth. It came away bloody and he shook his head in confusion.

Domitian watched him go. Not long now, old man. Not long. At the end he might find some compassion for his father, but not for the others who stood in his way. Titus had overshadowed him since he was a boy. After Vespasian's accession to the purple the situation had become worse. Instead of basking in the reflected glory of the Emperor,

4

Domitian had been kept in the shadows and forced to live on scraps. No Praetorian prefect's power for the younger son, just a few humiliating part-time consulships. Worse was the fact that, even after all these years, every time he looked into his wife's eyes he saw the face of another man reflected there. So there would be no compassion for Titus Flavius Vespasian when the time came, as it surely must, or for Gaius Valerius Verrens, who had tried to steal Domitia Longina Corbulo from him, only utter ruthlessness.

II

Southern Brigantia

Gaius Valerius Verrens, legate of the Ninth legion Hispana, walked across the grassy hillside as the fog began to clear. His bodyguard had tried to persuade him to stay away, but he insisted on inspecting the ground his men had just fought over. One of the legion's auxiliary flanking cohorts had caught a band of Brigante spearmen in the open as they waited in ambush. Bodies littered the ground in that curious, boneless attitude of the dead, limbs twisted into impossible positions and dull, sightless eyes staring at the sky. In places where they'd fought to the last the corpses were so thick on the ground Valerius was forced to take a wide loop to avoid stepping on them. Crimson blood trails showed where men had staggered or crawled from the field in an attempt to save themselves. This was what happened when lightly armed, undisciplined barbarians met hardened Roman soldiers in open combat.

'How many casualties, Barbarus?' He directed the question at the decurion who'd commanded the auxiliaries, a swarthy bearded veteran wearing the distinctive green cloak of the Asturian cohort.

'Just the three, lord, and a few scratches. But we killed forty or fifty of theirs.' He saw Valerius's look and shrugged. 'We tried to follow your orders about bringing in prisoners, but they just didn't want to surrender.'

Valerius called for his horse. The Ninth and its auxiliary cohorts and cavalry wings made up the eastern column of the twin-pronged northern campaign. Two more legions, the Twentieth and the Second Augusta, mirrored this advance up the western flank of the mountains which made up the spine of the island. Valerius had initially marched on the Brigante capital at Isurium, but the Ninth found the settlement empty of King Guiderius and his warriors. Rather than negotiating a treaty of surrender and taking hostages, Valerius was met by a group of stony-faced elders who claimed they could not act without their king's authority. When asked where he could be found, they would only say he was in the north.

His left hand instinctively strayed to check the binding on the cowhide socket that held the oak replica of his lost right one firmly in place on the wrist. Why was he chasing shadows in a stinking Brigante bog with enemies on every side when he could have been back in Italia tending his vines in the sun? The question provoked a wry smile.

The truth was there was more than one kind of enemy. The one who had driven him from Rome had proved much more dangerous than the tattooed savages lying dead on the grass. Not just to Valerius, but to his family. A man with Valerius's experience had the weapons to deal with most threats, but not an enemy with this kind of power. For the enemy was the Emperor Vespasian's son Domitian. Fortunately, Valerius also had powerful friends, including Vespasian's elder son Titus, who held the rank of consul and commander of the Praetorian Guard. Titus had arranged for Valerius to be appointed *legatus iuridicus*, the second most powerful official in Britannia and legal adviser to the governor Julius Agricola.

Yet within weeks of arriving on the island Agricola had manoeuvred Valerius into accepting command of the Ninth Hispana, one of four legions stationed in the province. He'd led his new legion in a bloody, brutal campaign in which Agricola had all but exterminated the

Ordovice tribe and destroyed for ever the power of the druids on the sacred isle of Mona. Agricola, with Vespasian's support, already had plans for the final subjugation of the mountainous north of Britannia. Instead, he'd experienced a year of delays and frustration as his forces recovered from their savage mauling at the hands of Mona's fanatical defenders.

Valerius had used the respite to hone the Ninth into a weapon that mirrored the qualities of its new commander: disciplined, aggressive, flexible and deadly. He'd also taken the opportunity to bring his family north to the legion's new base at Eboracum. He'd spent every possible moment with Tabitha, Lucius and his infant daughter Olivia, a dark-maned joy who, at six months, already had her mother's flashing temperament and was named for Valerius's sister. He felt a pang of regret as he recalled the moment he'd seen them off in the carriage to Londinium after the legion's celebration of *Augustalia*.

A trumpet blared and his chest swelled with pride as his legion marched into view on the valley floor below. He took up position on a hillock beside the track to watch them pass.

A legion on the march was an astonishing sight, even for one who'd seen it so many times, squirming across the ground like a giant centipede that only discipline, relentless industry and the brutal training of many years maintained as a single entity. In Valerius's mind the centipede's feelers were the scouts and cavalry patrols who ranged ahead and on the flanks of the long, snaking column, and the engineers who would forge ahead to decide the site of the next camp. Two cohorts of auxiliary infantry made up the head of the beast. In their midst marched Valerius's headquarters section and his personal guard, the *aquilifer*'s party, bearing the glittering eagle standard, and the *imaginifer* who carried the Emperor's image. The body consisted of close to five thousand legionaries, the unit's core of heavy infantry, divided into ten cohorts. A cohort was the legion's tactical heart, large enough to make a difference in any battle situation, but flexible enough to be used in part or in whole. The arithmetic of a cohort was simple. Eight men made up a *contubernium*, who shared a tent on campaign or a barrack block in the fort. Ten *contubernia* made up a century and six centuries a cohort. Only the elite First cohort defied this rule, consisting of five double-strength centuries: eight hundred men. In Valerius's experience it was unusual for a legion to march so close to a full complement of soldiers, but Agricola had agreed he could use replacements from the Second Augusta at Isca to fill the gaps in his ranks. A full cohort of that legion had taken over garrison duties at Eboracum under the command of Valerius's nominal deputy, a senior military tribune for whom he had little use, but with too many friends in high places to be replaced.

The centipede's tail consisted of the long column of baggage wagons and mules carrying everything eight thousand soldiers needed to survive – and to fight: flour, dried meat, olive oil and wine for the legionaries and auxiliaries; sacks of fodder for hundreds of horses and oxen; cooking pots and bread ovens; thousands of spare *pila*, the weighted javelins that would break a charge of bare-chested barbarians in an instant; *ballistae* and *scorpio* catapults, the dreaded 'shield-splitters' designed to cause havoc and dismay; pre-prepared timber for bridges; and forges and anvils for the armourers. Behind them came the rearguard, another two cohorts of auxiliaries. If Valerius cared to watch his legion pass by from nose to tail he would be here for more than an hour.

'Riders approaching.' Cornelius Felix, the commander of his escort, broke his revery. There was little urgency in the decurion's tone. No enemy horseman could have penetrated the cavalry screen undetected.

'It's Arafa.' Shabolz, the former Pannonian auxiliary, had the best eyes of any of them. Valerius had inherited the troops of his guard from his short time as *legatus iuridicus*. Eight cavalrymen from each of Britannia's four legions, hand-picked for all the wrong reasons. A motley band of misfits, they'd started out ready to spill each other's guts, but the balefire of battle had tested and moulded them. Valerius was happy to call them comrades, and in some cases friends. Shabolz was the best of them, a stocky Pannonian with a face carved from granite and a sidelock hanging from beneath his helmet that no dress regulation would compel him to remove. Originally there had been five Pannonians, but only three survived Agricola's invasion of Mona.

Valerius smiled. Arafa meant 'giant', but the man who answered to the name was Gaius Rufus, a Roman who lived as a Celt and, if he wasn't making the story up, the result of a union between one of the Emperor Caligula's slaves and the midget dancer responsible for his tiny stature.

From a distance the diminutive figure looked ridiculous perched on a full-sized Roman cavalry mount, but Rufus occupied the four-pronged saddle with all the ease and comfort of an emperor sitting on his throne. He was the legion's chief scout and a man who could range extraordinary distances into enemy territory. Valerius had sent him on a mission two days earlier. He could tell the moment he met Rufus's eyes it had been a success.

'I have him, lord,' the little man grinned.

'Where?' Valerius demanded.

'Patience, favoured of the gods.' Rufus's gimlet eyes glinted. 'King Guiderius has two problems. The first is that his army, like his tribe, is a patchwork of loyalties. They're also hungry. The last harvest was a poor one and the next is half a year away. For a strong king that wouldn't matter, but Guiderius is only king because none of the other candidates who want independence from Rome could raise the support to get rid of him. He knows he can only afford to attack you if everything favours him, or his army will melt away like the last snow of springtime. King Guiderius is not a confident man. He has heard about the fate of the Ordovices. That's why he's sought sanctuary in the north.'

'Thank you for the history lesson, but I still need to know where.'

Rufus dropped from his horse and used his foot to clear a space in the dirt. He drew his knife and bent over the patch of earth. Valerius dismounted to crouch beside him. 'We're here, and these are the mountains.' Rufus scraped a wavy line up the centre of the patch. He drew another line up the east side of the mountains and stabbed the point of his knife into the earth. 'Here. The original Brigante seat of kings, the

10

northern stronghold of Queen Cartimandua, and the tribe's traditional sanctuary.'

'How far is it?'

'For the legion? A long day on the road, but a prudent man would take two.'

Valerius studied the improvised map. 'Agricola must know about this.'

Agricola summoned the commanders of his legions as soon as Valerius arrived saddle-sore and weary at the temporary camp of the Twentieth. Valerius experienced a twinge of unease as he entered the governor's pavilion. His relationship with the proconsul of Britannia was more complex than he cared to admit. Even Tabitha wasn't aware of the full extent of his concerns. Agricola had originally greeted his new *legatus iuridicus* with a wariness that belied their previous service together; polite enough, but cold, offhand and just the right side of bad manners. The way he'd manoeuvred Valerius into command of the Ninth reeked of intrigue and conspiracy, and the passing of Valerius's predecessor something worse. Of course, the lack of welcome could be excused by the strain of his responsibilities. Britannia was a notoriously difficult province from which to prise a profit.

Agricola and two other men occupied the tent. The governor rose to welcome Valerius, followed by his companions. An amused smile flickered on thin lips, but didn't quite reach the steady grey eyes that always seemed to contain an element of question. A lawyer's eyes that saw everything, but took nothing at face value. Stockily built and of middle height, the governor wore his greying hair cropped short in a vain attempt to disguise its sparseness, and his brow still bore the impression where his helmet had sat not so long before.

'Verrens.' Valerius acknowledged the greeting of a dark, saturnine man in his early fifties with hair of a jet black that had nothing to do with nature. Tiberius Julius Ursus, legate of the Twentieth legion. If the rumours were correct his dealings with Agricola were even more strained than Valerius's. Ursus reached out a hand before withdrawing it in a nervous flutter as he remembered Valerius's wooden fist.

11

'Valerius.' The youngest of the three, plump and relaxed, with the face of a well-fed cherub, recognized the newcomer's presence with an inclination of the head and a smile that came as a surprise. Herenius Polio was a man with a bloodline that stretched back as far as Romulus. He commanded the Second Adiutrix and had previously treated Valerius with the detached condescension he maintained with all *new men*, even Agricola. Valerius returned the smile, but wondered what had brought about the sudden change.

Between them, Ursus, Polio and Valerius commanded three of Britannia's four legions, which, with their associated auxiliary units, combined the power of close to thirty thousand of the most disciplined and well-armed soldiers the world had ever seen. As long as Agricola had their support, he wielded a weapon so potent he was capable of marching on Rome with a fair degree of success.

Naturally, Vespasian and the Palatium, the great bureaucracy which ran the Empire's affairs, ensured that none of his commanders could fully trust the others. Ursus was Vespasian's man, hand and heart, and had served under the Emperor as a sixteen-year-old tribune with the Second Augusta as far back as the invasion. Valerius was known to be a client of Titus, heir to the purple, a newly appointed patrician whose influence, none the less, could only grow. Polio held his rank thanks to a combination of aristocratic alliances and his father's friends in the Senate, but he commanded a legion formed and constituted by the Emperor from the marines of the Ravenna fleet and known for their fierce loyalty to him.

'The scout, Gais Rufus,' Agricola's aide announced.

'Send him in.'

Gaius Rufus appeared a few moments later, entering the tent with a bow-legged cavalryman's swagger that might have looked incongruous on the small man, but that he managed to carry off like a Parthian Invincible. His eyes were red-rimmed and sunk deep with exhaustion, but they contained a twinkle that hinted he found his situation ripe for self-mockery.

'Bring the scout wine,' Agricola called to a hovering servant. Rufus accepted the silver cup and drained the contents in a single swallow. He sighed contentedly and wiped the back of his hand across his lips with a nod of thanks.

'Well?' The governor's voice was tight with anticipation.

'They call it Brynmochdar, lord, the Badger Hill,' Rufus said. 'It is a place associated with Guiderius's mother, Cartimandua, the Brigantes' greatest queen. I arrived in darkness and took refuge on a rise to the south I knew would provide a fine view of the fort when the sun rose. As I waited, I could hear the sound of shouting in the distance and see what looked like a thousand fireflies on the hill opposite.' He drew a long breath. 'They are there, lord.'

'How many?' Agricola demanded.

'Enough to be turning what I remember as a modest defensive position into one of the largest fortresses I have ever seen.'

'Impossible,' Ursus scoffed.

'Have you seen Maidun, lord?' The scout turned to him. 'The stronghold of the Durotriges where they made their last stand against our very own Caesar and the Second Augusta. Forgive me, of course you have, for you marched with him. Well, Brynmochdar is larger still, though the hill is not so steep, the walls so tall, nor the ditches deep.'

'How much work have they done?' Valerius had also seen Maidun and he'd wondered that even a Roman legion could take it.

'From what I could see, lord, they're concentrating their efforts on lengthening the line of ditches to enclose the hill. At the moment it's just a few feet deep with a low mound behind.'

'So we need to act quickly.' Valerius turned to Agricola.

'Yes,' the governor agreed. 'Before they have a chance to deepen the ditches and build a palisade.' Valerius saw a calculating look cross his face and felt a touch of unease. 'You should return to your legion, legate, and march north immediately. I will give you a *vexillatio* of two cohorts of the Twentieth to strengthen your force.' Ursus protested, but Agricola waved him aside. 'And I will personally join you at the Hill of Badgers for the siege.'

Valerius's heart sank as Rufus shot him a wry smile. His instinct had been right. Agricola couldn't resist the lure of glory. His beloved Twentieth would have the battle honour *Brynmochdar* sewn upon their pennants and any victory would be the victory of Gnaeus Julius Agricola.

'There is something else, lord,' Rufus interrupted. 'I captured a stray who thought to shirk the work at the camp, and put him to the question. He said King Guiderius's force is as numerous as grains of sand upon a beach and he would like nothing better than for us to attack him. The king has also acquired new allies.'

'New allies?' Valerius exchanged a glance with Agricola. Which of the tribes of southern Britannia would be foolish enough to ally themselves with a rebel who had no chance of success?

'He has been joined at Brynmochdar by a prince of the northern Celts, a champion of his tribe, along with a hundred of his greatest warriors. My Brigante said he is a giant, tall as a rowan and broad as a four-wheel cart. The sword he carries is as long as a chariot's centre pole and he can split an armoured man in two with a single blow.'

'Valerius.' Agricola was out of his seat and his fingers closed on Valerius's left arm, his eyes glittering. 'You must take him for me. Take him alive. This swordsman will be our gift to the Emperor.' Beyond the governor's shoulder Valerius saw Polio raise a sardonic eyebrow at the word *our*. 'He will be paraded through Rome for the eternal glory of Britannia's legions and suffer the fate of Vercingetorix the Gaul in the depths of the *carcer*. Alive, Valerius. I want him alive.'

Valerius nodded, not trusting himself to speak, remembering the man who had delivered Vercingetorix to Rome. Gaius Julius Caesar had proclaimed himself dictator and founded an empire. Just how high did Agricola's ambitions soar?

III

The two kings stood at the centre of what appeared to be a giant ants' nest. On every side men, women and children burrowed to dig or deepen ditches, gathered wood for palisades and quarried stone to build revetments where the ditches threatened to collapse, or to create paths through the bogs. Every tree of any size had been felled to be part of the defences and thorn bushes torn up to make the ditches more difficult to cross. Other tribesfolk carried sacks of salted meat, oatmeal and dried apples while still more drove individual cows, small herds of hardy brown sheep and squealing families of pigs into enclosures in the centre of the giant compound, where they mingled, moaning and jostling and making the air shimmer with the warmth from their reeking manure.

Anything that could be used as a weapon had been gathered from the surrounding area. The people had worked through the night and all the previous day in an attempt to complete the defences and provisioning of the fort in time. Yet Cathal noted they were fewer now than yesterday. Warriors preferred to fight and drink rather than dig, but still more feared what would happen to their families when the Romans came. An entire tribe had disappeared during the night with all its supplies.

It would have been difficult to find a greater contrast between two men. Guiderius, short and slight, with light brown hair that tumbled to his shoulders, had sad, wide-set blue eyes, a wispy beard and soft, almost feminine downturned lips. He wore a tunic and trews of finespun emerald cloth, with a chain of gold links at his waist and a heavy gold torc at his neck. In contrast, Cathal would have stood head and shoulders above most men and he loomed over Guiderius like a mountain crag. A chest like an ale barrel forced his tunic of rough, undyed wool apart at the neck and plaid trews encased his long legs to calves as massive as another man's thighs. Wild, raven hair chopped short at the brow and sides hung long at his back, and the narrow dark eyes took in and evaluated everything. A nose like a Celtic battle axe jutted above long moustaches that hung to his chin, and he had a rearing horse tattooed in blue on each cheek. What truly marked him, apart from his scale, was the sword he wore strapped to his back.

Taller than the man standing at his side, it had a two-handed grip bound in soft leather and fixed with spun gold and a blade as wide as a man's hand. Only Cathal could wield it. He called the sword Ghost Bane, because if a man looked closely enough the spirits of the eight strips of iron that created it were visible in the polished blade. The gold arm rings on his biceps were mere incidentals that proclaimed his authority in the unlikely event that any denied it.

Cathal ruled the Selgovae, the Hunters of the Forest, and he claimed tribute from every tribe between Great Cheviot and the lands of the Damnonii, even at times from his despised neighbours, the Votadini. He had come here with a hundred of his champions because his father had fought beside Guiderius's father and to see if what he'd heard about the Romans was true.

The men's vantage point was a fort within a fort, in fact the original fortification that had crowned Brynmochdar in the days of Guiderius's father's father's father, long before his mother Cartimandua had expanded it into a refuge during her struggle with Venutius. Guiderius had deepened the original ditches and created a stout wooden palisade with a fighting platform. This would be the position from which he conducted the defence and, if the need arose, the refuge where he would make his final stand. In Cathal's view the Brigantes should have concentrated on improving the existing defences and building huts for those who would instead suffer from lack of shelter. Guiderius insisted he must create a greater enclosure, large enough to house the warrior hosts of the Carvetii and the Parisii. They would come at his call, he insisted blithely, and he would have fifty thousand warriors to meet the Roman attack.

Cathal's eyes told him the Brigantes were several thousands fewer. Many were women and children and more were warriors whose heart was not in the fight. A king should not criticize a king, but still, he must try.

'You will not reconsider continuing north, lord king?'

'After all this effort?' Guiderius threw out an arm to encompass the workers in the ditch to his front. 'How many do you think would follow me?'

'Whatever their numbers they would be your best and your bravest,' Cathal said. 'Together we would destroy the Romans in the hills and valleys of my homeland.'

'Would you truly advise me to leave here?'

'I would take my people to the very ends of the earth before I would allow them to wear Roman chains.'

'I know you think I am a fool, Cathal.' Guiderius looked up into the fierce eyes. 'No, do not deny it. I understand why a man like you would believe that. I am not so blind that I cannot see how few of my warriors meet my eyes when I tell them we can win. That is why I had to come here. The elders have been spreading tales that the Romans are invincible in open combat. If I give them a wall to fight behind and their families to fight for they will be the equal of any legionary. The Romans can throw themselves against our spears from now until Samhain and they will gain nothing. I will bleed them until they offer terms.'

'The only terms they will offer your people are slavery and servitude,' Cathal said brutally. 'Your own words, Guiderius, of less than a week ago. You know them better than I. What price will they exact for this Roman blood you shed?'

Guiderius's eyes remained fixed on the distant hills, but his silence told Cathal he knew the answer well enough: his head.

Eventually, the Brigante ruler said: 'This is my land and these are my people and I will not abandon them, whatever the price. My mother shamed our nation when she sold Caratacus to Rome for a few more years of isolation, but of course they came back for more. Client state, they called us, a barrier between their *civilization*,' his lips twisted into a bitter smile, 'and the yet more barbarous tribes to the north. By my actions here I will repay my mother's debt and restore Brigante pride.'

Cathal turned to study their surroundings. Brynmochdar was a low hogback mound amidst a rolling landscape and not in itself a natural defensive position. He guessed it had originally been chosen as a gathering place, or perhaps a trading post, but its link to his mother blinded Guiderius to any flaws it might have as a fortress.

Guiderius's new rampart and ditch followed, as well as it could, the contours of the hill and would provide a formidable enough barrier if he were allowed to complete it. From what Cathal could see the ditch was too shallow and the earth mound behind it had crumbled in places, but there were not enough people to repair the damage. The stock pens stood on a flat area to the west of the original fort. Women and elders had begun to slaughter animals to provide meat for the thousands of workers' evening meal. The plaintive lowing of the condemned beasts shut out the thump of spade and mattock, and the combined stink of animal dung, blood and offal assailed his nostrils. For the moment supplies were plentiful, but Cathal could see that a breakthrough at a single weak spot could change that in an instant. One of the few genuine advantages was the number of streams that ran through the fort, although the Romans could nullify that by damming or contaminating the water further upstream. He remembered winter nights around the fire when his father Dugald had talked of his time with Venutius. The old man spoke of walls of shields and warriors fighting not man to man, as the Selgovae and the Brigantes did, but as a single combined unit. It

18

troubled Cathal that he couldn't divine what advantage this gave them, but Dugald had been sure. Certainly, Venutius suffered a great defeat and the Romans placed his head on a pole and paraded it around the Brigante settlements. No doubt his skull was someone's drinking bowl now. He prayed that would not be Guiderius's fate, because, despite the other's weaknesses as a man and a leader, he liked the little Brigante, but he feared it was a vain hope. 'At least shorten your perimeter. Your walls are too long and your ditches too shallow to be defended by the warriors you have.'

'When the Carvetii come . . .'

'I cannot stay and fight beside you.'

'I know,' Guiderius acknowledged. 'You must look to your own people now.'

'But I will do what I can.'

'Of course.'

'We will try to disrupt their supply lines. Make them think they are assailed from the rear.' He left unspoken the fact that his primary reason for remaining in the area was not to support Guiderius, but to study the Roman method of war. He intended to test his warriors against theirs, if he could manoeuvre a position that gave him a fair prospect of success.

'I have one request.' Guiderius sounded uncharacteristically hesitant.

'You may ask anything of me.'

'Take Gwlym with you.'

'The blind druid?' Cathal immediately regretted his offer. He remembered the malevolent, sneering features and red-rimmed, pus-filled eye sockets.

'He disturbs the men with his talk of Boudicca and Mona. They say he carries death with him.'

'We will be riding hard. It will be dangerous. Perhaps . . .'

But Guiderius would not be diverted. 'I will supply him with a good horse and a steady man to make sure he stays in the saddle. Do not make me plead, Cathal.'

'Of course.' The words choked in Cathal's throat. The king shamed him. For all his faults Guiderius was a good man and a good friend. If he could hold the Romans here and hurt them it might give Cathal's Selgovae another two seasons to prepare.

A shout went up from the south wall and Cathal looked up to see a flare of orange on a faraway hill. As he watched it quickly spawned a towering pillar of smoke.

'They are coming,' Guiderius said quietly. 'You should go.'

Cathal turned and clasped his friend's hand. 'Fare well, lord king. I wish you the joy of victory.'

'We will meet again, Cathal of the Selgovae.'

Cathal nodded.

But would it be in this world or the next?

IV

Valerius looked out from the hillside where Gaius Rufus had made his earlier estimate of the enemy strength and found himself in agreement with his scout. Brynmochdar was the largest hill fort he'd encountered in Britannia. It was an immense place. The walls encompassed more land than those of some great cities, probably three or four times longer than the ramparts of the original *colonia*. In the hazy dawn light it appeared dangerously formidable, but a closer look with a soldier's eye revealed a slightly different picture.

To his front warriors lined the wooden palisade several deep, long hair fluttering in the light breeze and spear points glinting, but away to the flanks he noticed that the numbers thinned out and some sections weren't manned at all. Anticipation welled up inside him as he studied the defences themselves. The palisade and shallow single ditches might have had *Salve* written over them for all the obstacle they posed to a legionary cohort. Beyond them lay a broad open space where thousands of people milled to find a vantage point to view the attackers. A mistake, because that human barrier would make it difficult for King Guiderius to move reinforcements within his perimeter. Cattle pens and rough supply huts thrown up in recent days further hindered internal movement. In the distance, close to the centre of the complex, he could see the raised mound of what looked like a more solid fortification. The inner stronghold called for some attention, but he'd worry about that when the time came.

Valerius had ridden to the fort with the advance party of two auxiliary cavalry wings. On the flat ground between the two rises a thousand troopers were laid out in their squadrons like a giant mosaic, struggling to keep their mounts still amidst the swarms of buzzing flies. The bulk of the Ninth was still on the march from the temporary camp a few miles to the south.

'Cornelius?' He called to the commander of his personal guard. 'Take two squadrons of Gauls and ride a quick circuit of the place. Make the defenders think you pose a threat despite your numbers. The odd rush at the walls when you consider it safe, but don't risk anyone. There's no point in losing men just to confirm what you see with your own eyes.'

'Legate.' Felix snapped a quick salute and rode off, shouting for Nilus, his trumpeter. A short series of calls rang out and two units of thirty men detached from the mass of cavalry and followed Felix east along the front of the low scarp defending Brynmochdar. Not a steep scarp, by any means, especially not at the great double gate where the raw, newly cut timbers shone like gold in the morning sunlight. Valerius remembered a hill fort he'd stormed a long time ago as a fresh-faced young tribune who still had his right hand. There had been lines of great ditches that funnelled the attackers into blind alleys and killing zones, hidden trenches filled with wooden stakes, and boiling water pouring from above. The gradient steepened with every step until each breath threatened to choke a man and his legs felt as though they were on fire. The rattle of arrows and boulders on the triple oak shields that were the only thing keeping the soldiers alive. Then the gate.

'Have the Second cohort find a suitable baulk of timber and fit it to the ram,' he ordered. 'Something impressive that will make them think we really mean to have that gate.'

The gate was the key. Not because Valerius planned to break through at that point, but because it was where he wanted the Brigantes to

22

believe he intended to break through. He waited patiently until a new blast of horns announced the arrival of his legion.

The front ranks of the Ninth marched into view in the attack formation he'd ordered. Three cohorts off to the east to threaten the walls beyond the gate; solid, compact slabs of heavily armed and armoured infantry almost five hundred men strong. Four more to form up directly opposite the gate, with the Second cohort and their ram in the centre. And, closest to Valerius but fifty or sixty feet below, a further three cohorts almost equal in numbers to the four opposite the gate, because one was the double-strength First.

The legionaries wore a mix of either chain armour vests or the more recently introduced *lorica segmentata* plate. Men favoured chain because it had fewer buckles, could be donned in seconds and was easier to keep rust free as long as you could access a few handfuls of sand. Others swore by the plate on account of its lightness and flexibility. They were willing to expend the time it took to strap on the thirty-four separate elements because plate would turn the point of a spear that would penetrate chain if the thrust was powerful enough. Beneath the armour, their tunics might once have been called red, but depending on age and wear covered every shade from off-white through pink and various combinations of terracotta to bright scarlet. They marched ready to fight, a pair of javelins on their right shoulders and left arms toting their big triple-layered oak shields, heads encased in polished iron helmets equipped with neck guards and cheekpieces. Every man carried a *gladius*, the legionary's deadly short sword, in a scabbard attached to the belt at his waist.

Four cohorts of auxiliary infantry, a further two thousand soldiers, stood in reserve, but Valerius was confident he wouldn't have to use them. He felt a surge of elation. The Brigantes were precisely where he wanted them, trapped in the great cage they'd created for themselves.

Agricola had promised two cohorts of the Twentieth and his own hallowed presence, but Valerius didn't plan to wait for either. This would be the Ninth's victory, and the triumph would be all the greater for the overwhelming numbers they faced, perhaps four or five times their own. The question was how many of the enemy were up for the fight?

Gaius Rufus had partially answered the question. The little scout had intercepted a tribe slinking away from the great fortress the previous night and they'd provided all the information Valerius needed about the scene laid out before him. King Guiderius commanded, probably from the central fort, guarded by every warrior loyal to him, and, of course, the giant barbarian prince whose presence so excited Agricola. It would be Valerius's pleasure to lead him to the governor at the end of a rope.

A thunder of hooves announced the return of Felix and his Gauls. The young decurion leapt from his horse and sprinted up the bank to join Valerius. 'You were right, lord, they don't have enough men to defend the whole perimeter in any depth. The northern ditch and palisade is unfinished in places. I'd suggest that a feint attack in the east to draw the defence and an all out assault in the centre would probably carry the walls, unless it's a ruse to draw us in.'

'There is always that possibility,' Valerius agreed. 'But judging by the lack of depth in the defences here in the south I doubt it's the case.' He drew the cavalryman aside. 'Pass on your recommendation to the commander of the Ala Petriana and the First Asturians, but as an order from me. Petriana to take the lead. They are to wait until the legion is fully engaged before they proceed with any attack.'

'Cohorts signalling they're in position, legate,' Valerius's second in command Quintus Naso announced.

No point in delaying any further. 'Order the artillery to loose,' Valerius said. A young signaller stationed further up the hill waved a red pennant back and forth above his head. Along the line, each *scorpio* and *ballista* team would be tensed for the signal.

A series of staccato thumps announced a volley from the closest machines and Valerius knew it would be being repeated all along the line. He had no siege towers to deploy and none of the large catapults Corbulo had put to such good use at the battle of the Cepha Gap. Even so, the legion's smaller missile throwers were capable of dispensing death on a horrific scale. He heard the first crunching impacts and the shrieks of the Celtic warriors massed in such tempting numbers at the perfect range for a flat trajectory. Half of the pieces were *scorpiones*, heavy, reinforced mechanical bows that could fire a big five-foot bolt four or five hundred paces depending on the conditions. 'Shield-splitters' the legionaries called them. They were well named and they'd be just as deadly against the painfully thin palisade. Skimming the top of the wall, where the bravest were cavorting and howling insults on their makeshift earthen fighting platform, the bolts would remove heads and smash skulls before spitting those further behind. Even if the aim was low the arrow was as likely to pierce the wall of wooden branches as not, and with the same results.

The stone-throwing *ballistae* which made up the balance of the artillery could be even more devastating to body and morale. The ten-pound missiles simply smashed through flesh and bone until the sheer number of victims slowed their momentum. Valerius had seen warriors torn in half, with great gaping holes in their torsos, men with ribcages torn asunder to reveal still-beating hearts; arms, legs and heads ripped from bodies. Even the splinters of smashed bone from the initial victims could maim those around them. Any missile which overshot the front ranks caused similar carnage among the thousands of women and children crowded behind the warriors to watch the legion deploy.

Valerius allowed the barrage to continue until the fire from the *ballista* teams began to slow. He could almost feel the urgency of the legionary cohorts as they stood in their tight-packed squares tensed for the order to advance.

'Have we had any word from Governor Agricola?'

'None, sir,' Naso confirmed.

Patience, Valerius, patience. He gave them another three volleys. 'Signal the attack.'

Above him the signaller waved a green flag three times.

Away to his right the four cohorts in front of the gate attacked in a sudden disciplined rush, but he had to wait a dozen frozen heartbeats before the flanking units began their slow deliberate march. Now the

Brigante king would be torn between sending warriors to reinforce his most threatened sector at the gate, or keeping them to combat the apparently less urgent hazard to the walls on either side. Valerius had massed his stone-throwing *ballistae* in front of the flanking cohorts with orders to concentrate their fire directly on the fragile wooden palisade. The resulting damage resembled a mouth full of rotting teeth, with gaps and jagged stumps all along the line, and mutilated, dead and dying Brigante warriors piled up behind. Yet thousands more stood behind the parapet of dead, tattooed, bare-chested and howling their defiance, urging the Romans towards their spears.

Valerius gave the gateway attack one last glance before focusing his attention on the main thrust. If the gate fell, so much the better. The left and right hand cohorts stood ready to capitalize on the ram's success, but they deliberately hung back a little to the side of their ostensible target. The centre pair of cohorts had already formed *testudo* as they approached the gateway under a hail of slingshots, spears, arrows and large stones. Stray missiles found gaps between the shields and left a few casualties crawling or coughing up blood in their wake. So far everything was going to plan.

Valerius's greatest hope of success depended on the three left hand cohorts. Theirs was the steepest part of the scarp, but also where the *ballistae* had done the most damage. He'd used all his experience to plan the attack. It was based on a much more difficult investment of Cremona more than a decade before, where the city had been defended by veteran legionaries and surrounded by stone walls. The First cohort led this sector of the attack. Eight hundred men deployed in five double-strength centuries, two in the van and three behind to form an arrow head. They advanced in *testudo* so the attackers within the carapace of linked shields could ignore the slingshots and spears that rained down on them. As they approached the ditch, the first two centuries transformed seamlessly into eight normal half centuries advancing in two ranks of four. Concealed in the ranks of one of the following cohorts three centuries of Thracian auxiliary archers moved to take up position where they could swamp the defenders with arrows. At first it appeared the foremost half centuries must be trapped in the defensive ditch and either slaughtered or forced to turn back. Instead, those in the van combined to create a sloping ramp of shields on to which the following half centuries leapt. Balancing on the trembling platform they immediately formed *testudo* and were able to tear at the shattered remains of the palisade in a perfectly timed assault. The defenders threw themselves at the locked shields, but all they won for their trouble was a handspan of *gladius* and a lingering death. Within moments the legionaries created a perimeter line a hundred paces wide. Even before it was complete the following centuries and cohorts poured over the human bridges to add their weight to the attack. Valerius saw a veteran centurion in their midst take control and suddenly the perimeter was expanding left and right and forward to create a greater tactical space to be exploited. As if by metamorphosis a cohort wedge the soldiers called a Boar's Head formed within the Roman bridgehead: a compact arrowhead of six centuries. With barely a pause for breath they charged to smash into the heart of the mass of stunned defenders. Simultaneously, the cohort on the right of the attack, which had been supporting the assault on the gate, took advantage of the confusion to make their own lunge at the walls in coordination with the expanding perimeter, causing yet more confusion and dismay among the defenders.

'Shit.' Valerius turned at Naso's muttered curse. Of course, it had all been going too well. When the Boar's Head smashed into the defenders a century detached and, driven by battle madness or simple over-enthusiasm, sprinted in open order towards the ultimate prize, the fort at the centre of the great compound. It was magnificent. It was brave. The type of thing Valerius had done when a battle was at its cusp. Win, and the man who led it was a Hero of Rome; lose . . . and you were dead. Hundreds of Brigante warriors erupted from a piece of broken ground on to the flank of the charging men and they disappeared in a welter of falling swords and plunging spears.

At last. On the far side of the fort, at the very edge of Valerius's vision, a ripple seemed to pulse through the mass of civilians taking shelter there. He recognized the emerald plumes of the Asturian cavalry wing in their midst, with what must be the Ala Petriana on their flank. Their only obstacle was the fleeing mass of women, children and grey-haired ancients, but the cavalry didn't hesitate and old and young alike fell shrieking beneath their swords. *It must be soon.* Valerius bit back the words. Even as he watched, the collapse began, slowly at first, but gaining momentum with every passing second. Drawn by the screams, the rear ranks of the multitude facing the initial breakthrough turned to go to the aid of their loved ones, followed by more and more warriors. Whatever organization existed among the defenders was gone.

'It is finished,' he said to Naso. He looked up at the sun and noted with satisfaction that the whole action had taken less than half of an hour. 'Let it be known that any who lay down their arms are to be spared.'

'There's still the central fort,' the camp prefect pointed out. 'It looks as if it might be a tougher nut to crack.'

'Tell them to bring forward the artillery.'

A diminutive figure rode up on a full-sized horse. 'Valerius!'

'Welcome, Gaius Rufus.' Valerius smiled. 'You are just in time to witness a great victory.'

'I know,' the little man said sourly, 'but in case you haven't noticed, while you've been enjoying the entertainment some bastard is attacking your baggage train.'

V

Cathal watched the battle until the point where the Roman formation divided and sub-divided to form a human ramp that allowed their comrades to cross the walls. It was enough. An exhibition of discipline, power and sacrifice no Celtic tribe could hope to emulate. Was any force on earth capable of stopping these people?

The image continued to fill his head as he rode to join his men in the little tree-lined gully where they hid not far from where the Romans had set up their baggage park. It lay midway between Brynmochdar and the temporary marching camp Cathal had studied the previous night and discarded as a possible target. He dismounted before he entered the gully and led his pony through the undergrowth and down to the shallow stream that cut eastwards to the far side of the hill. After a few minutes a shape seemed to sprout from the ground and he was staring into a pair of wide intimidating eyes caught between a mass of dark hair and a twitching beard.

'I don't mind you trying to scare me, Ranal,' the Selgovae chief growled. 'But you frighten my beast at your peril.'

The face creased into a grin. 'I just thought to surprise you, Cathal.'

'Well don't. You know I don't react well to surprise. I near took your head off. How are the lads?'

'They're grand, lord. But bored. They wish we could have stayed with the Brigantes. There were some lasses . . .'

'They're better off out of it.' Cathal's voice contained a brutal edge fuelled by what he'd watched. 'By nightfall those lasses will either be in Roman beds or wearing Roman chains.'

Ranal led him to a point where the gully widened and another stream joined it from a secondary valley where the warriors had corralled the group's ponies. Men wearing the same rough undyed wool tunics and trews as their chieftain sprawled on the damp ground or squatted in small groups. A few murmured a welcome, but most just watched in silence. They were Cathal's sword brothers and they had served and fought together long enough to need no words.

Cathal had equipped every man with the long sword that proclaimed him as a member of the tribe's elite. A champion. The Selgovae smiths had put every shred of their craft and their skill into creating those slim, ash-grey blades from the finest metal they could source, iron brought in finger-length ingots at great price from faraway Noricum. Cathal had ordered the felling of hundreds of trees to make the charcoal to heat the forges, and the sacred glades where the smiths worked rang with the clatter of hammer upon metal for an entire season. The swords made them rich men, but the fierce loyalty they bore him had not been bought, but earned. Cathal was their leader, but these men were a brotherhood. A brotherhood of the blade. All but one.

A dirty white robe drew Cathal's attention, like a maggot among a swarm of wasps. As his eyes became accustomed to the gloom he suppressed a shudder of distaste at the sight of Gwlym's pus-filled craters and filthy, food-stained beard. The druid's head turned, sensing his presence, and a smile flickered on the cracked lips. The Selgovae felt Gwlym's scrutiny and distaste turned to anger. It occurred to him that somewhere on the way north the priest might suffer an unfortunate accident, but that could wait. The gully took a sharp turn here and the broad bank that loomed over the clearing had collapsed to leave a mound of raw red earth. Cathal unslung his massive sword and handed it and his reins to Ranal before bounding nimbly up the mound until he could see a man lying among the bushes at the top of the bank.

'How many guards have they left, Colm?' he called softly.

'Too many,' the man said sourly. Colm was one of the oldest of the band, past thirty, but he had the eyes of a man ten years younger. 'Come up and have a look for yourself.'

Cathal took a leap to his left away from the collapse and wriggled his way upwards until he lay beside the other man. Colm parted the bushes in front of them so he could see down a broad, tussocky slope of rough grass. On the flat ground at the bottom of the hill, perhaps four hundred paces distant, a temporary township of tents and wagons sprawled across the landscape. Smoke from hundreds of fires rose to be tugged away by the breeze and Cathal guessed that, somewhere in that mass, smiths worked to repair armour and weapons and bakers were busy baking bread for the legion's evening meal. A tempting target, at first sight, for a man who had led more raids than he could see wagons. But that was before you noticed the bank and ditch that surrounded the baggage train and the hard-eyed guards who stood amongst the outer wagons. He looked closer, saw oval shields and chain armour. What the Romans called auxiliaries, mercenaries who fought for money and land, but no less dangerous for that.

Cathal stared at the camp with fierce concentration. He'd promised the Brigante king a demonstration, but nothing he could do here would affect the outcome at Brynmochdar. To attack the baggage train in camp would be to risk the lives of every man who followed him and those men could be vital to his cause in the seasons to come. The Selgovae would need leaders when the Roman eye turned north, as it undoubtedly would. And not just the Selgovae. It might be that the men who lay in the wooded dell below him were not just his bodyguard and his friends, but the foundations of an army.

Yet a promise was a promise and Cathal was a man of his word. He studied the massed wagons and their defences with even more care, seeking some weakness. His attack must necessarily be in daylight, otherwise it would be wasted entirely. Brynmochdar's defences would not last till nightfall. Anything worth taking or burning was stored in the centre of the camp and that meant breaching the walls.

The auxiliaries had cleared the land all around the camp so that even a mouse would have trouble approaching it unseen. As he watched, a man trudged from the gate and dropped into a crouch over a darkened patch that must be a narrow trench. Interesting. They'd dug their soil pit outside the walls. He considered the possibility for a moment before discarding it. Lifting a single man as he struggled to rid himself of a turd was hardly going to help Guiderius. His nostrils twitched at the faint scent of human excrement on the breeze. Yet that breeze also carried something else. A soft whinny.

For the first time his eyes were drawn beyond the circle of wagons and piles of supplies. Horse lines. His father had told him that every Roman cavalryman needed at least one remount and preferably two, so there would be hundreds of the beasts. The old man had talked in extravagant terms of the qualities of the animals he'd seen while campaigning against the Romans with Venutius. Of their beauty, their speed, length of leg and back, and depth of chest. The horses of the gods, he'd called them. They made the little ponies the Celts rode look like cattle and could run them down with as much ease. Cathal had sent emissaries south laden with gold in an attempt to barter in vain for a single Roman stallion. He'd even considered stealing one, but he was assured the Romans protected these revered animals with the same ferocity as the legions protected their eagle standards.

Yet now he was within touching distance of a Roman horse park with a hundred of his best men, and he had given his word to Guiderius that he would hurt his enemies. He gave a grunt of pleasure and Colm turned to him with a quizzical look.

'I know that sound,' he said. 'What have you seen in that dangerous great heap of manure you'd like to lay your hands on?'

Cathal grinned. 'I'd thought to relieve them of an anvil or two you could carry home and heft up Middle Hill as a gift for the sky gods.'

'Aye, that would be my talent right enough,' the other man said with lugubrious satisfaction. 'Beast of burden. Why do I have a feeling the reality is going to be even less appealing?'

'All of our lads can ride.'

'That would seem about right.' Colm's voice dripped with irony. 'Seeing as we came here on horseback.'

'But how many of them could ride a Roman horse, do you think?'

Understanding dawned on the other man's face. 'Ranal, Arwan, they're as good on a beast as any; say about half. But Roman cavalry horses? We ride without saddles and they have those great four-pronged monstrosities. And what about bridles? There'll not be a man without a broken bone before we reach the Cheviot. Better to kill them than steal them.'

Cathal considered the suggestion. It was good enough advice. Who knew what problems they'd cause among the hills. But killing those fine beasts? And killing took time. Besides, now that he thought about it he deserved one. More than one. 'Then I'm thinking we'll take fifty.'

Valerius's horse was blown out by the time the baggage camp came into sight. There'd been no chance to summon the cavalry, who were still in the process of consolidating the victory at Brynmochdar, so he'd gathered together what he had: Gaius Rufus, what was left of his escort – around twenty men – and a few aides. They'd galloped south to where he'd sited the baggage, close enough to supply the attacking troops but well beyond the range of any sortie from the besieged Brigantes. Or so he'd thought.

'Lord,' Rufus's shout broke the silence. He pointed to the east, beyond the fort. 'They're taking the horses.'

Valerius looked around. His signaller had gone with the men towards the fort. Too late to call them back.

'To me.' He led the way in a curve past the southern corner of the baggage circle with ten men at his back. Ten men against fifty, as it turned out. The guards assigned to the horse lines lay in the grass at the bottom of a shallow slope with their throats cut. Spare horses careering everywhere and the enemy already mounted. All except one.

If it hadn't been for that one, Valerius would have ordered the charge despite the odds. A towering figure holding an enormous sword in two hands as if it were a toy. He stood apart, silhouetted against the light, and faced ten mounted enemies as though willing them to come to him. Valerius had met Celtic champions before, faced them man to man, smelled their sweat and tasted their blood, and cut them down. This one was different. Not a warrior. An executioner.

'Leave them,' he said. 'We'll send the cavalry to hunt them down.'

He could feel the consternation in the men around him and even as he said it he knew it was a lie. The cavalry would take a day to recover after their charge and the battle that followed. The inner fort had still to be taken and the victory at Brynmochdar must be consolidated. Was it worth fifty horses to ensure that? The answer, of course, was yes, and it was a logical answer. But Valerius had a moment of doubt. Could his decision have been influenced by another factor as well as logic? Fear. It was a question he knew would come back to haunt him in the night.

But one thing he knew for certain. He would meet the swordsman again.

And one of them would die.

VI

From the walls of the inner fort King Guiderius watched helplessly as his outer defences disintegrated and his strategy for holding the Romans at bay was ripped to pitiful shreds amid a welter of carnage. The speed of it stunned his mind.

This was the greatest army a Brigante chieftain had ever led. At first he had smiled at the Roman commander's audacity in challenging countless thousands with a single legion. Then his heart quailed as he watched the efficiency and ease with which they crossed the walls that had been built at the cost of so much labour. Even then he had hope. Surely so few could not defeat so many?

How wrong could a man be? First the compact arrowhead formations of legionaries smashed the great mass of Brigante warriors into smaller segments, as if Guiderius's vaunted army had been a simple kitchen pot. Long triple lines of the great rectangular shields followed, herding the confused bands of warriors like cattle. Herding them to the slaughter. He could hear the combined grunt as the Romans won every pace of ground, and the screams of the men who died trying to hold it. As the lines moved forward they left a broad smear of blood and a carpet of writhing bodies in their wake. He understood Rome could be cruel, but he had never envisaged this merciless ferocity. The deadly little swords with their needle-sharp triangular points made no distinction between class or rank, bravery or cowardice. Men who threw down their spears in surrender died beside heroes who fought to the last.

A new round of panicked screaming broke out in the north. Guiderius ran along the earth parapet in time to see a column of Roman cavalry erupt on to the hill, brushing aside the few spearmen he'd posted there. Without breaking stride the big horses transformed from column to line, fanning out to the right and left. It was here the women and children had fled in their thousands to escape the deadly hail of missiles from the Roman artillery machines. Panic rippled through them like a breaking wave as the thundering hooves and bright spear points bore down on them.

'No!' The plea erupted from his throat without conscious thought, but no amount of words or prayer would stop what was about to happen. One rider appeared in advance of the others. He lined his beast on a dark-haired woman fleeing in blind terror with a baby in her arms. A sword flashed bright as it rose and fell and the woman crumpled. The infant flew from her arms and rolled for a few paces before it disappeared beneath the merciless hooves. A great howl from the charging cavalry sent a chill down the Brigante king's spine and he watched helplessly as the slaughter of the innocents began in earnest.

'Guiderius,' a voice screamed. 'You must help them.' The plea from his wife, Regina, shattered the wall of lethargy that seemed to surround the Brigante king.

'Every man who can hold a spear with me!' He snatched one of the seven-foot weapons from a rack on the parapet and raced for the gates with his personal guard sprinting in his wake. Warriors manning the walls rushed to join them.

A frustrating delay at the gate made him want to beat the gatekeepers aside as they toiled to remove the massive oak bar. Out on the muddy sward hundreds of women and children, the elderly and the infirm swarmed towards the fort in a great crowd, seeking sanctuary. Guiderius felt a moment of alarm that leaving the gates open might have been a mistake. But it was too late for second thoughts.

Ignoring the distant screaming he led his men through the fleeing Brigantes using the butt of his ash spear to thrust aside the tardy. The refugees had smashed the cattle pens in their panic and cows, sheep and pigs ran unchecked among the rest, their panicked cries adding to the cacophony.

Guiderius saw his opportunity in an undamaged section of fence. He dashed to one end of the wooden railing. 'Form line on me,' he screamed. 'Form line.' A hundred men had followed him. So few? But it must be enough. When the line was set he ran to the centre and forced the butt of his spear into the earth with the leaf-shaped iron point towards the enemy. He experienced a heartbeat of terror that the very people he was trying to protect would simply overwhelm the pathetic rank of spearmen.

The ground shook beneath his feet and thunder filled his ears. Emerald plumes bobbed and waved among the mob of fugitives and the cavalry were close enough now for him to hear the metallic *thwack* of sword on bone above the screams of the maimed. At the last moment the fleeing refugees veered to left and right away from the barrier of spears.

A woman ran across his front with half her face sheared away and one eye dangling like a glittering ornament. A gnarled ancient, eyes wide in disbelief, displayed the blood spurting from his severed wrists before he collapsed in the mud at Guiderius's feet.

Suddenly there were no more refugees, just a line of horses, their riders' bearded faces snarling beneath green-plumed pot helmets, bloody swords raised and ready. Guiderius tensed for the moment of collision that must sweep them away like chaff in the wind. Thirty paces. Twenty. He had to will himself not to close his eyes. Then a surge of blessed relief as the Roman cavalry wheeled away to the flanks in search of easier prey. One man rode along Guiderius's front within spear range roaring with laughter as he rattled his sword blade across the glittering points.

'Back,' Guiderius shouted, aware the respite might only last seconds. 'Back to the fort.'

They backed away, a walking fence of spears, with fleeing women and children passing through their ranks towards the safety of the inner fort. Guiderius had a view across the table top of Brynmochdar. His once proud warriors still struggled in the twin grip of the advancing legionaries and the cavalry who abandoned their slaughter of the civilians to end the last vestiges of Brigante defiance. From time to time, men burst from the trapped mass, fleeing blindly from the carnage, twisting and turning like hares, only to be overtaken and cut down by the heavy cavalry swords.

He felt a surge of relief. For the moment, it seemed, the fort had been forgotten. But even as the thought formed a squadron of cavalrymen decided to prove him wrong and charged the mob of refugees struggling at the gate.

'Lord king?' Arvirasto, the commander of his guard, shouted a warning, but he was pointing east. The cavalry charge had been prompted by a cohort of infantry who'd fought their way through the crumbling defences and were trotting towards the fort. Guiderius saw the danger in an instant. If the cavalry caused enough chaos and the legionaries reached the fort before he could close the gate it was over. All this slaughter would have been for nothing. At least if he defended the fort to the last he could make an end that would leave his name untarnished.

'Back,' he screamed. 'Force your way through to the gate. We must close the gate.'

He tore at the refugees in front of him, throwing them aside and striking out with the butt of his spear, uncaring whether his victims were women and children. His guard followed his lead, smashing their way with brutal intent through the helpless civilians. At last, Guiderius looked up to see wooden timber walls. Only a few more paces. A new rumble of thunder and shrieks from behind as the cavalry struck, accompanied by the familiar butcher's block sound of metal on meat.

'The gate,' he shouted to Arvirasto. With a grunt the big warrior threw away his spear and drew his sword, hacking left and right to clear a path through the shrieking crowd that blocked the gateway.

Guiderius stumbled on the body of a grey-haired woman, but he had no time for compassion. The guard reached the gate and held the terrified refugees at bay as Guiderius stepped inside. 'Close the gate,' he ordered.

The gate guards looked to where the king's personal guard still fought to keep the mass of people back, even as the Roman cavalry hacked their way through from the other side. 'But—'

'I said close the gate!' The words emerged as a panicked shriek and the men threw themselves against the double wooden doors. Arvirasto heard the squeal of the hinges and turned towards the fort. Too late. An auxiliary cavalryman appeared from his left and the last Guiderius saw of his guard commander was his startled features as his severed head leapt into the air.

Now it was a combination of cavalry troopers and his own guard trying to force the gate open. Guiderius hurled his weight against the oak planks, only for a pair of arms to reach through and rough hands take him by the throat. Wild eyes glared at him from a bearded face and he struggled in a grip that felt like iron claws. A spear thrust from behind Guiderius pierced the auxiliary through the eye. The death grip on the king's throat loosened, but the dying man's arms were trapped in the gate, keeping it from being barred. Someone appeared with an axe and hacked the arms off above the elbow, and others used their spear butts to smash the cavalryman away. The bar dropped and Guiderius collapsed to his knees and vomited.

When he looked up, he was the focus of hundreds of accusing eyes from every conceivable platform and vantage point.

'What will we do now, husband?' Regina stood a few feet away, her arms across the shoulders of their two daughters. Like their mother they were beauties, dark of hair and fair of skin even at eight and ten, and it made his heart lurch to see them. 'With enough food to supply five hundred people for a week, trapped in a fort that now contains five thousand and more.'

'What else can we do?' He pushed himself to his feet. 'We must fight.'

She went pale and the mixture of rage and despair in her eyes made him glad when she turned away with the children.

They waited for the inevitable assault as the sun climbed in the sky. Thankfully the Romans halted their slaughter and Guiderius watched the shattered remnant of Brigante might being led away in rope fetters.

Legionaries collected the few Roman casualties and carried them away, but the Brigante dead lay where they'd fallen. It wasn't long before the sickly sweet stink of corruption hung over the field, competing with the stench of evacuated bowels as the numbers in the fort quickly overwhelmed the capacity of the latrine pits.

It puzzled Guiderius that the Romans went about their business as if the fort didn't exist, but he used the respite to order an issue of food and water, and inspect his defences. He had more than a thousand warriors manning the walls, and more ready to replace those who fell. It composed a formidable host that he was confident, despite what had happened, could hold off any attack. A guard alerted him to the arrival of a senior Roman officer, splendid in a sculpted brass breastplate and with gold gleaming on his helmet. A trumpet sounded and the Brigante king felt a shiver as the legionary cohorts appeared from the direction of the outer gate and formed up a few hundred paces from the fort.

An emissary on a white horse approached, holding a green branch.

'Put a spear a pace in front of the beast's legs,' Guiderius ordered one of the surviving members of his guard. 'But make sure you don't kill him. We are not barbarians.'

The spearman did as he was ordered and the Roman turned away with a grim nod.

Still, the attack didn't come. Instead, a wail went up from the civilian occupants of the fort as the enemy began to deploy their stone-throwing catapults in a half circle around the beleaguered outpost.

Regina joined him on the parapet. 'You must surrender, Guiderius,' she insisted in a low voice. 'Your people have suffered enough.'

She had always been outspoken, but this was too much. 'I am their king,' he snarled. 'And I will say when they have suffered enough. We are not fighting for them. We are fighting for Brigantia. We are fighting for the name and the honour of Guiderius. This was where my mother bowed to the Romans. No man will ever say Guiderius did likewise.' He heard her draw in a breath as he turned away, but she said no more.

Your people have suffered enough. Part of him knew it was true, and they suffered more when the Roman missiles began to land amongst them. The fort was built on a succession of rises, each with its own rampart, but the refugees packed every available space, so any boulder or dart that landed within the confines was certain to cause casualties. It continued relentlessly all through the night. Only a single catapult at any one time, but none the less terrifying. Every second filled with terrible anticipation. The distant thump, a sudden rush of air in the darkness, then the crash, sometimes almost liquid, and the awful screams that followed. Man, woman and child, not one person within the confines of Guiderius's sanctuary had the respite of a single moment's sleep.

Guiderius spent the night on the fighting platform, setting an example to his warriors and trying to appear heedless of the danger. By the time the sun came up his mind was a curious mix of broken, jagged-edged confusion and numbed exhaustion. Gradually the compact squares of the legion became visible, as if they had stood there waiting all through the night. My bane, he thought. But there was something he knew he must do. He had to struggle to make himself think, and when he spoke his voice shook.

'Collect the dead from last night,' he ordered in a croak, 'and throw them into the ditch. And bring me something to drink,' he called as an afterthought.

When he heard someone coming up behind him he thought it was a servant bringing the water.

'Have you reconsidered, husband?' Regina's voice came as a surprise. 'Will you not surrender?'

'Never.' He turned towards his wife, intending to dismiss her. At first it felt as if someone had placed a red-hot poker against his neck two or three times. He tried to cry out, but he was choking. Still unwilling to believe what was happening, Guiderius put a hand to his throat and it came away dripping red. The front of his tunic was sheeted with blood. He spun, reaching out to Regina, but the strength was already fading from his legs and only his wife's slim form stopped him from falling.

'My daughters will not die for your honour, husband.' Regina drove the knife she held directly into his throat. Guiderius's world turned upside down and his last conscious image was the splintered planking of the walkway.

'Open the gate,' Regina commanded. The men of Guiderius's personal bodyguard stared at the woman still holding the bloodstained knife in her tiny, clenched fist. 'Are you deaf?' she spat. 'I said open the gate.'

Valerius saw the gates of the fort swing open and a small group of people step out into the morning sunlight.

'Hold,' he ordered, and the *ballista* crew stepped back from their catapult. 'Gaius Rufus, to me.'

'Are you sure, legate?' Quintus Naso said. 'It could be a trap. Let me go. Or one of the tribunes.'

Valerius studied the fort again. The Second cohort's centurion reported that at least five thousand civilians had sought refuge there during the final stages of the battle for Brynmochdar. He could only imagine what the conditions had been like when the stones and darts landed among them during the night.

'I think we'll be safe enough,' he said. 'Guiderius would have to be a fool or a madman to carry on fighting.'

He nudged his horse forward and Gaius Rufus took station at his side. He knew without looking that Felix and the men of his bodyguard would be a little way back, close enough to intervene if anything untoward happened.

As they drew closer he saw that the group was made up of a woman in a red dress, two children, and a group of four or five grey-bearded elders who hung a little back.

'Mars save us,' he heard Rufus mutter.

'What is it?'

'Her dress.'

Valerius looked again and realized that what he'd taken for red cloth was actually white, but so badly stained with blood that she might have bathed in it. And not just the dress. Her face was spattered with gore and her arms were crimson to the elbow. Valerius drew up in front of her. The two girls were weeping, but they kept their heads high in emulation of their mother. He scanned the male faces behind her, but none fitted the description he'd been given.

'Ask her where Guiderius is,' he said to the scout.

'I speak Latin perfectly well.' Her voice was firm and clear, the words tinged with only the slightest hint of accent.

'Then so much the better, lady,' Valerius said. 'King Guiderius?'

'I am his wife, Regina, and these,' she placed her arms round the girls' shoulders, 'are his daughters. Bryn?'

One of the elders stepped forward. Valerius blinked when he saw what the man carried.

'I offer my husband's head in exchange for our lives,' she continued, 'and those of our people. This war was his choice, and his choice alone. Those who followed him did so out of loyalty. Sadly, that loyalty was not repaid.'

'You may keep your husband's head. You have nothing to fear from me, lady. Once my clerks have questioned your people they will be free to return to their homes. The warriors who laid down their arms will be held until we decide which hostages to take for their future allegiance to Rome. Not your daughters,' he assured her, seeing her clutch the children closer. 'As queen you will be treated with as much honour as you were before this unfortunate misunderstanding between our peoples.'

'What will happen to us?'

Valerius held her gaze. 'Brigantia will be absorbed into the province of Britannia.' He saw her flinch. 'She will have her own tribal council but the leaders of her people will be required to live in administrative centres to deal with Roman officials.' This had been the plan from the start. Agricola's conquered tribes were to be taught Roman ways. The procurator's representative would lay out townships and force the farmers to build new homes within those precincts. There would be councils. Perhaps, in time, basilicas and forums. And taxes. The sons of the chiefs and the young hostages taken by the victors would grow up speaking Latin. The last great barbarian strongholds of Britannia would become as Roman as the cities of Gaul and Hispania. 'Your warriors' swords and spears will be melted down and turned into the tools they will need to rebuild their lives. They will live in peace with Rome and with each other. There will be reparations, but I am certain the governor will wish to see them reinvested in your country's recovery. For the moment, I will have you and your daughters escorted to my tent, where you will be given the facilities to bathe, and a change of clothing.'

'You are generous in victory.' She looked up at the tall, scarred soldier in the glittering breastplate and helmet, and took note of the wooden fist that confirmed her suspicions.

'Gaius Valerius Verrens, legate of the Ninth legion, at your service, lady.' Valerius bowed his head. 'I am only sorry that we had to meet in such unfortunate circumstances. May I also say that I am glad it was Guiderius my men faced in battle and not his queen. I fear you would have been a much more formidable opponent.'

'Not a bad day's work,' he said to Gaius Rufus as they rode back to the legion. 'A victory won at the cost of fewer than two hundred casualties, Brigantia falls into our hands like a ripe pear, and we have a queen better equipped to deal with Rome than her fool of a husband.'

'I'm not sure our illustrious governor will see it that way,' Gaius Rufus pointed out.

Valerius returned his grin. 'A pity we couldn't have given him that big northern barbarian to make up for the Twentieth missing out on the glory.'

'Calgacus.'

'Calgacus?'

44

'That's what the mules are calling him. Calgacus. The Swordsman. They say he took out three Pannonians with a single swing of that great blade while his men were lifting your horses.'

Valerius remembered the tall figure silhouetted against the light, and the easy way he held the huge sword. The Swordsman. It fitted him perfectly. Yet he felt an odd stirring of unease when Rufus spoke the name. His voice contained the same mixture of awe and respect men used when they spoke of Boudicca.

Calgacus.

VII

'So he is as formidable as the stories say. All the better when we finally bring him to bay.' Agricola had listened to Valerius's report of the siege with an equanimity the legate of the Ninth legion found surprising, given that he'd been denied any opportunity to share the glory. 'You did well, Valerius,' the governor continued. 'As neat a battle as I've ever heard and I approve all of your decisions regarding the disposition of the prisoners and the civilians. We will install Queen Regina at Iseur; it's close enough to Eboracum to keep her honest and will serve as an administrative centre for her tribe. Yes. In all the circumstances it's just as well that you acted with speed.'

'It is?'

'Yes. Because the campaign is suspended for at least one hundred days.'

'A hundred days?' Valerius frowned. 'But this victory gives us the platform to move north right away. There's nothing but mountains between the Ninth and Brigantia's northern border. You could secure it with a single cohort. If we do nothing for a hundred days we'll have wasted an entire season.'

'I'm aware of that,' Agricola said testily. 'But I'm afraid the conquest of northern Britannia is no longer our foremost priority.'

Valerius could barely believe what he'd just heard. Conquest had been Agricola's aim since the day he was appointed governor of the province. What could have changed?

'The news only reached me this morning and the men are not to know until they are back in barracks.' Agricola studied the other man's face. 'The Emperor is dead.'

Valerius should have felt grief, or at the very least surprise, but he remembered the frail shell of a man he'd last seen on the Capitoline Hill and he knew that death would have come as a relief to Titus Flavius Vespasianus Caesar Augustus. Then the true implication of the Emperor's passing knocked the air from him like a punch from a clenched fist. He stared at Agricola.

'Yes, Valerius. That means your friend Titus will be declared Emperor of Rome at the end of the formal mourning period. It will be Titus who decides whether we continue the campaign or not. In the meantime, I must return to Rome for consultations. You will act as governor of Britannia in my absence. It will be your task to organize the appropriate ceremonies and conduct them in my stead.'

Titus Flavius Vespasian looked down upon the shrunken features of his dead father and felt a huge weight on his shoulders that hadn't existed the previous day. A sad, wistful smile momentarily touched his lips. The old man looked at peace, almost relaxed, the look of sullen, frowning concentration that had been his permanent expression for the last few years gone. And little wonder.

Vespasian had often used Augustus's description of being Emperor of Rome as like 'holding a wolf by the ears' to describe the daily trials he faced. Now those same trials loomed over Titus like a mountain avalanche. His advisers would tell him he'd been Emperor in all but name for the last year and more, and they'd be right, but that wasn't how it felt. The decisions he'd made had been his decisions, but the responsibility for their outcomes lay with Vespasian. If he thought Titus had made a mistake, the Emperor would smile, tell him why, and act to correct it.

Now there was no Vespasian. Only Titus.

And Domitian.

He could feel his brother staring at his back. It sent a prickling sensation down his spine and the feeling troubled him. He'd always tried to treat Domitian with, at the very least, forbearance, if not liking, but the younger Flavius had never made it easy. A petulant child, he'd grown to become a sulky, and sometimes vicious, adult. Titus had never truly been able to comprehend the enmity that existed between his brother and his friend Valerius, though he sensed that Domitian's wife Domitia had her part in it. Yet that enmity was real, and on Domitian's side potentially deadly, he knew. His father had been able to give Valerius Verrens a certain level of protection, but Vespasian had taken care not to alienate his younger son entirely. Domitian, characteristically, had used this leeway to continue his campaign. In a few short weeks Titus would don the purple of an emperor of Rome, and then he would put an end to the antagonism for good. But first he must accord his father the proper rites and ceremonies he had earned so selflessly. Titus Flavius Vespasianus Caesar Augustus would join his predecessors Caesar, Augustus, Tiberius, Gaius, Claudius and Nero in the divine pantheon.

He pushed Domitian from his mind and remembered his father's final words. 'I think I am becoming a god.' A genuine smile this time. How typical of the man that he would face approaching death, and a vile death at that, with the contents of his bowels streaming down his thin legs, with a joke. Yet there was more to the words than merely a jest. Vespasian had known they would be remembered and repeated. They would make his rise to the godhead all the more legitimate, and that legitimacy would pass to his son, who would become Emperor in his stead.

Titus knew his advancement would not be universally welcomed. The views expressed by Marcellus and the late Caecina were more widely held than he could accept with equanimity, spread and encouraged by those who should know better. Yet Vespasian had prepared the way with the same meticulous attention to detail that characterized his military campaigns. Almost every day of his reign had, in one form or another, been devoted to ensuring an orderly transition that would place his elder son upon the throne of the Empire. Seven consulships, the appointment as Praetorian prefect, priesthoods beyond number, a triumph at his father's side, the hailing as Imperator by his legions. All Titus lacked was the title of pontifex maximus, high priest of the temple, and he would accept that honour on the day he donned the purple. Rome would thank Vespasian for ensuring a smooth transition, with none of the confusion and bloodshed that had characterized the reigns of his four predecessors. Titus would be proclaimed Emperor and his appointment confirmed by the Senate and people of Rome.

But the first question any emperor faced was: how long could he keep it?

That would depend on the legions. His generalship in Judaea had made him a favourite of the legionaries, but a man could never be too careful. History showed that the legions would follow the lead of the men who governed their provinces. Of these, the two Germanias, Inferior and Superior, were the most important, because they were garrisoned by eight legions, all close enough to march on Rome in less than three weeks, as the late and unlamented Caecina had proved. Priscus, at Colonia Claudia, was an old comrade of both Titus and his father, and could be trusted to keep his legions loyal. Corellius Rufus in Germania Superior was an unknown quantity to Titus, but he wouldn't move from Mogontiacum without Priscus's support or he risked pitting legionary against legionary on equal terms. That would invite either a bloodbath or the removal of Rufus's head, neither of which he suspected the proconsul would be prepared to risk.

Gaul and Hispania he could discount. Their garrisons were not strong enough to rebel against a sitting emperor. The Balkan legions were spread across their mountainous region and would take months to unite, so they could also be ignored for now. An image of a tall, silver-haired man swam into view in his head. Flavius Silva, in Titus's old Judaean stamping ground, was another old comrade and the hero of Masada.

Silva had revered Titus's father. Between them, he and Ulpius Trajanus, once commander of the Tenth Fretensis but now governor of Asia, could be relied on to keep Praianus, proconsul of Syria and a man known to have lofty ambitions, safely in his palace in Antioch. Logically, there didn't appear too great a threat, but who knew the undercurrents and intrigues those bald statements of fact hid. When he thought about it, Silva might be a welcome ally closer to home. The Senate still hadn't confirmed his triumph for his great victory. Yes, a triumph and a consulship would guarantee Titus a good man to cover his rear. In truth, Silva probably didn't need the incentive, but there were others who might. Aulus Veieneto for one, a greasy little worm, but one who had made himself a necessary part of government. Caelius, too, might be thrown a bone. And . . .

'You will share my first consulship as Emperor, of course, brother.'

'It would be my honour.' The tone didn't quite match the words.

Titus turned away from his father's body. Of course it would be an honour. For whatever reason, Vespasian had never chosen to grace Domitian with anything but a temporary suffect consulship. Titus knew his brother regarded it as a calculated slight, but had never had the courage to raise the matter directly.

'He was a good man.'

'He was a great emperor.'

Titus studied the other man for a long moment, trying to detect any hint of a challenge in the pale grey eyes. Of similar height to his brother, but with a slim, almost slight build, Domitian had sandy hair styled in tight curls. His jutting, rather fine nose marked him as a Flavian, but he had a weak chin he tried to disguise by thrusting it forward aggressively like a ship's ram. No challenge, but no hint of grief in the expressionless eyes either. The end had not been unexpected, Vespasian's *medicus* had predicted he wouldn't last the night. Still, there should have been some show of emotion for the man who had shaped their lives and raised them from the sons of a family of penniless equestrians to princes of Rome. Titus's throat tightened as he remembered the moment the slim hand had slipped lifeless from his grip. Now was not the time for suspicion. Vespasian had striven to create a dynasty. It was up to his sons to make it happen.

'Come, Domitianus, we must help the clerks prepare the official announcement. I intend to accelerate work on the great arena so we can stage a games on his birthday such as has never been seen since Nero.'

Domitian murmured his agreement as they walked from the room side by side. Titus would have been concerned had he seen the almost contemptuous sidelong glance his brother gave him, but his mind had already moved on to the dilemma that had eluded him earlier.

Britannia. Julius Agricola held sway over four legions on the gloomy island where Titus had served as a young tribune. Agricola was Vespasian's man, but the son had never taken to the aristocratic soldier. Titus regarded the governor as a subtly ambitious politician with more faces than a gambling die who had timed his defection to Vespasian's cause suspiciously close to perfection during the civil war.

His father had believed the province a backwater of little value and certainly not worth the services of four legions. Yet too much had been invested – in gold and blood – to abandon the place. Instead, Vespasian had ordered Agricola to emasculate and subdue the northern tribes, so that at least one legion could be withdrawn.

For the moment it suited Titus that Agricola continue to execute his father's strategy. A governor busy avoiding Caledonian skinning knives would be too busy to become involved in the political manoeuvring that would follow the succession. Yet in the longer term it might be better to have Agricola closer to hand. A new face replaced the governor's, scarred and savage, the lips twisted in a parody of a smile. One of the very few men he could call friend. Yes, it could do very well.

VIII

Londinium

She was being followed. It wasn't so much a possibility as a certainty. The years she'd spent carrying messages for Berenice of Cilicia had taught her to trust her instincts. And her instincts had saved her life. Yes, she was being followed. But by whom?

Tabitha clutched little Olivia closer to her breast and tightened her grip on Lucius's hand, but she continued her leisurely contemplation of the silversmith's wares. 'How much for this?' She released Lucius's hand and held up a slim bracelet to the hovering shopkeeper.

'That piece would be two *denarii*, lady,' he said. 'It is some of our finest work.'

Tabitha smiled. It was a pretty enough trinket, but it could never be called fine. 'I think you have looked upon my soft clothes and mistaken me for someone who uses gold *aurei* for loom weights.'

The man, a Greek or Armenian if she were any judge, pretended a look of shock. 'But lady, do I not have six mouths to feed? The silver itself is worth a *denarius*, the craftsmanship . . .'

'Still,' she said.

He sighed, a man used to oppression, but one who knew when a compromise was required. 'One *denarius* and four *sestertii* then. I would be robbing myself if I let it go for anything less.'

Tabitha contemplated the bracelet again, and shook her head. 'I will think on it, but first let us see if you have anything else that would suit me.' The shopkeeper held the curtain aside and she entered the darkened interior with the children, followed by her maid.

'Livia, please take Olivia and Lucius while I search for a present for the lady Domitia.'

The girl accepted Olivia, who at six months was already a squirming bundle of mischief, and took Lucius by the hand. Tabitha picked up a piece of jewellery and carried it to the door as if to inspect it in the natural light. She stood in the shadow and gently pulled the curtain aside, just enough to have a view of the far side of the street. A street of metalworkers, midway between the fort and the governor's palace, and busy today. The people she saw pass by were mostly Romanized Celts, with a scattering of off-duty legionaries, and the occasional exotic foreign merchant to be expected in a cosmopolitan trading centre. One or two slowed to study the wares on the silversmith's table, but at first she could detect no one taking an undue interest in the shop.

Then she saw him. He was standing in the doorway of a shop opposite and, like Tabitha, almost lost in the shadows. As she watched, another man appeared with a copper pan in his hand and began a conversation. She was no lip-reader, but from what she saw she could tell the second man was trying to sell the first the pan. The gestures became more animated and eventually the first man shrugged and stepped out into the light.

Short dark hair, medium build, not young, but not old either, the sort of face you walked past on the street every day without noticing. Not a slave or a servant – they acted in a certain way she could always recognize – and he wore the nondescript clothes of an artisan. His face was set in a frown of concentration and his eyes never left the front of the silversmith's shop. Had she seen him before? She didn't think so. But that meant nothing. The important thing was she had identified him and would know him again.

The question was what to do about it. Her first instinct was to leave by the back entrance. Most of the shop-owners lived behind their premises, for reasons of security, convenience and economics. Yet all that would do was alert whoever was having her followed. Her shadow would be replaced by someone else, possibly someone more competent.

'Do you have a boy who would send a message for me?' She reached beneath her shawl for her purse and pulled out a copper *as*.

'Of course, lady.' The man bowed his head.

'Then fetch him, please.'

'Cestus!' the shopkeeper called. A small tousle-haired boy not much older than Lucius appeared through a curtained doorway at the rear, holding a shabby piece of cloth. 'My son. He's a bright lad. You can rely on him.'

Tabitha pulled a ring from her finger and placed it in the boy's palm. It was a gold circlet set with a small gemstone and of obvious quality. Cestus was obviously fully aware of its value and he looked from the ring to his father with consternation, but the silversmith only nodded. 'You are to take this to the villa that stands by the broad stream, opposite the fort,' Tabitha told the child. 'The one with the eagle statues on the gateposts. You know it?'

'Yes, lady,' the boy said nervously. 'The quickest way would be through the cattle market and up by the baths.'

'Good,' she said. 'You will ask for Ceris, the Celtic girl. Say you come from the lady Tabitha, give the ring to her and ask her to return with you immediately and to bring Rufius. Immediately, you hear?'

'Yes, lady, but what if—'

'Ceris will understand,' Tabitha assured him. 'Now go. Your father will give you this *as* when you return.' When the boy would have pulled aside the entrance curtain she stopped him with a word. 'No, go out by the back door and return the same way.'

When he was gone the father turned to Tabitha. 'My lady, if I'd known you were the wife of the legate of the Ninth I would have—'

'It is no matter.' Tabitha rewarded him with her most forgiving smile.

'Now, we will spend a few more minutes studying this beautiful work, then go back outside and take a final look at the bracelet. I think I will buy it as a present for the governor's wife.'

When they stepped out into the sunlight the man who'd been watching the shop darted back into the metalworker's doorway. As she picked up the bracelet Tabitha heard a muffled conversation that ended with a snarled threat. She pretended to study the trinket for a few moments until she caught the unmistakable sound of someone entering the shop from the rear. 'Yes, I'll definitely take this,' she said to the silversmith.

Inside, the boy was waiting expectantly beside a slim, pale girl with close-cut black hair, piercing blue eyes and a sullen cast to her thin lips. Tabitha nodded to the shopkeeper to pay his son and drew Ceris aside. Livia, the servant girl, stood by the wooden counter with Olivia and Lucius, with a look of frank curiosity on her stolid features.

'I suppose you'll want this back.' Ceris handed Tabitha the gold ring. On another occasion the glint in the Celtic girl's eyes would have prompted a light-hearted exchange between two women who had formed an unlikely friendship despite the difference in race and class, but they had little time.

'Where is Rufius?' Rufius was Ceris's lover and a member of Valerius's escort. He'd been left behind with five others to guard the household while the legate was on campaign.

Ceris shrugged. 'He had to go to the fort. The boy said it was urgent so I came alone.'

Tabitha pursed her lips. It would have to be enough. 'Go to the door, but do not let yourself be seen. Tell me what you see on the street.'

Ceris did as she was asked. 'I see a man who thinks he is invisible,' she said quietly. 'And who has an unlikely interest in silverware, judging by the fact that his eyes never leave this shop.'

'He followed us here.'

'And now you want to know where he goes and to whom he reports?'

'If it can be done without exposing you to danger.'

'While he is concentrating on you it will be simple. The difficult part is when you return to the villa and he is on his own. Perhaps he will see the servant girl skipping along in his wake.' Ceris laughed. She wore a simple short tunic over a long skirt, and a shawl draped across her back. With a deft flick of the wrist she turned the shawl into a hood and bent her shoulders in a way that added thirty years to her age. 'But not the elderly matron hobbling from shop to shop. Give me to the count of a hundred.'

'We won't be returning to the villa just yet,' Tabitha warned as Ceris made for the rear entrance. 'I have business at the palace.'

With Ceris gone, Tabitha took a moment to compose herself. 'Now, how much do I owe you?'

But the silversmith would take nothing for the bracelet. 'Please let this be my gift to you. All I ask is that the governor's lady knows whence it came.'

'Of course,' Tabitha agreed. 'And I hope I can count on your discretion about anything which may have looked . . . curious today.'

The shopkeeper gave her a wry look. 'To a man of my calling nothing is curious and silence comes as second nature.'

'In that case, I will ensure that all the governor's friends are also aware of the quality of your merchandise.'

'Tabitha!' Domitia Decidiana greeted her with a radiant smile and a kiss on the cheek. She was a few years older than Tabitha and from a family that gave Agricola entry to the highest levels of Roman society. They'd become firm friends despite a certain reserve that existed between their husbands. 'And you have brought the children.'

Her delight couldn't have been greater. Tabitha knew Domitia liked little more than to spend an hour with Olivia wriggling against her breast. Yet her greatest joy was Lucius. She laughed to see his endless energy and restlessness, but look closer and you could see the shadow in her eyes. She had borne a son who would have been of a similar age, but died in infancy.

Eventually, Domitia handed Olivia back to the servant girl and she and Tabitha lay on couches to exchange gossip about acquaintances and the meagre news they'd had from their husbands. Eventually, Tabitha produced the bracelet.

Domitia accepted it with a little gasp of delight and immediately placed it on her wrist to hold it up to the light. 'It will go perfectly with my new dress,' she said.

Before the governor's wife could thank her, Tabitha told her that when the shopkeeper had discovered the identity of the recipient of the gift he'd insisted on giving her it for free. 'He seems honest, and his workmanship is of the highest quality. I said I would recommend him to you and your friends.'

'Of course.' Domitia smiled. 'We will arrange a visit.'

A servant coughed discreetly in the doorway. 'The governor's aide is waiting in the outer room.'

'Oh.' Domitia put a hand to her mouth. 'You must forgive me, Tabitha. I'm so forgetful these days. I'm to accompany Metilius to welcome some dreadful delegation of merchants. Julius hasn't made his decision whether to allow them an import licence yet, but we must maintain the proprieties.'

'Of course, Domitia.' Tabitha smiled. 'It is time we were going in any case.'

Before they could move they heard a boyish shout from outside the window. Tabitha stepped into the garden where a muscular young man was wrestling playfully with Lucius. Metilius Aprilis had long aristocratic features and crimped dark hair and wore a formal toga of the best finespun wool.

'Lucius,' she called. 'Stop manhandling tribune Aprilis. He'll have to change his toga if you step on it like that with your dirty feet.'

'My ladies.' The young man separated himself and bowed at the waist. Aprilis was the foremost of Agricola's circle of young aides. With the governor on campaign he wielded a power few men his age could equal, but standing beside Lucius he looked almost boyish. 'You must excuse me,' he said. 'I do believe Lucius grows an inch and more every time I see him and he likes to test his strength against me.' He laid a hand on Lucius's shoulder and the boy gazed up at him with a look that sent a twinge of regret through Tabitha that Valerius was so far out of reach. 'Now, Lucius, you must go with your mother. The governor's lady and I have business to attend to.'

This time it was Lucius who bowed low, aping Aprilis's earlier movement. Domitia laughed and clapped her hands, and the boy went to stand beside Tabitha.

Later, as they walked home, she told him: 'You must treat Metilius with a little more formality and respect. I know you are friends, but he's a very important young man.'

'I'm sorry, Mother.' Lucius bowed his head, but she could see he was holding back a tear. She placed a hand on his shoulder.

'I'm not angry, but save your wrestling for when he is off duty.'

As they approached the villa one of the sentries rushed to open the gate. Once inside, she sent Lucius to the kitchens and settled down on a couch to feed Olivia at her breast. Ceris appeared after a few moments and took her seat on a couch opposite. Tabitha could tell that something was troubling her.

'So?'

'He followed you to the governor's palace,' the Celtic girl said. 'And I swear by all the gods he never saw me.'

'Good. What happened then?'

'When you entered by the side gate, I thought he would wait and watch, but once he saw you were inside he walked on, looking perfectly pleased with himself. When he reached the servants' entrance by the kitchens he walked inside.'

'Into the palace?' Tabitha couldn't hide her surprise.

'Yes. When you came out I waited for him to follow, but he never did.'

'So he's still there?'

'Unless he used another gate I couldn't see. And there's more.'

'Yes?'

'As he went inside he met another man leaving and they greeted each other perfectly naturally, as if they were friends.'

IX

'If you do not destroy the Romans, lord king, the Romans will destroy you and your people with you.'

Cathal noticed the grudging acknowledgement of his title from the druid riding at his side and smiled. Clearly Gwlym sensed the animosity emanating from the men who escorted him. Perhaps he also felt the menace of this bleak, rugged valley with its bare slopes where the wind had sculpted the few remaining trees into twisted, tormented skeletons that looked as if they were fleeing its wrath.

They'd ridden north for two days after the slaughter at Brynmochdar across a patchwork of scree, heather and gorse. If his instincts were correct they should reach the meeting place where he would wait for Emrys before nightfall. This was familiar country to Cathal, disputed land claimed by both the Brigantes and the Selgovae, and sometimes by the Carvetii to the west. Rolling hills and deep, shadowed valleys with a thousand places a man could conceal a stolen herd. Despite the loathing they felt for him, none of the Selgovae would dare lay a hand on Gwlym, for that would bring the wrath of the gods down on themselves and their families. Yet not an hour past Colm had suggested setting the blind priest's horse on a path that led towards a sheer drop.

'If he is a favourite of the gods surely they will save him?' Cathal's sword brother suggested hopefully.

Cathal had shaken his head. For all his dislike of the wizened ancient, Guiderius had placed the druid in his charge and he would not betray that trust. Gwlym had arrived at the Brigante king's capital a friendless and helpless refugee, an outcast, and only his former status had saved him from being treated as such. The Brigantes had long ago cast out their druids to placate successive Roman governors, but they still retained a certain respect for the order. Gwlym's undisguised contempt for his companions inspired loathing and his pus-filled eye sockets and filthy habits provoked disgust, but none of them would have denied he had a certain power.

The feeling had grown with every hour they travelled. Cathal had been taught by his father that in battle a man must use every weapon at his disposal to defeat the enemy. What made Dugald different from other kings was that he understood knowledge was as important a weapon as any other. Knowledge of the terrain. Knowledge about his enemy's numbers and their dispositions. Were they hungry, sick or weary? A single piece of information could be worth a company of spearmen. It was what had allowed the Selgovae to defy the simultaneous pressures from the wild men of the north and the treacherous Votadini to the east. Gwlym had been brought to him by the gods.

'Perhaps they will be satisfied with the Brigantes for now,' he answered the druid at last.

Gwlym knew he was being taunted. His mouth twisted in a sneer that was accompanied by a snort of bitter laughter. 'The Romans will never be satisfied. They have an insatiable greed for power and land and slaves and gold: everything someone else has and they do not.' He paused to allow Cathal's silence to acknowledge the truth of his words. 'They also fear you.'

Now it was Cathal's turn to laugh. He had seen what the massed ranks of the legions could do even against a fortified position held by three times their numbers. Guiderius had made mistakes, but the truth was the result had never been in doubt. Everything about the way the

Romans fought was different. A Selgovae warrior would face his enemy man to man and sword to sword, sometimes fighting naked to prove his valour. The legionaries hid behind their wall of big shields, protected by their armour, and dealt out death with a cold efficiency that made Cathal shiver. Every movement was coordinated to create that moment when their pathetic-looking little swords darted out to gut an enemy. There was no honour in it. No individual bravery. Just slaughter. And victory.

His eyes drifted to his men, now comfortable on the backs of the big Roman horses they'd stolen. Every man a champion, skilled in the art of war. Not the Roman art, it was true, but perhaps that was the answer? If he could find a way to deprive them of the time and the space to create their impenetrable shield walls? If he could make them fight as individuals?

'What would you know, who has spent half his life running away from Romans?'

Gwlym ignored the insult. 'I know they and the Roman-lovers who support them cannot sleep safe in their beds until they destroy the threat of the barbarians in the north. They must either kill you, enslave you, or turn you into a pathetic replica of themselves as they have the Cantiaci, the Regni, the Trinovantes and the Catuvellauni. Every man of the four British legions must be paid and fed and equipped, which ensures this province will never provide a surplus. Only by total conquest can they bring about a peace that will allow them to withdraw one or two legions.'

'How do you know so much?' Cathal demanded.

'Do not make the mistake of believing I was always this pathetic, Cathal of the Selgovae.' What might have passed as a smile flickered on the thin lips. 'Once, the spies of the Arch-Druid Gwlym, high priest of Elfydd, gave him access to the very heart of Roman power in this land.'

Cathal stared into the distance, allowing the silence to lengthen. Eventually it came to him. They were approaching a stream and he signalled a halt to water the horses and allow the men to rest. He helped

Gwlym from his horse and led him to a grass mound beside a tree that sheltered them from the wind. 'Tell me about them. I want to know everything.'

The druid fixed him with the terrible pits of his eye sockets, but Cathal didn't flinch. 'They first came in the time of my father's father's father.' Gwlym's harsh voice took on an oddly sonorous tone. 'But they stayed only a season, like a dog pissing against a tree to mark its territory, stealing anything they could lay their hands on and taking hostages. A hundred summers passed before they returned, as near as anyone could reckon it.'

'Why then? And why here?'

'As to the why then, does not every great chieftain require to give his warriors victory from time to time or he will be a great chieftain no more? Claudius, for that was his name, had been in power for no more than a year. Perhaps his enemies were gathering about him like vultures and only glory would save him. Why here? Our people had traded with Gaul since the time of the Great Flood. We were known to the Romans as the Romans were known to us. What did they see? A fertile land, rich in all that Rome desired. Civilized and cultured, which no Roman could abide unless that civilization was Rome's, but also divided, king squabbling against king and chief against chief, which has always been our great weakness.'

'Fruit ripe for the picking.' Cathal saw it clearly.

'But fruit not without its thorns,' Gwlym corrected him. 'The people of Elfydd learned a new word. Legion. A red scourge that spread across the land like a bloodstain, burning and plundering as it advanced.'

'They must have swept everything aside.' The Selgovae king frowned. 'Divided and without forewarning, no single tribe could have stood against them with the hope of success.'

'And no single tribe did. You have heard the name Caratacus?'

Cathal shook his head.

'A warrior prince of the Catuvellauni, then the strongest of the southern federations. Caratacus persuaded the tribes to set aside their differences and unite against the Romans.'

'A remarkable man.' Cathal knew how difficult it was to keep even chieftains of the same blood from cutting each other's throats.

'More remarkable than you know. Caratacus and his warriors fought the legions to a standstill until the Emperor himself came from Rome with reinforcements. Caratacus devised a plan for their defeat on the banks of the mighty River Tamesa.'

The name meant nothing to Cathal, and no river in his experience was sufficiently wide or deep enough to hold back the legion he had seen at Brynmochdar for long. 'But he was defeated?'

'Not defeated,' Gwlym spat. 'Betrayed. Betrayed by kings bought with Roman gold. As Boudicca was betrayed after drowning the Roman-lovers in their own blood, just when she was poised to sweep Rome's legions from the lands of Elfydd.'

'Then if they cannot be defeated how am I meant to destroy them?'

'I did not say we could not defeat them,' Gwlym snapped. 'Only that our attempts to defeat them were betrayed.'

'That does not change my question.'

A pause as Gwlym brought order to his thoughts. 'The answer lies with the Ninth legion.'

'Guiderius believed the Romans he fought belonged to the Ninth.'

'That is true.' The druid's voice shook as he remembered a more personal betrayal that had led to his defeat and flight from the Romans. 'As were those who helped take Mona. The defeat of the Brigantes, Mona and Boudicca are all linked by one man. The commander of the Ninth legion. And when you defeat the Ninth all I ask is that you deliver him alive into my care.'

When you defeat the Ninth. Cathal stared at the druid, seeking some sign he was being mocked, but he could detect none. 'How will I know him?'

'By his armour, which will be more ornate than those who serve him, and, more important, by the fact that his right hand has been replaced by a wooden fist.'

'You said the answer lies with the Ninth, but you did not say why.'

'First Boudicca destroyed Colonia and slaughtered its defenders.'

Gwlym seemed to grow in stature as he relived the glory of his youth. 'Then she turned her anger on Londinium. But as her great horde advanced on the city her spies warned her that Suetonius Paulinus, the Roman commander, had ordered a force to march south from Lindum to intercept her.' The names meant nothing to Cathal and he didn't hide his irritation. Gwlym smiled at the Selgovae's grunt of annoyance. 'Patience, lord king,' he said. 'As the legion approached, a warrior host commanded by Mab, one of Boudicca's Iceni chieftains, lay in wait on both sides of a wooded valley. Before the men of the Ninth reached it, another much smaller force drew the Roman cavalry away, and Mab was undetected until he struck.' He sensed Cathal's renewed interest. 'Mab did not live to provide me with the details, but all Elfydd knows that six cohorts of the Ninth and all their auxiliary infantry were destroyed, and their standards taken. It can be done.'

'One cow does not make a herd,' Cathal protested, but he sounded thoughtful. 'A single moment in time when the gods favoured this Mab, never to be repeated.'

'No,' Gwlym said firmly. His clawed fingers hooked into the flesh of the Selgovae king's massive arm. 'A Roman prisoner taken by the Ordovices last year and put to the question told me of Varus, a general who lost three legions in the same fashion, and their eagle standards with them. Annihilated in a forest ambush by the king of the Germans. It can be done by a man who can draw followers to him. A man who knows and understands his ground. Who is prepared to give up territory for advantage. A man who has the patience to wait for the right moment. You, Cathal, are that man.'

'Is that what you told the king of the Ordovices, priest? You are not the only one who has spies. Guiderius learned of your ally's fate from the displaced families who fled Ordovicia, the ones who escaped slaughter and slavery.'

'King Owain's destiny was in the hands of the gods.' Gwlym dismissed the Ordovices' sacrifice. 'He failed because he underestimated the cunning of the officer who commanded the Ninth that day.'

'The Brigantes number five times the warriors of the Selgovae,' Cathal said.

'Guiderius is not Cathal.'

'And where am I to find these followers you speak of?' The king growled his frustration. 'Even if a man could manufacture that single moment of potential he would still need an army to exploit it.'

'You must look where other kings will soon face the same threat as the Selgovae: to the west, the east and the north.'

'Novantae backstabbers. Venicones cattle thieves. Caledonian wolves,' Cathal snorted. 'The Votadini?'

'Wherever a man can carry a sword or a spear. Once they understand what it means to lie in the path of the Romans they will join you.'

'Lord king?' The shout came from Colm. 'Look!'

'Get the horses ready,' Cathal shouted as he turned to follow the guard's pointing finger. At the far end of the valley, still perhaps an hour away, a thin column wound its way down the track the Selgovae fugitives had followed. Hundreds, quickly growing into thousands as the cavalcade thickened and lengthened. Not cavalry, thank the gods. 'Colm?'

'They're not Romans. I see bullock carts piled high.'

'What is this?' Confusion furrowed Cathal's brow.

'It seems not every Brigante is content to live under the Roman lash,' Gwlym answered, though the question was not directed at him. 'Perhaps these are the followers you seek?'

A shiver ran through Cathal at this evidence of the gods' faith.

'A start,' he whispered. 'Just a start. But maybe you will have your one-handed assassin yet, druid. And I my eagle.'

X

Londinium

A sinuous golden shape swam round Valerius in an elegant curve, brushing the back of his legs, dark hair streaming behind her like a banner before slipping up his body, taut, firm flesh hard against his scarred torso. Tabitha emerged before him with a look of such intense eroticism that he felt a fire burn at the very heart of him.

'Won't the—'

She stopped the words with her lips, her dark eyes never leaving his, and raised her legs slowly up his body so their hips met and her ankles locked behind his back. Valerius let out an involuntary groan as she began to move, almost imperceptibly, against him.

'We have our routine, O soldier come home from the wars,' Tabitha whispered through clenched teeth, as the pressure of her body increased slowly against his. 'No one will disturb us while we . . . bathe.'

The very touch of her body was almost too much and he could feel himself throbbing and twitching against her belly. She felt it too. Without warning she gave a deft twist of the hips that almost belied nature and she was on him, the fire transforming in an instant into a pool of molten gold.

'No,' she hissed as his hands went to her. 'Don't move. This is *my* welcome, husband.'

It took an hour, with various adjustments and refinements, before it ended with an explosion of activity that sent the water in the pool crashing over the tiles in waves. When the surface settled she lay back with her head against his chest, eyes closed. A contented smile on her lips, she let her body float effortlessly as he helped her drift across the *caldarium*, gently stroking her breasts.

'You've missed me, Valerius?' she whispered.

'Couldn't you tell?'

'It's been so long, I feared those native girls might have corrupted you.'

Valerius suppressed a laugh. When he'd finally arrived after his four-day journey from Eboracum she'd drawn him aside even before he could see his children and insisted he needed a bath. 'From my recollection of the last hour I doubt any Brigante girl could teach you anything about debauchery. How are Olivia and Lucius?'

'Olivia will be sleeping, and Lucius is having his reading lesson. Do you think my breasts are sagging?'

'They look perfect from here.' He pinched her erect nipple and she sighed.

'I expected you days ago.'

'When Agricola left for Rome I had to select our Brigante hostages and make sure everyone understood the system for prisoner release.' He turned her round and hugged her to his chest. 'And probably a dozen other things I've forgotten in my rush to get back to you.'

'I'm glad you did.' She studied her hands. 'I think we should get out now. Look, my skin is beginning to wrinkle.' He helped her from the pool and dried her body with a cloth. When he was done she wrapped herself in its folds, so she looked like the exotic Eastern princess she was. 'I'll send Marcus to oil and scrape you, and prepare the children to give their father a proper welcome.' She paused at the door and smiled, a beautiful genuine smile, filled with pure affection, that seemed to light up the room. 'It's good to have you home, Valerius.'

*

An early dinner with the children. Valerius cradled Olivia on his knee while he ate and Lucius attempted to maintain a decorous silence that came hard to an effervescent six-year-old. After months apart there were things that required to be discussed, but during the meal Valerius and Tabitha concentrated on small talk. When the servants had removed the dishes Lucius shot to his feet with a scrap of papyrus in his hand and a look of rapt anticipation on his face.

'Very well.' Valerius struggled to maintain a grave dignity while Tabitha grinned at him from the other side of the table. 'Continue.'

'*The Boy who Cried Wolf*,' Lucius announced in a high-pitched, nervous voice. 'There once was a shepherd boy who was bored . . .' He stumbled his way through the first few sentences of the Latin version of a story by the Greek writer Aesop, and tailed away as the villagers grew angrier at the vexing false alarms.

'That's very good, Lucius,' Valerius said. 'Has your tutor told you what the story means?'

'Yes, Father.' The boy blushed. 'It is about the importance of telling the truth.'

'And how is your addition proceeding?' Tabitha flashed her husband a warning. Lucius was already showing some of his mother's aptitude for languages, but numbers remained a puzzle to him.

'Not so well, Father.' The boy hung his head.

'Don't worry.' Valerius smiled. 'Attend to your lessons and it will soon become second nature. I was the same at your age.'

'Thank you, Father.' Lucius's face brightened. 'May I take Khamsin for a ride outside the walls before bed?'

Valerius looked to Tabitha, remembering We *have our routine* with a shiver of recollection. She nodded her assent. 'Very well. But take Rufius with you.'

'And don't try to lose him this time,' Tabitha warned.

The boy bowed and scampered from the room, calling for Rufius Florus, the trooper who had the unenviable task of acting as his personal bodyguard. Valerius handed Olivia to her mother. Tabitha unpinned her *stola* and placed the baby at her breast, where Olivia

68

swiftly fastened like a limpet. They lay back in companionable silence for a while, Valerius watching his wife and child and Tabitha watching him, enjoying the attention. After so many months of solely male companionship and constant decision-making, Valerius felt as if he'd washed up on an island in a sea of tranquillity.

'So I am the wife of the governor,' she said lightly.

'Acting, temporary . . .'

'And unpaid.' She completed the legionary's mantra with a smile. 'How did Julius react to the news of Vespasian's death?'

It was a natural enough question, under the circumstances, but Valerius sensed a deeper meaning and chose his words with care.

'It was difficult to tell in the short time I was with him. He'd had most of the day to digest the news and, of course, it wasn't completely unexpected. Certainly no tears or anguish. Concern, I suppose, at losing such a high-ranking patron. I've learned he's a man who can't abide uncertainty. I think that is why he was in such a hurry to report to Rome. To a certain extent his entire career depends on this campaign. Not to say his name. With Vespasian in power he could well have been awarded a triumph if he returned with Calgacus on a rope halter. With Titus, it might be different.'

'Calgacus?'

'A Celtic war leader who allied himself with the Brigantes.' He frowned at the memory of the giant silhouette against the sky. 'A huge man with an enormous sword and an even bigger reputation among his people. He will be a formidable opponent.'

She heard something in his voice and he saw a shadow pass over her eyes. 'Beware this Calgacus, Valerius.'

'Is that your god talking?' He smiled.

'No,' she said gravely. 'Elah Gebal would not set foot in this gloomy place. It is your wife. Rome may keep its honours and glory and conquest as long as I keep my husband. I know you too well, Valerius. You can never turn away from a challenge.'

He looked thoughtful for a moment, but when he spoke again it was to answer the question behind her original one. 'How will Vespasian's death affect my relationship with Agricola, such as it is? I don't know, but I suspect he will be more wary of offending me because of my friendship with Titus. For a man of his ambitions that would only be sensible. In the past he has been pleased to give me independent commands and then taken me to task when I availed myself of that independence. On the other hand, I've always made my decisions and dispositions based on situations and circumstances, so in truth it changes nothing.'

'You never take his feelings or his likely reaction into consideration?'

He looked puzzled. 'What have feelings got to do with war?'

'Oh, Valerius.' Tabitha laughed. 'Titus told me before we left Rome that he thought you were becoming more diplomatic as you grew older. You seem to have forgotten everything you've learned since you met Julius Agricola.' She shook her head in mock exasperation. 'Will our lives change now that you are a proconsul, however temporary?'

'I don't intend them to,' he said. 'My main responsibility will be to ensure the ceremonies during the mourning period are conducted properly, but the priests will do all the work. I'll operate from here as long as it doesn't interfere with your routine. Any receptions will be at the governor's palace. You'll see a bit more of Metilius Aprilis and his clerks, but that shouldn't be— Is something wrong?'

'No.' She drew the word out so that it took on a different meaning. 'Or possibly.' She hesitated. 'Metilius has been paying a lot of attention to Lucius. He often calls in to see him or take him riding. Lately he's been teaching him how to wrestle. Rufius is concerned.' She saw Valerius's expression harden. 'No, it's nothing like that, nothing physical. I make sure there's always someone with them. In any case, I'm certain Metilius isn't . . . like that.'

'Yes?'

'A woman can tell, Valerius.'

Olivia lifted her head with an audible pop and Tabitha shifted her expertly to the opposite breast.

'It's Rufius's job to be concerned. How does Lucius feel about it?'

'I haven't asked him, but he always seems pleased to see Metilius. It's just . . .' She frowned. 'A grown man and a six-year-old boy. It seems an unlikely friendship.'

'Very well.' Valerius gave it a moment's thought. 'I'll talk to Rufius and perhaps have a word with Lucius. Is there anything else?'

'I think . . . no, I'm certain I'm being followed.'

It shouldn't have surprised him after all their past experiences, but for some reason the breath seemed to freeze in his chest. 'Who?'

She told him about the man Ceris had seen entering the governor's palace.

'You didn't feel under any threat?'

'No, truly.'

'But he looked as if he belonged there and he didn't leave?'

'Not while Ceris was there.'

This was a problem of a different order and it would take some consideration. Valerius had a feeling he knew who was behind it. *Why* was a different proposition, with more than one possible answer. The one consolation was that circumstances had changed. A new order now prevailed in Rome, one that could swing the balance considerably.

'I should have told you earlier,' she apologized.

'Don't worry,' he assured her. 'I'll deal with it.'

XI

The summer passed in a blur for Valerius. When he wasn't involved in the ceremonies to mark Vespasian's passing, his greatest pleasure was to ride out far beyond the walls with his family to bathe in the cool, clear upper waters of the brook that wound its way through the city before emptying into the Tamesa.

He spent much of his time arbitrating disputes between rival priests vying for the positions of supremacy – and profit – during the multiple ceremonies mourning the Emperor's earthly passing and celebrating his deification. A team of scribes followed him around the city as he established who was officiating where and in what capacity, but he soon discovered that the clerks were themselves far from averse to accepting an incentive to alter the line of precedence. The procession of wailing priests who found their way to his door only stopped when he guaranteed that the next scribe caught taking so much as a *sestertius* would end up tied in a sack with a dog, a cockerel and a cat and thrown into the Tamesa. As Tabitha pointed out, the sight of Gaius Valerius Verrens in a towering rage was enough to convince any ink-stained clerk or lisping priest that he meant precisely what he said. The ceremonies would mirror, as precisely as possible, those being attended in Rome by Titus and Agricola. Statues of the late emperor in his various guises as priest, administrator and soldier had to be commissioned and food and wine ordered, for the events would be followed by a festival which every resident of Londinium and the surrounding area could attend. Somehow he also found time to decide on a site, confirm the design and consecrate the foundation trench of a new temple which would be jointly dedicated to Jupiter and the newly deified Vespasian.

Meantime, the work of governing the province continued. Britannia's *procurator* and *quaestor* were perfectly capable men, but he found himself relying more and more on Metilius Aprilis, who was seldom far from his shoulder during working hours. He'd spoken to Rufius Florus about the friendship between Agricola's aide and Lucius, but the cavalryman couldn't specify what made him uneasy, only that something did. Lucius, approached obliquely, was no more forthcoming, simply confirming that he enjoyed Metilius's attention. The young man himself was perfectly amenable, pleasant and professional. Valerius had to remind himself that this fresh-faced tribune had almost certainly either murdered or supervised the murder of his predecessor as legate of the Ninth. Caristanius Fronto had been discovered at the foot of an Ordovice cliff. Aprilis was Agricola's man, hand and heart; the question was whether he was also someone else's.

Just before Valerius arrived in Britannia he'd received information from a source close to Domitian. It appeared that Vespasian's son was in contact with a person of high rank in the province, probably a legate, and the name Verrens had been mentioned in their correspondence. Valerius discreetly checked the backgrounds of his three fellow legates. He discovered no direct link, though Herenius Polio, commander of the Second Adiutrix, was the uncle of an officer of Domitian's personal guard. That might have aroused his suspicions, but Polio had never treated him with anything but respect and gave the impression that any sort of intrigue was beneath him.

It must have been two or three days after the kalends of August when Quintus, his doorman, announced the arrival of a visitor who declined to come any further than the courtyard. Valerius emerged into the sunshine and felt a rush of pleasure when he recognized Gaius Rufus. They greeted each other like old friends and Valerius invited the diminutive scout inside.

Rufus laughed. 'I stink like an aurochs in heat and I have more fleas than an Asturian sheepdog. Your *atriensis* looked as though he might faint.'

'Then we'll sit out here.' Valerius grinned, glad of the chance to escape from his scrolls for an hour or two. 'Bring some wine,' he called to the servant. 'The biggest jug we have.'

Rufus licked his lips in anticipation. For such a small man he had a large appetite for the fermented grape. 'I would have been here a week earlier,' he went on, his tone becoming uncharacteristically serious. 'But an impulse took me to Colonia to sacrifice to the *genius* of my father. The older I get the closer I feel to his shade.'

'There couldn't have been any urgency.' Valerius dismissed the part-apology. 'When we visited last year I found the town changed, but the temple much the same.'

'No loose tiles in the *cella* these days.' Rufus's words stirred a mutual memory of fire and destruction that provoked a period of silent reflection.

'I thought only the priests had access to the *cella*?' Valerius said eventually.

'Since when has that been a problem for a man of my talents?' The scout grinned. 'I couldn't pass the place without taking a look.'

The wine came and they drank together, Rufus savouring every mouthful after his long journey and Valerius's mind flickering between the spider's web of responsibilities Agricola had bequeathed him. 'I take it this isn't just a social visit,' he said eventually.

'Calgacus.'

'Yes?' Valerius half turned to ensure Tabitha was nowhere close.

'He's a slippery one. As slippery as I've ever known.'

'I thought I told you to stay with the Ninth.'

'I reckoned the Ninth would eventually be heading north. Not this season, right enough, what with them cosying up the fort at Brynmochdar for the winter while the harvest is still being gathered. The Twentieth and the Second, too, once they've finished settling in all those Brigante prisoners you freed and building the forts that will keep them settled.'

'Where did he go?'

'I followed their tracks for two days. A hundred and fifty horses, but only a hundred of them laden. Then they took to the hills and I lost them for a bit. When I finally worked out what had happened it took me half a day to backtrack.'

'They doubled back on you?'

'Partly, but it surprised me because it was such a crude attempt at concealing their tracks. Then I finally worked it out. They'd split. The men on ponies took to the hills and those on our stolen beasts either doubled back, or more likely didn't go that way at all. It took a while to dawn on me that I hadn't seen a big hoof for a while.'

'A careful man,' Valerius mused.

'More than careful.' Rufus grinned. 'A proper fox.'

'He knew the big horses would be a liability in the hills,' Valerius said thoughtfully. 'But he wanted us to follow him there. So he sent the ponies into the hills and kept the horses on the flat where they could make ground on us.'

Rufus nodded in agreement. 'He didn't know you weren't going to follow with the legion, but he made certain that if you did he'd be able to stay one step ahead.'

'And now he's where?'

'There's more,' the little man said cheerfully, replenishing his wine. 'He's not alone.'

'No?'

'I tracked him to a valley, well hidden, but good water and grazing. It must be close to the border between the Brigantes and the Selgovae because he stopped to wait for the men on ponies. The last two miles of his tracks had been obliterated by thousands of feet.'

The cup froze partway to Valerius's mouth. 'How many thousands?'

Rufus shrugged. 'Five. Ten. Who knows.'

'Calgacus does,' Valerius said bitterly.

'I followed their trail on the way back.'

'Brigantes.'

'Not all of them appreciate your idea of Roman hospitality,' Rufus agreed. 'They must have set out as soon as you'd turned them loose.'

'Women and children?'

'Warriors, too.'

'How could you know from their tracks?'

Rufus laughed. 'How could anyone with his eyes not?'

'So I've provided him with an army.'

'The beginnings of one.' Rufus nodded.

Valerius stood up and looked to the skies. Scarlet-cheeked swallows and scythe-winged swifts slashed the air among the buildings, their screams of ecstasy echoing from the daub walls. Who knew where they went in the winter, but wherever a building rose they always appeared to build a nest in summer.

'I want you to take lodgings here.'

'For how long?'

'As long as it takes.'

'To do what?'

'To make a map. I want to know everything you've seen and everything you've heard about the country between Brynmochdar and the place you found them. And everything you've heard about what lies three or four days' march beyond. I'll give you a warrant for the *mansio* and send an engineer to help with the drawing.'

'All right,' Rufus agreed. 'But you haven't heard the best of it. Or maybe the worst.'

'What?'

'Calgacus has a druid with him. A blind druid.'

Gwlym.

Valerius had searched for the druid among the countless victims of Agricola's invasion of Mona. Failure had provoked a curious mix of relief and disappointment that the malevolent creature who had threatened his wife and child with the most hideous of deaths was gone from his life, but probably not from the world. At least he'd been able to content himself with the knowledge that Gwlym would never be in a position to threaten Tabitha again.

Now he was back.

For a few days it tormented him that the blind priest had probably been within *ballista*-throw of him at Brynmochdar. He took a little time each day to study the ever-growing detail as Rufus dredged his memory to add to the map of northern Britannia. In his mind the map became the key to not just the downfall of Calgacus, but also the druid's doom.

Yet all this was swept away when Agricola returned unexpectedly from Rome.

Valerius received a surprise invitation to the governor's mansion on the last day of August. Agricola hadn't been due to return for another two weeks and Valerius had his clerks hurriedly gather the documents required to update him on the current state of the province and the progress of the new temple. But when an aide ushered him into the governor's private offices Agricola, in an obvious state of agitation, showed no interest in the papers but dismissed the clerks with a wave of his hand.

'Aprilis will update me later.' The governor paced the room for a few moments with his eyes on the marble floor and his brow creased by a frown of concentration. His clothes were still travel-stained and Valerius realized the summons had come even before he had disembarked. 'The campaign will resume immediately,' Agricola said abruptly. 'The Ninth will continue up the eastern route in parallel with the Second Adiutrix in the west. While you're on the march Ursus and his Twentieth will complete the consolidation of Brigante country and the organization of the tribal lands into administrative townships.'

'But the ceremonies for Vespasian's deification haven't been completed,' Valerius pointed out.

Agricola stared at him with an odd look in his eyes. 'Titus has suspended the period of mourning for his father. That's why there was no point in my staying.'

Valerius shook his head. Such a thing was unthinkable. Unless . . .

'There has been a disaster — no, a catastrophe — in the Bay of Neapolis.'

XII

Rome

'It's not possible.'

'I'm sorry, Caesar.' Senator Ulpius Traianus didn't flinch from his emperor's gaze. 'Communications are still difficult in the area around the Bay of Neapolis, but there can be no doubt that the damage in many places is total. Whole communities – Pompeii, Herculaneum, Oplontis and Stabiae – destroyed so completely they might never have existed.'

Titus still couldn't believe what he was hearing. As a child he'd played on the slopes around the great villas of Stabiae and swum in the cool waters of the sea. His father had taken him to see a gladiator show at the amphitheatre in Pompeii. Whole streets, temples, villas, shops and factories. All gone. Yet there could be no mistake. Traianus had anchored off Neapolis on his way back from his province of Asia and walked the barren, sulphurous slopes of the volcano while the ashes were still warm.

'Survivors?'

'The Misenum fleet managed to pick up Pomponianus and a few others from Stabiae and it's likely that some people in the countryside fled south, but of the rest, none. They had nowhere to run. As far as we can tell the whole area to the south and west of the mountain is buried under ten feet of ash.'

Titus's mind reeled at the scale of the disaster and the resources that he would have to find to bring solace to the survivors. They would need roofs over their heads, food and water. He must arrange an immediate visit . . . He could feel Traianus's eyes on him.

'The Misenum fleet? Of course. Pliny.'

'Gaius Plinius Secundus died a hero.'

Titus struggled visibly to deal with this new blow. Pliny was the Empire's finest mind. Its greatest natural philosopher. He'd sent Titus an early version of his astonishing *Naturalis Historia*, ten volumes of incredible detail and insight that covered everything from astronomy and mathematics to metallurgy and mining. Titus barely noticed that Traianus had continued talking.

'I spoke to his nephew, Gaius, of course, and the commander of his flagship, the *Annona*. When he was alerted by the first eruption his first instinct was to go to the aid of his friend Tuscius, but when the scale of the event became clear he called out the fleet. They sailed through a storm of plunging rocks to Herculaneum, but the harbour there was blocked by some convulsion. The mariners wished to turn back, but Pliny wouldn't have it. *Fortuna favours the bold*, he said. If they couldn't save Tuscius and his wife, at least they could do something for Pomponianus and those trapped at Stabiae.' Traianus cleared his throat and Titus called for a servant to bring him a cup of watered wine. When his visitor had drunk the Emperor signalled for him to continue. 'They managed to reach Stabiae with some difficulty, but once they were in the harbour the wind changed direction and it was impossible to get out again. By now the fall of ash and rock had worsened, but Pliny remained calm. He said he would stay overnight at the house of Pomponianus and they would sail as soon as the wind turned in their favour. In the meantime, anyone with no other means of escape would be taken on board the ships of the fleet.' He frowned. 'As you know, Pliny was rather overweight and often struggled for breath. Despite his disability he refused a chair to carry him up the hill to the villa. Conditions continued to deteriorate through the night. Eventually it became clear the weight of ash on the roof of Pomponianus's house was unsustainable, and Pliny took the decision to return to the ships. Somewhere on the way down he lost touch with the rest of the party. Two slaves who had been helping him reported he had collapsed during the descent and passed away soon after. His body was recovered two days later and it was my honour to carry it back here to Rome.'

'Thank you, for your service to Rome,' Titus said. 'I am sure you must be tired after your journey.' He turned away and looked out from the palace window over the sea of terracotta rooftops on the Quirinal Hill. When Traianus was gone he called for his secretary. 'Make arrangements for me to travel to Neapolis. Six senators will accompany me. Military men, I think. I will need experts in supply, housing and road-building.'

'When do you wish to leave, Caesar?'

'In three days. First I must bury an old friend.'

XIII

'So Pliny is dead?'

'He died a hero,' Agricola confirmed, 'attempting to rescue the people of Stabiae.'

Valerius went to the window and stared at the clouds. It seemed absurd that Pliny would never look at them again, wondering where they came from, or how and why rain only fell from a cloudy sky. How could so much intelligence be wiped away in a single moment? Yes, they still had his books – Valerius had the entire collection, including the treatise on cavalry spearmen he'd helped Pliny write – but without the mind that created them the books would fade and decay and eventually the author himself would be forgotten. Pliny had sent him into mortal danger in Hispania, then saved his life on the dusty road from Asturica Augusta to Tarraco. They'd been friends for so long, arguing cases in the law courts and exchanging letters from distant lands, that it was impossible to imagine the world without the embodiment of that fierce, questing hunger for knowledge.

'I'm sorry . . . ?'

'I was saying that the Emperor is focusing all his attention on providing food and shelter for the survivors,' Agricola said. 'He plans to rebuild what can be rebuilt and replace what cannot. It is an enormous task which will require all his energies for months to come. He was of a mind to abandon the Britannia campaign entirely and withdraw a legion to Italia to help with the reconstruction of Neapolis.'

Valerius felt a moment of nostalgia for the warmth of the Italian sun. Would it be so wrong for the Ninth to be called back to carry out something worthwhile? Campaigning with Agricola wore a man down and, in truth, he sometimes wondered at the point of the operation. He'd seen little evidence of a threat from the northern tribes that warranted the attention of three legions. But Agricola quickly forestalled such wistful notions. 'Fortunately, I persuaded him otherwise. He has given us two more years to complete the subjugation of the north.'

'Is that possible?' Valerius didn't hide his scepticism.

'I have assured him it can be done, and that once the north is pacified two legions will be all that is required to maintain peace and stability on the islands.'

'You have promised him what you cannot provide,' Valerius persisted. 'Better to tell him now. Titus is the kind of man who would rather hear the truth. He will—'

Agricola's jaw tightened. 'Do you presume to tell me how to run my province, legate?'

'No, proconsul, I do not.' Valerius bit back the words that might have permanently destroyed their relationship. 'I merely offer my advice.'

'When I want your advice I will ask for it.' The governor made a visible attempt to contain his fury. Eventually, he said, 'I spoke in anger. Let us put this behind us, Valerius.'

Valerius nodded his agreement.

'I have not offered the Emperor the impossible, because you will make it possible. With the Brigantes destroyed there is no reason why we cannot advance at speed. Yes,' he said before Valerius could protest, 'I know there are a dozen tribes to the north who have not yet felt the power of Rome, but none of them matches the Brigante federation for fighting strength. Are we agreed on that at least?'

'Yes.'

'So, forget about your flanks. Push ahead as fast as your men can

83

march. You will have the full support of the fleet and every pound of supplies they can carry. Harry the tribes through the winter. Weaken them so that when spring comes we can advance at speed with all three legions and drive like a spear into the heartland of the Caledonians, who are the true enemy.'

'You know there are reasons why we don't campaign in winter. Valid reasons.'

'Of course I do.' He smiled, and a new Agricola appeared from behind the mask of command, 'But I am fortunate that I have with me the one man who can overcome those difficulties. If anyone can do it, Valerius, you can.'

Valerius saw there was no point in continuing the discussion. By ordering his army to go beyond the norms of war and carry the fight to the enemy in the dead of winter, the governor had shown that the taking of northern Britannia was not only an act of Imperial strategy, but an extension of his own vanity. Agricola would have his triumph if it cost the life of Valerius and every man who served under him. It was an act of desperation, perhaps even of madness. Should he make a personal appeal to Titus and warn him of the potential consequences? He had the means. But that would be a betrayal, not just of Agricola, but of Valerius's own principles. As a commander he had always counted on the loyalty and support of his subordinates; why should Agricola not be able to expect the same? He stood. 'In that case I should return to my command as quickly as possible. There is one more thing.'

'Yes?'

'I have reason to believe my family is being watched.'

'Watched?' Agricola frowned. 'By whom?'

'I don't know for certain,' Valerius admitted.

'Your wife is starting at shadows, then.' Agricola smiled. 'It is a trait in some women.'

'Not in Tabitha. A man followed her to the Street of the Silversmiths. She noticed him watching her and contrived to have him followed in his turn.' The smile had never quite reached Agricola's eyes. Now it froze in place.

84

'What did this *watcher* look like?'

Valerius repeated what Tabitha had told him.

'A description that could fit any one of a thousand of Londinium's inhabitants,' Agricola pointed out.

'He came here to your palace and was welcomed like an old friend.'

'What are you insinuating, Valerius?'

'I insinuate nothing.' Valerius held the other man's gaze. 'All I do is present the facts and the facts suggest that the man who followed Tabitha may be a member of this household.'

The governor tapped his stylus on his writing table. 'Very well. I will have the matter investigated. Will that satisfy you?'

Valerius knew he could expect nothing more. He bowed his head in thanks.

'I am sure we will find some innocent explanation.' Agricola rose and walked him to the door. 'Some foolishness by one of the servants. Your wife is a strikingly attractive woman, Valerius. It would be unfortunate, but not surprising, that she would draw a man's attention.' He hesitated as if a thought had struck him. 'Of course, I must also acknowledge the possibility that some member of my staff may have shown an over-enthusiastic regard for Tabitha's safety and decided to have her watched for her own protection while you were on campaign. Whatever the explanation, I hope you will accept my assurance there will be no recurrence of the event.'

Valerius stood in the doorway just long enough to let Agricola know that he would hold him to his promise. 'Of course, proconsul.'

Agricola waited long enough to ensure Valerius had left the palace before he called for his clerk. 'Send for my senior aide.'

Metilius Aprilis appeared a few moments later, clad in a simple tunic and carrying a bundle of scrolls. Agricola didn't invite him to sit.

'I thought I made it clear before I departed for Rome that Valerius Verrens was to be left strictly alone until I could gauge some idea of the new emperor's exact feelings towards him.'

Aprilis's cheerful expression turned wary. 'Have I done wrong, lord?'

Agricola repeated the description Valerius had given him. 'One of yours, I suspect.'

'Milo,' Aprilis hissed. 'The fool.'

'My instructions included his wife and his family, I believe.'

'Yes,' Aprilis acknowledged, 'but you also suggested that I spend the time considering his weaknesses. On reflection,' the young man recovered some of his former bounce, 'it seemed to me that Tabitha might turn out to be his greatest weakness. She is an easterner, with contacts and friendships within that community . . .'

'Are you suggesting she is some kind of spy?'

'No, lord,' the younger man hurried on. 'But she is, or was, a Judaean before her marriage to Valerius, and as we know, a Judaean is but one step from a Christ-follower.'

'Titus, like his father, is ambivalent on the subject of the Christ-followers.'

'But others on the Palatine are not,' Aprilis said with a significant look.

'Very well,' Agricola said after an interval. 'But this stops now. Titus Flavius Caesar Vespasianus Augustus has let it be known that the legate of the Ninth legion is a favoured friend. A single word from Valerius Verrens could have severe consequences for us both, Metilius. Do not forget that.'

Aprilis bowed. 'Lord.' After an interval he dared to raise his eyes to meet the other man's. 'And what of our friend on the Palatine?'

Agricola looked to the door, and when he spoke it was in a voice so low only Aprilis could hear. 'It was not deemed safe for me to meet him, nor to receive a letter, but a verbal message was sent. His enmity is undiminished, but the moment is inopportune.'

'So our brave soldier is safe for now?'

'As safe as any man about to embark on a winter campaign against a dangerous enemy in the mountainous north. Who knows what ills could befall him? But we must wish him well, Aprilis. If he succeeds it will be Gnaeus Julius Agricola who rides in triumph through Rome.'

'And if he fails?'

'If he fails, our emperor may have reason to revise his opinion of Gaius Valerius Verrens.'

XIV

The first autumn frost dusted the grass with silver and turned the ground hard as mortar on the morning Valerius rode through the gates of the temporary camp at Brynmochdar. Naso welcomed him with a guard of honour and a quizzical expression. Why would the legate of the Ninth turn up at the legion's winter quarters when he could be tucked up with his pretty wife in the comfort and warmth of his Londinium villa?

Valerius noted that his men had made themselves comfortable in the time he was away. Instead of the usual leather tents they'd built barrack blocks from wood salvaged from Guiderius's enormous folly of a hill fort, timber walls windproofed with moss and mud and thatched with layers of reeds. Naso's *principia* was constructed of the same materials, but somehow he'd managed to find a batch of terracotta roof tiles that gave the building an air of permanence.

'Camp prefect,' Valerius greeted his second in command. 'I see you've been busy.'

'We didn't expect to see you so soon, legate,' the other man smiled. 'But I'm sure we'll be able to find somewhere to put your head down.'

Valerius recognized a familiar face among the honour guard. 'Crescens, I hope you've been keeping out of mischief?'

'Of course, lord. May I ask if the lady Tabitha is keeping well?'

'She is, soldier.' Valerius returned his grin. 'And so is the lady Ceris.' Valerius knew that Crescens, once the most awkward of his bodyguard, had developed a recent attachment to Tabitha's Corieltauvi companion. Unfortunately the attachment was not returned by the lady and would earn him a dagger through his liver if Rufius Florus ever discovered its existence.

'Perhaps you'd like to escort the legate to his quarters, Crescens,' Naso suggested.

Valerius dismounted and handed his reins to a groom as Crescens took step beside him. 'What's been happening while I've been away, Julius?' Valerius nodded at the legionaries who looked up to watch their legate pass. 'The men seem suspiciously cheerful.'

'The lads are happy as pigs in shit, begging the legate's pardon.' Crescens grinned. 'Don't get me wrong, lord, the camp prefect keeps us busy, but living in barracks through a nice warm summer certainly beats marching twenty miles every day with some big barbarian out there itching to stick a spear through you. Our main job has been disarming the Brigantes and getting them settled back on their farms. A few thousand slipped away to the north. I reckoned they were gone for good, but . . .' he gave Valerius a sideways look, 'I have a feeling we might be seeing them again sooner than we thought.'

Valerius ignored the hint as the clatter of hooves on frost-hardened ground announced the return of a mounted patrol. A cavalry squadron. Thirty dust-stained, travel-weary men entered through the gateway, their horses surrounded by clouds of steam. A diminutive figure swathed in furs rode at their head. Valerius hurried towards them as Gaius Rufus unwrapped a cloth from his bearded face and slipped from the saddle.

'I didn't expect to see you so soon, scout,' Valerius greeted him. 'You have news for me?'

'I have news, lord,' Rufus confirmed, but his expression gave nothing away.

'Ask the camp prefect to join us in the *principia*,' Valerius ordered Crescens.

While they waited, Gaius Rufus heated a bowl of water with a glowing poker then buried his face in it. 'By Taranis's three heads,' he gasped, emerging from the steaming bowl just as Naso arrived, 'I thought my ears were going to freeze solid and fall off, and as for my nether parts . . .'

Valerius laughed. 'I think we've heard enough about those. In any case, I'd prefer to know what you've been up to since I sent you north.' He retrieved a circular leather tube from his baggage and opened it to reveal a roll of parchment, made up of several smaller sheets sewn together. When Valerius pinned it to the *principia*'s collapsible campaign table, Naso saw that it was a crude map. Valerius looked to Rufus. 'You'll recognize this. It's based on the information you gave my engineer in Londinium.'

Rufus studied the patchwork of dull brown, with its spots of deeper green, curling blue snakes and jagged peaks that could only be mountains. 'Yes,' he said, as his mind worked out the symbols and their meaning. 'I see it now.' He pointed to a small square in the lower portion. 'Brynmochdar.' He nodded to himself and his finger travelled northward. 'We followed the line of the mountains and turned west into the foothills following the path of the Brigante refugees to where they joined up with our horse thieves. Those fellows are cunning and tried to lead us astray more than once, but Gaius Rufus is too old and leery to be fooled by barbarian tricks. We stayed on their trail through what they call the Tinan Gap, here, to the very edge of Brigante country. Beyond it lies a softer land of rolling hills with fertile, well-watered valleys but few inhabitants because it is claimed by three or four tribes. Eventually there is a new barrier of more rugged hills, with steep scarps and narrow gullies that seldom feel the sun's light.'

'Ambush country.' Naso sucked his teeth, remembering the long, bloody march on Mona.

'Indeed, lord,' Rufus agreed. 'This is where I deemed it safer to leave the patrol. I forged ahead alone until my way was blocked by a hill fort that I judged as near impregnable as any of them is ever likely to be. Steep slopes on every side but one. I would judge it to be here.' His finger traced a route through the hills to a point where they fell away to a river valley.

'How far from the fort to this place?' Valerius pointed to an odd formation of three hills cradled in the blue curve of a river in otherwise almost empty country.

'It's impossible to tell.' Rufus gave him a shrewd look.

'You'll get to know it better before the spring. We all will.'

'So that's it.' Naso grimaced. 'I knew you must have a compelling reason to leave Londinium when the campaigning season was all but done.'

'Governor Agricola has ordered that we push northwards and campaign through the winter,' Valerius confirmed, ignoring the camp prefect's incredulous grunt. 'The Emperor has given him two more years to carry out the mission his father ordered.'

'Impossible,' Naso said. 'We have little or no information about the lands of the far north. There was no guarantee we could succeed in four seasons, even five. Now he wants it done in three. And in winter? The men will freeze on the march or starve in camp. We'll end up eating bloody snow and there'll be no forage for the horses. How can we ask them to build marching camps when the ground is frozen solid as year-old *opus signinum*?'

'It will be difficult,' Valerius admitted. 'But the governor recognizes that. That is why we will drive north through these hills before the first snows and build a new winter camp *here*,' he pointed to the river that curled round the three hills, 'at the river's highest navigable point. Ships will be waiting off shore to carry enough supplies and forage to last us through the winter. From the camp we'll launch fighting patrols into the territory of the Selgovae and the Votadini, burn their homes and supplies and weaken their ability to oppose us after the spring thaw.'

'Fighting patrols.' Naso didn't hide his scorn. 'In the snow?'

'It will keep the men warm.' Valerius allowed himself a wry smile. 'And if the ground is too hard to dig banks and ditches we'll build walls of snow instead.'

'Madness.'

'Orders,' Valerius corrected him. 'And the quicker we start the better it will be for all. I've requisitioned four hundred extra mules and a hundred ox carts from the Twentieth – yes, Quintus, only the Ninth and the Second are involved – so when we slight the camp we'll carry the timbers with us.'

'Very well, legate.' Naso set off for the door. 'I'll brief the centurions immediately.'

When they were alone, Valerius turned to Rufus. 'You have nothing to say, scout?'

'What more is there to say?' The little man looked up from his place by the fire. 'If we run out of *ballista* ammunition we can always throw snowballs at the Celts instead.'

'Can it be done?'

Rufus ran a hand through his beard and considered the map. 'We'll need to move fast. If we can get past the hill fort before the first snows.'

'We will.'

Rufus hesitated for a moment. 'There is something else.'

'What?' Valerius's voice was harsher than he intended, but he didn't need another problem to add to his already mountainous pile.

'Our Mithras-followers plan to initiate you into their number.'

Valerius froze. Rufus was no follower of Mithras – his gods were the gods of Britannia, ethereal creatures of the land and the air around him – but of course he would know the men who were. He'd proved himself as brave as any man in the legion and the bull-slayer's adepts recognized him as an equal. The pause gave Valerius time to reflect upon what was being offered. It was the greatest honour these men could do him. To become an adept of Mithras was to become part of a select brotherhood of warriors. Only the truly valorous who had proved their courage and risked death on the battlefield would be invited to go through the complex series of rituals and ordeals of the initiation ceremony. Even then, a single flinch would disqualify the initiate. To be asked was a testament of the Ninth's finest soldiers' trust in their legate. There was only one problem. He couldn't accept.

He turned to Rufus. 'You must make it known that the invitation cannot be made,' he told the scout. 'Because it cannot be accepted.'

Rufus looked stunned. 'May I tell them why?'

Valerius could have said that a legate could not be compromised by allying himself to a select handful of his men, or that the Emperor expected his generals' first and only loyalty to be to him, but neither of those things would be true. 'No.' He shook his head. 'They must be satisfied with that.'

Rufus hesitated a moment before giving a curt nod. As he left the tent Valerius heard him mutter: 'I'd rather be caught crawling into a Caledonian camp than do this.'

Why had he refused? A prudent officer fostered a good relationship with the Society of Mithras. His predecessor, Caristanius Fronto, had refused permission for the construction of a temple at Lindum dedicated to the bull-slayer. It had been part of the reason for the breakdown of his bond with his men. The rituals of the initiation ceremony were a secret defended by blood oath and curse, to be maintained on pain of death. Yet the ignorant would speculate and the jealous would deride or exaggerate. As time passed the truth became immersed in a fog of myth and legend, which suited the Mithras-followers just as well. But a man could not spend twenty years living among the toughest, bravest and best-disciplined soldiers in the Empire without learning something of the cult and its ceremonies.

Valerius knew, for instance, courtesy of a man who'd spent a week in the *valetudinarium* dying of fever, of the pit where the initiate crouched as the highest-ranking adept cut the throat of a bull to saturate him in the animal's blood. Half-heard gossip around a dozen different campfires told him that Shabolz, though a lowly trooper and a foreigner, was the Ninth's highest-ranking Mithraist, a master of the cult's deepest mysteries and probably the most respected man in the legion. And he knew of the moment in the ritual when the blindfolded, disorientated initiate, his mind reeling after two days without food and sleep, had a dagger placed in his hand, the point quivering with the movement of the flesh beneath, and was told, 'A child lies beneath your blade; strike deep and quick.'

In reality the child was no child, but a kid, its belly shaved to give the impression of human flesh, and the warm blood that spurted over the initiate's fingers was goat's blood. But that made no difference. The ritual required that the initiate *believe* he had killed a child to show his ruthless commitment to Mithras. Valerius had seen children die, on Mona and elsewhere. He'd heard his own men joke about exterminating vermin as they hunted them down and curse that they were harder to catch than the adults. But Gaius Valerius Verrens had never killed a child. He could *never* kill a child in cold blood. Valerius paid as much attention to the gods as the next Roman. He made the libation to the kitchen god because it was expected of him. He left a coin at the crossroads during his wedding parade because that was the tradition. As a legate he had paid for sacrifices, but Gnaeus Domitius Corbulo had taught him to also pay for the correct outcome. A sensible man never dismissed or deprecated the gods, but neither did he depend upon their aid. *A child lies beneath your blade; strike deep and quick.* Valerius knew he would never obey that order even if he knew the flesh beneath his knife was destined for the pot. Not for any man. Not for a god.

Not for Mithras.

XV

The six men sat against the walls of a barrack room close to the northern perimeter of the temporary fort at Brynmochdar. They were the legion's best and they were of all ranks, but rank meant nothing here. From outside came the sounds of the fort being taken apart, but it had been arranged that this block would be the last to be demolished. For the moment they were silent, lost in their own thoughts. The only sound was the soft hiss of the sharpening stone Shabolz was working back and forth along the length of the *gladius* he held across his lap.

This was a situation beyond their experience. They'd been certain Valerius would be unable to refuse the honour they sought to bestow upon him. Men had given up their lives to prove they were worthy of selection for the ordeals of Mithras.

'We should unmake it,' Honoratus, the legion's eagle-bearer, said.

Shabolz brought the blade up before his eyes and studied the bright iron, which had a peculiar blue sheen and took an edge like no other he'd ever known. It was a beautiful sword, the work of the legion's most experienced armourer, and a masterpiece of his craft, created from three bars of the finest carbon-rich iron from the foundry. The blade shone in the lamplight, as long as a man's arm from elbow to fingertip and with the triangular needle point that made something so beautiful

94

astonishingly deadly. It had a hilt carved from antler, wrapped in soft leather held in place with gold wire for a more comfortable grip. The pommel was also gold, worked into the shape of a bull's head. It was perfect. All it needed was the right man to wield it.

'Perhaps,' Shabolz conceded, continuing his study. To unmake it they'd bend the blade between two rocks, or, he mused, perhaps with this sword they'd somehow have to snap it. Then the two parts would be taken to a local shrine and either buried nearby or thrown into a pool to appease the gods. Mithras didn't deal in trinkets like this. It would be a pity . . .

One thing was certain. No other hand would wield it in battle.

He shook his head. Fools that they were to have had the sword made before they were certain Gaius Valerius Verrens would accept their offer.

'He should not have refused.' The speaker was Clodius, a centurion of the elite First cohort, a man who had been inducted into the society after proving his courage with the Twentieth legion during Agricola's first campaign against the Brigantes six years earlier. 'It will bring even more misfortune on a legion already cursed with ill-luck.'

'He didn't refuse,' Shabolz pointed out in his quiet voice. 'He made it known the offer would not be accepted before it could be made. He has done nothing wrong. If anyone is to blame it is we for assuming he would wish to serve the god.'

'Nevertheless,' the centurion persisted, 'it is a slight, an insult both to the god and to us who follow him. And it shows an unexpected weakness in our commander.'

'Not a weakness,' another voice growled. Hilario, Shabolz's fellow member of Valerius's bodyguard, a huge man with a sullen brute's face that disguised a sharp, if ponderous, intelligence. 'A different kind of strength. If the legate felt unable to accept our offer then he had good reason for it.'

Shabolz nodded agreement. 'I feel no insult and I see no insult to the god. By letting it be known through Arafa that the offer should not be made he ensured that no offence could be taken.'

'And the sword?' Clodius demanded.

Shabolz weighed the *gladius* in his hand. ' I think we will keep it,' he said, wrapping the blade and hilt in a piece of oiled leather that would protect it from damp and rust. 'Who knows, perhaps we will find a use for it?'

'No sign of them?'

'Nothing,' Gaius Rufus confirmed. 'They'll have scouts in the hills watching us, but their rearguard just melts away in front of us.'

'I'd prefer it if the bastards fought.' Valerius twitched his mount's bridle and they walked their horses down the sloping path to the valley where the legion's First cohort had halted to rest and replenish their water. Rain swept in chilled, misty waves from the north and every man except the scouts and the sentries huddled with their sodden cloaks over their heads. It had been like this for two days, progress frustratingly slow as the heavily laden ox wagons of the baggage train struggled through mud churned ankle deep by cavalry and infantry. Time was already against him. A mile lost today would contribute to an extra day's march in the weeks ahead. Valerius had considered leaving his baggage train and forging ahead with the legion, but he knew that if winter came early their lives might depend on the timber carried by the carts. 'They'll never have a better opportunity. We're strung out for miles and the baggage train wallows in the ooze like a drunken sow. Of course,' he flicked beads of water from the brim of his helmet, 'if they do, the cavalry will hunt them down and slaughter them before they can get into the hills.'

'Calgacus knows that,' Rufus grinned. 'That's why he won't oblige you. Not until he reaches the hill fort.'

'Why should he fight there and not here?' Valerius wondered. 'He saw what we did to the Brigantes at Brynmochdar. He must know that a few walls and ditches won't stop us for long.'

Rufus slid from his horse as they came to a bend in the river where floods had left a raised bank of sand. As Valerius joined him he cleared a wide area of debris and drew an elongated oval with his foot.

'This isn't Brynmochdar with its indefensible walls and scrapes of

96

ditches.' He picked up a piece of stick and drew three slashing strokes from south, east and west. 'It doesn't matter which direction you attack from, you'll be faced with an ankle-breaking open slope that'll sap your men's strength while massive boulders thunder down to batter them to pulp. When the survivors reach the top they'll have to fight their way through three lines of ditches filled with thorn bushes and stakes, cunningly positioned to allow the Celts to hurl spears into your ranks while you can't reach them. By now your cohorts are broken up and bleeding, the final ditch is filled with your dead and dying and still you must scale a sheer rock face the height of three men with a defended palisade on top. Too high for your shield platform tricks. You'll need ladders and plenty of them, but of course most of them will be lying broken on the slope and in the ditches. Calgacus knows he can't stop you completely, but he can buy time. By now he's wondering why you haven't already gone into winter quarters. Every day you take to overcome the Fort of the Bronze Gates is a day closer to your being forced back south by the weather.'

'I take it it's called that for a reason.'

'According to the locals it was previously named the Maw of Teutates because there was a superstition that anyone who entered uninvited was swallowed up by the god. More recently, Calgacus ordered his precious hoard of bronze be melted down and forged into plates to strengthen the gates.'

'Still, a couple of centuries in *testudo* with a battering ram . . .'

Rufus shook his head. 'We once talked of a place called Maidun. Do you remember the gates?'

'I remember them. Deep pits and false turns that led to nowhere but a cascade of flames or a volley of spears.'

'Then you know what Calgacus has in wait for you.'

Valerius pursed his lips. 'Could we bypass it? Leave them to starve?'

Rufus shrugged. 'You would then have the choice of leaving half your force to keep the garrison caged inside or using the same number to secure the valleys and river crossings that would give them access to your supply lines.'

'Then we attack.' Valerius made his decision. 'You say the northern slope is unclimbable?'

'So sheer a child could protect that rampart.'

'Then we attack from here, here and here.' Valerius pointed to where Rufus had slashed the sand. 'Two legionary cohorts and two of auxiliary infantry against each wall.' His face twisted into a scowl as he imagined the bloody escalade. 'That will leave four cohorts to exploit the breakthrough when it comes. We'll take losses, perhaps heavy losses, but I see no other option. We have to get past the fort before the first snow. How long to get into position to attack, unseen by the garrison?'

'Two days,' Rufus said decisively. 'But the Selgovae scouts . . .'

'Every cavalry trooper who can sit a horse will scour the hills on either side of our advance. Two days. You're sure?'

'Yes, lord.'

'Then we attack at dawn on the third. The gods willing we'll be in winter quarters in another week.'

'And Calgacus?' Rufus touched the little charm at his neck.

Valerius gave him a sour look. 'Let us hope he decides to command the defence himself. It might cost us more men, but it would rid us of a permanent nuisance.'

In the ghost hour before dawn Valerius stood with his command group and listened to the soft tramp of feet and the muffled jingle of metal as his legionary cohorts funnelled through the valley into their positions at the bottom of the ridge. Before them lay a steep climb of perhaps five hundred paces and he'd ordered their commanders to cover half that distance in the darkness at a silent crawl. Rufus had led them unerringly through the night, bypassing two palisaded defensive positions along the way.

Apart from a century that had lost its way and blundered into a bog the march had been without incident. The auxiliary cavalry squadrons reported no contact with enemy scouts, but that meant nothing. Valerius still had a niggling fear the Selgovae would be waiting at the top of the slope poised to turn the assault into bloody chaos. At the last minute he'd sent one of the reserve cohorts on a flanking march to cut off the enemy's line of retreat. Now he wondered if they'd have been better used supporting the attack. Only time would tell. When the remaining reserve cohorts were in position he ordered his signaller to check with their commanders that they were aware of the signals that would send them into battle. They'd be out of sight of the assault and the trumpet call would tell them where they were needed and demand an instant response. He rode along the lines, exchanging a quiet word with the men he knew, their positions in their cohorts fixed in his mind, asking after their welfare and the state of their equipment. They would suffer as much, in their own way, as the men currently crawling on their bellies up the slope out there in the darkness. Valerius knew the agony of waiting in reserve for the blast of the trumpet. Not knowing whether you were advancing to reinforce success or make a suicidal charge to stem failure. The frustration and the grinding in the guts. The looseness of the bladder and the bowels.

When he was satisfied with his dispositions he rode forward through the trees at the base of the hill, dismounted and handed his reins to an aide. 'You don't always have to prove yourself, Valerius,' Quintus Naso said, so quietly that only Valerius could hear him.

'You'll get your chance of glory soon enough, Quintus.' Valerius accompanied the words with a smile, but he found his lips were cracked and his throat dry as an Armenian salt pan. 'Water,' he called, and drank deeply when the aide passed him a goatskin. 'I'll be safe with the second wave. The men expect their eagle to be close by during an attack and they expect their legate to be with his eagle, isn't that right, Honoratus?' He couldn't see the *aquilifer*'s face in the gloom, but he could visualize the big man's shy smile. Quiet and thoughtful, Honoratus, but with a sword in his hand he could be a force of nature. No better man to carry and defend the legion's sacred symbol. The solid, leaden darkness gradually receded to a silvery veil and the shapes of individual men sharpened.

'Get ready.' He could hear the tension in his voice and the shadowy figures of his bodyguard moved into position around him. 'Send the signal, Quintus.'

No trumpet calls would announce the initial advance. Instead the messenger raced off to give the order for the right hand cohort to move. Valerius had ordered that the charge be made in silence until the attackers were detected. Each cohort would attack in line formation three ranks deep. When the cohort began its advance, the unit on its left would set off a moment later. It meant a staggered formation across and around the face of the hill, but Valerius saw that as positive. The defenders would naturally be drawn to the point of initial danger, weakening the other parts of their line. Or so he hoped.

Dawn proper, grey and unwelcoming. A glance showed the top of the hill concealed by mist. All the better. Time. 'Go,' he ordered. Honoratus set the pace, trotting diagonally towards the base of the slope, the eagle on his shoulder clearly visible now. When they hit the incline Valerius discovered it was even steeper than he'd expected. Within a few paces the rear of his calves began to burn. His sculpted leather breastplate was much lighter than the plate armour of the men surrounding him, but they had the advantage of youth and his breath rasped in his throat as he tried to maintain their pace. They advanced through the ranks of auxiliaries who would make up the second wave. Beyond them Valerius could see the backs of the legionaries trudging stolidly upwards, helmets wobbling with the effort of the climb, *pila* and shields at the ready. Despite the efforts of their centurions their lines were already ragged as a result of the rugged terrain.

Gaius Rufus had identified a small plateau behind the third cohort to advance and they made their way up across the rocks and scree and tussock grass. The leading legionaries would have crossed the brow of the hill by now and even with the mist their presence must be obvious to the defenders above. Yet there had been no alarm. No hurtling boulders bounding to shatter the advancing lines. Valerius strained to detect the screams and the crash of spear on *scutum* that would announce the joining of battle. Nothing.

Nervously, he checked his flanks as they reached the flat projection where he'd intended to pause. 'Keep going,' he ordered. 'But *aquila* to the rear.' He must know what was happening up there, but he couldn't risk the eagle to a sudden ambush.

'By the Lady's beard,' he heard one of the escort mutter – Hilario? – 'the bastards must be asleep.'

'If they're asleep it must be the sleep of the dead,' Crescens whispered.

Valerius remembered Rufus's reference to the Maw of Teutates and made the sign against evil.

They continued upwards.

'Lord.' A young messenger bounded down the slope towards them. 'Centurion Clodius says you must see this.'

By the time he reached the top the mist had all but cleared apart from a few wisps hanging in the air like wind-borne spider's web. Men stood around staring at the impressive ditches and successive walls. Not as large as he'd expected, but formidable enough. He could hear the sound of soldiers searching the few dozen roundhouses he could glimpse above the ramparts. One look at the gates confirmed what he already suspected. Bright splashes showed where the polished bronze had been nailed to the wood before being torn away by men in a hurry.

The fort was empty.

XVI

Cathal sat on a rampart not unlike the one Valerius had just crossed, lost in his own thoughts, staring south to where a column of white smoke marked the destruction of the Fort of the Bronze Gates. He snorted disdainfully at the pretentious names men gave to objects to make them seem frightening. His reinforced gates and high walls hadn't frightened the Romans.

Gwlym's head came up at the sound. 'You still haven't explained why you made an old man climb a mountain.'

'This is a special place. A sacred place. Can't you feel it?'

'I feel your fear.'

Cathal spat and the druid hissed what might have been a laugh. They'd dressed Gwlym in new robes, but nothing could dilute the sour stench of decay and corruption that hung about him. When they first rode into the little settlement of Mairos children had run in fear at the first sight of the pus-filled eye sockets and stretching, long nailed fingers. The village lay on a cleared strip of land snuggling in the bend of the river below the three hills. Beyond the river lay the eastern territories of the Selgovae and the ephemeral dangerous frontier with the Votadini, a people whose wealth was a result of their exploitation of land and sea and a combination of perfidy and broken promises. The

Selgovae and the Votadini had been enemies and rivals for countless generations and nothing would change that. Even now when the smoke from the enemy fires was visible on the horizon Votadini scouts sent by their chief Marro harried and probed west of the Selgovae boundary stones.

Yet Cathal knew that only by combining their strengths and those of every minor tribe within their sway could they ever hope to blunt the Roman attack. Despite the provocation he had swallowed his pride and sent emissaries to offer Marro an alliance. He must buy time.

He moved closer and took the ancient druid's hand in his. 'Where you sit,' he touched the hand to the heather-clad earth below them, 'is the rampart of a settlement which has been used by our ancestors since the beginning of time for the great festivals of Imbolc, Beltane, Lughnasa and Samhain. This is the north hill of three. The wall around the hilltop is gapped and decayed, the thatch of the houses patched and mouldering, for this is only a gathering place these days. Here the smiths forge the axes and swords that will be given in tribute to the sky gods. Middle hill, the highest of the three, is where the ceremonies take place and the offerings are made.'

'And the third?' Gwlym demanded. 'The realm of Taranis ever contains thrones for his cohorts, Teutates and Esus.'

Cathal bit back a surge of bile. How could he have known? The Selgovae chief's voice took on a sombre tone. 'Things are done on the third hill that none but the highest initiate may attend.'

'Then all is not lost,' the druid said. 'Your religion is the true religion and the gods are with you. With the correct sacrifice it is still possible we could condemn the red scourge to an eternity of suffering in the bowels of the earth. The blood of a virgin princess would be ideal. You have daughters to spare, I am sure.'

Cathal wasn't certain whether he was being mocked, but he drew a dagger from his belt with his left hand and the wizened priest froze at the touch of the point on his throat.

'If there is any further talk of sacrifice or threats to my family the only blood that will be spilled will be that of a dispensable druid.'

'That must be your decision,' Gwlym sniffed. 'But timidity will have its consequences just as boldness may lead to success. You were talking of the three hills.'

Cathal slipped his dagger back into its sheath. 'The bend of a great river cradles the three hills as a mother cradles a babe in her arms. We call the river Thuaidh and it provides an annual tribute of great fish and fat geese. Beaver and otters swim its waters and we harvest their pelts. A man could climb into his *curach* at Mairos yonder with the sun at its height and be at the ocean by nightfall, but only traders use the route these days. The Votadini hold sway over the lower reaches and they demand tribute for passage.' He raised Gwlym's hand and pointed it to the left. 'To the east, beyond the river a land of rolling hills, heather moor, rough pasture and fertile dale. Good farmland and well-settled open country with few trees, because my people hunger for land to till and plant, and farmers are greedy for wood.'

'No place to face the Romans, then,' Gwlym said, visualizing the terrain and remembering a similar landscape where Boudicca and seventy thousand of her warriors had died on the points of the little Roman swords.

'No,' Cathal agreed. 'But if I forge an alliance with the Votadini as I hope, I fear that Marro who rules them will insist we defend it. He too has farms on the Merse that pay him tribute and farmers who expect to be defended.'

'Then you must persuade him otherwise.'

'To the south,' Cathal ignored a suggestion with which he doubted he could comply, 'beyond Muckle Cheviot, lie the disputed lands and Brigante territory. I had thought to delay the Romans at the old hill fort, but if Guiderius could not hold Brynmochdar with thirty thousand men and more the Fort of the Bronze Gates could not be held by two thousand, no matter how valiant.'

'You could have hurt them,' Gwlym pointed out.

'Hurt them, yes. But at a cost I cannot afford. Two thousand of my best warriors trapped or slaughtered, but lost in any case.'

'Then there is nothing to stop them? Do you truly understand what that means, king?'

'I know what the Brigantes suffered.'

Gwlym spat a bitter laugh that emerged like a stubborn piece of phlegm. 'The Brigantes suffered nothing,' he sneered. 'They were clients who bowed the knee to Rome before the first arrow was drawn. Cartimandua bought them years of freedom with the life of Caratacus. Rome paid *them* a subsidy in return for keeping barbarians like you from interfering with them as they remade the south of Britannia in their own image. Their roads will be the chains that bind you, allowing them to move soldiers at speed in any weather while your horses and ponies are up to their bellies in mud. They will move you from your farms and settlements into *municipia* with basilicas and forums where your children will be taught to love Rome. You will wear Roman clothes, drink Roman wine and learn to be your own jailers. For that is the beauty of Rome's rule. Those ruled do not even know it is happening. You will obey Roman laws, take Roman names, make Roman lists that will identify everyone and every thing, so that Rome can tax you down to the last egg and the last bushel of barley. You will never hold another sword or throw another spear, Cathal, and one day you will wake up to find your sons and daughters are Romans. *That* is the reality you face.'

'Never.' Cathal's face had gone pale beneath the deep tan. 'But what can I do? A few rivers block their path: Owsnam, Jed and Tivyet. I have arranged for ambushes to be set and the fords to be defended, but nothing that will delay them for long.'

'You can fight.' Gwlym's voice took on a new urgency. 'You will fight them here. You must fight.'

'No,' Cathal said. 'Even if the hill could be made defensible there's no water and no shelter. We might last a few days, but then we'd be slaughtered like penned sheep.' It had been the most difficult decision of his life. 'If Marro refuses my offer of an alliance I will withdraw west.' He pointed Gwlym's hand to the right. 'There lies the great confusion of forest, hill, lake and valley that is the true heart of Selgovae country.

We have already moved granaries and cattle herds from the most threatened areas. My people were reluctant, but the experiences of our refugees convinced them they could never live under Roman rule. It is late in the season; the legions must withdraw south very soon. The first snows are not far off and if they are caught in the hills they will freeze, man and beast.'

'And if they do not withdraw?'

'You know them better than I, druid. You tell me.'

Gwlym thought for a moment, everything he had learned about the Romans running through his mind. 'They will choose a defensive position where they can build a fort and wait out your Selgovae winter in warmth and comfort. It will be on a height overlooking a river, probably near a ford. Ideally it would have hills nearby where they can site a signal tower.'

A shiver of anticipation ran through Cathal as the reality behind the druid's words dawned on him. He looked down towards the river. Not a mile away to the south-east, just beyond the shoulder of the great hill, lay a position that fitted the druid's description to the last detail.

A grim smile flitted across his rugged features. 'Then let us hope they do. Perhaps the Romans will find a Selgovae winter too warm for comfort – as warm, in fact, as the fires of Teutates' furnace.'

XVII

Dawn turned the gently rolling landscape to a glistening carpet of glowing gold. From Valerius's position by the hill fort the sight was enough to take even the most world-weary soldier's breath from his lungs. On the north side of a winding stream he could see the legion's camp laid out on the far slope hundreds of feet below. Neat rows of tents, horse lines, ovens set into the turf walls, six gates, each with a raised earth mound to deter a direct assault, and the legate's outsized pavilion his escort had cursed him for abandoning so he could be here, far above, at dawn. The sunlight glinted on the spears of the guard detachment and smoke rose in lazy spirals from the recently lit cooking fires. Gradually curiosity drew his eyes across the hills to the far distance and his heart seemed to stutter as he looked for the first time upon the silhouette that had come to haunt his dreams.

'Trimontium,' he whispered. The place of the three hills.

'Sir?'

'See it, Shabolz?' Valerius laughed. The sight had been hidden the previous day by thick haze. 'Three distinct peaks. Two quite sharp, the third flatter, but still perfectly visible. Trimontium. That is where we'll finally catch up with this Calgacus. If he is the kind of man I believe he is he will never give up his sacred place without a fight. Those hills will be our mark. If the gods are kind we will fight our battle before the freeze sets in and enjoy a comfortable winter in barracks.' He saw the Pannonian reach up and touch the curious crooked cross charm at his neck. 'Is something wrong, trooper?'

'With respect, lord, it never does to disregard the power of the local gods. The scout tells me they are all around us, in the water and the air. Calgacus would be a fool to fight us in open battle and my instincts tell me he is no fool.'

Valerius gave a mental curse. Of course Calgacus was no fool. Gaius Valerius Verrens was the fool, allowing his over-enthusiasm and the sight of a few hills to cloud his judgement. He looked back at the hills standing out like a giant milestone on the horizon. They would still be his mark, but he would treat them and Calgacus with more caution. Many a slip between the cup and the lip, as the legion's clandestine dice players said. He would not make the same mistake again.

'You're right, Shabolz.' He clapped the Pannonian on the shoulder. 'I will have the priests make a sacrifice before we break camp. Let us go down now. I'm so hungry I can feel my ribs sticking to my backbone.'

Shabolz smiled, but Valerius wondered if their relationship retained the warmth of a season earlier. Had his refusal to join the Mithras cult – yes, the invitation had never been given, but it could still be regarded as a slight – soured the bond he had with his men? Before he could consider the answer, Nilus, the signaller, alerted him to a rider forcing his mount up the slope towards them.

'It looks like Arafa,' Nilus said, confirming Valerius's suspicion. 'He's in a hurry.'

Valerius urged his horse down the hill and they met the little scout midway. A smile split his bearded face and removed the feeling of foreboding Valerius had experienced at the first sight of his approach.

'Lord.' Rufus saluted.

'What is it?'

'We have a visitor,' the scout grinned. 'And I think you'll want to meet him.'

Valerius delayed long enough to don his dress uniform, the breastplate and helmet glowing with gold and silver, the scarlet cloak and the sash that proclaimed his rank. Slaves rushed to decorate the *praetorium* with busts of Titus and Vespasian, brought on campaign in case he needed to entertain Agricola and his fellow legates. When the preparations were complete he stood beside a padded couch with Honoratus and the legion's eagle to his right, and eight men of his bodyguard, including the fearsome Hilario, arrayed behind him.

Gaius Rufus led the visitor into the room and a flicker of the dark eyes told Valerius he'd been right to go to the trouble of impressing the man. A face made up of sharp angles, nose like an axe blade, chin jutting like a ship's ram, a mane of walnut hair and moustaches that fell to his throat. He stood with his arms crossed, head held high on a long neck. A proud man, if Valerius was any judge, and not one to be taken lightly. He wore a heavy torc of twisted gold strands at his throat, and beneath his cloak of green plaid Valerius saw arm rings of the same precious metal. A long Celtic sword in an engraved scabbard hung on his right hip from a belt of golden links, and a short dagger on his left.

'His name is Aneirin and he is a prince of the Votadini,' Rufus explained. At the mention of his name the man nodded his head in what might be construed as a bow. 'King Marro, who rules east of here from a place called Chalk Hill by the River Thuaidh to a fort at Dun Eidin far to the north, sent him to bring fraternal greetings and declarations of friendship to the commander of Rome's armies. Aneirin,' Rufus bowed in his turn, 'tells me that the Votadini have long traded with Roman merchant ships – though I think they were more likely Gaulish. He warns us against a warlike tribe called the Selgovae who pollute the lands to the north and west and have been guilty of the worst kinds of depredations against the Votadini.'

'If the Selgovae are his enemy,' Valerius observed, 'he is a brave man to journey through their territory with an escort of just four men' – he waved a hand at the four stolid warriors who stood behind Aneirin, warily eyeing Hilario and the other guards – 'however brave and skilled.'

Rufus translated the words, which clearly pleased the Votadini envoy.

'I passed on your compliment to his bodyguard, but the original escort was actually about sixty men. When I met him with the patrol I suggested he left most of them behind. I didn't think it wise to come in with sixty strange warriors and risk our guest getting a spear in his guts from an over-zealous sentry.'

'You did right.' Valerius offered his own bow and Aneirin reciprocated. 'Please ask him to sit.' He gestured to a couch, but the offer was answered by a staccato burst from the thin lips and a flash of the dark eyes.

'Aneirin declines your invitation,' Rufus said through pursed lips. 'It seems to sit in your presence would in some way dishonour him. He does, however, present a gift from his king which he hopes will meet your approval and cement your friendship.'

Aneirin gestured to one of his bodyguards. The man stepped forward and handed him a leather sack that weighed heavily in his hands. Pulling a glinting object from its folds, the Votadini prince held out the gift and waited for Valerius to take it from him, his head bowed. Valerius looked to Rufus for guidance, but the little man just shrugged.

At last, Valerius approached the moustached Celt and accepted the offering, hearing the usual intake of breath as the man saw his wooden fist for the first time. A bull. A charging bull, worked in gold, so finely detailed you could see the flaring nostrils and feel the rage in the bulging eyes. It was heavy, but not heavy enough to indicate solid gold. Bronze, most likely, with a gilding of thinly beaten gold, but still a thing of astonishing beauty and workmanship. And a well-considered gift. For the bull was one of the symbols that marked the Ninth legion, a throwback to the days of its founding in Hispania and an initiation ritual that called for new recruits to vault the back of a charging beast. Yes, this Marro knew more of the Ninth than Valerius felt comfortable with.

'Extend my thanks in the appropriate terms,' Valerius told Rufus, with a smile to the Votadini. 'But perhaps I should know what else he wants apart from my friendship, for a soldier on campaign has little to offer another man apart from wine.' He signalled to a servant, who stepped forward and poured a cup which Valerius offered to the other man.

Rufus stifled a grin. He put the question to Aneirin, received a reply, and asked another question that elicited a longer and more animated answer.

'King Marro wishes to forge an alliance with Rome.' Valerius blinked at the outrageous proposition. Only Agricola carried the power of *imperium* to conclude a formal alliance, and even he would most likely consult Titus before coming to an agreement. 'His warriors will march beside your legionaries to wipe the stain of the Selgovae from this land for ever. Together you will slaughter the Selgovae spearmen and the king's sword brothers, enslave their women and children and burn their huts. All he asks in return is domain over all the lands east of the Thuaidh.'

'Is that all he said?'

'Oh, he listed the king's lineage all the way back to some Celtic god I've never heard of and hailed the prowess in battle of about a hundred individually named warriors, but I doubted you wanted to hear that.'

'Good.' Valerius smiled. 'You're sure he doesn't speak Latin?'

Rufus nodded. 'I'm sure. The first thing I did was insult him and he never blinked.'

Valerius cast a glance at Aneirin, but the other man just stared back. 'Then what do you think of this Marro's offer?'

Rufus considered for a moment, pulling at his beard. 'I think it secures your right flank, or at least well enough to mean you need assign only a light screen of cavalry to hold it. I doubt you want a rabble of Celts in your battle line. They have a tendency to pick out personal rivals and wander about the battlefield getting in the way.'

'My thoughts exactly.' Valerius nodded. 'Can you word a polite reply in a way that won't make him feel insulted?'

Rufus grinned. 'I doubt that will be a problem. Marro probably only made the offer so that he gets a share of the booty you win and can blood his warriors with minimal risk. I'll suggest he uses them to harry the Selgovae lands further north while we keep them occupied here. That should keep him happy.'

'And all he wants is the lands east of the river?'

'The only Selgovae farmland and pasture worth having, apparently. And he'd take it anyway when we've beaten them.'

Valerius ran his hands over the golden bull and exchanged a smile with Aneirin. 'This Thuaidh must be the river that flows past Trimontium. Ask him if it is navigable as far as the three hills and if he can guarantee free passage for our ships.'

'He says yes to both questions,' the little man said after a short conversation.

'Not an alliance, make sure he knows that. A temporary agreement between friends which may be formalized at some point in the future.'

The little man translated. 'Prince Aneirin agrees.'

'Then all that needs to be decided is a suitable gift to seal the contract.'

'It doesn't have to be much,' Rufus countered. 'The bull, pretty as it is, is a mere bauble and the agreement is more in the Votadini interest than Rome's. What about that chest of silver coin we recovered from the Brigante treasury?'

Valerius remembered the worn silver *denarii* from Claudius's reign given as tribute to Cartimandua in the time of Suetonius Paulinus. 'Very well, make it so, and send for the remainder of Aneirin's escort. We'll give them a feast to remember and send them home with sore heads in the morning.'

And as soon as they were gone the Ninth would march, with its flank secure and nothing standing between it, the place of the three hills and the destruction of the Selgovae.

XVIII

Scouts and engineers led the way, marking a path as they went that would one day be a road broad enough to take two wagons or eight legionaries side by side. Easy going for the most part, if you discounted the numerous bogs; gently undulating hills that plateaued into heathery moorland before the descent into the next river valley. Few trees, apart from along the watercourses.

They passed farms and scattered settlements of neat, well-maintained roundhouses of a type different from those in Brigante country, but all proved empty. It was as if the entire population had been swallowed up by the earth. Legionaries took delight in burning anything combustible, but after passing two or three blazing farms, Valerius insisted the rest be dismantled and added to the stock of timber for the new fort, and to see them through the winter. Well-used trackways proved that the valleys were the natural east–west highway for the native peoples, confirming what he'd learned from Aneirin the previous night. Such journeys would need to be monitored and controlled, and Valerius ordered the engineers to map out ground for fortlets that would be built and garrisoned once the Selgovae had been subdued. Life would go on for the natives; a different life, with Roman laws and Roman taxes, true, but one with its own benefits. But first they must experience the bitter taste of defeat.

At the height of every rise the three hills of Trimontium were clearly visible in the distance, like a giant altar, and with every rise they were clearer and closer. Near the end of the first day's march Gaius Rufus, who'd been roving ahead with his scouts, announced that a band of native warriors was lying in ambush at a place where two rivers met.

Valerius followed him to a point amid the riverside trees where they dismounted and crawled on their bellies amongst the reeds and clumps of stinging nettles close to the water's edge. When they reached their destination he sensed Rufus studying him and saw the little man grinning with delight at the sight of his legate swathed from helmet to sandal in clinging mud, his face blotched red where he'd come into contact with the nettle leaves.

'I don't see what's so funny,' he hissed. 'Show me what you have to and let's get back.' Rufus eased aside a fistful of reeds so Valerius could see across the burbling waters. 'What?'

'Two hundred of them,' Rufus whispered. Valerius looked again, but all he could see was sandy bank, reed beds and drooping willows, with a few ducks swimming contentedly in the centre of the river. 'There are two groups, one on either side of the ford. Look, you can see where a track has been worn over that pebble beach and up the bank.'

'I can see that, but I can't see the enemy.'

'A blind man . . . Don't worry, just trust me that they're there. A quick cavalry charge will sweep them aside, but I wanted you to see them.'

Valerius studied the position for a moment. 'No charges, I think. That would scatter them and I want prisoners I can question.' He began to squirm backwards towards the horses and Rufus followed.

When they returned to the legion's resting place Valerius called his camp prefect and auxiliary infantry commanders together to explain the situation. 'I'll leave this to you, Quintus,' he told Naso, 'but I want them all. Not a man must escape.'

Naso's eyes glittered and a grin split his face. He considered for a moment, then nodded. 'Decurion Barbarus, take your Asturians in a wide flanking movement on the left. Atticus, your mounted archers will do the same on the right.' He looked at the sky. 'It will be dusk in two hours. Make sure you're in position two hundred paces behind them in half that time. I'll cross with the Second cohort. You'll hear the signal just before we reach the far bank. That's when you strike. Remember we need prisoners and you heard what the legate said. Not a man must escape.'

The two auxiliary officers acknowledged their orders and set off. Valerius smiled. 'Very neat, Quintus. The rest of the legion will set up camp here and cross in the morning. If I'm correct we're about another day's march from the place of the three hills. Calgacus will be expecting a report from whoever he sent to ambush us. I plan to give him a surprise.'

Valerius watched from the south bank as the Second cohort crossed the ford as dusk began to fall. Six centuries. Four hundred and eighty men forcing their way in a column six broad through the fast-flowing, knee-deep waters, weighed down by their weapons and armour. They would outnumber their attackers, but they still made a tempting target for the Celtic ambush. Swoop, strike and fly would be their tactics. Swoop like a stooping falcon. Strike, every man making his mark in blood. Then fly before the defenders could recover and the Roman cavalry closed in.

The two flanking auxiliary cohorts should be in place by now. Another thousand seasoned veterans from Hispania and Gaul positioned like the jaws of a blacksmith's tongs to close and block the Celts' retreat. The head of the marching column reached the far bank and disappeared up the worn track into the undergrowth. A trumpet sounded, clear and long, followed by a roar and the staccato rattle of spear on shield. A second trumpet blast and a new cry, more visceral than the first. In his mind he could see the auxiliaries charging through the undergrowth to take the unsuspecting Celts in the rear. Victory. An annihilation. A small thing, barely worthy of the title skirmish. Yet two hundred of Calgacus's warriors would not fight again and two hundred wives and mothers would never know the fate of husband or son.

He waited for the howls of panic, the shrill cries of men pleading for their lives as they surrendered. But they never came. Instead the fight seemed to ebb and flow up and down the bank. Now muted and distant, then fiercer and certainly closer. Wounded auxiliaries and legionaries staggered into view and the men of Valerius's body-guard ran to help them back across the river to the waiting *medici*. It must have been an hour and close to dusk before the tumult finally faded.

Quintus Naso appeared with the Second's senior centurion and trudged wearily through the river to where Valerius stood. The centurion was cradling his right arm. Naso's helmet was askew and blood flowed freely from a cut on his cheek.

'Beg to report, legate,' the camp prefect gasped. 'The way is clear. But by all the gods, Valerius, they made us fight for it.'

'Well done, Quintus. Casualties?'

'We have five dead, around twenty wounded. The auxiliaries more. But not a man of the ambush escaped.'

'Prisoners?'

'I'm sorry, Valerius.' Naso shook his head at the memory of it. 'They made us kill them. These aren't Brigantes or even Ordovices who know when they're beaten. We had them surrounded and it was obvious there could be no escape, but not a man or boy threw down sword or spear. They fought in groups, back to back, frothing and snarling like rabid dogs. If it looked as if they were going to be overcome they cut their own throats or fell on their swords. The last of them, a group of about thirty, took refuge in that copse over there. That was where we suffered most of our casualties. Eventually, I decided to lead the assault myself. It was like hunting boar among the bushes, but a damned sight more dangerous. Come and take a look.'

Valerius followed him back across the ford and up the far bank. The track led through a mess of riverside scrub and bushes before running into scattered woodland. They met a pair of Gaulish auxiliaries, each carrying a severed head by the hair. Valerius frowned at the sight and Naso saw his look.

'They said it was their custom and I agreed they could take a few to decorate their tents and baggage wagons. I apologize if I did wrong, legate.'

'No, Quintus. If you hadn't given them permission they'd have taken them anyway. Just make sure they get rid of them before they really start to stink.'

It wasn't long before they found the first bodies. They'd died in groups, as Naso had described, their throats pierced by either Roman spear or sword or their own daggers, and each group was surrounded by blood spatters that appeared to give the lie to the camp prefect's estimate of the Ninth's casualties.

And that wasn't the only discrepancy between Naso's account and the picture it had created in Valerius's mind. From his deputy's description of their fighting prowess and selfless sacrifice he expected to see warriors in their prime, Calgacus's champions sent to deal the Romans a blow that would stop them in their tracks. This was very different.

'Greybeards,' he said wonderingly. 'And stripling boys.'

Naso nodded. 'They fought like wolves. Not a man or boy offered to yield or asked for mercy. This is a different sort of enemy, Valerius.'

XIX

Cathal stood by the river and watched a straggle of families and live-stock from his eastern lands struggle down the steep bank and cross the ford. Half a dozen men toiled in the waist-deep water, shoulders straining to heave a fully laden cart across the slippery submerged stones. The carter's family were among the more fortunate. The majority, man, woman and child, carried what was left of their lives in sacks across their shoulders as they trudged sullenly through the river. They kept their eyes down as they passed him and he could feel their resentment. Their silence oppressed him, but he had more important things to consider.

'Your ambush party should have returned by now.' Cathal turned to glare at the speaker. It was as if Gwlym had entered his mind and read his thoughts.

'There is still time,' he lied. He'd set little store by the chances of the men he'd sent to bloody the Romans at the Tivyet ford, but it was still a pity.

'Have it as you will, but do not mourn them.'

'They were brave men.' A mistake? Perhaps, but Gwlym had been right: he had to do *something*. He knew his people.

'The sacrifice of a few elderly warriors and unblooded young men

118

was worth it to show you still deserve to be your people's king,' the druid said airily. A pause. 'But not everyone is so impressed by your ability to wield a sword with such deadly ability. I have heard whispers.'

'Give me the names of the whisperers and none will live longer than tomorrow's dawn.'

'There, I have goaded you. Made you angry.' A cold smile flickered on Gwlym's thin lips. 'It is so easy with you mere brutes. I do so only to remind you that you must not let the Romans do the same.'

'There will be no repeat until I am certain I can truly hurt them.'

'Not before the thaw, then?'

'Not unless an opportunity presents itself,' Cathal rasped. 'But I will not rest while I seek out that opportunity. If it comes I will attack with every warrior I can spare.'

'It will come,' Gwlym assured him. 'The gods ask only that you take it.'

Cathal turned away, sickened by the contact with this sightless ancient, more dead than alive, who flitted between the dream world inside his head and the black chasm of his reality. Why was he so reluctant to rid himself of the druid? Because Gwlym understood the Romans in a way it would take Cathal decades to equal. And sometimes he spoke the words even Cathal didn't have the courage to utter.

Of more import was the return of the messenger he had sent to the Votadini, or more accurately the return of his head, contemptuously thrown at the feet of one of Cathal's patrols. There would be no alliance there. The same patrol had reported a growing Votadini presence in the hills of the disputed frontier country. Bands of horsemen and spearmen who hovered like buzzards over a rotting carcass, waiting to loot the farms of whatever their former occupants had been unable to carry.

'We have to move faster,' he urged a sweating Colm, who was supervising the crossing.

'We can only go as fast as the slowest cart, unless you want to leave them behind,' the older man spat. He hadn't slept in three nights and was as irritable as a cornered bear. 'They're tired, Cathal, and bewildered. They've lost everything and they don't understand why.'

'Don't waste your time on sympathy,' Cathal said. 'If they stay, the Romans will enslave them, if the Votadini leave them alive that long. They must be beyond the reach of either by daybreak tomorrow. How many more to cross?'

Colm shrugged. How could a man tell when there were so many squealing children and mewling babes? Easier to keep track of a herd of sheep. 'Five hundred. Maybe more.'

'Then we don't have time to cross them here. Guide them up the east bank and then take them through the hills. Cross at the meeting of the waters and try to get them as far as Eltref by nightfall.' It was a longer route, and a more arduous one, but it would keep them away from the Roman spears. 'I'll take men to defend the passes and meet you there when I can.'

Colm muttered his agreement. Cathal left him and walked up the slope from the river towards the roundhouse complex that was his seat of power in the summer months.

And the confrontation he'd delayed far too long.

Cathal's residence was one of seven buildings in the walled enclosure, including his treasure house, long since emptied of gold and silver to keep the tribe's wealth from Roman hands. His storehouses had also been largely cleared apart from the supplies needed to see them through to the refuge. The horses he'd stolen from the Romans had preceded the gold west, and would be dispersed through the hills for the winter. Too late in the season to breed them. That could wait till next spring. If there was a next spring.

Wood smoke filtered through the conical thatch of the largest house and he took a deep breath as he pulled back the heavy cloth curtain and entered. Drystone walls windproofed with clay stood to just above head height and provided support for the timbers that carried the roof frame. A ring of stout wooden posts held the planked floor of the living quarters above. In most Selgovae houses the ground level would contain pens for the owner's hardy cattle and scrawny .

brown sheep, but Cathal used the area to hold audiences and dispense justice from the wooden throne on a raised dais to his left. The scent of some mouth-watering stew drifted on the air and reminded him he hadn't eaten for hours. Hare if his nose didn't betray him. Young Dugald must have had the gods' own luck when he'd taken the dogs out on the hill earlier. A ladder leaned against the opening into the upper floor and he ran up it with surprising ease for such a large man.

Olwyn crouched over a cooking pot suspended above the fire, which glowed at the centre of a large flat stone from the river. 'Just in time,' she smiled, swatting a spark that escaped to settle on the rushes spread across the wooden floor. 'Dugald, fetch your father's bowl.'

The boy darted for a shelf on the far wall. He seemed to do everything at the run: a dark-haired blur of energy. No sign yet at ten he would ever attain his father's great build, but then his grandfather had been of middling height, and it wasn't just strength and skill with arms that made a king.

'A fine hare off the far meadow, Father.' Dugald grinned. 'He darted and jinked but Guidri had him in a trice.' Guidri was the boy's sight hound, a sleek, tawny mongrel with long legs, a sharp face that tapered to a pointed muzzle, and a vicious temperament. The dog looked up from its place beneath Dugald's sleeping pallet, fixed Cathal with a malicious glare and bared his teeth with a low growl.

Cathal grunted an acknowledgement as he took his seat on his wooden stool. Too much affection made a boy soft. No one was fooled, least of all Olwyn. She took the bowl and filled it with shreds of meat from the thin stew before placing it in his hands with a loaf of flat bread. Olwyn. Blue eyes that sparkled like the waters of the Thuaidh on a summer's day, hair the colour of ripening barley, and cheeks pink as an orchard's bounty. Beneath the homespun shift a slim body that still stirred him after a dozen years. A body that had borne her three children. The last had nearly killed her and the bairn survived but a day. A son. And a king could not have too many sons. Strong inside as any man, sometimes in the night the memory of that bairn robbed her of all joy and she would weep, not for the loss of it, but for failing him. He reached out and touched her hand.

Olwyn. Wife. Companion. Confessor. Adviser. A Brigante princess given in marriage to cement the alliance with the Selgovae. Their initial wariness had quickly been replaced by curiosity, curiosity by lust, and, very soon after, lust by love. Without her he would be as helpless as he would be without the great sword that hung in its scabbard from the wooden frame on the far side of the room.

'Have you brought me anything, Father?' A tousle-haired miniature of Olwyn poked her head round the partition that separated the room from the adult sleeping quarters. Berta, the second love of his life. Six years old and already a rare beauty.

Cathal smiled and reached into a pouch at his belt. 'Here,' he said. 'Another jewel for your collection.' He produced a stone he'd picked up earlier by the river. 'Look, you can see the gold and silver running through it.'

The girl ran to her father and studied the gift critically before skipping back through the partition.

Olwyn gave him a searching look that had nothing to do with the stone. 'You did not come here because of the smell of my cooking.'

Cathal glanced at Dugald, intently polishing the blade of a hunting knife. They'd agreed not to talk of the Romans in front of the children, but the boy was intelligent enough to understand what was going on around him.

'It is time for us . . . for you . . . to go.'

'Go where?' the shrill voice piped up.

The two adults exchanged a glance. 'It will be winter soon,' Cathal said. 'We must go somewhere more sheltered where there is ample game.'

'Into the hills?'

'I told you,' Olwyn whispered. 'I won't go without you.'

'We've already delayed too long.' Cathal kept his voice equally low. 'They will be here tomorrow or the day after. You must be beyond the meeting of the waters by then.'

'And you?'

'Their patrols are already probing west. That is where I am needed most.'

'Your family needs you most,' his wife hissed, but there was no anger in it. 'You will come? You promise?'

'I promise. Rodri and his band are already preparing a winter camp in the sheltered valley at Eltref, near the big loch. They won't come there, and if they do all the better. We will have plenty of warning and I can destroy them in the mountains. When can you be ready?'

'Let me gather a few things and we are ready now. I've had the wagons packed for a week.'

It was typical of her. Stubborn to the last, but prepared for any situation. 'You'll take the high road over the hills. It's closer to the line of the Roman advance, but faster going, and they haven't penetrated that far yet.'

'And we'll meet at Eltref?'

'Yes.'

'Very well.' She whirled away, bustling with energy. 'Berta, collect the things I told you to gather. You too, Dugald. We're going on an adventure.'

Cathal rose and took her by the shoulder. There were words that should be said, but somehow they stuck in his throat.

She met his gaze. 'I know,' she whispered.

XX

Rome

The tiredness came in waves like the knife-wielding Judaean *sicarii* warriors who haunted his dreams, a heavy, debilitating exhaustion that robbed him of the strength and will that made him the man he was: the emperor he wished to be. Titus Flavius Caesar Vespasianus Augustus felt old. He forced himself up, using his body slave for support and pinning the man with a savage glare that spelled out what would happen to him if he ever dared mention the lapse. Others bathed, dried, oiled, and dressed him in Imperial purple. Still another crimped his dark hair and wove an olive wreath worked in gold into its tresses. Food was brought, and though he could barely stomach the thought of it, he forced down what he could after the taster had done his work. He called on his father to give him the strength to carry out his duties on this day of all days.

Perhaps it was the strain of the office? His father had aged visibly in the last few years of his reign. But his father had been seventy and Titus was in the prime of his life at the age of forty-one. He knew he worked excessively hard to carry on the old man's work and the culture of effort and responsibility he had instilled in his sons. It had been Titus's good

124

fortune that as well as the position, he inherited the support of the army, which respected him for his victories as a general, the Senate, who would back him as long as he was strong, and the people, who loved him for being his father's son.

A slave handed him a cup of wine and for a moment he felt invigorated. It would hardly be surprising if the great cataclysm which had devastated the Bay of Neapolis had drained him in the same way as it had drained Rome's coffers. He had walked the evil-smelling pumice fields while the ash that had buried city, town, village, hamlet, villa and farmstead alike still drifted like filthy snow from a sky the colour of old lead. Countless thousands of dead lay beneath the all-enveloping carpet, so deep that not even the most devoted loved one would ever find them. Rich or poor, the volcano had not differentiated; they all died the same horrifying death. It had cost him friends and advisers, men like the heroic Gaius Plinius Secundus, the most intelligent man he had ever known, who had been killed in a forlorn attempt to save his friends.

Yet the dead, however exalted, were only a temporary burden. It was finding a way to feed and house the starving, homeless living that had taxed Titus, his officials, and the Empire's resources. There weren't enough craftsmen in all of Italia to replace the buildings that had been lost. He'd been forced to strip the Empire's fragile frontiers of legionary engineers and the army's experts in construction of every kind. Housing had been the first priority; temples and monuments could come later. Next came roads to carry the countless sacks of grain, olive oil and dried meat from Africa, Hispania and Aegyptus. Then docks to speed up the distribution of timber, lead, brick and roof tiles and all the other supplies needed to build rudimentary housing, but especially food and water for people stranded and on the brink of starvation. Midway through the reconstruction of Neapolis he had been forced to abandon his supervision of the project to deal with the aftermath of a fire that devastated four districts of central Rome. Bad enough to have such destruction at the beginning of his reign, but the blaze had the mob muttering doubts about whether he had offended the gods in some way.

A shuffling outside the doorway. 'Everything is ready, Caesar.'

Thank Jupiter, at last. He picked up the skirts of his toga and strode out into the corridor where they were waiting. A half turn to inspect the head of the long procession that would accompany him and a rustle as they bowed their heads. Some of them would be honouring the title, some the man, but he would not let that concern him today. This was his father's day. Domitian, his brother and fellow consul, stood at their head, accompanied, somewhat unusually, by his wife Domitia. Titus noted a hint of a smile on her lips as she raised her head; a look of support. Behind them the senior members of the Senate, aged dotards, mingled with Titus's *amici*, the men he could trust beyond measure and beyond politics. Glabrio, the redoubtable Clemens, his cousin Flavius Sabinus. More familiar faces, but ones that brought a flaring of the Imperial nostrils. Lucanus, Tullius and Rutillius Gallicus, whom he suspected of sedition he could not prove, too powerful to snub, who must be kept close.

'Very well.' He turned back to the master of ceremonies. 'We will continue.'

Slaves ran ahead sprinkling the marble floor with flower petals and scented water, but careful to keep them from his path lest he should slip. Two more waited by the doorway, flanked by two of his personal guard. As he reached it the soldiers saluted and the slaves swung open the double doors. A glare of direct sunlight made him blink and he was met by a wall of sound.

He'd refused the temporary *cryptoporticus* tunnel his advisers had wanted to construct to keep him apart from the mob and ensure his security. Twelve lictors were gathered in ceremonial formation with the bunched birch rods of the *fasces* that proclaimed the Emperor's *imperium* and control over life and death. Beyond them, he could see directly across the crowds and the open space to the wonder of the world his father had planned as his great memorial. Standing hundreds of feet high, it was the most magnificent arena the world had ever seen and the greatest feat of architecture. The outer wall alone consisted of three and a half million cubic feet of glistening travertine stone, held in place by three hundred tons of iron clamps. It rose, arcade upon arcade, each pierced by arched windows divided by statues of emperors, gods and generals. Every detail had been reflected upon and agreed by Vespasian or Titus, every bust, every column, every door and every window, an endeavour which had lasted ten long years. If anything would secure his father's divinity for a thousand generations it was the amphitheatre which would bear his name.

He must have halted, because Domitia Longina appeared at his side. 'Caesar? Are you well? You look pale.'

'It is all right, my dear.' Titus managed a smile as he resumed a steady pace. Members of his personal guard took step beside him, swords drawn and eyes beneath helmet rims seeking out any potential threat. Titus rested Domitia's arm on his, ignoring the *tsk* of disapproval from behind. 'I am merely overwhelmed by the magnificence of what we have created.'

'I fear it is more the matter of the hundred days that follow which overwhelms you, Titus.' She used his given name without fear of the consequences and he warmed to her still more. Small, barely reaching to his shoulder, she had a confidence, a presence, that made her seem much taller. Walnut hair, flecked with almost imperceptible strands of grey, framed high cheekbones, and dark eyes that never quite betrayed what she was thinking. Cool and poised, very different from the half-dead shipwreck survivor he had first encountered on a sun-scorched Aegyptian beach a decade and a half earlier. One might even say he'd saved her life. At the time she'd been under the protection of his friend Gaius Valerius Verrens. Titus sensed there was more to their relationship than protection, but that was none of his affair. Domitia Longina retained a beauty that still turned men's heads, much to the fury of her husband, but for reasons he had never fathomed, and that slightly disturbed him, Titus had always taken a more fatherly than carnal interest in his brother's wife.

'Perceptive as ever, my dear.' He turned his smile on the cheering crowds behind the protective lines of Praetorian guards. 'How could any man stand a hundred days sitting amongst the least cultured people in Rome, watching men slaughter each other, bored witless by leaping athletes and tumbling acrobats, and seeing so many wild beasts devouring and being devoured that one blends into the next. All this while one's Imperial backside turns numb on a block of cold Apuan marble?'

'You are right.' Domitia waved artlessly to the cheering bystanders and the acclamation grew to a roar. 'Caesar should not have to endure it. Your father would not have done. He would have shared the responsibility with you, taking perhaps one day in seven. Two at the most. As you must share it with my husband. He is, after all, also the son of Divine Caesar.' She glanced back at Domitian, three paces behind, his suspicious eyes never leaving them. 'He adores the games and the adulation of the crowd. You would earn his eternal gratitude.'

What was going on here? His smile remained fixed, but Titus's mind puzzled over Domitia's purpose in volunteering her husband's services. Was she trying to manoeuvre some advantage Titus couldn't discern? Did his cunning brother have some ploy in mind to gain greater public approval during the celebrations? Then some barrier dropped in her eyes to reveal a certain gleam . . . and he understood. Domitian did not love the games any more than he did, and would find the ordeal just as grim. Titus would appear on the days of the most important ceremonies and allow his brother to officiate on those of lesser significance. No advantage for you, little brother, just frustration. And Domitia? Domitia, who Titus had always suspected loathed her husband, would win seventy days of freedom from Domitian's unpredictable and, the Emperor suspected, threatening presence. It was exquisitely done. On the one hand begging an honour for her husband that could not lightly be turned down by either party. Two would profit, the other could only fume impotently at his fate. Domitian would never discover the true motive behind his wife's advances on his behalf, and even if he did suspect, what could he do?

He felt much better now, his mood lightened and the exhaustion only a memory. 'Come, brother.' He turned to wave Domitian forward. 'Join us. I have decided it is only right that you should share the honour of officiating over the opening ceremonies. In fact you should reap the greater part of it.'

'You have my thanks, Caesar.' Domitian bowed his head with a furtive glance at his wife.

The great amphitheatre stood on ground that had once been a lake where Nero had staged naval battles for the benefit of those he favoured, and had been known to feed those he did not to the giant Nile crocodiles he kept in his zoo. Much of the Domus Aurea, his grandiose Golden House, had been torn down to make room for the gladiator schools and the pens and cages where animals would wait to provide entertainment for the eighty thousand Romans who packed the towering stands. A plaque above the main entrance recorded that Vespasian had ordered the construction to benefit the people of Rome and paid for it with his general's share of the plunder from the sack of Jerusalem. In truth, it had cost much more, and they had been forced to impose the *fiscus judaicus*, a tax on every Jew under the Emperor's rule. Was it guilt for Jerusalem that kept him awake at nights? A great victory. One that had won him glory and fame. Yet it had cost the lives of hundreds of thousands of innocents: starving pilgrim families he'd refused to allow to leave the city. The loss of irreplaceable objects dear to the Jewish faith, and the utter destruction of the Great Temple, one of the architectural wonders of the world. Could he have done more to save it? The fire that had destroyed the temple had been started either by the defenders or by the attacking legionaries, but Titus had been so consumed by his triumph against great odds that he'd barely noticed at the time. Josephus, the captured Judaean general his father had spared at Jotapata, who was part of this procession, would have told him that the fall of the temple was pre-ordained and foretold by the Jew Christus, who had led a cult that denied the teachings of the old religion. This Christus had told his supporters: *There will not be left here one stone upon another that will not be thrown down.* And so it came to pass. A cleansing, Josephus called it. A necessary cull that would one day strengthen the Jews. Still, Titus sometimes felt as if the sack of Jerusalem was consuming him the way the flames had consumed the Great Temple.

One element of Nero's works which had survived still dominated the area between the Palatine Hill and the great amphitheatre. A great colossus of bronze over one hundred feet in height depicting Nero as the sun god Sol Invictus. Once covered in gold leaf, Vespasian had ordered it stripped to help offset the gold shortages at the start of his reign.

'You should tear it down, or at least have Nero's face chiselled off and replace it with your own,' Domitian whispered. Titus smiled indulgently. He knew his brother had often urged Vespasian to rid Rome of the great monstrosity, but the Emperor had always declined.

'Father always said he hoped his head would never be big enough to fit. It would not be becoming if I were any less modest. As he pointed out, brother, Nero is still popular among certain sections of the mob. Better not to tweak the wolf's ear unless absolutely necessary.'

By now the four storeys of the arena towered over them and the procession turned left into the south entrance, reserved for the Emperor, his closest *amici*, senators and Vestal Virgins. Titus had viewed the stadium from this position many times, but the combined effect of the crowd's adulation and the sight of such a great mass of people in such close proximity seemed to knock the breath from him. All around the stands soared high above, the higher the seats the steeper the climb, and every seat was filled: a head-spinning vision of row after row of screaming faces chanting his name.

'By the gods, brother,' he heard Domitian laugh. 'This makes the Circus Maximus look like a dusty provincial theatre.'

The lictors led them round the great oval of the arena floor, surrounded by an unscalable wall three times the height of a man. Famous gladiators from all over the Empire had been brought to Rome to entertain the crowds over the next hundred days. Only the best, bravest and most fortunate would leave these now pristine white sands alive.

Finally they completed the circuit and returned to the passage. A doorway on the left led to marble stairs. A new, even more powerful roar erupted as they emerged. Domitia steered him gently towards his seat beneath the gold cloth awning of the Imperial box on the podium. 'Sit with me,' he ordered as she turned to move away. He beckoned Domitian to join them. 'This is your day as well as mine, consul.'

Somewhere below a gate opened and they heard the thunder of hooves. The crowd heard it too. Their applause had dropped to the buzz of a disturbed wasps' nest, but now the sound grew again. A mixed herd of antelope and zebra galloped into view, their hooves rattling the wooden floor beneath the sand, followed by deer, bulls, buffalo and a pair of slab-sided, grey, horned monsters Titus recognized as rhinoceros. For two circuits they swept round the arena jostling for position, snorting, flanks heaving, zebras snapping at antelope, bulls slashing with their broad horns to right and left, tearing great gashes in any flesh unfortunate enough to be in their way. The blast of a horn brought a new crescendo of sound as a pair of gates opened at opposite ends of the arena. Two honey-brown streaks across the sands and two antelope were down, the fangs of a black-maned lion and his mate embedded in their throats. The herd milled in terror, seeking some sanctuary, only to burst into movement again as a massive tiger stalked slowly into view and crouched, tail swishing, the yellow eyes hungrily picking out his target, before three enormous leaps brought him on to the back of his choice, a zebra, which squealed in terror as claws like meathooks sank into its hindquarters before the mighty beast's snapping jaws bit into its neck and snapped its spine. Another pair of lions joined the slaughter, but as they tore into the flesh of their victims the larger rhinoceros, seemingly a spectator in this fight, charged across the arena floor and impaled the male with his horn, flexing his massive neck so that the lion, entrails streaming, was tossed the height of the podium to crash back on the boards mortally injured but still in killing mood.

And this was just the start. Nine thousand animals hand-picked from every corner of the Empire and beyond had been brought here to die in the arena's inaugural games. The slaughter would continue for the next hundred days.

Titus looked to his right where Domitia Longina sat, a model of composure, until you noticed the unnatural paleness of her skin and the delicate fists clenched so tight the knuckles gleamed ivory. Good. He took little pleasure from the spectacle himself, or the waste – the carcasses would be dragged from the arena and dumped in the festering rubbish pits out towards the River Teverone – and it pleased him to see that she had retained at least some of her humanity after all her years on the Palatine.

A pair of elephants stood, strangely lethargic at the centre of the killing ground, only reacting to any perceived threat. Titus called an aide forward.

'Have them removed and returned to their pens,' he said.

'Come, Titus,' Domitian snorted. 'Wouldn't that be the greatest spectacle of all?'

Titus ignored him and turned to Domitia with an apologetic smile. 'Their trainers allowed me to walk among them. A mistake, perhaps. I looked into their eyes and saw intelligence there, perhaps even understanding. Despite their size I believe they are gentle creatures unless threatened. It would be like killing a favourite horse.'

'Then I am glad, Caesar.' Domitia bowed her head. 'I understand that Vespasian's memory must be honoured, but I deplore unnecessary bloodshed.'

'Unnecessary?' her husband interrupted. 'Yet again you show the weakness of your sex. Every Caesar since Augustus has understood that if you don't entertain the mob and let them wallow in the blood of animals, criminals and slaves, they will very quickly seek out other blood to shed. Would you rather it was yours or mine?'

Domitia answered him with a stare.

'Come, my dear.' Titus stood and held out an arm to her. 'They are clearing the sands. If we are to survive the rest of the day we must have sustenance.' Men ran into the arena carrying baulks of timber and crosses, which they set into pre-prepared slots in the floor. A ragged column of verminous, skeletal creatures followed, their shackles linked by chains. 'The next hour will be filled by the execution of the condemned.

A necessary bloodletting, but hardly entertainment for the discerning. We will return for the gladiators.'

Domitia rose to her feet and joined him. As they left the Imperial box she chanced to look at her husband. Titus Flavius Domitianus stared at his brother's back, eyes filled with the same predatory hunger she'd seen in the hunting tiger's.

XXI

Trimontium

They'd been seeing the pillars of smoke all morning so Valerius knew what to expect. As he topped the rise beneath the loom of the three hills, nothing remained of the houses in the scattered settlement but blackened, smouldering timbers and glowing ash that scattered like drifting snow in the bitter wind. There must have been fifty huts cradled in the loop of the river. Beyond the settlement he could see his auxiliary infantry advancing in line to secure the far end of the valley. Another cohort had climbed the northern shoulder of the hills to protect the legion's western flank. Not that he expected any trouble with so many cavalry patrols out hunting the former occupants of these houses. Satisfied with his dispositions, a cluster of buildings within a stone wall drew his eye. A horse was tethered by the gateway and he rode down the gentle slope accompanied by his staff.

'Barbarian bastards haven't left us an ear of wheat or a grain of barley,' Quintus Naso grumbled. 'If you hadn't thought to bring our own timber we'd have spent the winter in tents foraging for twigs and been eating our horses by Saturnalia.'

'We might yet,' Valerius replied. 'The weather has changed this last few days. If the supply galleys don't arrive soon the river could freeze over. How much food and fodder do we have?'

'A week's supplies, perhaps a little more if we tighten our belts even further.'

'They'll come.' Valerius considered the hills to his left. 'Get a patrol up the northernmost hill and set up a lookout post. I want a watchtower and a signal station up there by dusk.'

Naso saluted and turned away, calling for his engineers. Valerius reined in beside the tethered horse and handed his reins to Shabolz. Off to his right the river flowed in a curving arc, deep, dark foam-flecked waters the colour of the beer the natives brewed. 'Check upstream and down,' he told the Pannonian. 'There must be a ford somewhere near here. We'll site the fort on the closest suitable piece of high ground.'

Shabolz acknowledged the order and Valerius strode into the walled enclosure. Gaius Rufus crouched among the still smouldering ashes of the largest house. 'Whoever lived here was important.' He showed Valerius a thin piece of metal he'd found among the debris. 'A gold pin from a brooch, I'd guess. It must have slipped between the floorboards of the living area. I doubt any ordinary Selgovae housewife would own something so precious, never mind ignoring its loss. And look at the layout of this place.' He waved a hand to the smoking heaps around him. 'Seven buildings. Storehouses and cattle sheds at a guess. No cow ever slept on the floor of this one. And look at that wall. The stonework is some of the finest I've seen in Britannia.'

'Calgacus?'

'Or someone similar. You can ask him when you meet.'

'That's not a subject for jest, little man.'

Rufus grinned. 'You think he'll just sit out the winter and leave you alone?'

Valerius shook his head and crouched down beside the little scout, sifting the warm ashes through his fingers. It had all seemed simple enough when he'd outlined his strategy to Naso at Brynmochdar. Create a place of sanctuary where the Ninth could sit out the winter, well fed and comfortable, and at the same time harry the Selgovae heartland and the eastern dales that supplied their granary. Kill every warrior they found and burn the farmers out so they would become a burden on Calgacus's stores. Either goad the barbarians into attacking or hit them hard when they inevitably emerged from their lair in the spring. But Calgacus had done the burning himself, leaving the Romans without a natural target, and gone . . . where?

'You followed their trail?'

'They went west. Some of those valleys are as tight as a mouse's arse-hole and twist so much you could end up following yourself. A veritable labyrinth like the place that fellow Theseus slew the Minotaur.'

'Do you think you could lead a fighting patrol to let them know we're here?'

Rufus sucked at his crooked teeth. 'How big a patrol?'

'I don't know. Whatever strength you think is needed to do the job. A full cohort and an auxiliary cavalry wing if necessary.'

'Those valleys.' The scout shook his head at the memory. 'Half a dozen river crossings. Bog and forest. These are *their* lands. They know every ford and every track. We go there, in whatever strength, and they get between us and help . . . Not many of us would be coming back out again.'

'All right.' Gaius Rufus had led two cavalry wings on a night march through mountains filled with Ordovice warriors. If he said it couldn't be done, best not to try. 'We go in as far as you think it's safe. Set up forts to block any movement through the valleys. A network of signal stations to warn of any major force that makes an appearance.'

Rufus dug at the ground with his knife, stabbing in the point and twisting. 'You'd need three forts, maybe four. If you garrison them with too few troops, there's the chance Calgacus would overrun one or all of them. Man them so well that he wouldn't dare and you're splitting your force and dangerously weakening the position here. If he stays home, the forts might as well not be there in the first place. If he comes out . . . well.' He waved a hand at their surroundings. 'This is where you should be fighting him, not in a place where the terrain strings out your col-umn for miles and leaves every cohort asking to be ambushed.'

'You're right.' Valerius laughed ruefully at his own foolishness. 'Maybe you should be the legate and not me.'

'I don't think you'd find a uniform to fit me,' Rufus answered with a grin.

Valerius stared downriver. 'So we just sit here all winter and do nothing.'

'Let me use the time between now and the first snows to get to know the country,' the scout suggested. 'Perhaps there is a way to get to the Selgovae wintering grounds without going through the labyrinth. If I can find a route to get two or three cohorts behind him or on his flank, we could drive Calgacus and his people away from their food and shelter. By spring they'd be so weakened an auxiliary cohort could defeat them.'

Valerius was about to reply when a voice hailed him. 'Lord!' Shabolz urged his mount towards them through what had been fields and gardens. Valerius went to meet him and Rufus unhitched his horse and followed. 'There is a ford just beyond the broad plateau there, legate.' The Pannonian pointed to a rise about a mile or two downriver. 'Better you see the rest for yourself.' Grinning, he helped Valerius mount the horse he led and the three men rode east. When they reached the rise, Shabolz pointed downstream. 'Look,' he said.

Valerius followed the pointing finger. Boats. Flat-bottomed and heavily laden. A long line of them, as far as the eye could see, straining against the current and driven by ten oarsmen apiece. His heart soared. 'The supplies.' He almost choked with relief. 'The quartermaster, Shabolz, and quickly. And men, lots of men. We need to get everything up here before dark. This is where we will build the fort.' He looked up at the three hills. 'Trimontium.'

'Of course, there is another possibility.'

Valerius turned, ready to snap at Rufus for questioning his decision. But the little man's grin stilled his tongue. This wasn't about the siting of the fort. 'What?'

'Do you think Calgacus will be content to stay in camp all winter and let you sit here in comfort?'

'No,' Valerius said. 'He won't. Not a man like him.'

'Then,' Rufus nodded to the supply boats, 'perhaps at some point we can provide him with an incentive.'

A dawning understanding set a string of possibilities flickering through Valerius's mind. Yes, it might work. But it was for later, when the snows came and the Selgovae were scratching around the frozen fields for the carelessly dropped ears from last year's harvest. He gave voice to his thoughts.

'Better if their bellies are resting against their backbones. While the weather holds, do as you suggested and seek out a way to take them by surprise. You'll have your choice of the auxiliary cavalry squadrons as escort. By the time you come back we will have built our nest for the winter and we will talk further of incentives.'

'Till the first fall of snow, then.' The scout saluted and rode north towards the auxiliary picket lines.

Engineers laboured to mark out the lines of a camp large enough to house the entire contingent on the gently sloping ground between the hills and the river. At last a stake marked the position of the *principia* and legionaries began erecting the headquarters pavilion that would be Valerius's home until something more substantial could be constructed. Others were already hacking at the ground with mattock and spade to excavate the ditches and raise the banks that would be the foundation of their defences in the coming months. They worked in their eight-man *contubernia*, each with his appointed task. Four men laboured in the ditches while the others carried out the essential tasks of preparing the camp: erecting tents, setting up ovens, digging latrines. Whatever his task, every man worked in his armour and with his sword at his side. They were in enemy territory now and Valerius had instilled in his legion the necessity of always being ready to fight off an attack.

He was about to set off for his tent and the dull but vital task of supervising the supply tallies when an aide drew his attention to a little group moving up the slope from the river. The figure at the centre wore the yellow cloak that marked him as an Imperial courier. Valerius felt a shiver of anticipation, but wasn't sure whether it was caused by excitement or foreboding.

A young man, as all the couriers were, cheeks shining in the chill air, he reached beneath his cloak as he approached and withdrew a leather scroll case. As he accepted it from the courier's hands Valerius recognized the imprint in the wax seal.

'I come direct from the Palatine,' the young man announced formally. 'Though I carried a second message which I placed in the hands of the governor in London.'

Valerius weighed the scroll case in his hand. Curiouser and curiouser. 'How is Governor Agricola?'

'He seemed well, sir,' the courier said. 'It was he who suggested I come by ship as the swifter alternative.'

'Then he has my thanks. He didn't suggest you might pause long enough to pick up a message from my wife?'

'No, sir.' The young man looked crestfallen. 'I didn't ... It was deemed urgent that I continue my journey as quickly as possible.'

'It is of no matter.' Valerius smiled. 'Come, I will read this in my tent and you can eat while I compose a reply.'

'I was told no reply was required, legate. Though I am happy to carry any message you wish. I must change ships in Londinium and I will be sure to call upon your family.'

'Then you are a prince among couriers. Shabolz,' Valerius called. 'Make sure this young man sups of the best from my supplies. The boats won't be returning tonight. You can stay in the *praetorium's* guest quarters.'

The courier spluttered his thanks. He'd spent the last eight days sleeping on the rough boards of a bucketing transport ship. Even the thought of the meanest cot made him feel quite faint.

Valerius hurried to his quarters and hesitated for a moment before breaking the seal. What lay inside might be merely friendly greetings, but the source also meant that the message had the potential to ignite life-changing events. He took a deep breath and worked the stiff leather straps with the fingers of his left hand so he could prise open the flaps.

XXII

Greetings from Titus Flavius Vespasianus Augustus to his friend G. Valerius Verrens, legate of Ninth legion Hispana. It has been too long, brother, since our last meeting. I cannot berate you, since I was the instigator of your absence from Rome, but I miss your forthright, countryman's conversation and the often unwanted, but never unregarded, advice with which you would ply me. You will have heard of the momentous events that have occurred since our parting. My father's end came as no surprise to either of us. The Purple had drained him of every ounce of his energy, but it was a comfort to me that he contemplated his impending death with such equanimity. He almost seemed to welcome his passing. It was part of his genius that he passed on his burden to me in modest increments in the months before his death. The immensity of the whole would have brought any normal man to his knees. As it is, I compare myself to that troubled king, Sisyphos of Ephyra, condemned to push his enormous rock to the top of the hill each day in an endless cycle of relentless toil, though I hope I have inherited none of the vices which brought him to that pass. If my accession has been welcomed by the gods they have a strange way of showing it. No doubt you know by now of the catastrophe which enveloped the Bay of Neapolis and took the life of our dear and trusted friend Pliny, but news may not yet have reached you of the disasters which followed, a fire which raged through the capital for three days and consumed, yet again, the Temple of Jupiter Capitolinus, that ill-starred shrine, and the return of the plague, which is interpreted as a punishment for my depredations against the Jews. Only a madman would seek the office I now hold. Yet how could one refuse it when it was offered? What kind of emperor should I be? – you will forgive me if I test you with the questions with which I nightly assail myself – not a Tiberius, a Gaius or a Nero, who used the office to encourage depravity and foster corruption, nor even a Claudius, who, for all his acknowledged attributes, allowed himself to be controlled by the former slaves of his household. Would it surprise you that I believe Vitellius might have become a truly great emperor had he survived? Possibly not, because he was, as I recall, also your friend. I have had access to his writings, which record his thoughts and aspirations, and found much to admire. Yet even he could not free himself from Caecina and Valens, the generals who truly grasped the reins of his power. No, the emperor on whom I shall model myself is that other Titus Flavius Vespasianus, my father. Within the constraints of his office he did everything he could to act in the interests of the Empire and the people of Rome. I will do likewise, and what son would not wish to outdo his father? Am I naive to vow that not a day of my reign shall pass that does not contain at least one act of goodness or kindness? I do not underestimate the difficulties – my brother Domitianus laughed at the suggestion I should no longer deal with informers, but I believe it a worthy aspiration, which I hope would have your approval. Now, to the substance of my missive. You may or may not be aware – I understand his relationship with his legates has been somewhat strained – that I have given Julius Agricola two years to complete his conquest of Britannia. What you do not know is that when his term of office is complete I have decided that you will replace him. I smile as I write this, remembering my father's reaction at your lack of ambition for consular rank, but I fear I must repeat his words now. It is not a question of ambition, but of serving Rome, or in this case your friend Titus. In short, Valerius, I need someone I can trust in charge of Britannia and its legions. You have the experience and merits to hold the position and by now you

know the province and its challenges. There is the question of your cur-
rent lack of consular rank, but there are precedents for such appointments
and in any case an emperor's word is law. I hope I do not flatter myself in
the hope that our friendship will be enough to ensure your acceptance
of the post, but if not I rely on your conception of duty, which I know
you hold dear. The issue of the consulship will be resolved upon your
return with your family to Rome, when every man will know the esteem I
have for you. Your son will be as my son, and every honour I can bestow
will be yours.

There was more, about why Titus couldn't remove Agricola immediately: the governor's friends in the Senate, and Vespasian's promise of a
triumph should he succeed in subduing Britannia. But Valerius's mind
had frozen at the words *Your son will be as my son.* Taken at face value,
just another endearment almost lost amid the avalanche of unexpected
and head-spinning honours. But look a little deeper, with an understanding of the Emperor's personal situation, and it became the most
astonishing suggestion of all. Astonishing? Almost beyond belief. With
potentially fatal implications.

Valerius studied the broken wax seal. Why hadn't he inspected it
more closely before he opened it. If other eyes than his had read the
letter . . . He shuddered at the thought of what might already be in
train. Titus Flavius Vespasian's first wife Arrecina Tertulla died of the
bloody flux shortly after their marriage. His second union, to Marcia
Furnilla, produced a daughter, Julia, but lasted for only two years before
Titus demanded a divorce. The greatest, and Valerius believed probably the only, true love of his life was Queen Berenice of Cilicia. Titus
had brought Berenice to Rome after the sack of Jerusalem, only for his
father to insist after a public outcry that he send her away. Valerius's
wife Tabitha, once Berenice's faithful handmaiden, had been her former mistress's only friend while she lived in the city. Tabitha was certain
it was only a matter of time before Titus summoned Berenice back to
his side. And that would be the end of it, if the lovers were discreet.
Titus could not risk the outrage of the Senate and the mob by marry-
ing Berenice, a Judaean who would not abandon her religion. Neither

could he acknowledge their issue. Titus Flavius Caesar Vespasianus Augustus would never father an heir.

Your son will be as my son.

It was a fact acknowledged in Rome, certainly by Domitian, that Titus would appoint his younger brother heir, but so far there had been no official announcement. Nor, judging by this letter, would there be.

'Titus, my old friend,' Valerius whispered. 'What have you done?'

On the face of it, the greatest honour any man could do a friend. Roman society accepted that rich, childless patrons would appoint suitable sons of their friends or clients as heirs to take their name and protect their fortunes after death. Lucius's face swam into Valerius's reeling mind. Young, not quite eight, and utterly guileless. A good child who might grow into a good man given the opportunity.

How long would he survive Domitian's wrath once the announcement became public knowledge?

Titus would take Lucius into the Imperial household to be educated alongside the children of Rome's most powerful families, just as Titus himself had been educated alongside Emperor Claudius's son Britannicus. On the Palatine, Lucius would be beyond Valerius's direct protection. Tabitha would be able to stay close, at least until Lucius reached the age when he was ready to don the *toga virilis* of manhood, but what real power would a mere woman have in a palace riddled with the agents of Domitian, even one as formidable as Tabitha? Gaius Caligula had killed his cousin and co-heir Gemellus and no man blinked an eye. Nero waited only four months after Claudius's death before he poisoned his stepbrother Britannicus. What chance would Lucius have?

No, he could not let it happen. He would apply for leave to return to Rome and put his case to Titus in person. Yet his son had the opportunity to become Emperor. What right did any father have to take that opportunity away without first discussing it with his family? At last, amid the whirlwind of thoughts and fears, objectivity returned. Titus would not make the announcement until he raised Valerius to proconsular rank, which gave him another eighteen months or two years. The immediate danger depended on whether Agricola or some other had read the letter, and if the information had been passed to Domitian. The more Valerius considered it, the less likely that seemed. Titus's suggestion was innocuously phrased, buried deep and couched in words that wouldn't be considered unusual between close friends. Nevertheless, he would take precautions. He knew it was impossible for him to abandon his legion when he had specific orders from Agricola to take the fight to the enemy through the winter months, so he called for his clerk and dictated an order detailing Hilario and three other trusted members of his escort to return to Londinium and join Tabitha's household guard. When the clerk had gone, he wrote a personal letter to Tabitha explaining the increase in security, but not the reasons for it, trusting that his wife knew him well enough to accept the decision without questioning why. If she was in the least doubt about the family's safety, he told her, she must take ship north at the first opportunity. He would issue a warrant that would give the household passage on any ship bringing supplies to the legions. They would be safer in the midst of Valerius's loyal legionaries than anywhere else in Britannia. Once they were with him he and Tabitha could decide on their next step.

A guard hustled a puzzled-looking Hilario into the headquarters. 'You are to carry this to the lady Tabitha and place it into her hands and her hands only.' Valerius handed him the letter. 'Do you understand, trooper?'

'Of course, legate.' The big man frowned. 'Into the lady's hands only.'

'Crescens, Regulus and Tiberius will accompany you, but you will command. It's all explained in the letter.'

'Tiberius?'

'Tiberius Mediolanum.' Named for his home city to distinguish him from the escort's other Tiberius, newly arrived and not yet fully integrated into the unit. 'You'll stay in Londinium serving the legate's family until you receive further orders, probably in the spring.'

Hilario struggled to suppress a smile, and little wonder. Valerius's orders meant he'd spend the winter under a proper roof, with a warm bed and baths and bars to hand, instead of shivering in, at best, a draughty hut huddled around a brazier that roasted one side of you while the other froze solid, breaking the river ice to bathe, with only dice, board games and the rude, soldierly pleasures that mainly focused on bodily functions and helped make barrack life tolerable to look forward to. The cavalryman noticed Valerius watching him and his eyes turned troubled.

'Maybe someone else would be better suited to the mission, lord?'

'No, trooper.' Valerius allowed himself a smile. 'I need men I can trust for this duty. Men whose vigilance will never waver.'

'Then you can count on me, legate.' Hilario raised himself to his full height.

'You'll leave at first light and I'll give you a cavalry squadron as escort as far as Brigante country.' Ideally, he would have sent the men by sea, but the commander of the supply barges had offered to attempt one more convoy from the supply ships before the weather closed in and that might mean another week before the fleet sailed south.

'I thank you for your trust, legate. May the gods protect you while I am gone.'

XXIII

The weather worsened and the temperature grew colder as the days dwindled towards Saturnalia. Snow showers became more frequent, covering the high country in a carpet of white, but Gaius Rufus refused to curb his ceaseless efforts to penetrate Selgovae territory. He led squadrons of auxiliary cavalry out on week-long patrols into the icy wastes of the upland moors, sometimes leaving them for days on end to forge ahead alone seeking out some unguarded river valley, gully or stretch of forest that would take him beyond the outer ring of guard posts Calgacus had set with such care and knowledge of the terrain.

He worked his patrols mercilessly and Valerius began to receive complaints from the auxiliary prefects that Rufus was wearing their men and horses to nothing. After each patrol he would return to fill in another section of the sand table Valerius had set up in his headquarters. Sometimes during his report his head would start nodding and his words would dwindle away. His ruddy features became bony and ever more skeletal behind the beard he wore, and if Valerius handed him a cup of wine his hand shook as he accepted it. When Valerius suggested he give up, his lips twisted into a fierce snarl.

'It can be done, Valerius. I know it can be done. I can find a way.' He lurched to the sand table. 'Beyond the three hills lies bleak moorland that was sparsely populated even before Calgacus ordered his people to burn what was there. Impossible for an army to cross without being seen. But go a little further south where the country is more broken and it may be possible to get as far as this river without detection.' He pointed to a line that snaked round the hills before turning west, then south of west. With his finger he traced a dog-leg from Trimontium that bisected the river where it was joined by another of the innumerable lesser tributaries that fed it. 'With care I believe I can get you there without Calgacus being aware of it.'

'Within striking distance?'

'I cannot be certain,' the little man admitted wearily. 'But I believe so.'

'And then?'

'That is the puzzle I have been trying to solve.'

His hand moved over the sand table. 'Calgacus is somewhere in this mass of mountains here. So close that I can smell his presence.' He turned to stare at Valerius with red-rimmed eyes. 'I remember you telling me you spoke to Governor Agricola of mountains as walls riddled with rat holes where an enemy can choose to emerge at will?'

'You remember correctly.'

'Well, here the situation is reversed. We must find a rat hole large enough to take a powerful column, or at worst two holes where columns can provide mutual support for each other in the event of attack. To divide your army further would be to invite Calgacus to destroy you in detail, are we agreed?'

Valerius nodded.

'Naturally, Calgacus knows this as well as we do, and while I must necessarily probe my way into his territory with the care of a man picking up a snake, he knows every track and gully. He understands his weaknesses as well as we understand that we must find one that can be exploited. That means every likely rat hole is watched by a guard post or a patrol of Selgovae warriors.'

'Then it is impossible,' Valerius said.

'Not impossible.' Rufus managed a semblance of a smile. 'It just means we have to find an *unlikely* rat hole.'

Valerius poured them another cup of wine. 'No rat hole is worth losing you, scout. Give it up.'

A proper grin, now. 'You see. That is precisely why I must continue.'

'Why?' Valerius said. 'I don't understand.'

'Because you care about the life of every man in this legion.' Rufus held his gaze. 'That is why most of us – the best of us – are prepared to risk ours for you.'

'Damned fool.' Valerius growled to keep the emotion from his voice. 'You will wait three days before you go out again. The Gauls will mutiny if I don't give them a rest. And if it snows you stay home, that's an order.'

'And one that I will gladly obey.' Rufus downed his wine and saluted. 'With your permission I will withdraw now, legate, lest I end up sleeping on your floor.'

Three days later Valerius watched from the parapet as the scout rode from the south gate at the head of a squadron of the Ala Petriana and turned south down the river. He waved a salute, but Gaius Rufus looked to neither right nor left.

After four days the patrol returned.

Rufus was missing.

Valerius interviewed the cavalry commander, Aulus Atticus, a prefect of the Ala Petriana, in his pavilion. Atticus hailed from Gaul, but his family had been Roman citizens for generations. He seemed absurdly young for his position, and when he removed his helmet and clawed a lick of sweat-plastered blond hair from his forehead he looked almost boyish.

'Tell me what happened,' Valerius ordered.

'It was as usual with Arafa.' Bleak resignation gave Atticus's voice a rebellious edge. 'Riding far into the night. In the saddle before dawn. No forest too thick, no gully too narrow for the Ala Petriana. We barely saw the sky for three days. And the cold,' he shook his head, 'Epona save us, the cold would have frozen us solid had we not made our horses lie down and slept together with them beneath our blankets. But he got us there.' His words took on a savage edge. 'He took us so close to them that we could smell their cooking fires.'

The young man took a deep, shuddering breath and Valerius called for warmed wine. When it was brought Atticus held his cup as if he feared someone would steal it from him.

'Continue, prefect. I must know everything.'

'We found a dell to shelter in for the night, neither horse nor man making a sound for fear of alerting the enemy. While we rested Arafa burrowed and squirmed this way and that like a stoat, or a squirrel, always seeking more knowledge of our enemy. When he returned before dawn he could barely mount his horse, but he said he believed he had solved the puzzle.'

Valerius had listened with increasing gloom, knowing the story must end with the loss of his friend, but now his military instincts intervened.

'Did he say how?'

'No.' Atticus shook his head. 'He did not have the time. When we left the dell we had to cross a track and we had the misfortune to encounter a small party of Selgovae heading east. They were no match for our numbers and we put them to the sword, but the noise alerted a much larger group. We were all but surrounded when Arafa took two warriors and shouted that he would create a distraction so we could get out. I tried to argue with him, but there was little time and he would not be moved. He charged the enemy and drew them away and we were able to make our escape. That was the last time I saw him.'

Valerius put his hand to his head and closed his eyes. 'Is there no hope?'

Atticus shrugged. 'With Arafa there is always hope, but . . .'

'Could you take me back there, with a full cavalry wing?'

'I could try. I'm not sure. But sir, have you not seen the weather?'

'Weather?' He'd been submerged in administrative work since daybreak.

Atticus went to the doorway and pulled back the curtain. Valerius looked out to discover every inch of ground and every tent carpeted in white. There had been a handspan of snow already. Any chance of recovering Gaius Rufus was gone.

He choked back a surge of grief, but his eye was drawn to two cloaked figures standing in the snow between a pair of Atticus's troopers.

'What's this?' he demanded.

'I hope it will be some compensation for your loss, sir, that we did not return empty-handed.'

XXIV

Cathal looked down at the stunted figure lying crumpled in the snow.

'So this is him?'

'He's been in and out of our territory spying out the land for weeks. We thought we had him a dozen times.'

'He looks a little scrawny for a wolfhound. Isn't that what you called him?'

'Make it a boarhound then,' Emrys grunted, 'with that face. He may not be big, but he has a boarhound's heart. He never lets up and he never stopped coming. He killed two of our best before I managed to bring down his horse.'

'If it is the midget you should burn him,' Gwlym hissed. 'He is a Roman-lover and a traitor to his people.'

'You know him?' Cathal demanded.

'I know of him. A fox and a shape-changer who slips between Celtic and Roman camps like a shadow, spreading his poison wherever he goes.'

'Then he interests me. At the worst he may be useful as an example to the Romans of what happens to their spies.'

'Put him to the fire now.'

Cathal ignored the blind druid and turned away as another man rode up on one of the small, sturdy Celtic ponies.

'Have you found them yet?'

The rider shook his head. 'But I have every spare man in the saddle and we will keep looking for as long as it takes.'

Cathal looked up at the snow drifting down through the branches and knew any tracks the Romans had left would soon be invisible. The figure on the ground lifted his bloodied head, groaned and let it fall back into the snow.

'Bring him to the settlement and make sure he is harmed no further, for now.'

As Cathal marched through his men his face remained set in an expression of fierce resolution, but unshed tears blurred his vision. He would get them back if it took all eternity. If they were alive.

Emrys picked up Gaius Rufus as if he were a child and followed in his chieftain's footsteps. 'You're safe for now, my tough little boar-hound. But I have a feeling it won't be long until you are wishing you were dead.'

Rufus tried to open his eyes, but it was too much of an effort, and in any case his head felt as if it had been split in two with an axe. The last thing he remembered was riding at a group of Selgovae warriors as they moved to cut the patrol off from its escape route. Fool, he cursed himself, getting yourself killed when they were probably already dead. Amazingly, he was not. Which seemed a pity. Maybe better to lie here quietly in the hope that they'd let him die in peace, rather than suffer the traditional, and infinitely more painful, fate normally reserved for spies. A vain hope, as it turned out.

'Free his legs and wipe the blood off his face.' A voice like river gravel being shovelled into a brass bucket. Undeniably Celtic, the words themselves intelligible, but the constituents warped or twisted so it might have been a different language altogether. A rough cloth scraped across his forehead. He bit back a cry. A different kind of pain this time, more of a stab, accompanied by a new dampness that ran into his eyes. 'Bind it.' The speaker was running out of patience. A scab must have been removed to create a new flow. 'And get him to his feet.'

The *medicus*, or whoever served him, was gentler this time, or maybe the bandage was just softer. Someone worked at the rope on his ankles and he opened his eyes as he was pulled to his feet and placed on a rough three-legged stool. The room swam for a few moments before he regained his focus. And froze. The man looming above him was probably the largest he'd ever seen and Rufus had no doubt as to his identity. A *giant, tall as a rowan and broad as a four-wheel cart*, his late informant had said, and he hadn't been exaggerating. The roof of the hut was somewhere up in the blackness above the central fire, but this man's head must have been close to touching it. Rufus reached up to examine his wound, but discovered that his hands were still bound.

'You hit your head on a tree,' the giant growled. 'But you will live. For now.'

Ah, that 'For now'. The scout looked around the hut. Two spearmen by the doorway, a wizened piece of gristle he recognized by description seated on a bench by the wall spearing him with pus-filled eye sockets. A woman holding a bloody cloth and leather water bucket, not hiding her hatred. No escape here. He settled back into his seat to enjoy the last few pain-free moments of his life in relative comfort.

'You kidnapped my wife and daughter and murdered their escort.'

'I didn't know she was your wife.'

'Would it have made a difference?'

'No.'

'No excuses? No pleas for mercy? If they harm them . . .'

'They won't.'

'You seem certain.'

Rufus shrugged. 'They have their orders.'

'The druid wants me to burn you.'

A chill ran through Rufus at the sudden, awkward turn in the conversation. He turned towards Gwlym and spat. The druid hissed and raised a finger with a long curling nail in the captive's direction, but Rufus only snorted with disdain.

'He enjoys burning people.' He hesitated, before deciding more information would harm no one. 'He wanted to burn the legate's wife and son on Mona. But the legate got to them first and then the legate wiped Mona clean of druids. That is why he scurried here like a chastened cur with his tail between his legs. His power, if he ever had any, is gone. You will find Gaius Valerius Verrens a formidable opponent, Calgacus.'

A puzzled frown flitted over Cathal's rugged features. 'Calgacus?'

'That is what they call you – the Romans – it means the Swordsman.'

Cathal considered for a moment. 'Yes.' Rufus saw something like pride in the narrow, serious eyes. The Selgovae reached across to stroke the great sword slung on a frame by the wall. 'It fits. Not the worst name to be given by an enemy. Leave us, Gwlym,' he said abruptly.

'You should kill him now,' the druid spat. 'Remember that soft words are part of his armoury. He will try to bewitch you. Do not mistake his size for lack of threat.'

'I said leave us.' Gwlym hesitated but eventually he rose and the woman escorted him from the hut. 'You can wait outside,' Cathal told the guards. 'If he so much as sneezes I will tear off his arms and you may feed them to your dogs.' The men grinned and disappeared through the curtain. Cathal studied Rufus for a long, disconcerting moment that told his captive he was perfectly capable of carrying out his threat. Rufus tensed as the big man reached down and removed a glowing branch from the fire, then breathed out a long sigh as the Selgovae used it to light a bronze oil lamp hanging from a beam. In the flickering light he noticed for the first time the blue tattoos on Cathal's cheeks.

Cathal went to the heavy bench on which Gwlym had sat, picked it up as easily as if it were a stick for the fire and set it down in front of Rufus. It had been a long time since the scout had felt small, such was the respect he inspired in his comrades, but with Cathal close enough to smell the sweat on his body he was reminded of his stature as never before. The hands that lay on the Selgovae's knees looked capable of tearing up entire forests, and he had a sense of enormous power lying at rest beneath the plaid tunic.

'Gwlym also says you are a traitor.'

Rufus considered for a moment. 'It is a point of view,' he agreed.

'I have lived among the Celts for almost as long as I remember. But I was born a Roman.' He smiled, pleased, despite his predicament, that he had surprised his captor. 'Born in the city of Rome among the great palaces of the emperors, the son of a slave. So, with respect, I would dispute the druid's opinion.'

'How did . . .' Cathal shook his great maned head. 'No, that is for later. Gwlym was right. Words are your weapons. I have a suspicion you could keep me talking here until we both die of old age. We will speak further, Roman, but first we must understand each other. I have a proposition for you. You must die, you understand that?'

'I understand.' Rufus glared back at the big man. 'I made a mistake. There is a price to be paid. I am prepared to pay it, whatever it is.'

'A good answer.' Cathal slapped his hands against his knees. 'Well, Roman, I will promise you a quick death and a good one, with a sword in your hand, but only if you tell me everything about the soldiers I face. Their numbers, their tactics, their leaders. What lies behind the walls of their fort. What plans they have for . . . Calgacus.' His lips twitched at the name, but his voice hardened immediately. 'But I warn you that if I catch you out in a lie you will suffer as no man has suffered before. One of your companions tried to escape and fell into the hands of one of my warrior bands. They included one who had lost his father and his brother in the fight at the Tivyet crossing. Before I could reach him they hung him from a tree by the heels and flayed every inch of skin from his body. He lives still, I believe. Of course, you may be too honourable a man to betray his comrades; as a warrior I can understand that. In that case, say so now and we will begin your instruction in the ways of the Selgovae.'

'No.' Rufus had his head down so his features were hidden and his shoulders shook. Cathal felt a pang of disappointment. The little man, whom he had believed so brave, was sobbing like a coward. But, when he raised his head, Rufus's face split in an enormous grin and he was laughing so hard tears ran down his cheeks into his beard. 'No,' he spluttered again, 'my honour can stand the stain. I will share with you everything I know about the Ninth legion, but I doubt it will do you any good.' He saw puzzlement in the dark eyes. 'Most of what I can tell you you will know already, for a man like you will have studied them on the march and seen how and where they make camp. You know you cannot beat them in a straight fight because of their superior discipline and weapons. Your only hope is surprise. Anything else I can tell you that you do not know serves the purpose just as well. If I reveal a weakness it will tempt you into an attack and that is just what my commander would wish. He would like nothing better than to face you in the open where he can annihilate you. You see, lord king, by complying with your wishes I am also complying with his. It might have been planned this way.' He rubbed his sleeves across his eyes. Cathal moved forward, intending to cut his captive's wrists free, then thought better of it.

'You are a strange people, you Romans. I doubt I will ever understand you. But hear this, little man: whatever you say, I *can* defeat your legionaries, and everything I learn from you makes the outcome more likely. Perhaps I will keep you alive long enough to see the commander of the Ninth kneel before me with his standard lying in the dust.'

'I would like that above all things.' Rufus bowed his head. 'For it would mean I was still alive with the sun on my face at the coming of spring. But if you make Gaius Valerius Verrens kneel you will be the first, and he will not kneel willingly.'

'Enough of this,' Cathal growled. 'We will begin. You were very certain my wife and daughter would not be harmed. How do you know this?'

'Because of the man you face.' Rufus spoke without conscious thought. He was already dead; why should he need to play with words? 'Gaius Valerius Verrens, legate of the Ninth legion Hispana, is a soldier bound by the twin chains of honour and duty, though it is his eternal burden that the one may not always be consistent with the other. In war he is relentless and can be merciless, but when the fighting is over he lives by a different code. His soldiers know that to be caught molesting a female prisoner in any way would condemn them to *fustuarium*, the most terrible and shameful of punishments: to be beaten to death by their tentmates. If your wife reveals herself to be a lady of rank she will be treated with honour and held in comfort, as Queen Regina was after Brynmochdar.'

'Where will they keep her?' Cathal tried without success to keep the eagerness from his voice, and Rufus noted another facet to this terrible warrior. The little scout had a memory of a love as powerful, but he kept it buried deep, and had never allowed it to recur lest it be accompanied by the same humiliation.

'They have tents in a stockade within the fort for valuable prisoners,' he looked up with a wry smile, 'though your warriors have been remarkably reluctant to surrender. It is on the north side of the fort between two of the granaries. If the legate knows she is your wife, she and your daughter will be provided with a room in his pavilion, which is the headquarters tent and his own living quarters. It is the largest structure in the camp and unmistakable. Attack before dawn, just before the change of sentries, and you might have a chance of reaching it. The wall on the river flank is probably the most vulnerable, because it's where you would be least expected.'

A dangerous glint of suspicion flashed in Cathal's eyes. 'You are remarkably forthcoming even for a man given such a powerful motivation to talk. Information I had expected, but now you give me advice and encouragement?'

'I told you, lord king. You are as aware of all this as I, and if we are aware of it so is Valerius Verrens. Once he knows his prisoner is your wife he will expect you, being the man you are, to come for her, and he will prepare a suitable welcome for you.'

'And I would go,' Cathal snarled. 'I would storm those walls with my sword brothers and we would cut through your camp like wolves in a sheep fold . . . but for one thing. I am a king. My love for my family must be secondary to my responsibility to my people. Without me they would be leaderless. Those who would replace me would either throw my warriors to be pointlessly slaughtered by the little Roman swords or sell their allegiance to Rome for a crock full of silver, like the Votadini.'

'Valerius went after his wife, though it was his duty to stay with his men. He crossed the raging seas and walked through fire and saved her from the druid's vengeance.' It was a provocation and both men knew it, but Cathal only tossed another branch on the fire and stared at the flames as the golden talons clawed the air and painted the walls of the hut with flickering shadows.

'When you speak of him I hear reverence in your voice for this man who sent you here to die. What bond can there be between a mere outrider, the son of a slave as you say, and a man who commands thousands?'

Rufus considered the question. He had a suspicion the conversation was coming to an end. An idea had been growing like a worm in his ear, but it needed to be carefully nurtured.

'We are both touched by the gods.' He watched Cathal's reaction and was gratified to see him spit in the fire. 'You have heard of Boudicca, who fought the Roman general Paulinus?'

'Even I, a mere barbarian lost in his northern fastness, have heard of Boudicca.' Cathal's words dripped sarcasm, but Rufus was undeterred.

'Gaius Valerius Verrens commanded the defenders of Colonia Claudia Victricensis, the legionary veterans' colony, a bare three thousand men. When Boudicca came she had twenty warriors for every Roman. They knew they could not win, but still they fought until they were cut down man by man. At the last, a dozen or so fought their way to the Temple of Claudius,' Cathal's brow creased into a frown at the unfamiliar words, 'where the town's remaining civilians had taken refuge. A sacred place made entirely of stone,' Rufus explained. 'With great pillars the height of oak trees.' He could tell the Selgovae believed he exaggerated, but he carried on in any case. 'They held out for three days. The Iceni fired the door and the heat was terrible. Valerius ordered what little water remained be poured on the door to stop it burning through. A hundred men, women and children trapped in a space barely larger than this hut, throats parched, hardly able to breathe because of the smoke, eyes watering, sitting in their own filth.'

'How do you know all this, Roman, son of a slave?'

'Because I was there.'

Cathal studied him with his serious dark eyes, seeking out the lie if one existed. He must have decided not. 'What is your name?' he asked eventually.

'They call me Arafa.' Rufus invested the word with pride and something Cathal couldn't read.

'This is like no Roman name I have ever heard.'

'It means giant.'

It started low in his belly, a heaving that expanded into his broad chest and eventually exploded in an enormous guffaw that threatened to blow the thatched roof from the hut. When the choking laughter faded Cathal reached out to pinch Rufus's arm. The little man stared at him.

'I was just checking that you truly existed. A man who made me laugh on the worst day of my life.'

'I exist,' Rufus assured him. 'For now.'

'For now,' Cathal acknowledged. 'And this Colonia. How did it end?'

'They would tell you there were no survivors. Boudicca ordered the slaughter of every living thing in the town. They even hunted down the rats.'

'Yet you survived.'

'We survived.'

'And that is your bond?'

'After Colonia, every day is a gift from the gods. I should have died twenty years ago. Valerius is the same. Men who have stared death in the face need never fear it again. Do your will, King Cathal.'

Cathal nodded slowly. 'You are brothers. Brothers of the sword.' He heaved himself to his feet, a towering presence that dominated the room. His gaze was drawn to the flames again and for a moment it appeared his eyes were on fire. 'I have not finished with you, Arafa. We will talk again.'

159

XXV

They were mother and daughter. The evidence was in the wild, corn-gold hair, the same intelligent, wary eyes, a distinctive mix of emerald and blue. It reminded Valerius of the colour of the Mare Internum where the shallows met the deeps, when the sun hit the water in a certain way. The same uptilted nose and the same delicate chin, set at just the right angle to show lack of fear, but not the outright defiance that might provoke some reaction from their captors. The girl would be a little younger than Lucius, long-limbed and gawky, with fine white teeth that seemed too big for her mouth. In the mother, the combination of features produced what Valerius could only call a sort of rustic Celtic prettiness. No conventional beauty in Roman eyes, but enough to make a man look twice in the hope of provoking a smile. Her cloak was slightly open at the neck and Valerius caught a glint of gold.

'Atticus, escort the ladies inside. I suspect you did well. Very well. And send for someone who can speak the Selgovae tongue.'

He smiled and stepped aside to let them pass through the curtained door of the pavilion. All he received in return for his gallantry was a glare from the elder and a look of aristocratic disdain from the daughter. Atticus met his eyes and shrugged. 'They've been like this since we

160

took them. Not a hint of fear after the initial capture, and they look at us as if we're something that's escaped from the sewer.'

Valerius followed the pair into the relative warmth and Quintus Naso appeared in the doorway behind him. 'I heard about Rufus. What do you plan to do?'

'Nothing, for now,' Valerius admitted. 'Once the snow stops we'll see, but . . .'

The camp prefect grimaced. 'He could be dead already. It's difficult . . .' For the first time, he noticed the cloaked woman and child standing in the centre of the room. 'What's this?'

'I'm not certain, but I hope to find out soon.' A guard ushered a man into the tent. He was probably the ugliest person Valerius had ever seen, the bulbous features and bulging eyes of a mating toad twisted into an obsequious, fawning grin. Short and squat, he held a leather cap twisted in his hands and his bowed head bobbed up and down with such regularity that Valerius wondered it didn't fall off.

'Is this the best you can do?' he demanded.

'No prisoners who speak the local tongue have volunteered, sir,' the guard said apologetically. 'Not that we've taken any. We picked this fellow up while we were still in Brigante country and he offered his services. Says he was a merchant, which is how he speaks the local lingo, but Arafa – the scout, I mean – thought he was on the run.'

Valerius ushered the interpreter forward. 'Ask them to sit down.' He waved a hand at a padded couch. 'And tell them we mean them no harm.' The man spluttered a string of unintelligible words, but neither the woman nor her daughter even looked in his direction.

'Then ask them if they would like food or drink.' The interpreter complied, this time accompanying his words with an eating motion, which made him look even more revolting. Again there was no reaction.

'Their names?' Valerius persisted.

Not even a flicker of an eyebrow.

'What will you do with them?' Naso eyed the prisoners warily. 'You know the standing orders are to send the best-looking women captives

161

to Agricola immediately.' His words were accompanied by a suggestive grin.

'It's not like that.' Valerius didn't often feel forced to defend the governor, but he couldn't let this pass. 'His wife likes to surround herself with beautiful things.' He pursed his lips. 'I'm not sure.' That gleam of gold at the woman's neck again. Welcome evidence that the Ala Petriana took his orders seriously. Another unit might have decided that a little light plundering didn't add up to molestation. It was also a hint of something that required some thought. 'You could argue that she was a little old to be a house slave.' Did he detect a flicker of emotion? 'There's plenty of room in the stockade,' he mused. 'Of course, they'd have to share it until the spring with the legion's defaulters and that century of Usipi auxiliaries who tried to desert. Still, they'd have a tent over their heads through the worst of the winter and it's better than what's waiting for them at the slave market.'

Naso nodded. He turned to the interpreter. 'Tell them . . .'

'There is no need,' the woman spat. 'This vile creature's grunting hurts my ears. I have pigs that speak the Selgovae tongue better. Yes,' she acknowledged the looks of surprise, 'I speak Latin as well as you do. I am a princess of the Brigante, descendant of Queen Cartimandua, and when I was young I spent time in Londinium as a hostage. I am also a queen.' She drew the cloak back to reveal an ornate Celtic neck torc of twisted strands of gold. 'And I had been led to expect better manners from the Roman officers I met in Londinium.'

Valerius and Naso looked at each other before bowing their heads in acknowledgement of the prisoner's rank. A guard hurried the interpreter from the tent, provoking a squeak of outraged dignity.

'Lady.' Valerius bowed again. 'Allow me to introduce myself. I am Gaius Valerius . . .'

'I know who you are.' She pointed to the wooden hand and the blue eyes flashed. 'That alone marks you as the killer of my uncle, Guiderius, even if your rank and status did not.' Valerius bit his tongue to stifle his denial. How had she known? Of course, Calgacus would be aware of Guiderius's fate, and the Brigante refugees who fled north would have confirmed it. 'I am Olwyn, wife of Cathal, king of the Selgovae, and this is my daughter the princess Berta. I ask that in all conscience you return us to our people, or at least allow my daughter to go.'

'I'm sorry, but you know that is not possible. Even if I were minded to do so, I would not expose you to the perils of the winter in this wild place . . .'

'This *wild place*, as you call it, is our home.'

'And your arrival poses certain political questions which I must consider. I am afraid you must stay with us over the winter.' He raised a hand to still the inevitable protest. 'You will have a room in this pavilion which will provide privacy and comfort for you both. In the spring I will send emissaries to your husband. Perhaps it is possible to end this unfortunate conflict without further bloodshed.'

'Cathal will not wait for the spring, Roman.' Olwyn's fury was so impressive her daughter laid a hand of warning on her arm. 'He will come for me when you least expect it, and when he does it will be your blood he spills, and that of all your hired killers.'

'That would be unfortunate,' Valerius said quietly. 'Because if it came to that all he would find would be the bodies of his loved ones. If I believed this fort was about to fall, lady, I would have one of my men cut both your throats. Goodnight. We will speak again tomorrow when you have rested. I will arrange for food and water to be sent to you.'

'Keep your food. I would not touch the filthy stuff.'

'Perhaps not.' Valerius met her gaze. 'But your daughter may feel otherwise. I will send men to prepare your quarters.'

He turned away and walked towards the doorway with Naso. 'I'll put together a dispatch to inform the governor of our catch.' The camp prefect grinned. 'Perhaps for once he will have reason to praise the Ninth.'

'No, Quintus,' Valerius said quietly. 'You will forget you ever heard the word queen. As far as this fort is concerned our guest is a lady of rank, a hostage for the life of Gaius Rufus.'

'But Rufus is most likely dead. The governor's orders . . .'

'Dead or not, I won't send Olwyn to Agricola,' Valerius insisted. 'As long as she is here she is worth her own weight in silver. Either her

163

presence will tempt Calgacus to attempt a rescue, in which case I will kill him or take him and break the Selgovae power for all time, or in the spring I will use her as a bargaining chip to drive a wedge between Calgacus and his people, perhaps even persuade him to give himself up in exchange for her life.'

Naso stared at him. 'You wouldn't kill her, Valerius, for all your threats. You're not that kind of man.'

'Perhaps I'm not the man I was, Quintus. In any case, make sure young Atticus knows to keep his mouth shut.'

'The trader?' Accompanied by a look that said: *Should I cut his throat?*

'Send him out with the next patrol into the wastes and make sure he doesn't come back.' He saw the look again. 'No, don't have them kill him. If the snow doesn't get him, the Selgovae will, and if by chance he survives . . . well, that will be up to the gods, won't it?'

Since the day they'd first met and he had heard Rufus's story he'd sensed that their fates were intertwined. How could they not be? The only two men to survive the destruction of the Temple of Claudius and the slaughter that followed. It seemed to Valerius that the gods had brought them together for a reason, just as they had saved them from a death that should have been inevitable. The knowledge that the scout was probably dead left a hollow feeling inside him. In a way, it was like the loss of his hand. Rufus, who had endured fire and slaughter and the loss of everything he loved, had become part of him. It was difficult to believe he was gone. Valerius still held out a slim hope and he intended to find out for certain. Tomorrow he would send a messenger under a flag of truce to inform Calgacus his wife and daughter were safe and that no harm would come to them as long as he didn't attempt a rescue. The threat would mean nothing to a man like the Selgovae king, but the messenger might get some hint of Rufus's fate. Of course, the messenger might not return, but that in itself would send a message. Every messenger knew the risk, and that was what messengers were for.

*

He left her for three days, ordering that no one who entered their quarters should communicate with the prisoners in any way. The servants who carried in their food and removed their night soil reported that both mother and daughter had ignored their offerings on the first day, but on the second attacked their rations with voracious appetite. Anyone who entered was plagued with demands to carry a request to the legate for their immediate release, or, at worst, an audience with him to discuss their situation.

It was mid-morning when he walked into the room. Olwyn's face switched to a mask of fury when she recognized him, but, oddly, the look softened as quickly as it appeared. The girl Berta barely glanced up, and she showed the listless quality Valerius had seen in animals caged for too long. He felt a pang of conscience when he remembered his son Lucius's boundless energy and the effect that being trapped for days on end like this would have had on him.

'I hope I find you well, ladies?'

'All the more so if you have come to tell us we may return to our people,' Olwyn snapped.

'Unfortunately, as I have said, that will not be possible, but' – Valerius waved towards the doorway where Shabolz had appeared carrying a large bundle of clothes across his arms – 'your husband has sent some changes of clothing and other essentials he felt you might require for your comfort.'

Before he could continue Berta leapt to her feet and rushed to inspect the skirts and tunics. 'Look, Mother,' she cried. 'My blue dress and your thick plaid cloak. He has even sent Mairaid.' She held up a worn cloth doll with straw-blonde hair. Olwyn didn't move, but Valerius could tell she was having to restrain herself.

'There is more outside still being unpacked,' he said. 'You may inspect it at your leisure. Cal— King Cathal sends his greetings and assures you that arrangements will be made for your return.' He missed out the part where the Selgovae chief promised her that if any harm came to them he would personally remove her captor's extremities one by one, leaving the choicest to be harvested by Olwyn herself. 'I have

165

assured him your welfare is safe in my hands and he bids you make yourself as comfortable as possible. He is sorry he is unlikely to be able to negotiate your freedom before the spring.' He saw the gleam in Olwyn's eyes and knew her thoughts mirrored his own. For different reasons they both hoped he would come long before the first thaw.

The messenger he'd sent to Calgacus, Dagwalda, one of Shabolz's Pannonian comrades, had recounted how he had been met by a Selgovae patrol mounted on the big Roman horses stolen at Brynmochdar. 'They blindfolded me and spun me round so I had no sense of my position before they led me to their camp. Some lesser lord questioned me, but treated me with courtesy. Eventually I was taken before their king, who questioned me again, and I answered as you had instructed, lord. I did not see Arafa, but there was an outbuilding beyond the perimeter of the settlement that I took to be a latrine, and I saw tracks the size of a child's leading there. A child accompanied by two adults and wearing what I took to be nailed sandals.'

Valerius knew it was possible the *caligae* had been taken from Rufus's dead body, but he chose to believe the little man was alive. The question was how to get him back. But that was for the future.

'Please let me know if there is anything else I can do to make your stay more comfortable,' he said to the queen. 'At least within the limits of this crude temporary camp.'

'Do you expect us to stare at four walls for the entire winter?' Olwyn demanded. 'Whether they are walls of cloth or walls of timber they are still walls. At least give us spindles and thread to help us pass the time.'

'Of course,' Valerius agreed. 'I should have thought of that. And when the weather is reasonable you may walk the streets of the camp under escort.' A faint hint of a familiar scent reached his nostrils. 'I will also arrange for a separate latrine to be built for you.'

Olwyn got to her feet and Berta ran to her side. 'Then I thank you.' The Selgovae queen's head twitched in a nod of acknowledgement. 'I doubt you treat all your female prisoners with such courtesy.'

'Not all prisoners are so noble in birth and bearing,' he assured her. 'Through no fault of your own you have become counters in the game

166

of diplomacy. It is possible your presence here may be instrumental in saving many hundreds of your people's lives. Your husband seems an intelligent and not unreasonable man . . .'

'For a barbarian, you mean?'

'Lady, my opinion of what constitutes a barbarian changes with every contact I have with the people of this island. King Cathal has a particular regard for you. I have a mission to complete. If that mission can be completed without further delay and bloodshed so much the better.' He turned to leave, then hesitated. 'You will have noticed that I do not require your promise that you will not try to escape. That is because I also have regard for *your* intelligence. Even if you managed to get beyond the gates, either you would freeze to death within a few hours or Shabolz and his men would ride you down before you had gone a mile.'

XXVI

Over the next few weeks Valerius would often see Olwyn and her daughter walking the circuit of the fort's walls, staring up at the three hills, or with their eyes on the south-west where Calgacus had his refuge. Wherever they went either Shabolz or another member of Valerius's escort would accompany them, at first dogging their footsteps like a faithful but unwanted hound, but later as part of the group. He noticed that the soldiers were shy in their company, but Olwyn would always engage them in conversation and set them at ease in a way that puzzled him. In his experience this wasn't the way prisoners, not even the most favoured hostages, treated their captors.

When he asked Shabolz about it, the Pannonian grinned. 'If the lady is here much longer she'll know more about this fort than you do. Aye, and the legion too. At first she'll talk about the weather, then she'll entertain you with tales of those great hills, sacred places she says. But then you'll find yourself talking about the fort and when the sentries change and where the armoury is. I hope I didn't do wrong, lord. I didn't think it would do any harm. Come the spring, when they leave us,' he gave Valerius a sideways glance, 'one way or the other, we'll be marching against these Selgovae barbarians and teaching them not to give us the runaround.'

Valerius shook his head. 'She has eyes and ears, trooper. Anything you tell her she can either see or hear for herself. She's only doing what I would do in her place.'

The next day he took the cavalryman's place beside Olwyn and her daughter at the start of their walk. Snow coated the hills in pristine white and the thin winter sun made them shine as if they were studded with diamonds.

'I did not expect to see you today, legate,' she said, but she didn't seem displeased. She wore the thick plaid cloak her husband had sent against the cold, with the wide hood draped across her shoulders so her hair glowed gold in the sun.

'The men are pleased you are taking such a deep interest in the working of the fort and their beloved legion.' He tempered the words with a smile.

'I hope you will not chastise them for indulging a lady's whims,' she said with mock gravity.

'Not at all,' he said. 'Their orders are to put you at your ease. You may go where you please as long as you are escorted. I want you to feel as if you are our guest.'

'A guest has the choice whether to come or go,' she pointed out. 'Whereas we do not.'

A pinprick of conscience. 'Forgive me. That is true.' He bowed his head. 'Then let us pretend you are a guest who is forced to stay by the peculiarities of the weather.'

'Is there a reason why you joined us?' she said abruptly, as if he'd reminded her of something she would rather not think about.

'I wanted to talk to you.'

'But you can talk to me at any time.' She gave him a puzzled look. 'All you have to do is wave your finger and I must appear before the commandant like any other member of your unit.'

'No, I wanted to talk to you about yourself. A Brigante princess, schooled in Roman ways, to be forced to marry and live among the Selgovae. It must have been a shock to you.'

'Why do you say that?' Olwyn stopped abruptly and stared at him.

She glanced back at Berta, but the girl's attention was on one of the dogs that had adopted the fort as its home. 'It was my duty, and if you knew my husband you would understand it was no hardship. He made me welcome and he treated me as his queen from the first moment, with respect and restraint, and he ensured his people did the same. I cannot say that of some of the Roman boys I encountered in Londinium.'

'Then I am sorry . . .'

But she continued as if she hadn't heard him. 'We had a home there.' She pointed north to where the little cluster of huts had been. 'We walked in the hills and we swam in the river and Cathal fished and hunted and we were happy. He built a fine house and gave me fine presents, and in time he gave me fine children. What more could any woman want than that?'

'What kind of a man is he?'

The question surprised and irritated her – he saw lightning flash in the blue eyes – but she didn't hesitate to answer.

'He is a great man and a great king. In the spring warriors will flock to his banner from north and south and he will drive the Romans from this land for ever. Yet he cares little for war. What he cares about is his people. In the main they are farmers, not warriors. He keeps the Votadini at bay and ensures they have peace to till their fields, he dispenses justice without fear or favour, and in return they give him their respect and their love. As a warrior he has no parallel, but that is not why he has no rivals. He is a king any man would follow, Roman. Even you.'

'I know he is a great king. I asked what kind of man he is.'

He could see the question perplexed her and for a moment he thought she would turn away. Instead, she met his gaze, and when she spoke, though there was no enmity in her voice, her words contained an unmistakable challenge.

'He is kind and fair,' she said softly, 'and for such a big man he can be surprisingly gentle. Do you want to know how he holds me in the night, Roman? Do you want to know what it feels like when he kisses me?'

'Enough,' he said. She'd made him feel sullied and dirty, the way a man sometimes felt after a battle with the blood of his enemies sticky on his skin and the taste of it on his lips, because the killing had been so easy. 'I did not mean . . .'

'You wanted to know your enemy,' she finished for him. 'So now you understand why I ask my questions of your soldiers in honeyed tones, even though I feel loathing for the uniform if not for the man who wears it.' A momentary hesitation. 'Why do you need what little we have, Roman, when you already have everything you require? The Selgovae are not rich. They are no threat to you. All we wanted was to be left in peace to harvest our crops, hunt our woods, take the bounty from our rivers' – she glanced to where Berta played with one of the stray's pups – 'and bring up our children. Is it because you are strong and the strong must dominate the weak? You would argue that it is essential to ensure the security of your province of Britannia. Yet you know nothing of the people against whom you march until you cross their borders and burn their villages. It cannot be greed, because we have nothing a *civilized* man like you could want. So what is left but fear? You fear us precisely because you do not know us. When you meet our unprepared warriors and put them to the sword you despise us as weaklings and cowards. And what comes next? I have heard what your Suetonius Paulinus did to the Iceni, the Trinovantes, the Catuvellauni and the Dobunni, and I experienced what happened to the Brigantes. The choice is between subjugation or annihilation. Our people must obey Roman laws and pay Roman taxes, they must live in Roman townships where our councils look and dress and act like Roman councils, our children must be educated as Roman children, so they will grow up as Romans. Even our land will be bound by your roads and your watchtowers, and our gods will be known by Roman names. If we do not fight, what will be left of the Selgovae but a name?'

Valerius could have argued that Roman rule could bring peace and prosperity as it had in Gaul and Hispania, Syria, Asia and Africa. If the Selgovae submitted to Rome her son would be brought up as a Roman aristocrat, with all the advantages that would bring in culture and learning and travel. Eventually, her people would live in warm stone buildings and worship in stone temples. They would grow rich manufacturing and selling essential supplies to satisfy the limitless appetite of the legions. But what did that matter if she was perfectly happy with what she already had? Would she consider it a price worth paying that the new world he painted could only be won at the cost of everything that had gone before, including her husband? For Cathal would not be part of it. Too great a prize, too influential and too dangerous to be allowed to stay free.

He shook his head and turned away. Her words followed him. 'In the spring, if not before, my husband will come here and he will kill you, Gaius Valerius Verrens. In a way that will be a pity. Your soldiers talk of you as a good man . . . for a Roman.'

XXVII

March AD 80

Gaius Rufus threw himself out of his vermin-infested furs and shook his shaggy head, scratching at the bites that covered his body. In the freezing weather that coated the hut walls with ice despite the fiercest fire, every biting parasite in the hut seemed to seek out the warmth of his body. It had become so irritating he'd even shaved the beard he'd worn for twenty years and more. Winter would have driven him mad if it had not been for his regular conversations with Cathal. The threat of a painful death had receded as he grew to know the Selgovae king better. Oh, Cathal would have his throat cut in a heartbeat if it would benefit his tribe or discomfit the Romans, but he would not inflict pain merely for the sake of it. Was there a different feel to the air today? He prayed not, but he knew he prayed in vain. Spring was coming. The day of decision approached.

Cathal had milked him of every detail about the Roman forces he would face in the spring. He knew the position of every sentry post, every plank of wood and every latrine pit of the fortress at Trimontium. And with every retelling he became more thoughtful. He knew Valerius's force was just one of three legions advancing north, and that the Ninth could be joined by either of the others at any time. The Selgovae were not the Brigantes. Brigantia was three or four times the size, with three or four times the population. Decades of acting as a barrier between the Romans and the barbarians of the north had created a standing Brigante army of thirty thousand hardened warriors. Rufus doubted Cathal could field an army a third as great. Most of his people were farmers and craftsmen. They had proved they were brave and they could fight, but fighting wasn't winning. Even if he lured a single legion into ambush it was unlikely he had sufficient men to destroy it, and he would lose so many in the attempt he wouldn't be strong enough to resist the next attack. Cathal never mentioned Olwyn or Berta, but Rufus knew of the gifts he had sent. The king sacrificed daily for their return, but in the fiercest winter in Selgovae memory had never found the opportunity to carry out the raid that might achieve it.

Gwlym would sit in the shadows, endlessly patient, listening to the discussions. At first he plagued Cathal with demands for an immediate attack, whatever the cost, but as the scale of the challenge became clear he limited his interventions to an occasional hiss or a sneer of contempt. Gradually it dawned on Rufus that Gwlym was as much a captive as he was, bound by the chains of his growing infirmity and his lack of options. The hunger for revenge that sustained him like a glowing fire had rested on the strength of the Brigantes and his ability to guide the malleable King Guiderius to victory. Now it was clear that Cathal alone could never defeat the Romans it was as if his old wounds were draining the life force from him.

Rufus heard a commotion and the cloth curtain covering the hut door was thrust aside. A massive bulk filled the opening, blocking out the fierce early morning sunlight. 'Still abed, Roman?' Cathal growled. 'Do you not feel it? We call this *an latha ath-nuadhachaidh* – the day of renewal. Come, the elders need the hut.'

Rufus drew a cloak over his tunic and *bracae* and wrapped cloths around his feet before donning his sandals. Outside the settlement was a hive of activity. Men and women carried great bundles of clothing and bedding down the slope towards the frozen lake. Elders and the younger children worked among the houses, clearing out the fur rugs that covered the earth floors. As he watched, Cathal's son Dugald was hoisted on to a thatched roof with the help of two of his friends. The boy clung to the thatch while a large fur was handed up to him. White smoke belched from the ventilation hole, suggesting the central fire had recently been banked up. Dugald dragged the fur up the slope to the apex and threw it over the hole, trapping the smoke. At the same time others pinned a heavy bearskin across the door.

'With Andraste's favour we'll drive out the worst of the vermin.' Cathal grinned. 'Sometimes we lose a hut or two to stray sparks, but they're easily replaced.'

A festival air pervaded the proceedings, and Rufus stepped aside as two men herded a squealing pig towards where a herdsman versed in butchery waited.

'Winter is not over yet,' the Selgovae chieftain said. 'But we will eat meat and drink beer tonight and soon the days will lengthen . . .'

His voice tailed away, and Rufus knew he was wondering what awaited his people in the spring. He had heard the whispers when he visited the cistern to chip away the ice and wash. The Romans occupied the ground by the river where once had stood the Selgovae capital. They controlled the sacred hills and had built a watchtower in the midst of the ancient settlement Cathal's ancestors had created. The priests calculated that Imbolc was less than a month away, but there would be no great gathering, no sacrifice and no ewes jumping through the ring of fire on the lower slopes.

Cathal led the way down to the lake and men used boulders to smash the inches-thick ice for a distance of twenty or thirty paces across the surface. Rufus looked on, puzzled, as others undressed and handed their clothes to the tribe's married women, who took the plaid trews and dyed tunics and giggled to each other as they compared the stature and attributes of the young warriors. One he recognized as Emrys, the man who might have killed him all those months ago, came to stand beside him and began to strip off. 'What are you waiting for, little man? It is not just the huts that are cleansed on the day of renewal.'

Rufus looked to Cathal and the king gave him a nod of encouragement. He shrugged and stripped off his tunic and the calf-length
bracae. When he threw his clothes to the ground he heard a grunt of
surprise and looked up to find Emrys grinning at him. 'Not so little
after all,' the Selgovae chortled. 'Now we know why the Romans called
you giant.' He called to a nearby woman and she gave a great hoot of
delight. 'Lucky we didn't strip you down when we captured you, or
we'd have had to keep you locked away in a cage.'

Embarrassed, Rufus followed Cathal down to the water's edge, running to keep up with the long-striding Selgovae. 'Don't hesitate,' the
king said, as much to himself as the captive Roman. 'And don't be too
proud of that great sword of yours.' He laughed. 'Ice water makes all men
equal.' With a howl he ran the last few yards and dived into the broken
ice and green waters, accompanied by a dozen of his sword brothers.

Rufus didn't wait to see the outcome, but sprinted in their wake.

When they were done, Rufus followed Cathal from the water and
accepted his clothes from a cheerful Selgovae woman. They dried
themselves with their tunics and as his body reheated Rufus found that
he'd never felt more alive. Every sinew seemed young again and his
body coursed with some kind of new invigorating power.

'It is good to be renewed.' Cathal, oddly sombre now, stared down at
him. 'Let us hope in your case it will be for good purpose.'

Before Rufus could react to the puzzling and slightly worrying statement, a groom brought one of the stolen horses down to the water's
edge. Colm, dressed in impressive new finery beneath a thick cloak,
took the reins and walked the horse to Cathal.

'You know what to say?' the king said. 'It must be expressed exactly
as I ordered.'

'Haven't I been sitting in my hut these last three weeks learning
every word,' Colm grumbled. 'I have it to the word and to the inflec-
tion. There will be no doubting what you intend.'

'Lord king! Lord king!' A new commotion as Gwlym brushed
through the crowd of women guided by a young Selgovae priest. 'You
must not do this.'

'Must not?' Cathal's face darkened. 'Who are you to tell a king what he must and must not do?'

'Then I humbly beg you to think again.' There was nothing humble about the druid's bearing. 'You gamble our entire enterprise on a single throw of the knife. There is nothing to be gained and everything to lose.'

'Nothing to be gained?' Cathal's voice had a dangerous quality, but Gwlym ignored the threat.

'You can find a new queen and she will bear you new daughters, and sons too. Your woman has spent a season among the Romans. A captive at the beck and call of a thousand soldiers. Her honour—'

'Is my affair,' Cathal snarled. 'I have the Roman commander's word that she would not be harmed or abused and I trust that word. Not so long ago you exhorted me to cut the head from the snake. What has changed?'

Rufus listened with growing bewilderment. Something was happening here he only partially understood.

'I would not have it at this price,' Gwlym persisted. 'He will play you false and we will all pay.'

'Enough.' Cathal walked back to Colm. 'I have made my decision.'

'Your pardon, lord king.' Rufus took step beside him. 'Perhaps I may be of service in this matter, whatever it is?'

Cathal's rugged features softened. 'I think not, Arafa. For you are already at the centre of it. Colm has the Latin and he carries word to your commander suggesting an exchange. Your freedom for that of my wife and daughter.'

Rufus's stomach lurched. This was what he'd tried to suggest to Cathal, ever so subtly, all those months ago, but so much time had passed that he could barely remember his words. Could it be? How would Valerius react? He tried to think back to their relationship. Had he imagined the bond that linked them after the Temple of Claudius? And Valerius, that fount of honour and duty, could not help but be torn even if his instinct was to accept. He dropped his head. 'I do not know if my commander will place so much value on a mere scout.'

177

'You are no mere scout, Gaius Rufus, as I have learned during your captivity. You are a Roman citizen. A man of intelligence, courage and sense. From what you tell me, the legate of the Ninth legion is of the same stock, and a man of compassion. I believe he will consider it a fair trade.' He looked down at the smaller man and for a moment Rufus felt he was being measured. 'You must pray it is so, because your life may depend on it.'

And the life of Gaius Valerius Verrens.

XXVIII

'Patrol coming in,' the sentry called from the gate tower. 'Looks like they have someone with them.'

'Call the legate,' the guard commander ordered. 'He'll want to know.'

Word spread quickly around the fort and by the time Valerius reached the ramparts a dozen others had already joined the sentries there.

'Haven't you people got work to do?' he snapped. 'This post has turned into a rest home. I swear the first day the snow thaws I'll have every spare man marching until he drops and the same for a week after. Now get back to your posts.'

'They're just curious, Valerius.' Quintus Naso climbed the steps to stand beside him. 'They mean no harm.'

Valerius grunted an acknowledgement. He knew he'd been as touchy as a caged tiger for the past two or three weeks and this was as close as his camp prefect would ever come to a rebuke. Was this what he'd been waiting for all this long interminable winter? The riders were close enough now to make out their individual features and he saw the patrol was commanded by a young, well-liked cavalry prefect of the Asturians called Flavinus. The stranger he was escorting carried a stunted conifer twig. More feet on the stairs and he turned to snap at whoever was coming to join the sightseers, only to shut his mouth like a trap when

179

he recognized Queen Olwyn, with Dagwalda at her side. She looked beyond the wooden stakes and he saw the moment her eyes lit up in recognition.

'You know this man, lady.'

She licked her lips, uncertain whether to reply, then: 'He is Colm, a trusted companion of my husband.'

'Then we should prepare to make him welcome.' Valerius turned and strode down the stairs, Quintus at his side and Olwyn and Dagwalda in their wake. 'Have him brought to the *principia*. You'll need to be there, Quintus, and a clerk to take notes. Four guards should be enough . . . Not you, lady,' he added, forestalling the inevitable suggestion. 'Escort the lady and her daughter to her quarters, Dagwalda. And make sure she has no contact of any kind with this emissary. Do you understand me? Not even eye contact.'

'Not even eye contact,' the Pannonian muttered. 'Lady.' He waved a hand in the direction of the *praetorium*. Olwyn let out a growl of frustration and marched off, leaving him to catch up with her as he could.

'What do you think's going on?' Naso asked.

'I have a suspicion Calgacus wants his lady back.'

'And will you assent? The governor will—'

'Hear about it in good time, Quintus. We both know he has spies in this camp who will send him the news the first opportunity they get. But that will not be until a proper thaw. This decision is mine and mine alone. As to whether I'll assent, that will depend on what King Cathal has to offer.'

They passed the *praetorium* and entered the *principia*, the fort's administrative centre. Flavinus had confirmed that their visitor spoke adequate Latin and no interpreter would be required. Naso called for the most competent clerk and Valerius took his place behind his portable campaign desk. To his right was the entrance to the *sacellum* where the Ninth's eagle and the other unit standards were kept, along with the legion's pay chest. To his left stood the large sand table Rufus had created with such painstaking care. A pair of crossed standards stood on display behind him, but the room's only other decoration was a painted marble bust of Titus Flavius Vespasian.

Four members of Valerius's escort flanked the Selgovae ambassador as he entered the room. Colm had pushed back his cloak to display a thin gold torc at his neck that announced his status, and a finespun blue tunic. When they came to a halt a few paces before the desk the Celt thrust out his chest and glared at Valerius. Thick dark hair shot with hints of auburn hung to his shoulders and his moustaches reached below his chin.

'You came here under a branch of peace. What is your business with us?'

'Colm ap Gryffud ap Owain ap Gryffud seeks an audience with the commander of the Ninth legion on behalf of Cathal ap Dugald ap Donal ap Guidri, king of the Selgovae, and ruler of these lands.'

'You have your audience, Colm ap Gryffud,' Valerius said. 'You may tell King Cathal that I will be happy to accept his surrender at any time and in any place of his choosing. And that I will give guarantees for the safety and security of his people under Roman rule.'

Colm was perfectly accustomed to the ritual exchange of insults before a tribal battle and he cheerfully ignored the Roman version. 'The offer I make on behalf of King Cathal is such that it might be better acknowledged in private.' He allowed his eyes to linger ostentatiously on the clerk, before turning to the guards on either side. 'Not for any dishonour it would bring my king, but to allow the legate of the Ninth legion, Gaius Valerius Verrens, Hero of Rome and holder of the Corona Aurea, the opportunity to consider it at his leisure and without outward interference or pressure.'

It occurred to Valerius that the use of his titles could indicate that Rufus might still be alive, but Naso bridled at once.

'This barbarian insults Rome and the officers of this legion,' he snapped. 'Worse, he expects us to be stupid enough to leave you alone with him. Have him taken away and whipped, then throw him out in the snow.'

'No, Quintus.' Valerius saw the twitch of a smile on Colm's thin lips.

'King Cathal has left the choice to me. Let us humour him. You will of course stay. Clerk, you may leave us. He's been searched, I take it? Then a single guard will suffice. Shabolz, I think.' He waited until the others had left the tent before speaking again. 'You should know that Shabolz is very quick and that I give him leave to kill you if you even think of moving in the wrong direction. Do you understand, Colm ap Gryffud?'

'Of course, lord.' Colm bowed. 'You have made yourself very clear.'

'Then make your king's offer.'

'Cathal ap Dugald thanks you for the care you have taken of Queen Olwyn and his daughter Princess Berta and asks you for their return. In compensation he offers the return unharmed to his legion of the scout Gaius Rufus, known as Arafa.'

'A lowly scout for a queen and a princess?' Valerius laughed to cover his relief at this confirmation that Rufus lived. 'This bargain seems very one-sided to me. Perhaps we should ask for the return of the horses you stole from us at Brynmochdar to make it more equitable.'

But Colm wasn't finished. 'In addition, when the exchange is made Cathal ap Dugald challenges Gaius Valerius Verrens, Hero of Rome,' he allowed the final three words to drip sarcasm, 'to resolve their differences in single combat at a place and a time of the legate's choosing.' Neither man reacted to Naso's spluttered 'No' and Colm continued. 'My king says there is no honour in the Roman way of fighting. A true warrior fights man against man and sword against sword and the greater champion wins. Should Gaius Valerius Verrens emerge the victor, Cathal ap Dugald pledges that his people will lay down their arms and submit to Roman rule. If Cathal wins he would expect nothing more than your promise that the Ninth legion Hispana will withdraw to Brynmochdar for a season.'

Naso continued to fume, but Valerius tapped his lips with the middle finger of his left hand. 'Am I to assume that this single combat will be to the death?'

Naso produced a strangled croak. 'Valerius, you can't . . .'

Valerius held his right hand up for silence. He saw Colm's eyes widen slightly at the sight of the wooden fist and smiled.

'Thank you, Colm ap Gryffud. Clearly this offer raises questions which require my deepest consideration. Shabolz, take King Cathal's emissary to the tribunes' quarters and offer him food and hospitality.' The smile stayed in place, but the voice hardened. 'He is to speak to no one, and what you have heard does not go beyond this tent.'

'Of course, lord.' Shabolz's eyes had a strange glint that puzzled Valerius, but he didn't have time to ponder it.

'Then leave us. The camp prefect and I have much to discuss.'

Naso waited until the two men had left. 'You can't be seriously considering this, Valerius,' he exploded. 'Calgacus would cut you to mincemeat before you got within a sword's length of him.'

'Perhaps,' Valerius said thoughtfully. 'But he's offered me what I've wanted all winter. The chance to end this without further bloodshed.'

'But that isn't what Agricola wants and we both know it. Even if you defeat this monster, Agricola wants a triumph and you aren't awarded triumphs by conducting a successful negotiation. He'll take as much bloodshed as we can give him.'

'Do you think I should be afraid of Agricola, Quintus?'

'No, of course not. Not when you have the support of the Emperor. But I'm asking you not to commit suicide, because that's what it will be if you decide to accept Calgacus's ludicrous challenge.'

'You think I can't beat him?'

'I've seen him fight. I know you can't beat him.'

'Then what would you advise?'

'By all means agree to a negotiated settlement, but agree it in exchange for Olwyn. If he accepts, Calgacus wouldn't dare kill Rufus.'

'But that still leaves Calgacus with ten thousand Selgovae and the gods only know how many Brigantes under his command.' Valerius rose and went to the sand table, running his finger up the line of the river valley to the west. 'Most of them are farmers, I know, but he has a core of seasoned warriors. Agricola would never leave them in his rear while he marches north. You know him as well as I do. One way or the other he'd break the truce.'

'That may be true.' Naso rubbed a hand across the iron-grey bristles on his chin. 'Very well. Agree the exchange and demand the return of the horses to put a better face on it. We can do what we always planned to do and take care of the Selgovae in the spring.'

'At what cost to my honour?' Valerius marched to the doorway. 'One way or the other it will become known that Calgacus issued this challenge and I refused it. The legion already believes it has been cursed by bad luck; would you also have them call their commander a coward? Think of it, Quintus. There is no other leader capable of uniting the tribes of northern Britannia. Calgacus does not realize that yet. When he does, he will become ten times as great a danger to us.'

'You are no coward, Valerius, and the men know it. There is no dishonour in refusing an insolent challenge from a painted barbarian. Even if there were I'd rather your precious honour was slightly tainted than carry the word to your family that you are dead.'

Valerius closed his eyes for a moment. 'I'm sorry, Quintus,' he said. 'I was being selfish. I'd forgotten this was about more than just me.'

The words carried an apology, but Naso knew that tone. 'But you mean to fight him anyway?'

'What if, by allowing me to choose the place and the time of our meeting, Calgacus has given me a greater advantage than he realized? An advantage that could be the death of him?'

XXIX

. . . take comfort from the fact that I died doing what I believed was right, and not in some vain quest for an illusory glory. Your loving husband, Valerius.

Valerius blew on the parchment to dry the ink. He studied what he'd written to Tabitha. It was all wrong; how could it not be? But he didn't have the words to convey what needed to be said any better.

He laid the letter aside and sat back in his chair. No sleep tonight. The days when he could sleep soundly before a battle were long in the past. Too many memories. Too much knowledge and experience of what might happen and what could go wrong. He had made what preparations he could to give himself the best possible opportunity, but the truth was Calgacus was going to kill him. A memory of that great sweeping sword scything the air made him wince and he reached for the wine flask. No. The left hand froze in mid-air. Wine might still the voices in his head for a time, but they would not banish them for long. Wine slowed a man's reactions and muddled a man's mind long after he drank it, and Valerius would need all the wit and speed he could find tomorrow. Speed, stealth and subterfuge. Those were the only things that would save him.

Man against man. Sword against sword. The only man he could

remember facing in single combat was his friend, Serpentius of Avala, veteran of a hundred fights in the arena and the fastest, most skilful warrior with a sword Valerius had ever seen. He remembered the dusty arena at Cremona, the hot sand and the blazing sun, the ring of contorted faces screaming for more blood in a place already drowning in it. He had never had a chance against Serpentius and he knew it. His fate had been inevitable and so it proved. The former gladiator had killed him. And saved his life. There would be no such deceit in the morning.

Serpentius would have told him he was a fool and he would have been right. He would have suggested posting a hidden archer to put an arrow through Calgacus's throat before they first crossed swords. He would have been right about that too. But that wouldn't be honourable and Valerius's actions had been driven, for better or worse, by honour and duty since the first day he'd worn the toga of adulthood. They had brought him here. If he died, his son would be raised a patrician, the highest Roman class, and it was important that Lucius knew he had died an honourable death and a good one.

Titus's letter flashed through his mind. How could he have forgotten the offer? Would it still hold after he was dead? He prayed not, but there was nothing to be done about it now. Something coursed through him that was not excitement or anticipation, something that turned his guts to water and made his legs feel weak. He slammed the wooden fist on to the table to banish the jagged, corrosive edge of pure fear.

'Lord?' Felix, the commander of his escort, unusually tentative.

'What is it?' Valerius took a breath to regain his composure.

'The lady . . . Queen Olwyn has asked to speak to you.'

A moment of confusion. Why? What good did she hope to do? His mind agreed to the request, but the words that emerged from his mouth were 'No. Send her my apologies'. Anything she had to say would do nothing to help. There was no turning back now.

He noticed that Felix was still standing by the doorway. 'I said no.'

'Trooper Shabolz also begs an audience with you, legate.'

Valerius closed his eyes. More nonsense. This Mithras thing raising its head again at the time when he least needed it, no doubt. But Shabolz was a comrade and a valued one. A wise commander did not alienate his best men, even when he was going to die when the sun came up. 'Send him in.'

Felix disappeared and a tall figure marched in wearing full ceremonial uniform, the chain armour polished to a gleaming silver that glinted yellow and gold in the shimmer of the oil lamps, and a long cavalry *spatha* sheathed on his hip. Shabolz held his iron helmet beneath his right arm, and the sidelock that distinguished the Pannonians from other men hung to his left shoulder. In the crook of his left arm he held a narrow bundle wrapped in leather.

'You look well, soldier.' Valerius managed a smile. 'But I'm intrigued to know why you have gone to so much trouble.'

Shabolz drew himself up to his full height. 'We wished you to know that we have sacrificed to the god in your honour, lord. You cannot join us in the ceremonies, we understand that, but the warriors of Mithras hold you in their heart and know you are with us in spirit.'

'I'm honoured.' Valerius struggled with the words. 'I had feared refusal might be taken as a slight. I am glad that's not the case.'

'There could be no refusal because no offer was made, lord,' Shabolz said. 'The god is all-seeing. He took no slight. Tomorrow you fight Calgacus.'

Valerius froze at the abrupt change of course. 'It seems the whole world knows.'

'He is a great swordsman, worthy of our respect,' Shabolz continued. Valerius nodded slowly, wondering where the conversation was going. 'It seemed to us that a man facing a great swordsman should carry a great sword.' He placed his helmet on the table and flicked the leather so it unrolled to reveal the contents. 'A warrior's sword.'

Valerius looked down at the gleaming object on the table. 'It is beautiful.' He heard something like reverence in his voice. Almost involuntarily, the fingers of his left hand closed on the hilt and he rose to his feet, staring at the culmination of the armourer's skills. A deft flick told him instantly how perfectly balanced it was. His own *gladius*

187

was a ceremonial affair, hilt-heavy and clumsy in the hand, and he'd borrowed Naso's sword for the morrow's combat; a workmanlike weapon, but one that did him no dishonour. This was different. A double cut, backhand then fore. The edge hissed through the air like a whispered endearment. It felt like a living thing in his hand. A living thing that had always belonged there. As long as his forearm and with a blade that shone blue in a way he associated with only the finest of swords. The grip beneath the soft leather had been carved from bone or antler, and the pommel was a latticework of spun gold worked in the shape of a bull's head. He knew immediately it was too much. Too valuable. A commander couldn't accept such a gift from a single faction among his soldiers. Yet to refuse it would be the ultimate insult to the men who chose to honour him like this. It was a great sword. Such a sword as the world seldom saw. The kind of sword a man deserved to take into battle against a warrior like Calgacus.

'A gift fit for an emperor,' he said quietly, still taking in the fine lines and the razor edge. He looked up into Shabolz's eyes. 'I will carry it with pride and try to do those who presented it honour.'

'That is all we ask, lord.'

'Once again your commander shows he is no fool, Gaius Rufus.' Cathal squinted into the low morning sun across the fractured, buckled river surface, frozen and refrozen countless times over the winter. The Meeting, where the waters of Thuaidh and Etryk mingled and became one. Sunlight glistened on shallow pools of water where the ice had melted. Treacherous, the Selgovae mused: a leveller. In the still air they could hear the measured trudge of nailed boots carving a path through the foot-deep compacted falls of the previous months. A column of legionaries six broad emerged from the trees on the far side of the river, armour and spear points glittering, their breath clouding the chilly air around them. Two officers on horseback led them, followed by an escort of cavalrymen, and Cathal's heart stuttered as he recognized the two diminutive figures in their midst. He smiled down at the little man. 'Prepare yourself.'

'You do not have to do this, lord king.' His prisoner's voice was so low only the two men could hear. 'I have formed an affection for you. I do not wish to see you die.'

'And I for you, Arafa. Only one man will die today, and it will not be Cathal of the Selgovae.'

They turned at the brittle clatter of hooves on the ice. One of the Roman officers had broken away from the column and spurred his way across the frozen river. It was broad here, a hundred paces and more, and his mount's hooves skidded on the treacherous surface, so he had to slow his showy gallop. He reined in below the raised bank where Cathal stood. Rufus recognized Quintus Naso.

'My commander asks if you wish to withdraw your challenge?'

Rufus looked expectantly up at the giant Selgovae, but Cathal stared across the river and said: 'Translate.'

Rufus repeated the words in the Celtic tongue and Cathal laughed. 'Why? Is he frightened of me?'

The men around him joined in the laughter. Naso's horse fidgeted nervously. 'Stay still, damn you,' the Roman muttered. 'Our prisoners will cross to the west; your prisoner,' he nodded to Rufus, 'to the east. We will have arrows trained on them. If there are any tricks they will be killed.'

'I too have archers,' Cathal said after Rufus had translated. 'I would regret killing you, Roman,' he said to the little scout.

'That is very reassuring, lord king.'

Cathal nodded to indicate he should move to the river's edge a little way downstream.

Rufus bowed his head. 'I cannot wish you Fortuna's favour in this thing, lord king, but I will wish you a good death and a quick one.'

Cathal kept his eyes on the far bank where his wife and daughter were being led down towards the river. 'What more could any man want?'

A Selgovae warrior pushed Rufus none too gently down to the water's edge. He kept his eyes on the far bank, and when Olwyn and Berta began walking across the ice he propelled the Roman scout forward.

189

'Go. And think yourself fortunate, little man. If Cathal hadn't taken a liking to you we would have cut you into little pieces and fed you to the pigs.'

Rufus walked gingerly across the broken surface, avoiding thin patches where he could see the water flowing beneath the ice. His nailed *caligae* slipped and slithered as he went. He considered taking them off and walking in his foot cloths, but thought better of it. Just one falter might provoke those bowmen Cathal had mentioned. Better to fall on your arse than to have an arrow up it. He could see Olwyn and Berta walking in the opposite direction on a parallel path perhaps fifty paces to the north. The queen made stately process, as befitted her rank, looking neither right nor left, but Berta skipped and capered and called to her father. As they drew level she caught sight of Rufus and waved to him. He waved back, grinning at the realization that shaving his beard had made her mistake him for a boy of her own age. Ah, to be young again. The cohort was spread out along the river bank to his front, six full strength centuries of the Second, he knew, because he recognized the commander, Centurion Tiberius, by his build: a man so squat he could almost be called square.

As he approached the bank he saw Valerius dismount and walk down the slope towards him. The legate wore an unadorned iron helmet and his cloak was thrown back to reveal a common legionary's *lorica segmentata* plate armour. A good choice, Rufus decided: light, flexible and better protection than chain from that terrible sword he'd watched Cathal practise with day in and day out throughout the winter. Still, for all his brave words to Cathal, Rufus doubted it would do anything more than prolong Valerius's life for a very few moments. Why had Valerius accepted the Selgovae king's challenge? He must know it was tantamount to suicide. Not, he prayed, for his sake. He would rather have died than endanger Valerius. What was the life of a lowly scout when set against the legate of a legion, a Hero of Rome, and a husband and father? No, there must be another reason, something more pressing. Something that made the sacrifice worthwhile.

Valerius strode towards him with a warm smile and the wooden fist stretched out towards him. 'Welcome home, scout.' Rufus felt a prickle behind his eyes, but he blinked it away. He took the outstretched hand and shook it.

'A nice morning to commit suicide, lord, if you don't mind my saying so.'

Shabolz stepped up behind Valerius and unclipped the brooch pinning his cloak. Valerius pushed it back from his shoulders and the Pannonian caught it before it hit the ground. 'Does no one think I can defeat this barbarian?'

'Watch out for the thrust, lord,' Rufus said quietly as he checked Valerius's armour for fit. 'This is one Celt who likes to put a point on his sword. And when he spins take a step back, especially if he spins slow. He has a way of reversing direction faster than you can blink.'

'How will I know if it's fast or slow?'

Rufus shrugged. 'Just try to stay out of his way.'

'I can't kill him if I stay out of his way.' He looked over Rufus's shoulder and saw Cathal clutch his wife and daughter to him. Olwyn stepped away and an animated conversation followed, in which he liked to think she was trying to persuade her husband to avoid combat. If she was it did no good, because the Selgovae waved them away and unslung the great sword from his back. 'What did you say?'

'I said you'll definitely be committing suicide if you wear iron-shod boots on the ice.'

Mars' arse, why hadn't he thought of that? 'Quickly then. Shabolz, fetch me a pair of felt-soled boots. I saw someone in the third century wearing a pair that looked as if they'd fit.' He bent to unlace his *caligae*.

'You have my thanks, lord.' Rufus's voice had a brittle edge to it. 'If I can repay you . . .'

'You have repaid me by surviving, Gaius Rufus. The debt is paid.' Shabolz arrived with a pair of leather shoes with felt soles. Valerius removed his sandals and slipped into the new shoes. 'A little large, but they'll do.'

'Here, lord.' Rufus sat in the snow and hauled at his foot cloth until a strip tore away. 'Pad them with this.'

But Valerius was already walking out on to the ice.

Just come back alive. Did he say it or only think it? He glanced at Shabolz and saw the same look of anguished despair he knew adorned his own face.

XXX

A silence so intense it hurt the ears. A thousand eyes watched their progress, but for Valerius they might have been the last two men in the world. One foot in front of the other. Keep going forward, because if you stop you might never move again. Calgacus was like a giant cat, his long strides eating up the ground so he was a third of the way across before Valerius had made half that distance. Mars' arse he was big, and that fornicating sword . . . Breathe, keep breathing, ignore the churning in your guts and the icy chill in your groin as cold as the river that flows beneath your feet. A battle could be a thing of joy, marching shoulder to shoulder with men who were your comrades and your equals, for impending death made all men equal. Comfort in the physical presence of men you trusted with your life. Even an army marching to certain defeat could take a certain ironic pleasure in their situation. This was different.

He had never felt so alone. It was as if he were one of the new recruits sent out into the parade square to take on the legion's wrestling champion. That interminable walk that could only end in humiliation. No hoots of derision here, no yells of advice or encouragement. Just the terrible unnerving silence, broken only by the crunch of ice beneath your feet. No bloody nose or bruised ego at the end of it, either. Before the sun reached its height blood would spill on the virgin ice of the river. A sharp creak beneath his feet made him glance down to see the dark waters rushing a few inches below a clear patch. The heat of the sun warmed his back, the sun he hoped would blind Calgacus for the precious moment he needed to kill him. Spring was not far away. The thought sent a shiver running through him. Would he ever see it? A vision of Tabitha's face sprang into his mind and he clung to it for a moment like a drowning man clutching a wooden spar. He gritted his teeth and squared his shoulders. Let the gods decide.

No vision now, but a voice that rang through his head. Old Marcus, the *lanista* who had trained Serpentius, and had died on the ill-starred field of Bedriacum. *Don't fight like a left-handed man or a right-handed man. Fight like a killer.* And now here was Serpentius himself. *I like fighting big men. The bigger they are the further they have to fall.* Oh, old friend, how I wish you were here to fight at my side. Even better, how would you like to take my place, you who relish fighting big men?

The thought made him laugh and the sound rang unnaturally loud in the morning silence. Calgacus was close enough for Valerius to make out the expression on those rugged eagle's features. He was smiling, but at Valerius's outburst the smile took on a wry, puzzled quality. The Selgovae had reached the centre of the river now and he stopped and waited for Valerius to come to him. He was dressed in a simple homespun tunic with plaid *bracae* laced tight at the calf and his enormous feet were bare, but all Valerius could think about was the great blade planted in the ice in front of him. Man against man. Sword against sword. Should he draw his *gladius*? No, not yet, leave it until the final moment. That showed confidence. Had he tested the draw? Would that beautiful, deadly length of polished iron even slip free of the scabbard? Calm. Feel the heartbeat slow.

Soldiers speak of battle madness, that terrible, visceral relish for the slaughter that can so consume a man he will not even feel his wounds before he drops dead from lack of blood or falls beneath his enemy's final blow. Valerius had experienced precisely that other-worldly ecstasy in the final moments after Boudicca's warriors burst into the Temple of

Claudius. But there are different kinds of madness. What he called up now was the cold, detached certainty that had made Serpentius the lethal killer he was. To find this a man had to reach into the very centre of his being, allow his mind to clear and drain his body of all emotion. The result was like being at the core of a flawless gemstone. A coldness that started at the heart and grew and expanded to fill every void of the mind and the soul. Valerius came to a halt a few paces from his enemy and stared up at him. But now he saw not a giant, but a victim. He reached across and drew the blade from the scabbard on his right hip.

Calgacus stood leaning on his great sword as relaxed as if he were taking the morning air. He ran his eyes over Valerius like a man considering a cow in a market stall before his gaze fixed on the *gladius*. 'A fine sword, Roman, but a fine sword in a weak hand won't do you any good.'

To Valerius's puzzlement he spoke a stumbling but perfectly decipherable Latin.

'I surprise you.' The big man smiled. 'That is good. It was a long winter, but your Arafa was a good teacher. I will miss him.'

For answer Valerius used his left thumb to press a protrusion on the wrist of his wooden fist. A thin sliver of bright iron snapped from the middle knuckle.

Calgacus laughed, the great chest heaving. 'Are you planning to do some sewing? I thought we had come here to fight.'

'I did too.' Valerius lifted his sword and shifted his stance to get a better grip on the ice.

'But first I must thank you for looking after my wife and daughter through the winter. She said you were kind and fair.'

'I only did what was right.' Was this some kind of warped strategy to break his concentration?

'Yes, but others might not have. For that reason I promise you a quick death.'

Valerius didn't answer and the Selgovae raised his mighty sword two-handed so it was poised above his left shoulder. He bounced right and left on his feet, light as a dancer, seeming not to move, but Valerius found himself being turned despite his reluctance.

'You thought to blind me with the sun,' Calgacus said conversationally. 'But I am so much taller than you I am looking down, and, of course,' another dancing step and Valerius's head filled with light, 'with two simple steps it is you who are blinded.' Valerius instinctively stepped back and he felt the draught of something hissing past his throat. A mix of roars and boos from a thousand gaping mouths greeted the first attack of the contest. When his vision cleared, Calgacus was staring at him, the sword poised. 'That was a mistake, my Roman friend. I tried to make it easy for you.'

'I thought we came here to fight, not talk.'

In answer, Calgacus's great blade flicked out at Valerius's eyes, but he had been waiting for the pass and he rolled his body so the point went past his shoulder. *Beat the point and your opponent is dead,* his first arms master had said. Now he put the theory into practice with a lunge aimed precisely at his enemy's stomach. It was a joyous stroke, with all his weight behind it, a killing stroke that paid no attention to the legionary's belief that three inches of iron was as good as a foot. He could almost feel the moment the point penetrated flesh and sliced deep into the viscera, the muscles closing in spasm on the terrible blade that had pierced them. Yet a heartbeat later the dirt brown blur in front of him had been replaced by white, and he staggered past his victim, turning in an instant on the slippery ice to parry Calgacus's counterstroke.

But the Selgovae chief stood three paces away, leaning on his sword again. A broad grin splitting the savage features.

'So,' he said cheerfully. 'The wasp has a sting. Good. It has been many a year since I fought an enemy worthy of my efforts.' He lifted the sword in salute. 'Cathal, king of the Selgovae.'

Valerius raised his *gladius* in turn. 'Gaius Valerius Verrens, legate of Ninth legion Hispana . . .'

'Hero of Rome and holder of the Corona Aurea.' Calgacus completed his title. 'It will be an honour to kill you, Valerius Verrens.'

'And you, my lord king.'

Valerius held his gaze and the most fleeting of shadows in the dark eyes told him the blow was coming. But from where? He was ready to step right or left to avoid the attack, but he waited a second too long, frozen in place by the knowledge that he'd misread his opponent. No scything diagonal sweep from the flank this time, but a full-blooded overhead swing on an arc that, armour or no armour, would slice through the right shoulder and cut him, flesh, bone, sinew, heart, lungs and entrails, to his hip bone. Only Fortuna's favour placed his sword hand in a position where he was able to half parry the blow with the angled blade. It forced Calgacus's sword from its chosen path so it ripped through the edge of his tunic and hacked a roundel of flesh from the point of his right elbow. Yet he barely felt the pain of the wound. The shock of the collision jarred his wrist so he almost dropped the *gladius* and sent a lightning bolt of agony up his arm and into his shoulder.

Even as Valerius reeled from the first strike Calgacus reversed his mighty blade and drove it upwards. If Valerius had stepped away as the Selgovae expected the edge would have cut him in half. Instead, he stepped forward inside the killing arc. Too close to bring the edge of his sword across the bulge of Calgacus's exposed belly as he intended. So close he could smell the sweat on the Selgovae's clothing and the acrid scent that taints a man after a battle and is the essence of exhilaration, excitement, self-preservation and fear. His head was on a level with Calgacus's chin and he hurled himself forward to smash his iron helmet into the unprotected face, simultaneously trying to work the *gladius* round to force the point through the cloth of the king's *bracae* and into his groin. As he scrabbled with the sword Calgacus managed to land a glancing blow on Valerius's helmet with the pommel of his own weapon.

Valerius's world seemed to turn sideways, but some instinct told him this might be his only chance. Giving up on the sword he worked the wooden fist into a position where the little knife blade rested on Calgacus's inner thigh. As he tensed for the thrust Calgacus must have felt the prick of the knife point, because he hurled himself backwards with an angry shout, his feet skidding on the ice until he fell with a mighty crash that shook the surface. Expecting Valerius to follow up his success the king flailed frantically with his sword until he realized there was no threat. Valerius remained where he was, breathing hard, face flushed with the joy of partial victory. They stared at each other while the ice creaked and they heard an ominous crack. Valerius studied the surface below his feet, but he could see nothing but ice and slush.

'A friend of mind had a saying,' he taunted Calgacus. 'The bigger they are, the further they have to fall.'

'We'll see who falls next,' the king replied, wiping a smear of blood from his smashed lips. 'And we'll see who walks away.' He forced himself to his feet and, eyeing the place where he'd fallen, took a step back and waited for Valerius to come to him.

'Oh, no.' Valerius shook his head. 'This is your fight, lord king. If you want to kill me come and get me. Your people are getting impatient and mine don't much like standing around in the cold.'

'Very well, Roman, if you're so keen to die.' Calgacus edged his way forward, sword held upright in front of him in a position that gave him the flexibility to attack from any angle. Valerius moved to his right, always keeping the *gladius* between himself and his enemy. Calgacus made a few tentative cuts that Valerius parried with ease and had the watching legionaries hooting with disdain. But Valerius noticed a mocking half smile on his opponent's lips. The man was *enjoying* himself. But there was also something ominous about that smile. It was the smile of a someone who knew that all he had to do was keep fighting and he would eventually win. His moment would come.

And that put a different perspective on this game of hunt the rat. Valerius couldn't just wait for Calgacus to choose his moment. He was already feeling an ache on the inside of his forearm and it would only get worse. He'd tried two or three attacks, only for the Selgovae to dance out of range and counter with a scything sweep that made Valerius back away in turn. There had to be a way. He noticed Calgacus seemed to be favouring his right leg. Was he tiring? An old wound? He darted in, forcing Calgacus to turn quickly. Yes. There was definitely something awkward about his movements.

He looked up into Calgacus's face. The smile had faded. Now was the time. He waited his chance. He feinted left. Calgacus moved to block the attack and Valerius rolled inside the point with a cry of triumph, his own point reaching for the giant's throat. But the Selgovae's block was only a ruse and before Valerius could strike he'd taken half a step and was bringing the enormous blade scything down on top of Valerius's head. No time to parry. No time for anything but to get his sword in the way of the blow and pray. He was dead. He must have closed his eyes because he never saw the blades meet. All he felt was a massive impact powerful enough to have broken his arm and something clanged against his helmet, leaving his head ringing like a bell. He staggered backward, his mind whirling as if it were at the centre of a snowstorm. A blow from that sword would have cleft his helmet in two. But where was the pain? Where was the blood? More important, where was Calgacus?

Exactly where he'd been as he delivered the blow, as it turned out, staring in bemusement at the jagged stump of his great iron sword, snapped a third of the way up the blade. Valerius looked in equal bewilderment at his own weapon. The only sign of the contact was a dull band across the centre of the polished iron.

Calgacus's face split into a huge grin and he looked towards Valerius. 'I was wearying of carrying so much metal, Roman. This will do just as well.' The grin stayed in place but the dark eyes hardened. 'Let us finish it.'

Before he'd completed the sentence Calgacus launched himself across the ice in a rush and Valerius was forced to fight off a flurry of blows in the space of a heartbeat. It was as if what had gone before had merely been some kind of game. Now the Selgovae attacked with a relentless, deadly ferocity that reminded Valerius of Serpentius. The truncated sword made little difference. If anything it made Calgacus more dangerous, for the jagged, saw-toothed break could take a man's throat out as easily as a needle point. In battle, Valerius had always relied on his speed and an instinctive aptitude for swordsmanship, but in battle, even if he was outfought, a man could always hope that some comrade would come to his aid, or a pocket of resistance provide sanctuary, however short-lived. Here there would be no aid and there was nowhere to hide.

Somehow he managed to survive the onslaught, but he was conscious of an ominous silence from the Roman bank. His legionaries, every man a veteran, believed it was only a matter of time before their commander lay dead on the ice. *The bigger they are the further they have to fall.* He ducked a vicious slashing cut, but where Calgacus expected him to recover Valerius allowed his momentum to take him down in a frantic roll that allowed him to stab upwards into the Selgovae's groin. Again, Calgacus was too quick for him. The big man leapt away and landed two-footed on a patch of ice and slush where they'd fought previously.

This time the crack lasted a dozen heartbeats and the sound froze both men in place.

Valerius saw the consternation in Calgacus's eyes as the ice gave way beneath his feet and plunged him into the freezing waters below. At the same time he felt movement under his own boots and took a hurried step back. Calgacus clung to the fractured edge with one hand, determined to hold on to his broken sword with the other, and for a moment it seemed he would be swept away. Valerius moved towards him. He would never know whether he was moved by the Selgovae's plight or a desire to finish the fight for good, because at that moment the gap between them widened and a lurch almost made him lose his footing. As he moved back, Calgacus finally dropped his sword on the ice and used both hands to haul himself, gasping and shivering, to safety. He forced himself to his feet. Astonishingly he was still smiling.

'Another minute and I would have killed you, Roman,' he called across the dark, swirling waters that separated them.

'No,' Valerius gasped. 'I think I just about had you.'

Calgacus laughed, looked at the void between them as if he was contemplating attempting the leap, then walked away.

'Calgacus?'

The Selgovae half turned. 'Yes,' he said. 'Arafa said you called me that. The Swordsman, eh?' Valerius could see he liked the name. 'From an enemy almost a compliment.'

'Make terms now,' Valerius urged him, unsure in his own mind why he was making the effort. 'Become a client of Rome. I will do what I can to ensure you remain a king and your people will live in peace under the Empire's protection. Otherwise . . .'

Calgacus hesitated for a moment before shaking his shaggy head. 'Perhaps if it was only you, but Rome . . . I do not think so.'

'In the spring then.'

Calgacus nodded. 'The spring.'

As the Selgovae king walked back towards his family and his warriors Valerius turned to see Quintus Naso, offering a thick cloak. 'It was a good offer,' Naso said.

'No,' Valerius accepted the cloak. 'It was a very bad offer.' He saw the question in Naso's eyes. 'Agricola would never have honoured the terms. One way or the other Calgacus would have been dragged to Rome in chains and the name of Gaius Valerius Verrens would be dragged behind him in the mud.'

XXXI

Spring proper was late that year and Valerius spent a further two months of frustration in Trimontium before it finally arrived. Emerald buds clothed the skeletal trees and the first wild flowers began to peep through the leaf mould on the forest floor. Still the ground was too wet to open the campaign against the Selgovae in the marshy wastes of the western valleys. By the time the messenger reached him from Julius Agricola the men of the Ninth were heartily sick of attacking the steep flanks of the three hills.

Naso joined him while he opened the leather scroll case and watched as he read the contents.

'The governor is back with the Twentieth at their winter quarters in a place called Luguwaliom about four or five days' march to the southwest of us. He's ordered me to a conference to discuss a joint campaign against Calgacus. You'll need to prepare the legion to march immediately on my return, Quintus.'

'The legion has been ready for a month, legate, as you well know. My biggest problem will be reining in the auxiliary cavalry.'

Valerius returned his grin. 'Send orders for Rufus and my escort and a full squadron of the Ala Petriana. No point in taking any chances. The Selgovae are bound to have scouts covering the south of the country.'

Naso left and Valerius turned to the letter that had arrived with the first supply convoy to make its way up the Thuaidh from the coast. He smiled as his eyes ran across the neat lines of exotically inscribed and slightly archaic Latin that identified Tabitha's correspondence. The scroll was only the second he'd received since he'd sent Hilario south. Tabitha reported that, though he'd found London lively enough at first, he was now bored with city life and pined for his old tentmates and a chance to cross swords with a proper enemy. There'd been no further incidents and Metilius Aprilis kept a respectful distance. Whether that was because of Hilario's ferocious presence and the increased security in the house or the regular missives from the Emperor tendering his kindest regards and affection she wasn't certain. This last comment provoked a frown of concern. If, as Valerius suspected, Aprilis or some other was having Tabitha's messages read before they reached her, he prayed Titus was careful with his words. However, Tabitha never so much as hinted that her correspondence might have been tampered with, and she had much more experience than Valerius with such hole-in-the-corner techniques. She ended with a cryptic suggestion that Agricola's winter sojourn in Londinium might have resulted in something more tangible in his wife Domitia than appreciation of his frequent companionship.

Valerius certainly hoped that was the case. He had a feeling that, Titus's favour or not, the governor's reception for his legate of the Ninth legion Hispana might not be as warm as he would wish.

They set out to the sound of trumpets on the Tubilustrium, the last day of the Quinquatria festival dedicated to Mars. Thanks to the guide's knowledge of the road and the regular switching of remounts it took just two and a half days to reach their destination.

Even before Valerius had washed and donned his ceremonial toga, an aide appeared at the curtained door of his room in the pavilion of Julius Ursus, legate of the Twentieth. 'The governor suggests it is too late in the day to begin a conference of war,' the young tribune said. 'But he asks you to attend him as soon as you are ready.'

Valerius noticed the suggestion that the timing of his arrival had delayed their meeting, the use of *attend* rather than *join*, and the unnecessary pretence of urgency. All suggested rebuke or were deliberately designed to annoy. 'Very well,' he said evenly. 'Tell the governor I will attend him as soon as I've seen that my men are properly settled.' Agricola wasn't the only one who could play games.

When he finally entered the governor's quarters Agricola was seated at his desk dictating orders to a clerk. Valerius expected him to dismiss the man, but Agricola merely finished the orders and welcomed his visitor with a tight smile.

'I wanted to speak to you alone, Valerius, so that you could give me a report of your operations against the Selgovae over the winter, and your plans for the spring offensive. My clerk will take notes for my report to the Emperor. Is that acceptable to you?'

'Of course.' Valerius wondered for a moment whether to congratulate the governor on his impending fatherhood, but thought better of it. 'Though I fear my report will be shorter than you would like.'

'Yes?'

Valerius explained how the Selgovae had melted away before his advance, and described the attack on the empty hill fort and the frustrating winter that followed. 'Every settlement we would have attacked and burned they had already destroyed. Every cow and every pig that we would have taken had either been driven off to their mountain fastness or slaughtered and used to contaminate a well or a spring. The only course left us was to send out patrols to take what prisoners they could and harass the Selgovae wherever they found them. We killed a few when they raided our camp intent on burning our supply of timber, but I fear that was the limit of our success.'

Agricola waited until the clerk's nimble fingers had completed their work and his stylus no longer moved over his wax tablet. 'Yes, I can see that would be frustrating for a man of your . . . qualities.' He hesitated, and his voice became suspiciously mild. 'But I'm confused. Is something not missing from your account?'

'Missing?'

'I'm led to believe that the legate of the Ninth legion Hispana has made a treaty in my name with a tribe called the Votadini. A chief named . . . ?' He looked to the scribe.

'Marro, lord?'

'Yes. *King* Marro . . . sends me his fraternal greetings and offers me exclusive trading rights with his people. He appears to believe I am his equal.'

'I made no alliance.' For a moment Valerius struggled for words. 'No treaty. The Selgovae were my priority – as they were yours – and so I came to an informal agreement with the numerous tribe capable of threatening my right flank.'

'You sought this agreement? I thought my orders were clear. In Britannia under my stewardship Rome does not negotiate. It dominates.'

'I did not seek any agreement, but one was offered and I dictated the terms.' Valerius cursed himself for sounding so defensive. 'A Votadini representative approached my camp when we reached the edge of Selgovae territory.'

'And what did he offer, precisely?'

'He gave assurances of friendship and asked for an alliance with Rome.' Valerius saw Agricola's eyes harden. 'Which I refused on the grounds that only the governor of this province has the *imperium* to form alliances on Rome's behalf. I was also conscious of your clear orders on the subject of negotiation.'

'Yet you did negotiate.'

'I believed, as a general of one of the Emperor's legions, that I had some latitude in nullifying the threats on my front and flank.' Valerius didn't hide his irritation and Agricola blinked at the mention of the Emperor. 'King Marro offered the services of his warriors, which I rejected. Instead, I suggested he took them to harry the settlements of the northern Selgovae, thus simultaneously depriving Calgacus of potential reinforcements and taking the Votadini far from our current supply lines.'

'Very well.' Agricola clasped his hands together before him. 'And what did King Marro ask in return for these services?'

'He asked for domination of the Selgovae lands to the east of the

River Thuaidh. I agreed, because in my opinion he would have taken them anyway while we were busy with Calgacus.'

The governor sat for a few moments, his eyes on the other man, before he nodded. 'Yes. Yes, I see your dilemma. I endorse your decision, but Valerius,' his voice softened again, 'you do understand that the Votadini will have to be dealt with in time and that by then your generosity in this matter of land may have strengthened them substantially.'

'Thank you, proconsul.' Valerius felt very tired. All he wanted was to get back to his tent, have a meal and get some rest.

'Now.' A different tone suggested something had changed and suddenly the room seemed to go cold. 'Tell me about this fight – this duel – with Calgacus, king of the Selgovae, the man I sent you to capture.'

'I . . .' Valerius closed his eyes.

'You deny it took place?'

'No.' How could he when Agricola had just provided proof that he had a spy somewhere in Valerius's headquarters? Perhaps even in his household. 'I believed I had the opportunity to subdue the Selgovae without further bloodshed. Calgacus . . .'

'Come, Valerius, spare me no details.' Agricola sat back in his chair with a complacent smile. A smile that said *I have you now, and not even your friend Titus will save you from my wrath.*

'Calgacus sent an emissary under a branch of truce . . .'

'So many emissaries seek you out, it's almost as if they believe you are the governor in my stead. What reason did this emissary have to believe you would entertain him?'

'It was not like that.' Plainly there was no point in prevaricating. Agricola already knew the details. Valerius told him about the loss of Gaius Rufus, and the capture of Calgacus's wife and daughter. How the approach had been made and how he had accepted. He kept his account of the fight with Calgacus short, hinting that he had never been in any danger and would have triumphed had the ice not broken. Agricola's eyes reflected his unconcealed disbelief and Valerius

206

realized the spy had not just heard about the fight, but must have witnessed it.

'So let me summarize,' Agricola said. 'You agreed to exchange two of the most valuable hostages in Britannia for an entirely expendable half-Celtic scout . . .'

'With respect, governor, Gaius Rufus has provided invaluable service and advice in this and other campaigns, as the governor well knows.'

'Not only that,' Agricola continued as if Valerius hadn't spoken, 'but you – the legate of a Roman legion – offered yourself in single combat against a tribal leader who is currently the most dangerous man in Britannia, and not just because of his prowess with a sword. Have you any idea of the effect it would have on the people of this benighted province of mine if it became known Calgacus had butchered a Roman general? Have you? He would immediately become the hero every Celt on this island would cheerfully march behind and die beside. Every tribe, in the province and without, would have heard about his victory within a week and every minor chief and petty king would have sought him out in a month. Forget Spartacus, a mere slave, followed by slaves. Calgacus is a warrior and a leader. Fortunately a warrior who currently leads a mere ten thousand warriors. Your death, Gaius Valerius Verrens, would have provided Calgacus with another fifty thousand willing spears. Your pointless, idiotic death, Hero of Rome, brought about by nothing but your own vanity, might very well have plunged Britannia into a bloodbath that would have finished Boudicca's work for her.'

The accusations and recriminations came at Valerius like a shower of arrows on the battlefield. His only shield had been his certainty that what he'd done was justified, but Agricola's cold anger shattered that defence. The rebuke was made more painful by the fact that Valerius now understood that, from the governor's point of view, it was entirely warranted. Every arrow hit its mark and the barbs bit deep.

'I did what I thought was right . . .'

'You thought to enhance your reputation,' Agricola rasped. 'Nothing more. In fact, Valerius, you did not think at all. Were you blinded by her beauty? I know you are susceptible to such things. Did she seduce you with her soft words . . . or was it her soft body?'

'No, it was not like that.'

'A real Roman general with iron for a backbone would not have hesitated to use mother and daughter to force Calgacus to abandon his pointless resistance and surrender himself. If you had built a pyre around their feet he would have come to you on his knees.'

'No, you don't know him . . .'

'I know he is as hopeless a romantic as you are, or he would never have offered to meet you in single combat in the first place with all the risks it entailed.'

Valerius took a deep breath. 'If the governor has lost faith in me I will resign my position immediately.' The words fell from his mouth like stones and it was as if he were listening to someone else say them. He was giving up his legion. He was no longer commander of the Ninth. All the energy drained from him and he felt an emptiness such as he'd only ever experienced in the terrible, bloody dawn after a battle. 'If you would permit it I will take the time to say farewell to my men before I return to Londinium.'

Agricola stared at him, lips clamped tight in a line that might have been scored by a knife point, but gradually the anger faded from him.

'No,' he said. 'I do not think so. Though even your friend the Emperor wouldn't rescind my order if I chose to issue it, against charges so serious and showing such flagrant disregard for military and political principles. The truth is I have no one on the island capable of replacing you.' He paused. 'Your past is too deeply embedded in the shadowier corridors of the Palatium for me to trust you fully. Who knows where your loyalty truly lies? But I always thought I could trust your instinct for command and your fighting qualities on the battlefield. Do not betray that trust again. We will meet with the legates in the morning. Let us speak of this no more.'

Valerius stepped from the governor's tent into the sunshine at the centre of a whirlpool of uncertainty. He didn't know where he wanted to go until his feet carried him towards his quarters. Shabolz and Dagwalda took step by his side and he could feel their consternation. Had he changed so much in a few short minutes? He remained a legate, but what real authority did he have? A commander must have faith in his own judgement or he could not function properly as a leader of men. Titus wanted him to succeed Agricola as governor of Britannia. That aspiration seemed laughable now. Had Agricola been correct? Was it possible that Valerius's impetuous acceptance of Calgacus's challenge might have cost Rome the entire province? They would never know, but Agricola had seemed certain enough. There was nothing feigned about his anger.

He arrived at Ursus's pavilion and dismissed the two guards. Inside he turned left into his quarters. A tall figure in a formal toga stood by his cot, studying the sword Shabolz had presented to him.

'They say Calgacus's sword is as long as a man is tall,' Herenius Polio, commander of the Second legion Adiutrix, commented. 'Is that true?'

'Not now.' Valerius managed a smile. 'But it was before, if the man is very tall.' He didn't know Polio well enough to call him friend, but their shared rank and experiences made him more than a casual acquaintance.

'And you fought him with this?'

'Do not be deceived by the length of the weapon, Herenius. It is probably the best sword I have ever owned. Better even than the *gladius* Suetonius presented me with after Colonia. That iron cut Calgacus's blade in two.'

'That blue sheen.' Polio brought the metal close to his eyes. 'They say it is a sign of incredible strength. What is it the armourers believe . . . ?'

'That a certain mix of charcoal and bone creates the effect. If only one could reproduce that mix.'

'But they never have.'

Valerius took the sword from his hands and placed it back in its rack. 'To what do I owe this visit?'

Polio pointed to a jug sitting on a small table beside two cups. 'I thought you might need something to bring a little joy into your life

209

after your audience.' He smiled. 'The finest Falernian I could find in the governor's personal supplies. Rank has to have its privileges, don't you think?'

Valerius went to the table, poured two cups and handed one to Polio. 'To rank, then.' He raised the cup in salute. 'So you knew about my audience before I did. And the subject matter?'

Polio took a sip of his wine and released a contented sigh. 'A good choice, even if I do say so myself. I doubt there is a man in the camp who doesn't know the legate of the Ninth had been summoned to be lectured on the subject of overreaching himself. I see you survived unscathed.'

'Relatively.' Valerius sensed the question in the statement and considered for a moment before answering it. 'Perhaps the governor had a point. He certainly thought so.'

'So you accepted your chastisement without protest. I salute you.'

'I offered to resign my command, but he refused to accept.'

'Then our leader is less of a fool than I thought.'

'You don't like him, Herenius.' Valerius lowered his voice. 'Why would that be?'

'It's not a matter of liking. It's a matter of trust. I do not trust Gnaeus Julius Agricola to act in the best interests of my legion.' He saw Valerius's wry look. 'Why should he, and isn't that a commander's prerogative? Perhaps you're right. But at the very least I would prefer to be sacrificed in the best interests of the Empire and not for the advancement of our governor.'

'Titus trusts him, or he wouldn't be here.' A wary flash of blue eyes from Polio made Valerius wonder just how well informed he was. 'Why shouldn't we?'

'You've just returned from being lectured by him for doing nothing but your duty and you don't know?' Polio laughed, but there was little humour in it. 'It astonishes me that you can be so innocent and have survived what you have, Valerius.' The Adiutrix's commander paced the cloth-covered floor. 'This campaign is not about defeating the Selgovae,' he said carefully. 'Or subduing what is left of Britannia. It is wholly focused on furthering Agricola's career. When the history of our deeds is written there will be no mention of Herenius Polio, Gaius Valerius Verrens or Julius Ursus. They, however valorous, or however great their contribution, are to be forgotten. He is so obsessed by the notion of a triumph that it fills his thoughts and dreams night and day. You've seen the way he has his clerks record every word and every deed?'

Valerius nodded.

'That is not to allow a comprehensive account to be written. It is to ensure he remembers which actions to justify, which to claim credit for, and where to apportion blame. Do you wonder that your audacious attempt to bring the Selgovae to heel by killing their ruler inspired nothing but fury? If you had defeated Calgacus with that little sword nothing he could do would have stopped you taking your place in the pantheon of Rome's greatest heroes. Romulus reborn. Horatius defying all at the Pons Sublicius. You would have had a statue in the forum and been feted across the Empire. Yet all Agricola can talk about is your vanity, a lack of judgement and the consequences of failure, which he multiplies until they rival Varus in Germania. I . . .' his face dissolved into a sheepish grin and he took a sup from his wine cup, 'have talked too much. A legate doesn't have much opportunity to talk freely, unless it is to his equals, and I have overindulged. Ursus keeps his thoughts to himself and doesn't entertain mine. I just wanted you to know that you should not place too much emphasis on our governor's rebukes. It is you who have been wronged, not he.'

'You are very free with your speech, Herenius.' Valerius looked pointedly at the tented doorway.

'Oh, it is of little import. Our friend knows how I feel.' He stepped in close and put his mouth to Valerius's ear. 'His obsession is destroying him. He is falling apart. There may be a time when independent action is necessary, and you are his deputy, for better or worse. Know that you have my support when . . . if . . . the time comes.'

He pulled on his cloak. 'Tomorrow he will ask your opinion of his plan, but it is already decided. The Second is in camp a little north of here. My scouts have found a way into Selgovae country from the west, but I've been ordered to advance north against the Damnonii who have already sent envoys pledging peaceful passage for our troops and asking for client status. In a few days, a week at the most, Agricola will launch a simultaneous attack which will crush Calgacus's forces like a nut caught between the hammer of the Ninth and the anvil of the Twentieth. I believe he has already dictated the victory dispatch. All that is required are the details.' He laughed as he went out. 'If I am wrong about our leader, you will be hailed as Valerius Verrens, Hammer of Rome. Think of that.'

'I doubt I will ever see it carved on a triumphal arch,' Valerius said ruefully, but Polio was gone.

XXXII

Another foggy pre-dawn in the bowels of a damp river valley on the edge of the reduced Selgovae lands. Valerius suppressed a shiver, but experience told him the mist would burn away when the sun came up.

Quintus Naso sat his horse on Valerius's left side, a calming presence and constant reassurance that everything had been prepared. They'd made the night march in silence and, they hoped, Calgacus's scouts were still unaware of their presence. Daybreak would be the signal for the attack.

'Are you sure the forts aren't defended?' Valerius said quietly to Gaius Rufus, who rode at his shoulder. A pair of redoubts guarded the slopes at the head of the valley and he didn't want any unnecessary casualties.

'They were yesterday, and the day before,' the scout replied. 'A garrison of fifty or so men in each, but they're empty now.' Still Valerius didn't seem convinced. 'I got close enough to look into their latrine pits,' Rufus said. 'The newest shit is two days old. Does that satisfy you?'

For reply, Valerius worked at his chin strap with his left hand and studied the sky, which unless his eyes deceived him had become appreciably lighter.

'Tell Cornelius to bring the escort forward. And remind the cavalry commanders of their orders.' Agricola had decreed that any civilians found still on their farms were not to be harmed. He planned to set up a veterans' colony at Trimontium when the conquest was completed. The veterans would be given farms in this valley and he wanted the land maintained in good condition. Rufus turned his mount and rode off to the rear.

'Ready, Nilus?'

Valerius's signaller licked his lips. 'Ready, lord.'

'On my signal.'

Cornelius Felix rode up with the thirty men of Valerius's escort just as a glowing ball of pink rose up directly ahead of the legion. The mist lifted as if a curtain had been pulled back and light filled the valley.

'Legion will advance,' Valerius called to his signaller. In the same instant Nilus's trumpet brayed and the call was echoed by the legion's *cornicines* down the line and the cavalry trumpeters on the flanks.

Asturian and the Gaulish auxiliaries of the advance guard trotted past in open order carrying their spears at the trail. The First cohort followed close behind, identified by its double-strength centuries of a hundred and sixty men apiece. Valerius and his escort slipped into the gap behind them, already occupied by Honoratus, the *aquilifer*, and his eight-strong guard. The column passed without incident beneath the two Selgovae watch forts, circular earthen ramparts perched like falcons' nests on each side of the valley, and emerged into a broad vale that hugged the north bank of the river.

Here the forest had been cleared and the remains of small, burned-out farmsteads dotted the fields and meadows their former occupants had tended.

'Which cavalry *ala* is covering the hills there?' Valerius pointed south beyond the river.

'The Ala Petriana, lord.'

'Still no sign of the enemy?'

'Nothing. Not even their scouts.'

'He has something interesting in mind for us, then.' Valerius reached up and the fingers of his left hand brushed the scar on his right cheek, a nervous habit he was trying to break. 'Gaius Rufus,' he shouted. 'Attend me.'

The little scout spurred his mount forward. 'Legate.'

'I'm disappointed in Calgacus. I thought he'd have given us a prod by now.'

'Yes, lord.' Rufus waited for the inevitable question.

'Where do you think he's most likely to make a stand?'

The scout smiled to himself. They'd already discussed this a dozen times, but he understood that Valerius felt the need to visualize what they faced with the utmost clarity.

'There are two prepared positions before the great lake where the king has his winter compound,' he said. 'The first is perhaps three miles ahead, an earthen bank and ditch with a rough palisade that stretches from the river to the hills, where its flank is protected by a steep scree slope.'

'A formidable position, then.'

'Indeed, lord, but not so formidable as the second, which consists of a pair of ditches a dozen paces wide and just as deep.'

'He will hold the first until he believes he has caused us sufficient casualties to weaken us, then draw us on to the second where he will hope to destroy us,' Valerius predicted. 'It's a good plan, but he doesn't know Agricola and the Twentieth are advancing from the west.'

'But not fast enough to assist us, lord,' Rufus pointed out helpfully.

'I want you to join the cavalry on the right flank. Take a squadron and forge ahead until you have a view of Calgacus's first defence line. I have an idea that might deprive him of one of his battles, but first I need to know how many men hold that first line.'

'Yes, lord.'

As Rufus rode off, Valerius felt Naso's eyes on him. 'It only occurred to me just now, Quintus, but this position reminds me of Corbulo's battle against the Parthians for the Cepha Gap.'

'Ten thousand legionaries and auxiliaries against the Parthian Invincibles and their King of Kings.' Naso had heard the stories.

'If we can find some way to outflank the first line on the river side, we may be able to take the second before it's fully manned and while they're still unprepared.' Valerius smiled. 'The Ninth's hammer may not require Agricola's anvil after all.'

'*If* we can find a way.'

'Let's see what the scout comes up with before we make our decision.' He studied the countryside around them. 'It almost seems a pity to fight a battle in such a beautiful place.'

Naso nodded distractedly as they rode past another burned-out farm. 'You can't blame Calgacus and his people for being so keen to hold on to it.'

'You have sympathy for him, Quintus?'

'I enjoy soldiering, Valerius, but I've never felt terribly comfortable playing the conqueror. I'm no lord, like you and Polio and Ursus. All I'm looking for is a little personal loot to supplement my pension so I can sit back and watch other people doing the work during my hopefully prolonged retirement. To be honest, from what I've seen of the Selgovae my share of the plunder is likely to consist of a few rusty ploughshares.'

'And slaves, Quintus. Our leader,' Valerius silently rebuked himself for echoing Polio's contemptuous phrase for Agricola, 'the governor has demanded an enormous haul of Calgacus's warriors for the markets in Rome. It seems the trade had prepared for a glut from Brigantia and now they're desperate for labour to man the fields, the mines and the brick factories.'

Ahead of them the leading auxiliary unit moved from column into skirmish formation as they approached a rise in the ground that hid the way ahead. The Asturians spread out across the valley in a loose screen and advanced warily until they had a view of the dead terrain. A signaller sounded the all clear and the column breathed again.

'I'm all for the *denarii* a good strong Selgovae slave would bring,' Naso agreed in his lugubrious fashion. 'But I've seen the bastards fight. You'd be safer trying to capture a cobra with your bare hands.'

Another hour passed before a warning shout came from ahead. Valerius ordered the column to halt. 'Have the legion ready to form line on my signal,' he told his aides.

Naso rode up from the rear where he'd been chivvying a lagging cohort. 'What is it?' His eyes scanned the horizon where the auxiliaries waited, poised to return to the column at the appearance of an overwhelming force of enemy warriors. Instead a small column of horsemen came into view and trotted through their open ranks. As they approached Valerius saw the familiar figure of Gaius Rufus at their head.

'You have news, Rufus?' he called out as the scout approached. But the expression on the other man's face told him something was not right here. Why had the patrol been able to approach from directly ahead, across ground that should have been swarming with the enemy? 'How strongly is the first defence line held?'

'It's not.' Rufus's tone testified to his bafflement.

'What do you mean, it's not?'

'We rode as far as the first line and not a single warrior in sight. I walked the entire length of it and it's never been manned. So we continued on to the double ditches. The same. Not just abandoned; never occupied in the first place.'

'And that's not all,' Rufus continued. 'The people here have stayed on their farms – not the fighters, but their entire families. They're tilling their fields and planting their crops. They acted as if we didn't exist.' Valerius noticed a ragged Celt on a small pony sitting in the midst of the auxiliary cavalrymen. 'You.' Rufus pointed to the Selgovae and spat a volley of Celtic. The man slid from his horse and approached, clearly terrified. When he reached Valerius he went down on his knees and made a long speech in the sing-song tones of his people.

'He says King Cathal told them to stay on their farms,' a glint of humour twinkled in the scout's deep-set eyes, 'and promised that the legate of the Ninth legion would ensure they came to no harm. They would live in peace under the Empire's protection.'

Valerius cursed under his breath as his own words came back to plague him. 'Ask him how long Calgacus has been gone and how many warriors he has with him.'

'He says the king started sending supplies north by hidden routes the day after your fight on the ice.' Rufus shrugged. 'King Cathal himself left three days ago with his sword brothers and every able-bodied man capable of fighting. He left behind a small band of warriors to man the forts in the lower valley until they heard us approaching.'

'Hidden routes?' Valerius eyed the grovelling man.

'He claims he's never left the farm, except to take his pigs to the king's market.'

'Find these hidden routes for me, Gaius Rufus. Find them and follow them.'

But he knew it was too late. Calgacus was gone, like a ghost in the night.

XXXIII

'Keep going.' Cathal thought his voice would tear his throat it was so ragged. Two days and two nights without pause he had been driving them, ever since the Selgovae sword brotherhood had reassembled, exhorting them to greater effort, denying them food and cajoling stragglers. 'Keep going. They cannot be far behind us and we must not be trapped in these hills.' He didn't know whether the Romans were following them, just as he didn't know they would send their cavalry north to block the passes where they spilled out on to the valley of Abhainn dhub, the Dragon river. Yet his instinct told him a man like Gaius Valerius Verrens would never give up the chase. 'We will rest at daybreak, but not before.' And not for long.

Selgovae and Brigantes, they counted more than ten thousand strong. The supplies they carried should be sufficient for three days, but despite his orders not to eat he knew they would dwindle fast. When men carrying sacks of barley or oats felt themselves weaken their natural instinct was to fill what pouches they had and abandon the rest to those coming behind. If a man's belly twisted into knots with hunger his response was to reach into his pouch for a handful, raw or not, to ease the pangs. Cathal had been forced to place his strongest men among the stragglers to recover the depleted sacks and discourage the slow from eating. The grain, what remained of it, was recovered, but it meant the weakest, those already struggling, became weaker still until they could barely put one foot in front of the other. It was these men Cathal had dropped back to encourage, but he could see his efforts were doing little good. One by one they fell or lay down. His instinct was to help them, but he hardened his heart and left them without a backward glance. Most would die of cold and hunger; the survivors would catch up eventually.

Only to Olwyn did he confide his fears. 'I had hoped to replenish at least some of our food from the northern clans,' he told her. 'But my writ holds little sway here, where I am just a name and they distrust southerners as if we were a different tribe.'

Even that small hope had been extinguished the previous day when they'd passed a burned-out settlement, the bodies of its occupants stripped bare and mutilated. Smoke pillars on the horizon marked dozens of similar atrocities.

'Votadini.' Emrys spat. 'Marro, like the backstabber he is, senses our weakness and sends his carrion crows past the boundary stones to slaughter and plunder.'

'Any of our people who escaped will be in hiding,' Cathal agreed. 'Even if we could find them they would be loath to part with their stores to a man they barely acknowledge as their king.'

He understood that retreating, fleeing, running from the Romans, call it what you will, had weakened his authority. The manner of it had weakened him further still. Cathal rode one of the big stolen cavalry horses, and Olwyn, Berta and Dugald another. His was the only family he had allowed to accompany the Selgovae warriors into exile. He knew the decision had provoked dissent and anger among his followers, including his closest allies. Even his sword brothers would barely meet his eyes. The minor chiefs of the tribe, who had always resented his popularity, grumbled among themselves while their war bands swelled the numbers of the stragglers and, worse, deserters. Yet Cathal had no regrets about his decision. The Romans had taught him the value of Olwyn and the children and he would not allow himself to be torn between family and tribe again. There would be repercussions, he understood that, but he would deal with them when the time came.

The sure-footed Roman mare he rode was no affectation or symbol of his kingship. She was the only reason he could cover three or four times the ground, be the beacon that brought strength to the struggling, and be on hand to deal with any of the myriad crises that accompanied such a march. Twice he'd pulled men clear who had stumbled into a bog in the dark. On another occasion Arwan, the sword brother who had helped him carry off the horses, fell down a steep slope from the narrow mountain path and broke his thigh. Only the mare's strength had allowed them to recover him so his injuries could be tended. Sadly, he'd died an hour later. Cathal refused to allow his friends to bury him. Instead they put a sword in his hand and covered the body with a few rocks, hoping to return when the Romans were defeated. Word of the tragedy spread quickly through the column and the death was regarded as an ill omen. It was a bad injury, but seldom so immediately fatal.

Another reason for the curious glances he received was that he insisted on carrying the jagged stump of Ghost Bane slung from his back. Men believed it was sentiment for a weapon that had served him well, but the truth was very different. Cathal kept the sword as a reminder that his judgement was as fallible as any other's and his great strength did not make him immortal. He would admit to no man, or woman, just how close the Roman had come to killing him and how he sometimes woke sweating with the feel of the little knife point pricking his groin. Only Gwlym had sensed it. The druid told him his survival was the work of the gods and another sign that he had been chosen to do their bidding. One day they would demand repayment. It was one of the reasons for his decision to retreat north when he had learned of another legion probing his outposts to the south-west. A dead man could not serve the gods.

Cathal's smith, Finngail, offered to forge a new and stronger Ghost Bane, but the king had refused. He understood now that though the mighty sword struck fear into lesser men, against a true warrior like

221

Gaius Valerius Verrens it was crude and awkward, inviting defeat and death. He remembered the darting point of his enemy's blade and knew he could never match the speed and skill that drove it. He must find another way. That was when he'd noticed the big hammer Finngail used to work the hardest metals. On the face of it, little subtlety there, but it was compact, and in the hands of a man as strong as Cathal a weapon of flexibility and power.

The smith reluctantly agreed to part with a tool that had become part of the lore and mystery of his craft, but he agreed on condition that he could first make it a weapon fit for a king. He'd lengthened the handle to improve the balance and transform it into a true instrument of war. An antler-bone lining to the socket of the hammer combined with a bonding resin of Finngail's own invention ensured the head would never come loose. By some miracle of the craftsman's art he inlaid the face and sides of the head with gold in patterns that matched the rearing horses tattooed on Cathal's cheeks.

They were entering a broad valley when Olwyn pushed her mount shoulder to shoulder with his. Berta perched half asleep in front of her on the horse's broad shoulders. Dugald, who never seemed to run out of energy, walked alongside with a hunting bow he'd pledged would provide tonight's supper. 'How much further?' she asked.

'It is five years and more since I journeyed this far north,' Cathal admitted. 'Another day and we will be able to stop for a proper rest. I believe we must cross the plain between the mountains and the river by night, then travel another two days north and west until it is fordable and we can cross.'

'And you think the people of the lands beyond the river will welcome us?'

He understood the doubt in her voice. The Selgovae had welcomed the Brigante families who had fled north seeking refuge because Cathal had felt he owed it to Guiderius. Not all kings would be so magnanimous. There had been grumblings among his people, and even one or two fights. Yes, he could offer an army of seasoned warriors, but some rulers would perceive them as a threat. Such a force could affect the balance of power in any kingdom. Relations with the kings over the river had never been easy, because ownership of the border marshlands had been disputed by the Damnonii, the Selgovae and the Votadini for longer than any could remember. They had become a refuge for oath-breakers and thieves who did not hesitate to raid northwards into more fertile lands where the pickings were easy. But Cathal's father had led an expedition to clear them out and to this day, as far as Cathal knew, the marshes lay empty.

'No,' he admitted. 'I do not think they will welcome us. But I hope to persuade them that the threat from the Romans is so great that it is vital to add our strength to their own. I will offer to be subordinate to their king like any other chieftain.'

'And if they do not accept?'

'Then I will seek safe passage through their territory.'

'If they will not accept you as an ally they may not allow it,' Olwyn pointed out.

'That is true.'

Berta shifted in her seat and Olwyn adjusted her grip on the reins to hold her more securely in place. 'You would not consider forcing your way through?'

'That would start a war. I would be doing the Romans' work for them. Besides, the men are too weak and we need to replenish our supplies.'

'Then we may be trapped.' Her logic was remorseless. 'The Romans will come eventually.'

'I hope it does not come to that.' Cathal tried to instil some confidence in the words, but he knew how weak and helpless he sounded.

'What does Gwlym say?'

'He says that with the gods' help I am destined to become ruler of all the northlands.'

She nodded. 'Then perhaps it will be so.'

Cathal felt the first stirrings of anger. Had it really reached the stage where even Olwyn must place her faith in the ravings of a blind priest so weakened by age that his meat had to be chewed for him by a slave before it could be swallowed? Yet until this exchange, Cathal had never fully comprehended the true hopelessness of their position. A prudent king would have made overtures to those beyond his northern boundary from a position of strength, not when he'd been forced to flee his own lands like some ragged vagabond or outlaw. His confidence in his own personal strength had blinded him to the might of the Romans. He had believed an alliance between the Selgovae and the Brigantes would be powerful enough to destroy the invaders, or at least drive them south again. Even when Guiderius and his army had been defeated by a fourth of their number his pride would not allow him to accept the same could happen to his Selgovae. It was only after the battle on the ice and hearing the shrewd observations Olwyn had made during her captivity that reality dawned. When the Twentieth legion had begun to infiltrate his territory the inevitable choice had been between slaughter, surrender or flight. He had believed he had a plan, but after two days in the saddle that plan turned out to be a hollow shell. When would he ever be able to keep his assurance that he'd return to free his people from the Roman yoke? What was the mighty Cathal of the Selgovae now, but another ragged refugee?

He felt Olwyn's hand on his arm. 'This is not the time for doubt, lord king,' she said quietly. 'Your people depend on you. Your family knows you would never betray that trust.'

Cathal straightened in the saddle and his hand went to the great hammer hanging in the pouch at his belt. What was he without her, the iron core at the heart of his being, the elixir that gave him strength? He could never fail her. He would succeed in this or die trying.

At dawn the next morning a scout who could barely keep his place in the saddle called him forward to the crest of the next hill. Cathal followed him up the slope, and when they reached the summit a great vista was laid out before him. He had a clear view north across a small range of lesser peaks and then the plain, but what drew his eyes was the glittering salver of the open sea away to his right front and the broad chasm of a great estuary. He followed its course westwards to the point where it narrowed into the winding coils of the Abhainn dhub, the Dragon river, so called because from the hills above it twisted and turned in seemingly impossible loops across the kerse bogland like some enormous serpent, until it widened to create a giant maw that swallowed the sea.

They rested that day in the shelter of the final valley before the plain. Cathal could almost feel the discontent among his followers ebb away with every hour of relative leisure. Somehow they had come to believe that once they reached the river their ordeal would be over. Partly it was whispers spread by Gwlym of Cathal's bond with the gods, partly the knowledge their strength was fading and it *must* end.

The night march was a disaster.

Despite the full moon their guide somehow led them in what must have been a full circle. When they came to rising ground after many hours of marching the men simply assumed they'd reached their destination. They crawled into the nearest shelter and fell asleep where they lay. Cathal had an inkling of what had happened, but he knew there was no forcing them back into movement now. He wrapped himself in a blanket with Olwyn and the children and took what sleep he could. Daylight found them in the centre of the plain on a bald hill open to all, with the coastal hills clearly visible in the middle distance.

'We cannot stay here.' Cathal made his decision. Without even breaking fast they continued their journey. At last they reached the hills and turned west. Along the coast tendrils of smoke marked the site of a few fishing villages. Emrys suggested a sweep to relieve them of their catches and stores, but Cathal refused his permission. The fisher folk would simply take to their boats at the first sign of the raiders and he didn't want to antagonize people whose help he might need in future. A mile and more of dull grey water separated them from the far shore and a pair of large boats were just visible in the centre of the river. The glare made it difficult to make out the detail, but they could hear some kind of rhythmic chant on the wind and his instinct told him they were like none manufactured by Celtic hands.

A few miles on they skirted a vast bogland on the fringes of the river.

Thick beds of dense reeds clogged narrow channels flanked by slick mudbanks, and beyond were dark, glittering pools dotted with a few tree-covered mounds of high ground. Another long-buried memory stirred, of flighting ducks and laughing netsmen covered in filthy black ooze. Ahead, like a low wall, the range of hills that was all that separated them from the Damnonii, where the column finally turned north.

They crossed a deep river valley and climbed again. A curious, long-abandoned stone dwelling or storehouse, dome-shaped and taller by far than Cathal's palace, confirmed they were on course. At noon the following day they stood upon a rise and looked out over a new place of the three hills.

Unlike the sacred hills of the Selgovae, these were not part of a single whole, but separate entities spread across a marshy plain split by the writhing coils of Abhainn dhub. The first rose up before them like a sleeping bear, the great head to the north and the feet to the south, and according to lore marked the river's lowest ford. To the west of it the second appeared to be little more than a rocky outcrop, but its height made it as clear a landmark as the first. The third hill matched the scale and shape of the first rather than the second and stood on the far side of the river where the Abhainn dhub turned back on itself with such agility that it almost made a complete loop. It stood out against a backdrop Cathal had been trying to ignore, because it reminded him of the imminent meeting that would decide his fate and the fate of every man who accompanied him. On the north side of the river a great mountain range ended abruptly as if it had been chopped by a giant axe. These mountains provided a viewing platform from which to observe the comings and goings of anyone on the south bank. For the past two days pillars of smoke had split the still air to mark the progress of the Selgovae column.

Cathal felt the eyes of his closest advisers on him. 'We will make camp on the high ground,' he told Emrys. 'Tomorrow we will explore the ford and see what awaits us beyond the river.'

XXXIV

Valerius and the Ninth marched west until they reached the great lake beside which Calgacus and his people had spent the winter. Something like five hundred homes clung to the hillsides around the lake, squat, windproof buildings of stone and timber, roofed with heather so they blended in with the landscape and almost invisible but for the smoke from their cooking fires. Some of the huts in the scattered settlement were abandoned, but families occupied most and Selgovae farmers worked the fields, seemingly unperturbed by the Roman invasion.

'You don't think it's strange that he burned everything in the east to keep it from us, yet now he presents us with his entire tribe?' Naso asked.

'He's changed his tactics,' Valerius said. 'When he burned his settlement at Trimontium he thought he could beat us. Now he knows he can't, not with the forces he currently has. I think he's known about the advance of the Twentieth for days, perhaps weeks. It made up his mind for him.'

'I still don't understand it.' Naso frowned at the figures scratching in the fields. 'Not that long ago these men were fighting like wolves for every inch of their land, armed only with axes and hoes. Now it's as if they've turned into sheep.'

The same thought had occurred to Valerius. 'Calgacus couldn't take the women and children with him, they'd have slowed him down. But he couldn't leave them behind to starve without their men. They were prepared to sacrifice their lives. It says something about his kingship that he was able to persuade them to sacrifice something even more valuable – their honour.'

'Can we trust them?'

'That's for Agricola to decide,' Valerius said. 'If it were me I'd make the fort at Trimontium permanent and build an auxiliary outpost here. Which reminds me: send out detachments to demand the surrender of all swords and armour. They can keep their spears for hunting. Tell the commanders not to be heavy-handed and not to expect too much. I suspect Calgacus will have collected every weapon of any value.'

Gaius Rufus returned the next day with a report that the governor's arrival was imminent and that his own bid to follow Calgacus had ended in failure. 'It doesn't get any easier,' the little man said wearily. 'He must have sent his warriors out in groups and given them different routes, because the hills and valley bottoms are criss-crossed with trails that double back on each other and merge before dividing again. Who knows who was going in which direction. The scent is cold, Valerius.'

Valerius expected an explosion when the governor learned that his prey had slipped the trap, but Agricola was almost jovial. 'So the wolf has escaped and he's taken his pack with him? A temporary setback.' The words were accompanied by a grim smile. 'And a battle won is a battle won no matter the calibre of the opposition.' Valerius exchanged a mystified glance with Naso. They'd heard nothing of any battle, but if Agricola noticed anything he ignored it. 'We surprised some kind of blocking force as they were setting up their defences,' he continued. 'But the Second cohort made short work of them. May this Swordsman enjoy his freedom, because it will be short-lived and hungry.'

They entered the *praetorium* tent of the temporary encampment and servants brought food and wine. Agricola poured olive oil into a bowl and dipped a crust of newly baked bread into it. As he chewed, one of his aides set up a frame that Valerius recognized from his first visit to the palace in Londinium. When the frame was complete the aide unrolled a large scroll.

'Good,' Agricola said, but whether he was referring to his underling's efforts or the wine he drank to wash down the bread wasn't clear. 'So.' He studied the map and picked up a pointer the aide had left to hand. Much more of the parchment had been filled in since Valerius had previously seen it. He vaguely recognized the outline of the terrain they'd marched over. Two pieces of red twine flanked the island's mountainous spine and he realized they plotted the approximate marches of the three legions. 'I believe we are somewhere near . . . here.' Agricola darted the pointer at the map midway between the ragged ends of the two pieces of twine. 'And our prey has fled into the mountains to the north . . . here. If he stays where he is I intend to starve him until he is forced to either surrender or commit to battle. If he moves north he will undoubtedly find there are bigger and more powerful wolves waiting for him. They will tear him apart, and if they do not, we will take him in our own time.' He met the eyes of Valerius and Naso in turn. 'But it will not be this year.'

'Sir?' Naso's features mirrored his confusion.

'I intend to spend this campaigning season consolidating what we have, building up our supplies and training our men for what is to come next year.'

'But Titus . . . ?'

'Yes, legate, the Emperor gave me two years and I intend to meet his wishes with a single decisive campaign that will sweep all before it. Next year. We are in danger of leaving three powerful forces intact in our wake. *King* Marro and your Votadini friends here in the east, Valerius. The Novantae in the south-west, who are more numerous and their lands far more extensive than I had been led to believe, and the Damnonii, here in the north-west. Should they decide to combine or form an alliance with Calgacus they could cut all three legions off from their supplies and attack us from four sides. I will not let that happen. We will use this campaigning season to bind these lands and their peoples so tight that they are unable to move a bushel of wheat without

229

Roman sanction. Our task is to secure everything north of Luguwaliom and south of the two estuaries which form the narrow isthmus here. Engineers of the Twentieth are already marking out sites for forts in the country of the Novantae. Meanwhile, Polio and his Second Augusta will carry out a similar programme in the lands of the Damnonii. You, Valerius, will make permanent your camp at Trimontium and establish new forts in this valley, on this river . . . ?'

'The Thuaidh.'

'The Thuaidh. Where did you say Marro had his capital?'

Valerius stepped closer to the map frame. 'Here,' he said. 'Where the two rivers meet. Chalk Hill.'

'A fort that will dominate Chalk Hill and keep Marro honest in the matter of our supply line from the sea. Then you will turn your attention north. Drive a road up the east of the mountains to the estuary and build a second fort on Votadini territory in a suitable position and close enough to the sea to become our northern supply base. Once that's done all three legions will supply men to build a third road, across the isthmus, thus ensuring our ability to be supplied from east or west as the situation desires. You understand my stratagem?'

Valerius nodded thoughtfully. 'The roads contain the tribes within their own lands and at the same time give us the ability to strike at them swiftly from any position along these routes. We're also in a position to reinforce or expand the occupying forts at need. Do you plan to disarm them?'

'No,' Agricola chewed his lip. 'We will do it in time, but it might be overly provocative with all this building going on at or within their gates. Do you agree?'

'I think the governor shows commendable wisdom and restraint.'

'Good. Now, I will carry on immediately to inspect your fort at Trimontium and prepare dispatches for Rome. I'm sure you have much to do. By the way.' Agricola's face broke into a tired smile. 'You may congratulate me, Valerius. I am to be a father again. I thought your wife might have told you. It seems I was the only person in Londinium unaware of the impending event.'

'Then may the gods smile upon you,' Valerius said, genuinely pleased for the other man.

He followed Agricola out into the open and watched the governor leave the camp. A swift visit. He should be grateful. He walked towards the parapet and Naso took step beside him. Together they watched the cohort make its way down the slope to the river.

'*I think the governor shows commendable restraint,*' the camp prefect said quietly. 'I almost choked.'

'What do *you* think?'

'I think the same as you,' Naso growled. 'It's madness. The logistics alone are impossible, never mind finding the manpower while we're keeping a lid on the Votadini and the Selgovae. Where will we find enough gravel to bed forty miles of road? Or the timber to build another three forts. And who's going to garrison them? It'll take every auxiliary infantryman we have. And all the time Calgacus is left to strengthen his position.' He grimaced. 'I'll draft a letter for Terentius Strabo and ask that the Second Augusta send every auxiliary they can spare us. And we'll need to free those lunatic Usipi on licence.' He hesitated. 'What do you think?'

'I think we should probably get started.'

XXXV

Sleep would not come, and before dawn some instinct took Cathal up a winding path through the bushes to the head of the sleeping bear. The summit was a rocky plateau cleared of the bushes and scrubby trees that clung to the lower slopes. In the torchlight a blackened circle showed where a large fire had burned at some time in the past. White flecks among the charcoal made Cathal suspect it might have been a funeral pyre. His hand flew to his hammer at the sound of approaching footsteps.

'You shouldn't wander off on your own,' Olwyn chided him. 'I was worried.' Four of his sword brothers accompanied her and together they stood and waited for the dawn. As the sun rose they were greeted by a layer of mist that covered the entire valley, from which the northern outcrop protruded like an island in a silver lake.

'Look,' one of the guards called as the mist began to clear. From their vantage point high on the rock they could see across to the far side of the river. A man-made timber causeway ran arrow-straight through the marshes from the far-off outcrop to a broad swathe of raised ground directly opposite. As they watched, an enormous mass of warriors emerged from the dispersing tendrils of mist to take station along the bank. At first they were silent, the only movement the fluttering of cloaks in the light breeze, spear points packed together as closely and as numerous as ears of corn in a field. Then a shout went up as someone noticed the figures on the hilltop. The shout had barely faded away when it was replaced by a roar that swelled and grew and echoed from the rocks about them. Men battered their shields to add to the tumult and brandished their spears or made obscene gestures hinting at the fate of any man trying to cross the river.

Cathal felt Olwyn's fingers clutch his hand. 'So much for our welcome,' he said. 'Take the lady back to the camp and keep her safe.'

'Should I bring the men up?' Emrys asked.

Before he could answer Olwyn reached up and caressed Cathal's cheek. 'Take care, husband,' she whispered.

He held her for a moment. 'If anything goes wrong,' he replied just as quietly, take these men and make for the hills. Go south and seek out the Roman scout Arafa. He will ensure no harm comes to you.'

He released her and she hurried off downhill. 'No, Emrys,' he finally said. 'Form them up out of sight behind the hill. Send scouts upriver to see if there is an alternative crossing. If they want a fight it may be that we can surprise them from the flank. Tell Colm to bring my bodyguard and meet me at the bottom of the hill with my horse. And bring the druid,' he said as an afterthought.

Emrys moved off and Cathal turned his attention again to the men across the river. So many. Too many to fight. But such a host if the right man led them.

Colm and his guard were waiting at the base of the hill, all mounted on the big Roman horses, with Gwlym on a small Celtic pony guided by a lead rope. Cathal turned to a nearby bush and snapped off a leafy branch before pulling himself up into the saddle.

'What is happening?' the druid demanded. 'These fools refuse to tell me, but I can smell your confusion, Cathal of the Selgovae.'

'For once you may come in useful, priest,' Cathal growled. 'You boasted that you are schooled in every dialect spoken by the tribes of this island. Does that include the Venicones?'

'Of course,' the blind druid replied with unconcealed disdain. 'Though

233

it is so close to that of the Selgovae a child could decipher it. They call themselves An Taghadh, the Chosen, conceited fools. Their ancestors came here from Armorica when they were attacked by—'

'It is enough that you speak it, without providing a history lesson.'

They rounded a shoulder of the hill and a new roar went up as they came into sight of the massed ranks of warriors on the other side of the river. 'Now, I understand.' Gwlym almost chortled. 'Quickly. Tell me how we stand.'

Cathal described the great force spread out before them. 'A thousand or so hold the far bank, with many more in column behind them. They number about half as many again as we do,' he said, explaining his own dispositions.

'Oh, I doubt we will need the help of your brutes.' Gwlym's empty eye sockets scanned the far side of the Abhainn dhub. 'Where is their king?'

'We aren't close enough to tell,' Cathal said.

'Then he is not much of a king, but then,' the pus-filled orbs seemed to seek Cathal out, 'neither are you. I'm sure you will do very well together. Still, we must find him, and when you do I need to know if there is a priest. No king should ever travel without a priest to save him from his follies.'

They advanced along a rutted track that led to a ford. The river here was probably a hundred and fifty paces wide and even this far inland was affected by the tide. At high tide the ford would be impassable, but now Cathal could see what looked like cobbles through the clear water. An important crossing then, though little used these days, it appeared. They stopped just short of the fast-flowing stream.

'The king?' Gwlym persisted.

'Have patience, priest,' Cathal snarled.

'Nervous, lord king?' the druid suggested mildly. 'And so you should be. From here they smell like twenty thousand hungry wolves.'

'There.' Colm swallowed. Across the river the armed multitude parted to allow a two-wheeled chariot to pass, accompanied by a guard of thirty or forty warriors, naked to the waist and carrying shields and spears. To Cathal's astonishment the king's face was hidden by a crude mask of beaten silver and the two ponies pulling the chariot wore horned metal caps, designed to make them look like monsters from another world. He described the scene to Gwlym.

'Yes, yes,' the druid said impatiently. 'He is known as the Argento Rìgh, the Silver King, but what about the priest?'

'The man driving the chariot may be a druid. He wears a white robe, but he is young for a priest.'

'Good, that is all I wanted to know. Now go and say your piece.'

'Aren't you coming with me?'

'You will understand him as well as you understand anyone.' Gwlym didn't conceal his impatience. 'I may consent to clean up your mess, but only for the sake of that clever wife of yours who has taken to treating me like an equal and not some aged relic.'

'Colm?' Cathal tried to hide his confusion. 'Go ahead. And make sure they can see that branch.' Colm urged his mount into the stream. Cathal unslung his sword and removed the belt that held the hammer and dropped them to the ground. 'Ranal, you and Liam stay with the druid.'

He followed Colm into the water, accompanied by the remainder of his guard. Despite the feeling of placing his head in a wolf's slavering jaws, Cathal had no real fears for his safety. It would not, of course, be the first time the green branch of truce ended up with the bearer lying in the mud coughing up blood, but never when ten thousand warriors waited at the emissary's call. The remaining Selgovae would view Cathal's death as a declaration of war and bring fire and sword to the Venicones lands with a ferocity mere hunger and desperation could never duplicate. Cathal was also conceited enough to believe his reputation as a warrior would be known to the Venicones. The Silver King's bodyguard spread out to create an open space where the two rulers could meet, but he didn't step down from his chariot. Cathal had heard of these archaic machines which had gone out of use amongst the Selgovae a dozen generations ago, but he had never seen one. In truth, such a flimsy vehicle would be a liability in the type of rugged landscape that surrounded them. He could only think that, like the mask, it was a customary trapping for Venicones kings. A pair of glistening white skulls hung from one side of the chariot and two snarling, half decomposed heads from the other. The only frightening thing about them was their stink.

The Argento's priest, a long-haired young man of impressive stature, placed a half circle of finger bones around the king's chariot, leaving a gateway wide enough for a single person to pass through. He hissed at Colm and the bodyguard and the Selgovae shifted uneasily under the muttered threats. 'Stay here,' Cathal told them. 'Listen to every word and watch every gesture. Remember them. What occurs here could be the difference between life and death for all of us.' Handing the branch of peace to Colm, he dismounted and stepped forward into the half ring of bones. The druid bowed his head in welcome. Two guards remained with the Argento. One of them, if not quite of Cathal's height, was at least as broad. The warrior glared at the Selgovae king, his lips twisted in a sneer of contempt. Cathal ignored him and advanced until he was three paces short of the nervously skittering ponies. He could see the glitter of eyes behind the mask.

'I see you, Cathal, lord of the Selgovae.' The king of the Chosen had a high-pitched voice and Cathal realized he was much younger than he'd assumed. 'I see you and I wonder what has brought you to my land with an army. Surely it cannot be a hunting trip with so many men? But perhaps I am wrong?'

'I greet you, Argento Rìgh, High King of the Venicones and the Taexali.' Cathal ignored the calculated lack of acknowledgement of his own kingship, and dignified the man in the silver mask with an inflated title he doubted he deserved. He noticed for the first time the pair of massive silver armlets that circled the king's upper arms, each of which must weigh as much as the smith's hammer. 'I honour you and your ancestors. I come not as an enemy, but as a friend, though I fear I come with news of grave import for your tribe and mine . . .'

'Wait.' The king raised a hand. 'Should not a petitioner and a *friend* come bearing gifts for him he petitions?'

'I am no petitioner, lord king.' Cathal smiled at this new provocation.' But I do come bearing gifts. I bring an army – the very army you described – to fight at your side against the approaching threat.'

'I see no threat.' The Venicones turned his head ostentatiously from side to side. 'Except the one before me. What is this threat to which you refer?'

'Not long from now, lord king,' Cathal gave his voice new volume and a harsher edge that made the other man stiffen, 'a *Roman* army will march in my footsteps and they will not come as friends. They will come to establish dominion over the Venicones and the Taexali. Your sons and daughters will be their hostages and your people will be their slaves. If you are fortunate, lord king, they will allow you to keep your titles, but you will rule only through them, and to them you will pay a fifth of your wealth until they decide to take more . . .'

'I have heard of these Romans,' the Argento Rìgh interrupted. 'And the exaggerated stories of their prowess. In fact did I not hear that the Selgovae people even now bend the knee to them while their king and their *protectors*,' he gave the word a sneering quality that raised the hackles on Cathal's neck, 'flee north, so panicked by these legions that they even run from the feral dogs that call themselves the Votadini? I do not fear the Romans. I have warriors of my own, like Giulan Marbh here,' he waved a languid hand in the direction of the massive guard, 'who has killed bear with his own hands. Have you killed a bear, lord Cathal?'

Cathal took a deep breath. 'Say what you will of me, lord king, but do not defame my warriors or my people. And do not make light of the threat from the Romans. They *will* come, and the Venicones and the Taexali do not alone have the strength to defeat them.' His gaze turned to Giulan Marbh and he didn't hide his contempt. 'Romans are not so easy to kill as bears. If you do not wish me as an ally, give me leave to pass through your lands with my warriors to make common cause with someone who does.'

A high-pitched laugh gurgled from behind the mask. 'Am I so naive that I will invite the sword threatening my belly to move behind my back? No, Cathal, *lord* of the Selgovae, I do not give you leave. As to your fate, and that of your warriors, I must think on it. You may go now.'

The contemptuous dismissal lit a dangerous fire deep inside Cathal, but he knew anything he said would only make the impasse worse. Perhaps there was—

'Lord?' Colm called. 'The druid.'

Cathal looked to the far side of the river where Gwlym fidgeted on his horse, making barely decipherable gestures.

'Lord king,' Cathal turned. 'I believe my druid wishes to consult with yours on matters of mutual interest to them.'

'Then he may approach,' the Venicones ruler said. 'We are, after all, not uncivilized.'

Cathal waved to Gwlym's guard to bring him forward and remounted, leading Colm and the others back across the stream. They met the priest halfway and the druid called out as he passed, 'I congratulate you on your diplomacy, Cathal, king of the Selgovae. How many enemies does one man need?'

Cathal found Olwyn on the high ground beyond the rock outcrop supervising the completion of a temporary shelter. She hung a thick curtain across the entrance and turned with a smile, but her pleasure only lasted as long as it took to read the expression on his face.

'It did not go well, husband?'

Cathal took her hands in his. 'He is not interested in making an alliance and I do not think he will allow us free passage through his lands.'

Olwyn drew him inside the crude hut and they sat together on a cushion of ferns she'd arranged in the corner. 'Then move west at nightfall and cross the river further upstream,' she said, ever practical.

'I've just had a report from the scouts who've been patrolling in that direction. The lowlands beside the river are nothing but a trackless waste, miles wide and full of bogs, quicksand and bottomless ponds. If we tried to cross in the dark we would lose dozens, perhaps hundreds of men and we might never find a way to the other side in any case. It is finished. We can either stay here and starve or turn back and meet the Romans.'

'No,' she snapped. 'Not while you have a single breath in your body, Cathal *bhon chridhe mòr*. You will go north. Gwlym has prophesied it. Where is the druid?'

'You must not—'

'He insisted on seeing you, lord.' Ranal appeared in the doorway, Gwlym at his side. The scrawny figure sniffed the air and the head swivelled as if the empty eye sockets were taking in everything about them.

'You make yourself comfortable.' Gwlym's lips wore a thin smile. 'That is good. We may be here for some time.'

'The Venicones king would not change his mind?'

'Of course not. He's not stupid. He did, however, agree that you and your men may stay here unmolested until Beltane.'

'Beltane?' It was almost a full year.

'He will also provide you with three months' supply of grain so that you do not go hungry. Are you not grateful to me, Cathal of the Selgovae? You do not seem so.'

Cathal snorted. 'My teeth are seeking the grit in the loaf.'

'Is it not obvious,' the druid crowed, almost as if he were enjoying himself. 'He could leave you here to starve, but he provides you with sustenance, which gives—'

'Strength. He wants us to be strong. Why?'

'Why, he asks?' Gwlym groaned. 'A child would be quicker.'

'Because he wants us to fight the Romans for him.'

'Of course.'

'We stand between the Romans and the river. He expects us to fortify the high ground and defend it to the last, leaving the Romans so weakened that he can cross the river and either destroy them or drive them away.'

'Can you fault his strategy?'

'I cannot.' Cathal laughed, a humourless bark. 'But I would rather be a willing part of it than a sacrificial lamb. He sustains us through the fighting season, and if by some chance we survive, he will allow us to starve through the winter, before fattening us up for the next contest. He is using us as his guard dogs.'

'Enough of this talk of starving,' Olwyn snapped. 'He has given you time, and with time anything is possible. Look around you. The hills are cloaked with timber we can use to build a fortress and more permanent huts. We do not have to use all the grain for food. If we plant now we will have a crop to harvest by Samhain. The river is filled with fish, the reeds swarm with ducks and the high ground with deer. There are beavers and otters to provide us with furs. You are the Selgovae – the Hunters of the Hills. Make good that boast.'

'Ever practical Olwyn.' Cathal treated his wife to a wry smile. 'Always a solution to a problem.'

'Oenghus, the Argento's druid – a clever man for one so young – talked of a great bounty from the sky gods as summer wanes,' Gwlym agreed.

'Time and strength,' Cathal mused. 'A prudent man could make good use of such commodities.'

'And cunning,' Gwlym whispered. 'There is much to be said for cunning.'

'If only the Romans give us time.'

XXXVI

Londinium, October AD *80*

'So you think the governor's plans have more to do with Domitia's condition than high strategy?' Tabitha gently stroked Olivia's dark hair as the little girl slept with her head in her lap. Valerius had arrived that morning, five days after embarking at the mouth of the Thuaidh. Difficult to believe his daughter was almost two years old now. Valerius had been astonished at the progress she'd made, waddling around on her stubby little legs with an insatiable curiosity. The wet nurse had to watch her every moment, lest she wander out of the door to make another muddy exploration of the gardens. She had a smile that made his heart glow and a habit of shrieking her version of 'Mother' every time Tabitha walked into the room. He knew other men who believed girl children were an expensive waste of time until the day they could be married off for whatever benefits they could bring. All Valerius felt was a dull regret that he'd yet to hear the word 'Father' from her lips.

'It's difficult to know,' he replied. 'Every time we meet I see a different Agricola. Last year it was north, north, north, drive your troops until they drop and campaign through the winter. This year it's as if he is challenging Titus to remove him if he dares. We could have advanced a hundred miles in the fine weather we've had this summer, but now it's consolidate and resupply.' He smiled. 'Build, build, build. I can't think of any other reason why he would risk Titus's displeasure by losing a full campaigning season.'

The flames of the fire flickered in a draught, sending ghostly patterns round the painted walls of the room and making the eyes of the marble busts gleam so they seemed to come alive. Below their feet lay a hypocaust system that circulated warm air beneath the floors and up the walls, but on chill afternoons like this Valerius preferred the physical comfort of an open fire.

'I know what you mean,' Tabitha said. 'There appear to be many different Julius Agricolas. One day he can be so calm and sensible, the next it's as if he's filled with some inner power. A light in his eyes like a candle that's burning too brightly and about to explode.'

'How is Domitia?'

'She is well, but very big and very worried. She had a difficult birth with Julia and lost a boy stillborn. It could be in the next two or three weeks. I've told the midwife who will attend her that I'm to be called at any time of the day or night. She is glad of the governor's presence. It may have been she who persuaded him to pause. She thinks he works too hard.'

'She may be right,' Valerius conceded. 'No detail is so small that it doesn't require his personal attention. He wears out an aide every month with his constant planning and scheming. The last time I visited him he'd just returned from a trip to the coast and swore he'd been able to see Hibernia, though his aides told me it was more likely some smaller island or a distant peninsula that hasn't been mapped yet. Now we must plan to invade it. All it would take is a single legion, he says, and I would be able to present the Emperor with an entirely new province. This at a time when Titus has no interest in expansion because he already has enough trouble on the Rhenus frontier.' Tabitha yawned. 'Am I boring you?'

'Not at all.' She smiled. 'You know the sound of your voice makes me relax. We were parted so long and I have missed your presence so much I want to hear everything.'

'And I.'

'You first,' Tabitha said. 'All I have is domestic tittle-tattle about cats bringing in live rats and screaming maids leaping on couches and tables. How has it been for you?'

'You might think it would be dull. An entire campaigning season without a single skirmish, never mind a proper battle. Your husband reduced from directing cohorts to chiding new recruits on the depth of their roadside ditch. Yet there was something idyllic about this summer. The sun on your back, barely a shower of rain, curlews and lapwings whirring and mewing in the still air on the high moors and the soporific buzz of insects in your ears; the men working hard, but happy and at ease in a land without threat, unless you happened to step on a sleeping adder, and swimming in the cool, clear waters of a river at the end of a long day sweating in the sun, with all around you a patchwork of green, more shades and tones of green than you could count. All that was missing was you.' He grinned.

'Enough of your flattery.' She smiled back. 'Six months without drawing a sword and Gaius Valerius Verrens was content?'

'I was too tired to be anything else. It was relentless. The task Agricola allocated to the Ninth should have been impossible.'

'And in all that time no word of this Calgacus?' An innocent enough question on the face of it, but with just the faintest hint of something more hazardous.

'You may have heard some outlandish stories,' he ventured.

'About a Roman hero who volunteered to sacrifice himself in single combat against a mighty barbarian giant as tall as an oak tree?' she said with exaggerated sweetness. 'Yes, husband, I have heard whispers of this tale.'

'Events like that are often magnified in the minds of those who weren't in attendance.'

'Events like that?'

'Fights.' He tried to deflect whatever was coming with a laugh, but didn't quite succeed. 'Combat.'

'Was he as tall as they say, and as broad?'

'Probably. He was a big man, yes.'

'And his sword?'

'At the beginning it stretched, oh, from me to you.'

'At the beginning.' Two perfectly curved eyebrows rose in unison. 'And in the end?'

'Perhaps half that, a little more.'

'But still dangerous. Some say . . .' The correct words seemed to elude her, but she persisted and eventually they came. 'Some say they fought for the heart of a lady?'

The most dangerous question of all, but Valerius recognized that it provided his way out. 'Then they say wrong.' He laughed. 'They fought for the life of a miserable little half-Celtic scout who'd been foolish enough to get himself captured.'

Still she wasn't entirely convinced. 'Not to kill this giant, this Calgacus, and force the surrender of his tribe?'

'That too,' he could not lie to her, 'but mostly it was to get Rufus back. Agricola was most put out.'

'You shouldn't do things like this, Valerius,' Tabitha said seriously. 'You're too old to be making grand gestures. You're a husband and a father. You must think of us.'

'Too old, eh?' he growled.

'Well.' She studied him. 'Perhaps not that old. You look leaner and fitter. Hard work seems to agree with you. I think I'll make use of that. Tomorrow you can chop wood for the fire and harvest the last of the apples in the orchard, and when you're finished outside perhaps you'd take a look at the hypocaust for me.'

'Don't we have slaves to do those things?' Valerius protested.

'When will you learn, Gaius Valerius Verrens? You are my slave.' The way she looked at him when she said it made his throat go dry. 'As I will prove tonight.'

'I'm planning to take Lucius hunting tomorrow. He says he has found a coppice where a small herd hides during the day.'

She smiled at his earnest tone. 'Good. You should spend some time together.'

244

'There is one other thing I must tell you.' Valerius got up and went to the door, checking none of the slaves or servants was within hearing distance.

'I'm intrigued.' The tone was light, but her dark eyes told him she recognized the significance of his precautions. He dragged his couch towards hers so they could sit almost head to head and, in a low whisper, told her about Titus's letter, the possibility he might make Lucius his heir and the threat that could pose. She listened without comment, but he could see she understood the danger they faced.

'So that's what your cryptic note about increased security was about?'

He nodded.

'Do you still have the letter?'

'I burned it as soon as I'd read it.'

'That was best,' Tabitha said. No complaint, he noted, that he hadn't tried to inform her of the true scale of the danger. She knew that such a message could have placed them all in even greater peril. 'Domitian can't be aware of his brother's intentions or he would have acted by now.'

'That's my instinct.'

'So we are safe for now. We also have time. Titus isn't the kind of man to separate a child from his father. If, as he says, he plans to appoint you governor in Agricola's place he won't take Lucius until your period of office is over. Would it be acceptable in Rome for an emperor not to name his heir for so long?'

'Titus is in his prime and in good health,' Valerius said. 'If the gods are kind he could rule for twenty years and more. He won't be in any hurry and he's not the type of man to be pushed.'

'Good. How sad that the greatest honour Titus could do our son is also the greatest threat. There is no question of refusing the Emperor. In Rome there will be ways we can protect Lucius . . . or,' her eyes turned dangerous, 'to strike at the heart of the threat.'

Valerius quailed at the thought of what Tabitha was suggesting. 'We can make that decision when the time comes, but it would have to be a last resort.'

'Of course,' she said. 'In the meantime I will make alternative plans as you suggested. We may not have time to warn you, but if we disappear without warning, follow us to Emesa.'

They discussed other ideas, but came up with no answers. Eventually, they retired to the bedroom, where Tabitha fulfilled her earlier vow, and Valerius fell into an exhausted sleep. But it was not long before he was disturbed by a vision of a savage, grinning face and the glint of a sword edge slicing towards his throat at incredible speed.

'Valerius?'

He opened his eyes. 'Yes?'

'You cried out in your sleep,' she said. 'What were you dreaming about?'

'Calgacus.'

XXXVII

The Romans gave Cathal the breathing space he'd prayed for, but he discovered trouble did not need to wear a red cloak and carry a short sword.

At first everything went to plan. Men stripped the hillsides overlooking the river of timber to build the rough huts and shelters they would need to survive the winter. But before they began work on the houses the Selgovae dug a curving ditch from the edge of the marshes on the eastern side of the high ground to the top of the closest hill. Sweating warriors created a bank from the spoil and topped it with a palisade of newly hewn raw wood planks. Later they would dig a second ditch, Cathal decided, and perhaps a third.

While they constructed the wall others planted a third of the mouldy grain grudgingly provided by the Venicones and stored the rest in raised granaries for rationing over the coming months. Of course, it would have to be supplemented by what nature could provide. And that was what brought the first clashes.

Olwyn had been right. The nearby marshes and the river at first supplied what appeared to be an endless bounty, but that was an illusion. Ten thousand mouths take a great deal of filling, as Cathal quickly discovered. At first the men came home carrying enormous nets of wildfowl, baskets of trout, eels, salmon and pike, and with roe deer stags and wild pigs slung across their shoulders. But the survivors of this initial slaughter soon became wary or moved elsewhere to safer ground where they would not be harassed by the newcomers. Inevitably, the Selgovae were forced to range further afield to provide meat and fish for the plate and the smokehouse. East, to the great wetland they'd skirted on the trek here, and the lower river, and west where the river narrowed and the marshland was even greater in extent and much more dense. Not quite impenetrable, however, as they discovered when the hunters began to probe its outer reaches. Cunningly concealed poles marked paths where a man could range deep into the reeds if he was prepared to be submerged to the chest on occasion. And elsewhere they discovered plank tracks that linked patches of open water and reed beds where the ducks gathered in the greatest numbers. But the Venicones had long regarded the reed beds and the pools as their own. Had they not marked the paths and their forefathers not built the wooden board-walks? Hollowed out the log canoes moored ready to be paddled to the less accessible regions of the swamp?

It started with a dispute over a starved otter caught in someone's forgotten trap. A pair of Venicones hunters stumbled upon a lone Selgovae emptying the wicker tube and claimed ownership. Insults were exchanged and then stones, before the outnumbered Selgovae made his escape still laughing at his good fortune. But the next time he checked the trap four or five Venicones lay in ambush and gave him a salutary beating that left his ribs bruised and his nose bleeding. The assault in turn drove his outraged friends to plan their revenge, which resulted in a pitched battle on a sandbank and split heads on either side. Cathal heard rumours of friction between his people and those from across the river, but he was too busy planning his response to the inevitable Roman appearance to take much notice.

It was only when they brought Ranal staggering into the camp with half his guts hanging out that he understood the dispute had escalated far beyond a few scuffles. They laid Cathal's sword brother on a cot and covered him in a blanket. By the time the king reached him blood had soaked through the thick wool and Ranal's flesh had taken on the dull yellow pallor unmistakable to anyone who had seen it. 'What happened?' he demanded.

'There were twenty of them and we were about to set to,' one of the warriors who'd accompanied the wounded man explained. 'Ranal knew you'd disapprove.' Cathal winced at that fatal truth, but he didn't interrupt. 'He challenged their leader to a fight. Man to man. The Venicones bastard drew a knife and the next thing we knew they were rolling around and the rest of us roaring Ranal on. There was this scream, like a woman with a baby stuck halfway, and the Venicones staggered back with the blood spraying from his neck. His mates took him away and it was only then we saw what he'd done to Ranal.'

'Did I kill him?' Ranal croaked.

'That you did,' his friend assured him. But Ranal's eyes had already dulled.

'We should slaughter the bastards.' Another voice came from the rear of the hut. 'There's a gang of them camped on the far side of the big pool. We can burn them out tonight.'

'There'll be no burning and no slaughter.' Cathal looked down at Ranal and closed the dead man's eyes gently with his fingers. 'Fetch Colm and tell him to bring a green branch. It is time I talked to the Silver King again.'

When he went to meet Colm it was Olwyn who led his horse. 'What will you do, Cathal?'

'Make an agreement.' He vaulted into the saddle. 'What else? I should have foreseen this.'

'Do not blame yourself, husband. You can't be everywhere.'

'See what happens when I'm not?' He reached down and touched her cheek. 'Whatever happens and whatever it takes, it stops here or we'll have a war on our hands.'

They rode down to the river with Colm in the lead, Cathal accompanied by ten of his bodyguard. The Venicones kept a guard of about fifty men on the ford and Colm advanced into the waters of the Abhainn dhub calling out the king's name. A bearded young man with his dark hair coiled in a topknot emerged from one of the guard shelters. 'You may advance, lord king, but the Argento Rìgh has decreed you may only be accompanied by four men.'

Colm growled at the restriction, but Cathal waved the first four men forward and together they crossed and urged their horses out on the north bank. When they reached the huts the young warrior was already in the saddle with ten of his men. Cathal noticed the slim gold torc at his neck and the quality of his accoutrements and decided that, despite his age, he was a man of some consequence. 'A single guide would have sufficed.' Cathal nodded ruefully in the direction of the other riders.

'Not every Venicones is as well disposed to Cathal king of the Selgovae as I.' The man smiled. 'There are some who would prefer you did not meet our king.'

Cathal noted the warning, but knew better than to acknowledge it. 'You have the better of me?'

'My name is Donacha ap Arrol, and my father holds lands yonder at Goirtaincabar.' He waved a hand towards the north-west. 'We have responsibility for defending five miles of the north bank, though the marshes do most of the defending for us.'

'Was it your man . . . ?'

'No, those were poachers. You did me a favour by ridding me of a nuisance.'

'I doubt others feel so relaxed about his loss.'

The young man didn't answer but led the way to the raised causeway that ran between river and marsh towards the high ground to the north. 'This is our food store.' Donacha nodded towards the marsh. 'The king created much resentment when he placed you in a position where your men were bound to make use of it.'

'A man cannot live on fresh air,' Cathal growled.

'No, lord king, you mistake me. I did not think to apportion blame. What I mean is that I believe the king erred when he kept you south of the river.'

'You would have done differently?'

'We have ample lands to the north that have never felt the coulter.' The young man shrugged. 'True, they border the shit-eaters of the high lands, but who better to keep them busy than the celebrated King Cathal of the Selgovae? There,' he pointed to a spur that jutted from the highest peak of the escarpment, 'is the fortress of the Venicones.'

'It looks formidable.' Cathal sounded suitably admiring.

Donacha caught the irony and smiled. 'The Argento Rìgh believes our warriors will be able to line the mountain and throw the Romans back into the Abhainn dhub.'

'After they have waded through Selgovae blood,' Cathal pointed out.

'Naturally,' Donacha agreed. 'But I am not so certain. I have heard of these Romans, but I do not know what to believe and what not. Perhaps you could enlighten me. For instance, I am told they do not fight honourably, warrior against warrior. Is that true?'

'That is true,' Cathal acknowledged. 'They fight in what they call centuries.' He recalled the words of the midget scout Arafa. 'Eighty men acting as one.' He saw the look of puzzlement on Donacha's hand- some features. 'Think of eighty of your warriors facing eighty men with shields that protect them from shin to throat, wearing chest armour and iron helmets. The shields are locked together to make a continuous wall.'

'Then we would break the wall with our strength and our courage.'

'Perhaps.'

'Or our bravest would leap over the wall and cause panic and death, allowing their comrades to slaughter the cowards.'

'Not cowards,' Cathal assured him. 'And in any case, behind the wall of shields is a second line of men ready with iron-tipped spears waiting for just such an attempt.'

'I see,' Donacha said, and Cathal saw he was familiar enough with battle to be able to imagine the carnage as the Roman spears bit into the exposed throats and groins of his champions.

'As I understand it,' the Selgovae king said, 'even our bravest can only break a shield wall perhaps once out of a hundred times. For the most part they will hammer at the shields with their swords, or use spears to

251

try to blind the defenders. The warriors following the initial attackers are equally brave and in their desperation force those in front against the shields.'

'Then their weight must break the line,' Donacha suggested.

'They would eventually,' Cathal agreed, 'but for the little Roman swords, no longer than a man's forearm.'

'A pitiful weapon,' the younger man said.

'In the open, yes,' though Cathal remembered the gleaming point of Valerius's *gladius* probing and seeking and wondered if that was true. 'But imagine if each Roman simultaneously heaves his shield forward at an angle,' he made the motion with his arm, 'thus creating a gap to his right front, and stabs forward into the exposed flank of his enemy – because most of our warriors wear no armour, of course.'

'A coward's way of fighting.' Donacha sounded perplexed.

'True, but a very effective way. The warrior falls and is replaced by the next.'

'They use our own courage against us?'

Cathal nodded.

'But there must be a way to defeat them.'

'Let us hope so.'

The Venicones king's palace stood behind a wooden palisade on a shelf of land four times as long as it was broad, set a third of the way up the hillside overlooking the river valley. From the walkway of his walls he had a clear view south to the reclining bear outcrop and its smaller sibling behind the river. To his left Cathal could see the third of the hills and the long causeway leading down to the ford. He could imagine the Argento looking out from his eyrie and obsessing all the long hot summer over the enormous cuckoo, in the shape of Cathal's followers, he had invited to share his nest. By now, with trees shedding their golden coverlet, he would have expected the Romans to have either destroyed them or been repulsed, but neither of those things had happened. Instead, the Selgovae grew stronger with every passing day, untouched even by the hut sickness Cathal had seen decimate large gatherings who stayed in a single place for too long. Not only stronger, but more numerous. Over the past month contingents of ragged, exhausted warriors had approached the gate in the palisade or appeared from over the hills asking to join King Cathal's force. They were disaffected men of the Damnonii and the Novantae who had tasted Roman rule and wanted nothing to do with it. Even amongst the Votadini, men of honour sickened by Marro's collaboration with the invaders rode north to join their old enemy. Cathal made each and every one of them welcome. The Argento knew all this, but seemed powerless to stop it, and at one time Cathal had even wondered if the king himself was responsible for the provocations in the marshes. However, he had concluded they were too minor to constitute any kind of strategy.

The Argento lay back on a wooden throne on a platform in his palace, an enormous two-storey roundhouse hung with pelts and furs. The exotic mask was gone, revealing a thin, worried face, protruding ears and beady black eyes that reminded Cathal of a puzzled weasel. He guessed the king would be close to his thirtieth year. A young woman sat by him suckling twin babes, but for all the attention she gave him Cathal might not have existed. Six of the Argento's bodyguard, the same big, bare-chested men with thick moustaches who'd accompanied him to the ford, stood at his back. They included the glaring Giulan Marbh and each held a spear in his right hand. Oenghus, the druid, sat on a stool at the king's right hand. Cathal noted some form of almost invisible greeting between the priest and Donacha, and guessed the two men were brothers.

He bowed his head in the direction of the throne. 'I have come, lord king, to seek ways to end the constant and dangerous dispute between our warriors on the hunting grounds.'

'There is a simple way to end it,' the king said peevishly. 'Tell your men they may hunt in the hills, but stay away from the marshes and the river.'

'Perhaps that would end it, or it may be that hungry bellies make the situation worse,' Cathal said.

'Then what do you propose? Are we to take their knives? Insist they bow to each other as they steal each other's catch?'

253

'First I would offer the lord king a gift.' He held out a hand and Colm placed a bag of soft leather in his palm. Cathal pulled at the draw strings and withdrew an exquisitely worked torc that shone buttery gold in the lamplight and drew a gasp from at least one person in the room. The Argento's wife's eyes, if she was indeed his wife, looked as if they were on sticks. 'This was made for my father's father and has a place of honour not just in my tribe, but in my heart.' It was a lie, but the necessary kind of lie that went by the name of diplomacy. 'I hope you will accept it in honour of our ongoing friendship.'

He walked forward and placed the torc in the Argento's hand. The king weighed the piece and held it out to his wife, who abandoned the children and took it, cooing over the weight and the fine workmanship. The Argento feigned uninterest, but Cathal knew he had impressed the younger man. Oenghus met his eyes and he thought he caught a hint of approval.

'Go on.' The king nodded.

'I suggest nothing as complex as disarming our men, or teaching them manners.' Cathal allowed himself a smile. 'A simple dividing line, the course of which would be agreed between our two most experienced hunters. If any man crosses it without reasonable cause he will be brought before a court which will meet to dispense justice the day after the first full moon of each month.'

'Yes, I could see how that would work.' The King's eyes glittered. 'Nothing like removing a man's hand to teach him not to stray. Or even more salutary, Giulan can crush his skull slowly with his bare hands.'

'I would suggest the arbitrators of justice should be our druids. They are oathsworn to be impartial.' Another lie, but Oenghus, who Cathal guessed had his own reasons for seeking contact with Gwlym, murmured his approval. 'I stress it would be a purely temporary arrangement. I have no wish to be your guest for any longer than is necessary.'

'Very well.' The Argento smiled for the first time. 'And to cement our agreement I suggest a further exchange of gifts.'

Cathal sensed a trap. 'I wish nothing more from the king than his continued hospitality and friendship.'

'But I seek something from you, Cathal of the Selgovae.' The Venicones couldn't keep the sly glint from his eyes. 'A pair of your fine horses hitched to the yoke would add to the magnificence of my chariot, don't you think?'

Did he notice the faintest nod of the head from Oenghus? And if he did what did it signify? 'Very well.' Cathal produced a defeated sigh and the Argento's triumphant grin almost split his face. 'But,' the Selgovae continued, 'they are in poor condition at this time of the year. You may visit my stables at Beltane and take your choice. My grooms will ensure they are at their finest. I can do nothing less.'

The Argento scowled, but he knew he'd been outmanoeuvred. He rose to his feet and waved a dismissive hand that froze in mid-air at a sharp, rhythmic shriek from outside, quickly echoed by a dozen others. The Venicones king rushed past Cathal to the door, his eyes eagerly scanning the sky above.

Cathal ignored a grimace of warning from Donacha and joined the king in the doorway. He looked up to see a skein of about a hundred geese flow smoothly from their V formation and swoop down in a curving dive to land with a series of splashes on a pool in the marshes below. They preened their feathers and settled with a curious contented honking call.

'Royal birds.' The intensity in the Argento's voice matched the fire in his eyes and Cathal had to disguise his astonishment. 'Any man who takes the king's bounty must deliver his catch to me on pain of death – any man on either side of the river. Do you understand, Cathal of the Selgovae?'

'I understand.' Cathal saw no point in arguing with so consuming a passion.

Donacha explained it on the ride back to the river. 'The annual migration is what keeps him on the throne,' the young warrior said. 'The geese come in their countless thousands to overwinter here. He only allows a certain proportion to be hunted and the smoked birds are held in the royal treasury to be dispensed through the winter. In hard times the king's favour can be the difference between life and death.'

He gave a sad smile that made him look much younger. 'So make sure your men are warned, lord king. The Argento is not as harmless as he sometimes appears.'

'I will,' Cathal assured him, but as Donacha turned away he had a feeling the final sentence was as much a warning for himself as for his hunters.

XXXVIII

Londinium, October AD *80*

Valerius flinched at another long, drawn-out cry from inside the building and tried to concentrate on the workers extending the port above the bridge. Only smaller craft could negotiate the relatively low space between the piers, but it would ease congestion at the main wharf downstream. The river traffic seemed to multiply daily, with ships arriving from Gaul, Hispania, and every major city with a port on the Mare Internum. Twenty years earlier there had been three or four warehouses huddled behind the original dock; now there were scores, and every street with a warehouse had its bars and brothels, food shops and cheap apartment blocks to house the workers who laboured in them.

These men filed in a constant stream to and from the merchant ships that lined the wooden quays, shouldering enormous *amphorae* of wine, *garum* and olive oil. At a pinch, a Roman legion would march with a few thousand quarts of native beer in its collective belly, but it would march further on sour wine. And no rations were so welcome that they could not be improved by a generous helping of fish sauce or a dash of olive oil to soften the jaw-breaking *buccelatum* biscuits. Crates of fine red pottery from the factories in Gaul; sacks of spices that filled the air with their pungent aroma; baskets of one-size-fits-all leather sandals from Hispania that would fall apart on the first wet day; swords and armour forged in a dozen provinces to equip Britannia's legions and auxiliary cohorts. Wooden cranes hoisted great slabs of the finest Asian marble from deep in the holds to clad the ever-growing number of public buildings and floor the homes of the richest merchants.

Traders flocked to Londinium from all over the Empire to tout their wares, bringing slaves from even further afield: men so black they could almost be called blue, from the heart of trackless Africa; Scythians, short, stocky and narrow-eyed; blond giants from the freezing north of Germania; hawk-nosed, beetle-browed Parthians, and sultry, perfumed *hetaerae* from the fabled Indus. A man's ears could be assailed by a dozen different languages as he walked along a single street. But – Valerius gritted his teeth at another demonic howl – may the gods save him from being assailed by this.

'Mars' wrinkled scrotum,' he muttered: Serpentius's favoured epithet. 'How long has it been? Three hours?'

'Nearer four,' suggested his companion seated on the stone terrace overlooking the foam-flecked muddy waters of the Tamesa. 'Is it always like this?' Rufius Florus asked.

'How would I know?' Valerius laughed. 'Tabitha wouldn't let me within a mile of the house when Lucius was born, and I was in Lindum for Olivia's arrival. Didn't Ceris give you some idea?' They were wrapped in heavy cloaks against the bitter east wind, but anything was better than the claustrophobic, over-heated rooms of the palace with that din echoing from the walls.

'She calls them *the mysteries* and won't tell me anything,' Rufius confessed. The young cavalryman was a reformed thief who'd chosen service in Valerius's bodyguard in preference to violent retribution from his former comrades. 'All she says is that nature must take its course, but sometimes it needs a little help.'

If it was like this for two men with so little stake in what was happening, what was Domitia Decidiana Agricola suffering? She'd gone into labour just before dawn and Valerius had accompanied Tabitha and

Ceris as they rushed to Tabitha's friend's side. They'd met the white-faced governor at the door and Valerius had suggested they spend the day riding and hunting in the open country outside the city walls. Instead, Agricola insisted on staying close to his wife. Valerius knew they'd lost one son and he prayed to every god he could think of that there would be no repeat of that tragedy. He'd left Agricola at his desk staring at a piece of parchment, but he was fairly certain the governor would not have read a single word in the endless hours that had passed since.

Another long bout of screaming felt like an iron nail running down the inside of the skull.

'I have a request to make, legate.'

'Yes?' Valerius was grateful for the distraction.

'I'd like to rejoin the escort squadron when you go back north.'

Valerius looked at him in surprise. 'What will Ceris say?'

'It's her idea.'

'Ah.' Valerius nodded his understanding. The unfathomable mysteries of the human relationship conveyed perfectly in so few little words. 'In that case I'll consider it.'

'It's awfully quiet all of a sudden.'

'So it is.'

A new wail, high-pitched and angry. A baby's howl of outrage at being dragged from the sanctuary of the womb.

The two men spontaneously stood and Florus grasped Valerius by the shoulders and hugged him tight, disengaging himself after a moment with a sheepish grin. Valerius grinned back, filled with some transcendental, primordial joy by the arrival of a new life into the world, whatever its worth. He reached into his purse and drew out a large coin. 'Here.' He handed the gold *aureus* to his companion. 'Go to the Street of the Silversmiths and buy Ceris a present. A special present, mind, one that shows how much you appreciate her. You make a good team. Tell her I need you here. For the lady's protection.'

'I will, lord.' Florus laughed out loud as he bounded toward the east gate. 'Surely I will.'

Valerius heard footsteps and turned. Tabitha stood in the doorway with a look of utter weariness on her face, aged a dozen years in a single morning. Her honey-brown skin had taken on an unnatural shade of grey, and drying blood coated her halfway to the elbows. Gore spattered her linen dress and at some point she'd wiped her hand across her forehead leaving a scarlet smear.

He stepped towards her and took her into his arms before she fell, half carrying her to the terraced embankment where he'd sat with Florus. When he'd got her seated he sat beside her with his arm around her shoulders. She closed her eyes and sat with her chin on her breastbone, utterly spent. Her whole body shook and he could feel the tension in her like a *ballista* racked and ready to fire. In the next second a great convulsion racked her and she vomited among the plants at her feet.

'That bad?' he said quietly.

She didn't open her eyes. 'Worse.' At last she looked up at him, saw the question in his eyes. 'A boy,' she said, though there was no joy in her announcement of this joyous news. 'He was stuck fast and had to be forced free. At times we thought they both must die.'

'Now it's over,' he stroked her hair, 'and they live. The gods be thanked.'

'Yes, they live,' she said. 'But Ceris believes Domitia will never be able to have another child, and if she attempts it she will certainly die in the process. And only the gods know the harm done to the child. His poor head was damaged in the ordeal, but Ceris assures me it will resume its shape eventually. You are not to mention any of this to Agricola, my love. He is not to see mother or baby until both have recovered.'

'How much does he know?'

'Only that they must be left alone for now.' She hesitated. 'He wept when I told him, Valerius, wept in a way that concerned me. Give him an hour before you congratulate him on his son – he is to be called Julius after his father – and, if you can, persuade him to go north again as soon as possible. Domitia needs time and solitude. There may still be more suffering to endure and I am not sure he can bear it.'

XXXIX

Rome, December AD 80

'I always think Saturnalia sets a dangerous precedent, brother, don't you?' Domitian's tone was perfectly harmless and the words were pleasant enough, but they contained that element of challenge Titus always found difficult to ignore. The younger man tugged irritably at his *pilleus*, the rather ludicrous felt cap everyone in the room wore, perched at a precarious angle on his head. Normally, the conical cap was only worn by freed slaves on the day of their manumission, but on this day it was a sign that, nominally, every man and woman was equal.

Below the Imperial dais, in the palace's great dining hall, the members of Titus's inner circle cheerfully dispensed food and drink to their household slaves and exchanged banter in a familiar fashion that would seem a distant memory in just a few days.

'Look at them, acting as if they own the Palatine,' Domitian continued. 'Drinking like sows, arguing with their masters. Playing dice and haggling over which gift they should receive. I saw Acilius Glabrio giving one of his wife's maids an expensive gold chain. All it does is give them a taste for freedom, and we know what happens when that taste turns into a hunger.'

261

'It's only once a year for a few days, husband.'

Titus noticed that Domitia Longina seemed to be enjoying herself. That pleased him, because she'd been pensive and troubled of late and it affected her looks. 'Try taking the privilege of a hundred generations away from them and you will learn the true meaning of danger, brother,' he said cheerfully. 'They look forward to these six days all year long and they have come to believe they are entitled to them.'

'That is exactly what I mean.' Domitian leaned forward on his couch, waving his cup so wine spilled on the table. 'A sense of entitlement in a slave is entirely inappropriate and can lead to a lack of respect. On the other hand, I suppose it gives one a chance to single out the trouble-makers for future retribution.'

'Wearing a *pilleus* for an afternoon of pleasant company is a small price to pay.' Titus reached across and playfully knocked the cap over Domitian's eyes. 'Just be thankful that we at least are not expected to serve our slaves. I'm not sure I would remember how.' He laughed, thinking that it had been months since he felt so cheerful and ener-getic. 'Though I see old Philippus, your *atriensis*, down there. Perhaps I'll ask you to serve him his soup.'

Domitian chuckled dutifully and his wife put a hand to her mouth to stifle a laugh.

'When are you going to hold the ceremony to confirm Father's div-inity?' Domitian manoeuvred the conversation to what he thought was safer ground. 'He's been in his grave for eighteen months now and still no proper tomb.'

'I was going to talk to you about that.' Titus smiled. 'I plan to move him from the Mausoleum of Augustus to the family vaults next year, but first we have to turn them into a resting place fit for an emperor' – he raised his cup to his brother – 'for a dynasty. I would like you to look after that, Domitian, and I want you to organize the divination cere-monies. They'll begin in July and last for the usual hundred days.'

It was an enormous task and Domitian felt as if all the wind had been knocked from him, but what could he say? 'It will be an honour, brother.'

'I thought you'd say that.' Titus looked around the hall seeking out a particular face. Yes, there he was. 'Flavius Josephus,' he called. 'Yes, you. You're not deaf, are you? Don't sit there looking so glum, come and join us.' He summoned a passing servant. 'Move the spare couch next to my brother.'

Josephus looked warily around the table, not certain if he was the subject of some kind of jest. Domitia's welcoming smile put him more at ease and he slipped on to the couch next to Domitian. The servant placed a gold cup before him and filled it with wine. The Judaean had oiled his beard for the festival and, like the others, he'd relinquished his formal toga for the colourful dining clothes that were appropriate for the occasion. In his case, the voluminous smock had a rainbow sheen and was cut to make him look like an Eastern potentate, which was what he'd intended.

'What do you think of it all?' Titus waved an expansive hand across the thronged hall. 'It must seem quite strange to you, even after all these years.'

'On the contrary, Caesar.' The Judaean tugged at his beard. 'I find it rather entertaining to see masters fawning over their servants for a change. As you know, certain elements in my home country were very enthusiastic about notions of equality, and even common ownership.'

'The Christus fellow, you mean.'

'Indeed.' Josephus bowed to acknowledge Titus's grasp of the subject. They'd served long enough together in Judaea for Josephus to be aware of the new emperor's interests . . . and prejudices. 'Your immediate predecessor but four,' he bared his teeth to show that his use of words was a small, harmless jest, and in no way intended as a slight to Titus's father, 'took vigorous steps to stamp them out in Rome, but I believe they are still active in Galilee.'

'Being in Rome doesn't appear to have done you any harm, Jew.' Domitian ignored his wife's stare to reach across and lift Josephus's arm to show off the massive gold bracelet adorning his wrist.

'Indeed.' Josephus smiled. Outwardly he took no offence, though his hand twitched for a knife to push into that scrawny throat. 'I will always be grateful to your father for inviting me here for the good of my health. I find the proximity of the Tiber and the water from your fine aqueducts most invigorating.'

Domitian snorted, and even Titus stifled a laugh. Every man in Rome knew that if Josephus so much as set one foot on the soil of Judaea enough of his enemies remained to ensure that his life would be measured in minutes. The members of no less than three different sects were certain he had betrayed the secrets of Jerusalem to Titus, and had thus been equally responsible for its ultimate destruction.

'And you, my lady.' Josephus turned his dark eyes on Domitia. With her, he always played the father figure, though she was certain his inclinations were far from fatherly. 'You are in such fine colour that one would almost say . . . but of course, I will not.' Domitia felt herself redden and the Judaean raised a speculative eyebrow. 'I do believe I saw you coming from the palace kitchens again the other day?'

Domitia darted a warning glance at her husband, but Domitian's attention was on the increasingly drunken revels below. Josephus realized his mistake and artfully changed the subject.

'What news of Britannia, Caesar? The last word was of a great victory and I understand we must congratulate you on being hailed Imperator yet again. What is it now? Sixteen times, and each more deserving than the last.'

Titus's smile froze momentarily. The initial reports from Londinium had indicated precisely that, but he had his own sources and there were hints that the 'great victory' might not be all it appeared. 'Fifteen,' he corrected. 'You flatter me. But that was always one of your great strengths.'

'Indeed, lord—'

'Yes.' Domitian's bray cut across the conversation. 'What are you going to do about Britannia? Two years you gave that sluggard Agricola, and now we hear he's *consolidating*. Building forts as if he's some kind of engineer. He shouldn't be consolidating, he should be advancing. He should have rounded up each and every barbarian male on the island by now and shipped them off to the slave market at Ostia.'

'It may be that there are extenuating circumstances.' Titus suddenly felt tired. 'The governor's wife has recently borne him a son and it would be a callous emperor,' he bestowed a weak smile on Domitia, 'who begrudged one of his officials a few weeks with his wife at such a time.'

'At the least he should have ordered his generals to do what he was not prepared to do himself.'

'Perhaps you are right, brother,' Titus pinned Domitian with his solemn grey eyes, 'and it is time for some new blood. I have been considering a replacement for some months now, though in all conscience I cannot make the change until Agricola has had his two years and a chance to win a triumph.'

'Who?' Titus could see Domitian running the potential candidates through his mind, wondering who would provide him with the greatest advantage.

'Gaius Valerius Verrens was the man I had in mind.'

Domitian spluttered into his wine cup and a flash of alarm appeared in Domitia's dark eyes. Titus had a momentary twinge of regret that in his clumsy eagerness to astonish Domitian he'd caused her pain or alarm. Domitia Longina and Gaius Valerius Verrens had a history of which Domitian was perfectly aware and would like to expunge permanently from memory.

'A mere plebeian?' Domitian found his voice. 'A man who has proved himself little more than a brute? You would appoint someone as proconsul of Rome who turned traitor not once but three times during the civil war?'

'Careful, brother.' The words were accompanied by a half smile, but the iron in the voice was unmistakable. 'I am perfectly aware of your dislike of the man, but do not let that cloud your judgement. Much of what Verrens did or did not do during the late war was at my bidding or our father's. He is, as you well know, an *eques*, from a venerable family of knights, and our father esteemed him enough to award him patrician status before he left for Britannia. Between them, he and Josephus here handed me the keys to Jerusalem. In our long acquaintance I have found him to be both loyal and honest, a rare enough combination to single him out for overdue advancement. He has a long history of service to Rome and our family, both as a diplomat and as a fighter.'

'And,' Domitian struggled to keep the sneer from his voice, 'he is your *friend*.'

'Yes, he is my friend.' Titus went dangerously still. 'And I can assure you, brother, I have discovered that an emperor cannot have enough true friends. You may argue that he is not of consular rank, but that is soon resolved. I intend to appoint him a suffect consul next year; the only question is whether he should share it with you or me.' He grimaced at some internal tumult. 'But we will speak of this no more. I ask your forbearance and your discretion. It would not be right for Agricola to hear of his replacement from anyone but myself. Now,' he raised himself to his feet and two aides rushed to his side, 'if you will excuse me I have much reading to do before nightfall. Domitian, you will close the banquet for me?' His brother inclined his head in acknowledgement of the honour. 'Good.' Titus smiled. 'And be so kind as to have a jug of that excellent Falernian sent through to help me with my labours.'

He bent to kiss Domitia Longina's hand and she watched him go with a smile that disguised her concern. She'd been pleased to see him so energetic and voluble after so many months of lethargy, but there'd been something unnatural about his eyes and the way his mood swung so violently.

Domitian gestured to the man who had been serving them. 'Take a jug of the Falernian to the Emperor's private quarters. The best, mind. Not the tavern slops we've been serving to the slaves.'

Only the practised eyes of Josephus noticed the silent message that passed between master and servant. Even he couldn't divine the true meaning, or, for that matter, where he stood in the ever-changing ebb and flow of palace life. In any case, what could he do?

The servant retrieved a full jug from a long chest behind the Imperial table and covered it with a white cloth. On the way to the Emperor's quarters he found a junction between two corridors where he was certain he couldn't be seen. He pulled back the cloth over the jug's mouth and, with a last look to ensure he was alone, reached into his tunic and pulled out a cloth sachet. His fingers worked at the thread ties to open the mouth and he poured the contents into the jug, shaking it to help them dissolve.

He took a deep breath – he would never get used to this – and carried the wine to the Emperor's apartments.

'Good.' Titus looked up from his parchment as the man was ushered in by his guards. 'Put the wine there and pour me a cup, then you may go.'

XL

Emrys waited silently in the darkness where the bowed, drooping branches of a willow touched the black water. He wasn't sure how much longer he could suffer the freezing cold that had long since turned his submerged legs into numb, useless blocks of dead flesh and was working its way up his body. A man groaned nearby with the pain of it and he hissed for silence. His fingers stroked the thin strands of hemp that made up the net, folded just so in the water in front of him, and he vowed to go home as soon as he could no longer feel the rough fibres. Yet the contented mumbling was not too far away and for men who'd been living on the summer's smoked fish for five weeks it was a temptation beyond reason. Even the thought of that sweet, pale flesh flaking away from the breastbone had the saliva running down his throat.

Closer now, and closer still. The darkness was total, a stygian black that even the light of the stars couldn't penetrate. His decision and his alone. And it must be made by using a combination of ear and instinct. An occasional whimper amongst the soft chirring made him think of a dog dreaming by the fire. He knew this branch of the swamp well and he had a picture in his mind of what was in front of him. But was it a true picture?

'Now!' Two pairs of hands propelled the circular net into the air, swinging and turning, carried upwards and out by the stones attached to the outer strands. A sharp squawk of alarm accompanied by a frenzied thrashing and a beating of wings. Emrys and his companion forced their way through the water and carefully checked their catch.

'Four,' he chortled. 'I told you it would be worth the wait. That's twelve for the night. Just about worth freezing your balls off.' They dragged the net full of outraged squawking birds to the bank, taking care not to leave any way to escape. Once they were on dry land Emrys removed them one by one and chopped off their heads with a flick of his knife. They gathered up the net and the night's haul and set off for home by the now familiar walkways. But not before Emrys had seen a shadow detach itself from one of the trees and disappear back into the night.

It didn't affect his mood. They would eat goose tonight.

Cathal had called a council of his war chiefs on his return from meeting the Silver King and told them of his agreement, with a stern admonition to abide by it. But he also knew a hungry man would not look out on such bounty for long before his belly urged him to take advantage of it. So he chose not to see. When the Venicones king's outraged wails of broken promises were conveyed to him he would be able to say with truth that he knew nothing of these charges. As far as he was aware, there was no poaching of the king's geese.

'This fish is good tonight.' He smiled over the fire at Olwyn.

'Yes.' She tore at a piece of leg meat with her strong white teeth. 'I believe Dugald helped catch it.' Her son shot her a glance of alarm from his place among a bundle of furs and swiftly dipped his head before his father could look in his direction. Berta snored gently a few feet away.

'My father told me of a trader who visited Mairos once,' Cathal said. 'He had skin as black as night and decked himself in furs even in the heart of summer because he claimed his body could not stand our chill winds. He told outlandish tales of the birds and beasts he'd seen on his travels. One of them was of an odd creature: a fish that flew above the waves. Can you imagine such a thing? Yet I do believe this is the very same.'

They grinned at each other, but the smiles vanished at a sound outside the doorway. Olwyn was by the children even before the knife appeared in Cathal's hand. 'Lord king?' He relaxed as the curtain was drawn back and Colm's stolid face appeared in the entrance. 'The druid says he must see you.'

Gwlym slipped inside uninvited and placed himself in front of the fire as if he could see it as well as any man in the room. 'Careful, priest, or you will be scorched,' Cathal admonished him. 'I don't much mind if you set yourself ablaze, but the hut would go up with you.'

'I have walked through the sacred flames of Pencerrig,' Gwlym said scornfully. 'No fire can harm me.' His voice changed without warning to take on a mystic quality. 'I come with a warning, Cathal ap Dugald. The Argento Rìgh's patience is at an end. He has convinced himself that the Romans will not come and that he needs you no longer. They will come for you tonight.'

'How many?'

Gwlym shrugged. That was not his affair. 'Enough.'

Cathal called for Colm. 'We will have visitors tonight from across the water. Where will they come, do you think?'

'They have canoes downriver,' the guard said thoughtfully. 'But that would mean they'd have to cross the palisade. So from the west, I would say, through the marshes.'

Cathal considered. 'You are right. From the marshes.'

'We'll cut their throats before they get anywhere near you.'

'No,' the king said. 'Even if they don't return I want whoever sent them to believe they might well have succeeded. And this is my fight. I will deal with them alone.' He heard a hiss from the corner of the hut. 'Hush, Olwyn. My sword has been idle for too long. A king must prove himself from time to time or he will no longer be a king. You, a princess of the Brigantes, know that well enough.' He took his scabbard and the shattered sword from its frame, and buckled the belt with the war hammer at his waist. 'Let us hope they do not keep me waiting,' he said with a grim smile.

＊

270

They came quietly, big men, swift over the ground, who knew how to plant their feet to avoid the snap of a twig, the crunch of an acorn or the telltale rustle of the leaves that carpeted the damp ground. Only a warrior equally capable could hope to detect them. Cathal felt a moment of regret. Men like these should be his allies. They should be killing Romans together, not butchering each other. He thrust the thought aside. Tonight they were the enemy. Six of them. He fixed them in his mind, noting the relative positions, the distance apart, the likely reaction when . . . Without another thought he rose from the ground in the centre of the assassins, the great blacksmith's hammer already swinging as he spun on his toes. A jarring impact and a wet smack, before he reversed the spin and raised the hammer high, bringing it down with a bone-breaking crunch on head or shoulder, he wasn't certain which. It didn't matter. The weight of the blow would either kill or disable. He danced forward. They were aware of him now. Their minds would be racing, every shadow a threat. A spear point came out of the darkness and he swayed aside as it brushed his beard, the hammer already scything to stave in the bearer's ribs and drawing a terrible cry from his victim. A bull's roar and two shadows rushed at him. He brushed aside one spear with his left hand and snapped the other in half with a blow of the hammer, reversing in the same instant to bring the head upwards in a swing that took his attacker square on the jaw.

Torches flared and a roar went up as a hundred Selgovae warriors surged out of the darkness. Cathal blinked. One man was on his knees, his hands clutched together in supplication and a dark stain on the crotch of his *bracae*. Another stood, staring in bewilderment at useless hands that flopped from his broken wrists. Two lay dead, but two more lived, though their time left would be short and painful. One lay face down, shivering like a storm-swept rowan, four or five shattered ribs jutting stark white from his side and a dark pool staining the ground beneath him. The other lay on his back, what was once his face a smear of beard, bone, crimson gore and broken teeth, breath whistling from the approximate position of his mouth.

Cathal stood among them, huge and invincible, the great hammer

271

red with the blood of his victims. He knew the bards would already be making up songs that would ensure his feat this night was remembered for countless generations. 'Finish them.' He nodded to the dying men, and two Selgovae stepped forward drawing their knives. Two of his warriors hustled the man with the broken wrists to kneel beside the other.

'Mercy, lord king,' the uninjured man pleaded. He glanced at the other who spat at him with contempt. 'I will pledge allegiance to you and fight at your side.'

'Druid!' Cathal called and Gwlym was led into the circle of light. 'These men came to murder me, but they also had another purpose?'

'They did, lord king,' Gwlym acknowledged.

'State it.'

'They were to kill your wife and children.'

Cathal stared down at the two men and the look in his eyes was awful to behold. 'Then there can be no mercy.'

The first man bowed his head, his shoulders shaking with terror, but the other stared into Cathal's eyes with a wry smile on his lips. He was still smiling when the hammer descended with such terrible force that it spattered bone and brain for a dozen paces.

Cathal barely paused to draw breath. 'Gather the host at the river bank and wait for me there,' he ordered Emrys. 'Vodenos?' he called to the leader of his Brigante contingent. 'You will command your people and the Damnonii, Novantae and Votadini. Stay clear till the last of the Selgovae have moved to the north bank, then cross in their wake. I will send guides to give you instructions.'

An hour later Cathal's horse picked its way carefully through the rushing waters of the Abhainn dhub towards the Venicones guard post on the north side of the ford. The river was thigh deep and heavy with snow melt and the current would test the men who came behind, but there was no helping it. He must act now. His sword brothers accompanied him, or as many as the big Roman horses which had survived would mount. With every step he expected to be met with a hail of spears out of the darkness.

Instead, a familiar voice called out, only just audible over the rush of the river. 'King Cathal? Is that you?'

Cathal breathed a sigh of relief. 'And who else would it be, Donacha of Goirtaincabar? Is all ready?'

A lamp flared to illuminate Donacha and a score of men waiting on the far bank. 'Everything is as you ordered it, lord king. We are fortunate. The Argento has decided to wait till daylight before he delivers his ultimatum to whoever now rules the Selgovae.'

'Then he is in for a surprise.'

'He is, lord king. The lights here will not alert the king's supporters, but the rest of your advance must take place in darkness. Your warriors will need a steady man to lead them. Oenghus' – his brother appeared at his side and nodded a greeting – 'will guide your men along the causeway and down the edge of the marsh to block any escape to the Alauna valley to the west. They need fear no opposition. The guards are our men.'

'I wish you well in your negotiations, lord king,' Oenghus called as Emrys and the first of the Selgovae squelched out of the river at the head of the long column of faceless shadows.

'Perhaps half as many again will follow them,' Cathal told Donacha. 'Can you find someone to guide them to the top of the escarpment and a position where they can deter any reinforcement from reaching the Argento?'

'I can, lord,' the young man assured him. 'But I doubt you will need them. The Argento believes the tribes of the Venicones are assembling on the hill ready to join him at dawn. Half of the chiefs are already committed to you; the rest have been persuaded to await the outcome of your . . . discussions . . . with the king. Many feel he has dishonoured us by ordering the death of your wife and children.'

'All the same,' Cathal insisted, 'I will feel better when they are in position.'

'Then it will be so.'

They waited until the last of the Selgovae passed before making their way along the causeway in their wake. When they reached the bottom of the track that led up to the palace complex, Cathal turned to Donacha. 'I cannot order you to do anything, but it is my belief it would be better for our future dealings if you are not seen to be involved in this.'

'Then I will do as you advise, lord king.' Donacha stepped aside to let Colm and the king's sword brothers follow Cathal up the winding track into the darkness.

Cathal had been told that only the king's bodyguard, a few loyal retainers and the more sycophantic members of his court would be in the palace complex at this time of the night. The Silver King had no close family among his power base. He'd killed two brothers within weeks of being crowned and any uncles and cousins hurried into exile before they shared their relatives' fate. Cathal's own force numbered fifty, every one a sword brother with at least ten years of service. Others had pleaded to accompany him, but if his plan worked they wouldn't have to fight at all. He wanted no accidental massacre to anger the Venicones and complicate his plans for the succession. The gate guards were Donacha's men and stepped aside to let them pass.

'Let no man interfere with what happens inside,' Cathal said. His sword brothers stayed obediently in the shadows as their king marched straight ahead. Two of the Argento's personal guard stood sentry in the torchlight outside the palace doorway, and they straightened at the sound of his approach. Their spear points were aimed at the intruder's heart, but their eyes widened in astonishment as they recognized the giant figure.

'I am Cathal, king of the Selgovae, and I seek an urgent audience with the Argento Rìgh.' The guards exchanged a panicked look before the first turned and ran inside. Cathal smiled at the remaining warrior and punched him hard in the side of the head. He marched past the falling body and his bodyguard swarmed out of the darkness to follow him inside.

The Argento Rìgh sat on his throne listening in irritation to the guard's stammering report. The king's face went pale when Cathal burst through the curtained doorway followed by a stream of warriors who lined the walls behind him. Off-duty bodyguards sat drinking from clay beer pots at rough benches to either side of the throne. Recovering from their surprise, they rose to meet the threat to their master, only to freeze as Cathal's hammer swung in a slow half circle to encompass them. Warily, they resumed their places. All but one.

Cathal stared at the man on the throne and the sentry moved nervously away.

'What . . . what reason can there be for this unmannerly intrusion?' The Argento struggled to maintain his dignity and his nerve, but Cathal could see his mind working. How had Cathal survived? How had the Selgovae managed to breach his defences? And more important, what were the implications for him? 'Whatever has brought you here is surely not so significant,' he managed a weak smile, 'that it cannot wait until morning.'

'I believe it is, lord king.' Cathal moved forward a step. To his right he sensed a hand sliding towards a racked spear. 'I come here to seek redress for a great wrong. Armed men appeared at my camp tonight, sneaking treacherously out of the night. Assassins who would have murdered me, my wife and my children had I not killed them first. I am here to demand justice and seek redress in the way our people have always done. Man to man and sword to sword.' He sheathed his hammer and reached behind him to draw his sword from its scabbard. The sight of the splintered stump of metal drew a burst of nervous laughter.

The Argento shifted in his seat. 'It is an affront to draw a weapon in the king's presence.'

'Not when it was the king who sent the assassins who would have killed my family,' Cathal said quietly. 'Will you fight me, lord king, or are you too frightened?'

'Kings do not fight.' The man on the throne's eyes flickered to his left. 'That is why they give champions women and silver.'

Cathal was turning long before Colm's shout of warning. Giulan Marbh's spear was angled to take the Selgovae in the armpit with all the snarling warrior's strength behind it. Cathal brushed the point away with the ease of a man swatting a fly and stepped forward to meet the Argento's champion. Giulan shrieked as the jagged edge of the sword took him just below the breastbone, the point forced upwards through flesh and sinew into his vitals. It was a killing blow, but a crimson rage filled Cathal's skull and he roared as he forced the blade ever deeper, pushing Giulan Marbh back through his horrified comrades, sending tables clattering until he reached the far wall and could go no further. Still he worked the blade, though Giulan was long dead, his heart severed in two. Using all his enormous strength Cathal ripped the sword upwards and outwards, sending blood and viscera spraying across the hall. At last, the giant Selgovae stepped away, allowing Giulan's torn remains to slump to the floor. He turned, face and arms dripping gore.

The sight entirely unmanned the Argento. With a howl of terror he leapt from his chair and raced to a separate chamber at the rear of the hall. Cathal signalled to his men to stay where they were and followed the king. He pulled back the curtain to see the fleeing man disappearing through a panel cut in the wall. The Argento's wife looked up in horror from her cot and clutched her twin sons to her breast as Cathal charged past. The panel was too small for a man Cathal's size and he simply hacked at the wattle and daub with his sword and kicked an exit through the shattered wreckage.

By now the Argento was a mere shadow slipping through the scattered huts of the complex, but he was making enough noise for ten men and Cathal had no difficulty following him. The Venicones king sprinted to the steep bank at the rear of the plateau and Cathal reached him as he began clawing his way upwards. The Selgovae dropped his sword and drew his mighty hammer from his belt. The Silver King of the Chosen never saw the blow that crushed his skull.

XLI

Where was Agricola with the Twentieth and the Second? The towering hill at Dun Eidin loomed, for all the world like a great sleeping lion, above the temporary marching camps of the Ninth and its associated auxiliary units. Valerius had sent word six weeks earlier that he was ready to advance north and suggesting a convergence between the three legions for a single devastating attack. Together they would smash the might of Calgacus if he attempted to oppose the river crossing Gaius Rufus had identified thirty miles to the north-east.

Instead, Agricola insisted on continuing his probe in the west of the country. His shipmasters and scouts reported that all that awaited him there was an inaccessible wasteland of mountains, lakes and valleys that made Siluria look almost welcoming, but that didn't deter the governor.

Valerius and his officers eased their frustrations by pushing their troops to the limit. Calgacus might well have been weakened over the winter, but it was now April. Whatever deprivations his forces suffered, the fine weather would provide an opportunity to recover. Fine weather that was being wasted by the Romans.

Valerius looked to the clear blue sky knowing that in minutes it could be obliterated by dark clouds, and a howling wind could turn the nearby sea into a whirling maelstrom. The coastal tracks were dry, but how long would that last in a country that had as many types of rain as the days of the year? On the march from Trimontium they'd been flayed by horizontal storms that forced men to walk in a stoop, drenched by a fine drizzle that penetrated even the most heavily lanolin-coated cloaks, and near hammered into the ground by hailstones the size of slingshot pellets.

And still no Agricola.

A sharp trumpet call from the signal station on the hill raised his hopes and he ran up the lower slope in time to see a column marching in from the west. Cavalry outriders and the compact cohort formations immediately identified it as a legionary unit. Soon the numbers confirmed a full legion. Valerius searched the country beyond it for evidence of another, but he searched in vain.

'Have the stores opened and food prepared,' he told one of his aides. 'And mark out a camp on the far side of the river.' He called down to his escort on the flat ground below. 'Fetch me my horse, Shabolz. We'll ride out to meet them.'

'Looks like the Second, lord,' the Pannonian cavalryman called back. 'The legate always likes a little extra space between his cohorts, and the baggage is lagging as usual.'

The hawk-eyed Pannonian was right. When they'd covered a mile or so Valerius could see that the lead cohort's shields carried the unmistakable flying horse symbol of the Second Adiutrix on their faces. A small group of riders trotted out to meet them. 'I'm sorry to have left you cooling your heels here for so long, Valerius,' Herenius Polio called with a smile. 'But take that scowl off your face, because the blame, if blame there is, lies elsewhere.'

'I'm just glad to see you, Herenius, although I expected you to have company. Still, I hope this means we'll be able to strike camp soon. My men have been here for so long they're putting down roots.'

'As to that . . .' Polio shrugged. 'Perhaps we may ride a little ahead.' He smiled his apology to Valerius's escort. 'Your general and I have much to discuss and I'm sure you would rather not be bored by our ramblings.'

Valerius nodded, and Shabolz and the other troopers held back as the two legates put a little distance between them.

'Your instinct is right, Valerius,' Polio said. 'We move out at dawn the day after tomorrow. You'll have had your scouts working hard, I've no doubt?'

'The key is the river crossing,' Valerius told him. 'That solitary hill you see dominating the landscape ahead is Dun Eidin. The river at that point is two miles wide and might as well be the open sea as far as we're concerned. It narrows the further north and west you travel, but just when you think it could be bridged you discover it's still tidal. The first ford is two days' march upstream. Decent high ground on the south side of the river, but on the north bank the valley bottom is marsh and mudflats, reed beds and pools, quicksand like as not, cut by streams and ditches.'

'A nightmare.'

Valerius nodded. 'And once they've struggled their way through two miles of mud our mules will have a hillside to climb, with a few thousand of Calgacus's warriors at the top of it.'

'Still,' the other man considered. 'We should be able to do it with two legions.'

'Better with three.' Valerius's statement held an unmistakable question.

'Agricola is obsessed with catching the Celts between his hammer and our anvil. Despite what he's been told he believes there must be a western route through the mountains. He's had Ursus and the Twentieth slogging up one valley after another for the last month, then slogging their way back down again.'

'How much opposition are they meeting in the west?'

'In a word: none. Every valley is the same. A few scattered huts or a house built over a lake for better security. An old man who calls himself king of his extended family, and a few dozen sheep or cattle. According to Ursus it has given our governor much to ponder. How do you create a provincial government in a place with no natural centre, where every man thinks he was born to rule, but none has the power or the allies to

279

dominate all the rest? The geography makes it difficult; the social structure, if you can even call it that, makes it impossible.'

'Then why doesn't he just give up and come and join us where the Twentieth can do some good?' Valerius didn't hide his frustration.

'You haven't been listening, Valerius.' Polio clapped him on the shoulder. 'I told you he's obsessed. He's like a ram that sees its reflection in a polished bronze door. No amount of argument will convince him that he can't win. So we go it alone, and, strictly between us, maybe it's better that way.'

They set off two days later with the Ninth in the lead on the high ground close to the coast and the Second a little further behind and covering the hill country to the west. They made good progress on the first day, but coastal marshes forced them to use the same path on the second. The two legions stretched out so far Valerius knew the last man wouldn't have quit the marching camp before those in the van reached their destination. All that long day he had the feeling of being watched from the escarpment across the river. It made him nervous and though he hid it behind the mask of command, one man wasn't convinced.

'You don't have to worry about this side, legate.' Gaius Rufus sat his horse as if he was on a drawing room couch. 'I checked all the way to the ford again yesterday and there's not a Selgovae to be seen. A few renegades in those hills behind us, but not enough to do us any harm.'

'It's not those hills I'm worried about. It's the ones across there.' Valerius nodded to the north.

'Aye.' The little man grinned. 'That's where he'll be. Eyeing us like a hawk about to make his stoop.'

'The governor thinks Calgacus and his people starved over the winter and they won't have the strength to face us.'

Rufus shook his head. 'Maybe if we'd pushed them hard last year and forced him across the river before he was ready, but I reckon they ate as well as we did and probably slept a bit sounder.'

'What makes you say that?'

'They may have burned all their huts . . .' Rufus gave a snort of laughter. 'Calgacus really doesn't want to give us anything. I think he may not like you, legate.' He spat to one side. 'But you can't hide the sign of ten thousand men and you can't hide fields. Those fields had been cleared, planted and harvested and they must have produced an abundance because one or two of the grain silos I found were still full. If you think you're going to be hungry you don't leave a single seed behind. I had a look through their rubbish pits and they weren't wanting for meat or fish either. No, I reckon Calgacus ended the year as strong as he began it. Maybe stronger. One of those renegades I mentioned told a story about bands of warriors, Damnonii and Novantae, he thought, marching through the hills to join him. Hundreds of them.'

In the afternoon of the second day Rufus persuaded Valerius to ride ahead with his escort and soon they could see the massive outcrops the scout told him marked the crossing place. Not long after, they came to the curving line of ditches between the riverside marsh and the high ground that marked the outer defences of the Selgovae encampment. 'That's what's left of the palisade.' Rufus pointed to regular piles of blackened ash in the ditch. They rode over the ditches and on to a broad plateau of flat ground that covered the area between the largest outcrop and the hills. Ash circles dotted the spring grass like some obscene murrain.

'It's not like the Celts to make such a thorough job of slighting their encampment,' Naso said.

'I think you'll find this Celt is a bit cleverer than most,' Rufus informed him.

'Ten thousand warriors.' Valerius looked towards the rocky outcrop. 'I wonder why he didn't fortify that hill. Let's go and take a look.'

'Maybe he thought he didn't have to.' They rode into the dip between the plateau and the rock. 'Once he knew we weren't coming before winter there'd be no need, unless . . .'

'Unless he feared an attack from the tribes across the river,' Valerius completed the sentence for him. 'But he didn't. And they left him unmolested for an entire year, clearing the hills of timber and deer, the river of fish and fowl. What does that tell us?'

'He came to an agreement with whoever rules north of the river.' Naso urged his mount up the slope.

'Yes,' Valerius acknowledged, following his prefect up the track. 'But what kind of agreement? And what did Calgacus have to bargain with? Did the northern king agree to let the Selgovae travel through his territory?'

'That would depend on whether he intended to fight us.' Rufus joined them at the summit.

Valerius contemplated the wooded slopes beyond the outcrop on the far side of the river. 'If he does, why let ten thousand seasoned warriors slip through his fingers?'

'We need to get heralds across there as soon as we can,' Naso said grimly. 'If they come back with their heads still attached we'll know he intends to treat with us. If they don't . . .'

'We'll know it's not just Calgacus and his Selgovae who are waiting for us in those hills,' Rufus grinned as if the prospect appealed to him, 'but Mars only knows how many thousand more of the tattooed maniacs.'

Valerius frowned. 'Can we get someone across to carry a message to the king for me?'

Rufus shook his head. 'Not yet. Not unless they can fly.' He pointed to the marshland directly in front of them. 'See that brown scar that leads from the high ground there out into the marsh? I think it might have been a roadway, but it's been torn up. It means there must have been some kind of crossing point, but they've probably destroyed that too, or left us something interesting to find. Either way, it might take days to pick your way through that marsh.'

'But there's a definite crossing further west.'

Rufus nodded. 'Shallows just above the tidal reach, where a tributary stream joins from the north.'

'Then we'll cross in the morning.'

'But we can't walk on water,' Naso protested. 'That marsh would swallow a full cohort and you'd never know they'd existed.'

'That's why we have engineers, Quintus.' Valerius smiled. 'So that we don't have to. A log road. Two log roads. One for each legion. They're common enough on the Rhenus frontier where the lowlands are much like this. A floating platform that will allow us to get the men and horses across. We can worry about the baggage later.'

'I'm more worried about where we'll find the trees.' The lugubrious camp prefect studied the bare hillside to the south.

'Plenty in the hills beyond,' Rufus said cheerfully. 'And I'd prefer getting my hands blistered gripping an axe than leading the first century off the end of your log road. They're likely to get a warm reception.'

'They are.' Valerius fixed his gaze on the sloping hillside two miles distant. 'But we'll worry about that when the time comes.'

XLII

Cathal stood on a promontory of the great escarpment that gave him an uninterrupted view far to the west, but it was the land just across the river that interested him. On the rising ground just beyond the silver waters of the Abhainn dhub the glint of armour marked one long, snaking column, while another flanked it a little further west. They looked so insignificant from here, like so many ants. He almost felt as if he could reach out a hand and crush them between his fingers.

Yet he knew them well enough now to know he was seeing two full Roman legions and all the foreign mercenaries who accompanied those dangerous animals. It would be another day and more before they reached the ford, and he had left a force there that he hoped would make them think before crossing immediately. If he guessed right they numbered at least twelve thousand infantry and close to four thousand cavalry. Every man a fully armoured, seasoned warrior skilled in the disciplined, highly organized warfare he still did not fully comprehend, and which, for all the confidence he showed to Emrys, Donacha and Oenghus accompanying him, he did not know how to defeat.

Worse, the warriors from the Novantae and Damnonii who had joined him over the winter brought word of not two legions, but three.

So where was the third? Below him a large galley powered its way upriver against wind and current and he felt a shiver of dread. Was it possible such vessels might carry that many men and horses? After all, these were Romans, who had come from nowhere to strike terror in the land. Who had driven all before them as they advanced northwards. If they had somehow crossed the river further east, they might even now be behind him, cutting off his retreat. The sight confirmed what he'd already known deep in his heart.

'We are still not strong enough to oppose them.'

'But . . .'

Oenghus put a hand on his brother's arm to silence him. Cathal understood Donacha's reaction. No warrior wanted to admit defeat before a spear had been thrown or he'd heard the clash of swords.

'Tell us what you wish us to do, lord king,' the priest said.

'We will go north and I will find more men to join us.'

'Where?' Donacha demanded. 'The people of the coastal lands are simple farmers and fishermen. They care not who rules them as long as they are allowed to till and harvest and cast a net.'

Cathal took no offence at the Venicones warrior's question. If anyone had the right to ask it Donacha did. Not two days earlier Cathal had assembled the war chiefs of the Venicones and the tribes who paid tribute to them at the great gathering stone at Pendreich. All knew of the Argento's passing. Some of them welcomed it, most understood it, and those who did not harboured more puzzlement than resentment. What they were prepared to resent was an outsider appearing in their midst and declaring himself their overlord, a giant with ten thousand warriors at his back or not. They were a proud people and they were prepared to fight to prove it.

'You have all heard what happened,' he had told them. 'And you know the reason for it. If a man's family is threatened by assassins who come like thieves in the night, is he not duty bound to take his revenge on those who ordered it?' That brought a growl of agreement, if not approval. Every man there understood the blood feud. It was also Cathal's good fortune that, in his quest for security, the Argento had purged the Venicones of those of his own blood who might have wished to avenge him. Even the possibility of future retribution no longer existed. The Argento's wife had been found dead with her throat cut, apparently having smothered her sons before taking her own life. Cathal had his own suspicions about the tragedy, but he didn't allow them to diminish his regard for Donacha and his brother.

'I am not here to impose myself as your king,' Cathal continued. 'That is for you to decide, though I would commend to you Donacha ap Arrol, a man well known to you, and of great reputation.' It was a risk, but one Donacha and Oenghus insisted was worth taking. They had been preparing for this day long before the Selgovae had been forced from their lands, and enough of their supporters, persuaded or bought, salted the crowd to raise a great roar. 'If, as already seems clear, he is your choice, I offer myself as his war chief, to help him lead your warriors and mine against the Romans.' He preempted the question he knew would be in their minds if not on their tongues. 'Why should you fight the Romans? Do not listen to me, but to a man who has been fighting them for twenty years and more. A man of great power. A druid of Mona, no less, and steeped in the lore of the people of this island.'

Oenghus and the young acolytes who revered him had already been at work among them. Now Gwlym stepped before the scarred warrior chiefs on the hillside to reinforce the arguments in his harsh voice. He told them how the Roman roads and Roman watchtowers would be the chains that bound them, and Roman soldiers would take away the swords that made them the warriors they were. Roman officials would extract four times in tribute what they voluntarily paid to their king. Every cow, sheep, egg and grain of corn would be recorded on a Roman list, and from each the Romans would wring a profit. Roman courts with Roman judges would arbitrate their disputes, and any man who objected – high or low – would feel the sting of a Roman whip. Even the greatest among them would no longer be his own man, and the rest would be little more than Roman dogs, curs to be fed scraps when they obeyed and kicked when they did not.

Cries of 'No' went up with each new revelation, and Cathal knew he could depend on the majority of them, at least for now. They were like a pack of war dogs straining at the leash. The next challenge was to teach them patience. When Gwlym stopped speaking, he stepped forward once more.

'We will fight the Romans,' he promised, 'and we will defeat them. But we will fight them when I say so, and we will fight them in the way I say. It may be that we will not fight them here.' A confused silence followed, which he allowed to stretch out until one tribal elder could stand it no longer.

'We must not let them take one pace on to our land. Throw them back into the river. Make it run red with their blood.'

'A fine sentiment, lord. Where would you stop them?'

'On the raised ground by the ford,' another cried.

'And how many of your warriors would you position there?'

'A thousand,' the first chief suggested. 'It would hold no more. But others would wait on the causeway to reinforce them.'

'And they would be your greatest champions? Men forged in war. Spearmen of valour and repute.'

'Of course. Who else would deserve the honour?'

'And the Romans would fight with each other for the honour of slaughtering them.' Cathal's voice rose to a harsh, sneering bray. 'The sky would darken and the arrows of their archers would fall like hailstones on to that crowded mound. Their infantry would march through the waters of the Abhainn dhub invulnerable behind their shields and kill the survivors with their heavy spears. Yes,' he forestalled the inevitable interruption, 'you would throw more warriors forward to die an honourable and avoidable death. And the same would happen. Again. And again. And again. And while they are dying more Romans will be crossing upriver and devising some stratagem to cross the marshes unseen. It would be like trying to put out a fire with one drip of water at a time. Our bravest and our best would die for nothing.'

'So we will not fight them? We will abandon our lands to them? What about our honour?'

Cathal raged inwardly. He could have told them he cared nothing for their honour, only for victory. That their honour would win them nothing but death. But he curbed his temper.

'There is a greater sacrifice and more honour than throwing the lives of your young men away in a battle that can't be won,' he told them. 'And that is accepting that your duty to your people is better done by taking a backward step than a forward one. By curbing your instinct to throw yourselves into the fire for the sake of your individual reputation. You are all brave. I am sure you have proved that a hundred times. Now all I ask is that you have the courage to do what is right.'

The mood had been solemn as he moved away from the stone, but Donacha and Oenghus had walked among the tribal leaders and gathered their warriors along the edge of the swamp, waiting for the Romans. Now Cathal reaffirmed his decision.

'We go north and we seek out those in the high lands. We need warriors, and from what you tell me they are warriors, for all their primitive nature.'

'Warriors they are, Cathal, king of the Selgovae.' Donacha's voice was filled with grim portent. 'But do not think you can bend the shit-eaters to your will as you do the foolish Venicones. You will find not one twisted king, but a hundred, and you will need not one ambitious usurper like me, but a hundred more. They are not like us, or like you. In the high lands every man is king and every family his kingdom. You think to take an army in your grasp, but it will be like closing your hands on fog. Better to fight with what you have.'

'We are not enough,' Cathal repeated. 'I hear your words, Donacha, but nothing will change that. We must find more men, with more swords, if we are to defeat the Romans.'

'Then it is decided.' Oenghus came between them. 'We will move north and whatever will be, will be.'

The younger men moved off and Cathal was left looking out over the river to where the spear points twinkled. They would abandon the river and move north. Now was not the time.

*

How long did it take for a man to know he'd made a mistake? In Cathal's case it took less than a week. They marched north in a loose column and each day the Selgovae king would either mark the possibilities for an attack in his mind or seek some way to find a new ally. Possibilities there were aplenty, but certainties – and he needed certainty – there were none. Donacha and Oenghus assured him the people of the high lands were there, watching their every move, but each time Cathal took his sword brothers into the hills all they found was empty huts and glowing embers.

No huts now, for the Selgovae and the Venicones. In the fresh spring air they slept under blankets wherever it was most comfortable or, in the cases of the commanders, in tents. By night Olwyn lay by Cathal's side and she could feel his growing frustration.

'Donacha was right,' he confided in her one morning. 'It is like grasping early morning fog. I must have men, sword bearers, but how can I bring them to me when I cannot even find them?'

She considered his dilemma, in the same sensible, intuitive way she considered everything. 'Perhaps your reputation goes before you even here, Cathal, husband, king. Everywhere you go a hundred men accompany you. These are simple people. Let them see the true Cathal. Strong enough to make his own pacts without a hundred swords at his back.'

Another valley, a deep score in the earth flanked by sheer walls of unyielding grey stone, with a lake running through the centre like a polished iron blade, and fields of sprouting kale and barley hacked from the hard earth along the shore. This time only Gwlym and eight men accompanied the king, the guards' swords sheathed and hidden beneath cloaks. More empty huts and glowing embers, but for once they stayed long after the embers dimmed and went cold. The big Roman horses danced nervously beneath their riders as they waited for what seemed an eternity.

'Over there,' a man hissed.

Cathal looked to where two figures had appeared from what must be a hidden gully further up the valley. As they approached he could see they were tall, spare men, bare-chested, wearing ragged plaid trews or *bracae*. The elder, hawk-nosed and hollow-cheeked, had a mass of wild, unkempt hair that might have been white, but was so matted and caked with filth it was impossible to tell. Faded tattoos of outlandish figures and shapes covered his chest and stomach. His companion had the same predator's features, but his hair and moustaches were the dirty russet colour of a year-old fox pelt, and the tattoos were fresh. They were unarmed apart from a wood-handled knife that hung from a belt of twisted fibre at the younger man's waist. Cathal described them to Gwlym.

'Take me to them,' the priest said, dismounting, and Cathal guided him across the springy turf to meet the pair. The older man snarled what might have been a greeting and revealed a mouth inhabited by two blackened teeth snapped off close to the gums. A conversation followed in a language that at times seemed familiar, punctuated by grimaces and hand signals on the part of the tattooed men. Eventually the druid grunted something and turned to Cathal.

'I believe the elder is called Bruda. He claims to be a king of the Caledonians. The younger is his son, also Bruda, and this,' the pus-filled sockets made a half circuit of their bleak surroundings, 'is his domain. He also claims lordship of three more valleys – he calls them glens – but I am uncertain of the details, because, though their speech is similar to ours, they regurgitate it like a dog vomiting.'

'Did you tell him why we are here?'

'I did.' The druid's thin lips twitched. 'He asks why he would ally himself to a man who comes with fewer warriors than he commands himself, a ragged creature, who, though large, is running to fat.'

An involuntary growl rose in Cathal's throat. The younger man's eyes narrowed at the sound and his hand twitched for the knife. Cathal forced his features into a smile.

'Tell them that I lead an army of twenty thousand warriors.'

'The number would mean nothing to people like these.' Gwlym chortled. 'I told him there would be much gold when our enemies are put to the sword. In reply, he asked me what use was gold, other than to decorate his women and make them fight among themselves even more. Besides, he prefers them naked.'

Cathal shook his head. They were wasting their time. What good would these men be anyway? They could barely feed or clothe themselves. Still, he would not give up yet. 'Have you told him what will happen when the Romans come?'

'Of course,' Gwlym snapped. 'He thinks of them as just another tribe. He likens them to a man who rules over a glen five days' march north of here – it may be more – who sent emissaries announcing himself as the High King of these lands and demanding his loyalty. King Bruda simply killed the messenger and heard no more of it.' Young Bruda growled something to his father. 'The word Roman means something more to him. He is reminding his father of a story he told him when he was young. In the time of King Bruda's father a traveller appeared in the valley seeking the tribe's support.' Gwlym went very still and his tongue flicked out to lick his lips.

'What is it?'

'He told them the spirit of the hare and the horse and the wolf were with them, and would bring down the wrath of Andraste on their enemies. He was a druid.' Gwlym's voice dropped to a whisper. 'A druid of Mona.'

'What happened to him?'

'Bruda is uncertain. He can't remember whether his father fed him and sent him on his way, or, more likely, killed him – in which case I suspect they ate the poor man.'

More warriors filtered from the gully mouth to the west. 'I brought gifts of silver,' Cathal told the druid. 'Is it worth leaving them?'

Gwlym shook his head. 'No. It would not change his mind and he would probably lose them. But Colm has a skin of beer strapped to his saddle he thinks I don't know about. They would appreciate that and it would do no harm.'

'Then give it, with my thanks.' He turned and walked back to his horse.

'Do not despair, Cathal, king of the Selgovae,' Gwlym called. 'Did you learn how to wield a sword in a single day? This is but the start. Olwyn was right that you needed fewer men, but she forgot that you still must be able to project power. Bruda would probably never have joined you, but others may. Yet it is not enough to seek them out in their dozens and their scores. We must find a way to bring them to you in their thousands.'

'And how will I do that?' Cathal demanded. 'Is this a prophecy you give me or the kind of hope that keeps a hunter expecting a deer to appear round every corner of the track?'

'It is neither,' Gwlym said airily. 'But there will be a way. Perhaps if these poor creatures will not listen to a man, they will listen to a god?'

XLIII

A week had passed since the rearguard Cathal left to make a show of defending the line of the Abhainn dhub caught up with the main force and reported that the two legions had crossed and set up camp on the north side. Yet there had been not a word of a further Roman advance.

Once more his mind had spun with the potential disasters the third 'lost' legion might cause to his scattered and, he would be the first to admit, disorganized forces. The war chiefs of the Venicones, while undoubtedly brave, had differing ideas of discipline and their responsibilities to their forces. Most had thought to ensure their people were supplied with spears, at a minimum, though too many men for Cathal's liking carried reaping hooks, woodsmen's axes and even wooden pitchforks. Shields and helmets of bronze or iron were virtually unknown except among the chiefs like Donacha and their personal bodyguards. Food was an abiding problem. It quickly became clear that, apart from the few days' rations they carried with them, the men expected Cathal to provide food, or sanction expeditions into the local countryside to raid farms and homesteads to find it.

Since the families of one of the Venicones sub-tribes that made up Cathal's army invariably occupied the houses and owned the cattle, goats and pigs the raiders sought, he did everything he could to deter these excursions. Fortunately, his Selgovae had stockpiled sufficient seed and dried fish and meat to last them for some weeks, but Emrys and his men didn't hide their reluctance to part with their carefully hoarded supplies to less practical and deserving allies. Cathal knew he had to find an alternative supply soon or his 'army' would begin tearing itself apart.

For the moment, then, the Romans posed a lesser problem than his allies. But for the sake of the plan that had been forming inside his head he couldn't allow his Celts to get too far ahead of the enemy. Two days' march, at most, would be enough, and less if the terrain and the circumstances allowed it. He called a day's rest halt and joined Colm and his men on a patrol back along the route they'd come. He'd made no attempt to hide their tracks, so there was no reason the Romans couldn't follow him. Yet after six hours in the saddle there was still no sign of them, even of their patrols.

When he returned to the Selgovae camp he was puzzled to find Olwyn in Gwlym's shelter and in deep conversation with the druid, and more so when they made a joint appeal for a further day's rest. There was no reason not to, unless the Romans made a sudden, and apparently unlikely, thrust, so he gave his permission. The cause became apparent the next afternoon when Olwyn asked to speak to him. Her request came as such a surprise, given the lack of formality in their relationship.

She came into his tent carrying a basket and, not so surprisingly these days, accompanied by Gwlym. They were followed by Cathal's smith carrying a second, clearly much heavier basket.

'You may leave us, Finngail.' Olwyn dismissed the craftsman when he'd set down his burden. 'But your lord will hear of your part in our doings and no doubt reward you.'

'What is this?' Cathal smiled. 'Have I missed the Imbolc gift-giving this year?'

'It is a gift indeed, lord king.' She didn't return his smile. 'We hope it meets your approval.'

'You may remember that when we met the odious Bruda and his

son,' Gwlym said, 'I mentioned the projection of power? With the help of your good wife, I have been giving the matter some thought. The question was how to make your presence even more imposing without the addition of sheer numbers, which might intimidate those you were attempting to impress. This,' he waved a hand towards Olwyn, who was delving into the heavier basket, 'is our answer.'

She emerged holding a metal helm that glittered silver and gold in her hands. And much more than a helm. Beneath the rim it incorporated a full face mask of silver, a much more subtle representation than the one worn by the Argento Rìgh, and from the flanks a pair of wings the length of a spear point projected vertically to give it a mystical look. 'It is only a Roman cavalry helmet taken as booty in some raid,' Gwlym said dismissively. 'But Finngail took great delight in giving it a coating of silver and adding the accessories. Donacha was happy to part with the Argento's bauble. The whole is modelled on my memory of something similar Boudicca captured at an auxiliary cavalry barracks.'

'You expect me to wear this? To fight in it?'

'Wear it?' Gwlym sounded indignant. 'Of course. But if you wish to fight in it I'd suggest removing the mask – Finngail assures me it is simple enough. It would impair your vision, and I believe the late departed auxiliaries only used them in ceremonial parades.'

'But to what purpose?' Cathal was still confused.

Olwyn grunted as she withdrew a second object from the basket. A massive shirt of linked iron rings large enough to fit even Cathal's great frame and polished so bright that it matched the helmet in brilliance. 'We spoke of the Caledonians not listening to a man,' Gwlym continued. 'But perhaps to a god. Wear this on our next mission to find more allies and no man could doubt your power, no matter how few warriors accompany you.'

'But it's absurd.' Cathal looked from Olwyn to the druid. 'I will look a fool.'

'No, lord king,' Olwyn assured him. 'You will look like Taranis come down from the clouds to lead us to victory.' From the second basket she drew out a cloak of the deepest, darkest green. Cathal recognized the fine wool of her most cherished dress and saw the twin lightning bolts embroidered across the back. 'We will find something similar, though less grand, for your escort to wear, so that they provide a fitting accompaniment to your rank. There is one thing more.' The curtain twitched back and Finngail returned, carrying an enormous sword across his arms. Cathal's heart stuttered as he recognized an exact replica of Ghost Bane, broken fighting the Roman on the frozen Thuaidh. 'I took the liberty, lord king,' the smith said. 'I hope I did right?'

Cathal accepted the sword and swung it so the bright iron blade hissed through the air. His eyes glittered with the sheer joy of it. 'You did right, smith. The gods could not have made finer.'

A week later, Cathal picked his way through another fractured, bog-ridden valley at the head of his bodyguard, with Gwlym at his side. Their route took them along the flank of a great lake dotted with what at first looked like islands, but in reality were houses built on wooden platforms. The occupants watched the little column with suspicious eyes and drew in the plank bridges that connected them to their fields. Herd boys took fright and drove their beasts and skinny sheep away from the approaching riders.

Emrys and Colm had found the valley and the location fitted the flimsy geography supplied by Bruda, but Cathal held out little hope. This was their third expedition in as many days and the new allies he'd attracted numbered barely a score. The flamboyant costume he wore and the power it projected had been a surprising success, but the sparsely populated valleys and their piecemeal rewards made him wonder if it was worth the effort.

Even as the melancholy thought formed, a smudge of smoke at the head of the lake drew his attention and his interest revived. It came from some sort of building complex on a rocky outcrop overlooking the valley, positioned so it resembled the Venicones sanctuary above the crossing of the Abhainn dhub. As they advanced up the lakeside he became aware of a substantial settlement behind a wooden palisade on the lower ground beside the lake.

He exchanged a glance with Emrys. This was very different from what they'd come to expect.

Gwlym must have sensed their interest. 'What is it?' the druid demanded peevishly. Cathal explained what he could see and the priest nodded. 'Yes, that is what Bruda described to me. Perhaps this is the gods' reward for a sore arse and the dullness of your conversation.'

A worn track led through cultivated fields to the gateway of the lower settlement. Cathal's bodyguard tensed as the double doors opened and fifty spearmen emerged to bar their way. Cathal murmured news of this latest development to Gwlym. 'Continue,' the druid said. 'I believe we will be safe enough.'

'I hope you're right,' Cathal grunted as he led the little column forward. 'Whatever happens, no man will draw his sword until he hears my order. Is that understood?'

Emrys led a chorus of agreement.

Yet the closer Cathal came to the waiting men the less he feared a confrontation. The way they stood and the manner in which they held their weapons presented no sign of a threat to a warrior who understood these things. They weren't so much a guard as a guard of honour. Big men, with the tawny thatch that appeared to be the mark of these mountain dwellers, chosen for their stature, and with pride in their bearing. Each warrior carried a seven-foot ash spear and wore plaid shirt and trews, with a bronze torc at his neck that presumably proclaimed some special status. But what truly distinguished them was that, like Cathal's own guard, each man wore an iron sword on a belt at his waist. Their expressions were proud and fierce as hunting wolves and they made Bruda and his son seem like feral dogs by comparison. A barked order confirmed his impressions as the warriors separated to form two lines ahead of him and reveal a delegation of three older men.

Cathal drew to a halt fifteen or so paces short of the waiting elders. He didn't dismount, but used the height advantage to survey his surroundings. Within the enclosure he counted something like seventy heather-thatched, conical roofs, and about a hundred men, women and children drifted from the double gates to stare at the exotic newcomers. The slopes of the closest mountains had been cleared of timber, but those in the distance glowed a bright, verdant green. The hillside to his right rose in a series of walled terraces to a smaller enclosure occupied by the stone buildings he'd originally seen from the lakeside. None of the walls by themselves would stop a determined assault, but the amount of work that had gone into constructing them must have been enormous. Like Cathal's helmet they were an expression of power. Only a man of enormous authority could have persuaded his people to give their time and labour to build this eyrie.

He sensed the three elders approach, but he ignored their presence and continued to stare at the fort on the hill. Instead, Emrys came forward and guided Gwlym to meet them. At first they seemed bemused by the druid's presence, but eventually a conversation developed between Gwlym and the youngest, a tall man with a thick brown beard. Eventually, Emrys escorted the priest back to Cathal.

Gwlym's thin lips were set in what might have been a grimace, but Cathal knew was actually an expression of extreme complacency. 'His name is Rurid and, like Bruda's, these people are known as the Caledonians. Unlike him their king has heard of a mighty warrior whose footsteps make the mountains shake, a sky god whose very voice is enough to draw lightning from the clouds and whose horses are fleeter than the swiftest arrow. He wonders why you have wasted your time among the petty carrion and oath-breakers of the outlands when he is so obviously the man you seek.'

'I assume you replied with suitable subtlety?' For the first time Cathal allowed the dark eyes of the silver mask to drift over the delegation.

'I told him that even a god preferred to test himself against the weak before he approached the strong. I also said you looked forward to dealing with an equal.'

'Good.' Cathal allowed himself a slight nod of acknowledgement towards the three men and they visibly relaxed. 'How much have they learned about why I'm here?'

'They appear to know precisely why you're here.' A troubled frown

298

creased the blind druid's forehead. 'In fact, I have a feeling they've been expecting you for some time.'

Rurid spoke again and Gwlym translated his words. 'He invites you to an audience with his king, if it pleases you to accompany him to his palace on the hill. He apologizes for the inconvenience, but King Crinan is indisposed and never leaves his stronghold, except to walk the walls and survey his lands.'

Cathal's mask hid his grimace of disappointment. He had hoped for an ally who would lead his warriors in battle. If Crinan was so aged and infirm he couldn't leave his house that complicated things. Still, he dismounted and handed his reins to Colm. 'Tell him I will be pleased to make the climb, accompanied by you and three of my guards.'

Gwlym translated the words and Rurid nodded gravely, taking step with Cathal as the escort closed in behind them. A pathway of wooden planks led through the houses and granaries and Cathal noted that the people were well enough fed, and well clothed. Women in brightly coloured dresses spun thread on spindles or worked looms with the finished product. Men, young and old, sharpened and polished unfinished swords and spear points with specially selected stones while they drank from clay pots. The sound of rumbling quern stones added to the familiar background noises, and the scents of cooking and smoke from the perpetually burning hearth fires hung in the air.

The track led to a gateway through the first of three stone walls that held the terraces. Here the clamour of hammer against iron was almost constant and heat blasted from furnaces outside huts built from stone. Blackened, bare-chested men sweated and grunted over glowing bars of metal, massive arm muscles flexing as the hammers rose and fell.

As they climbed, Rurid chattered away in his oddly familiar but, to Cathal, almost entirely incomprehensible tongue while Gwlym translated. 'King Crinan once held extensive lands in the low country,' the druid explained, 'which is their name for the fertile coastal plain. An unfortunate disagreement with an elder brother led to his exile in the mountains. Yet such was Crinan's popularity that many of his people followed him to this valley. He was also able to attract – I believe the proper term may be abduct – the tribe's finest metal workers, who brought with them their extensive contacts amongst those who supply the ingots without which no sword can ever be forged. This is the foundation of King Crinan's prosperity and gives him overlordship over all the tribes of mountain and plain.'

'He controls the trade in weapons in the north?'

'So it appears.'

Cathal looked around thoughtfully as they crossed the third terrace to a stone hut much larger than the others. 'I am beginning to wonder why he provides such a warm welcome for a potential rival,' he said, so quietly that only Gwlym could hear him.

'That had also occurred to me,' Gwlym admitted. 'But I have a sense for these things and I do not feel that Rurid is deceiving us.'

In King Crinan's compound there was no sign of industry and the huts that surrounded the main structure appeared to be occupied solely by warriors. Two of them stood guard at the doorway of the king's house and they stepped aside at a word from Rurid. Cathal ordered his guards to remain where they were and walked inside with Gwlym. It was only natural that the interior of a hut should be part filled with smoke, but the drifting clouds in King Crinan's house obscured almost everything from view and an odd, sweetish scent tickled Cathal's nostrils.

He felt Gwlym's hand on his arm. 'Do not breathe too deeply, lord king,' the druid warned, 'and keep your wits about you.'

Rurid led them forward as if there was nothing unusual about the scene. Gradually, Cathal made out a number of shadowy figures in the smoke. It took a few moments before he realized they were almost entirely female. Flame-haired seemed to be King Crinan's preference, and six of the most beautiful women Cathal had ever seen lay draped across low cots dressed in thin shifts that were as useful as the drifting smoke in covering their attributes. A seventh woman was coiled in the lap of a grey-bearded man of late middle age who sat on a raised throne in the centre of the room. Her shift had slipped from her shoulders and he fondled a round breast with one hand while drinking from a silver cup with the other. Cathal's head spun and he felt an irrational urge to laugh.

For a moment he wondered if it was all a dream. Gwlym's bony fingers sinking into his arm brought him back to reality and he realized Rurid and the king had been speaking. Crinan was staring at him with wide, unblinking eyes.

'King Crinan welcomes you to his palace and offers you his hospitality,' Gwlym announced. 'He has been waiting for you these long years and your appearance surpasses even the description he was given. He honours you as a great warrior and a servant of the old gods. Together you will rid the land of the Red Scourge, of which he has heard so much, but never seen, and your names will be sung in the halls of the great until the end of time.'

Cathal shook his head in an attempt to clear it of a new wave of confusion that had nothing to do with the pungent, sweet-smelling smoke. 'I don't understand. How can—?'

'You have come.' An urgent, high-pitched cry from the far edge of the room. 'I told them you would come, but only the king believed me.' The speaker appeared like a wraith from the smoke. A withered ancient with a wispy fringe of white hair that clung to the back of his bald head like the last snow in the shade of a mountain. Tears flowed from rheumy pink eyes over the cracked, leathery skin of his cheeks. It took a moment for Cathal's reeling mind to understand that, though the words spilled from him like a river in spate, the old man spoke a language perfectly comprehensible to him. 'Twenty winters I have waited for this moment, tending the fires of hope kindled in the halls of Pencerrig by Aymer, high priest of my order.'

Cathal felt Gwlym stiffen at his side. 'What is it?' he whispered.

'He is a druid,' the priest whispered back. 'An emissary sent from Mona in the years before Suetonius Paulinus bathed the sacred isle in blood.' He raised his voice. 'What is your name?'

'I am Amergyn, son of Gluingel. "Carry the word with care, but carry it far," Aymer told me. "When the time is right the gods will send a sign. You will carry the spark and the gods will provide a leader. The wrath of Andraste will rain from the sky . . ." '

'The wrath of Andraste.' Gwlym's voice was filled with puzzled awe. 'Yes, that was it.'

' ". . . the people will rise, and the Red Scourge will be purged from this land for ever." Others like me would rally the tribes of the south, he said, but mine was the most difficult task. The greatest trial. The wild folk of the north must be convinced the Romans were as much a threat to their freedom as to that of every other tribe on this island. Trial indeed,' the old man sighed. 'I was robbed and stripped bare, driven from forest and glen, starved, stoned and enslaved. Time and again I almost lost faith, and time and again I remembered Aymer's words as I walked through the cleansing fire. "The wrath of Andraste lives through you. You must prevail. At the last call on the spirit of the hare, and the horse." Finally I reached this valley and King Crinan listened to my plea. He ordered his priests to make a sacrifice and said his gods supported me. We would wait for the sign. And we have been waiting since.'

'Lord king,' Gwlym said formally, 'remove your mask.'

Cathal still didn't fully understand what was happening, but the druid's voice contained a certainty that couldn't be ignored. He reached up and lifted the silver faceplate on its hinges. Amergyn gasped and Crinan rose unsteadily from his throne. Cathal didn't move as the Caledonian king stepped forward and raised a hand to run his fingers over the tattoo on his left cheek.

'The spirit of the horse,' Amergyn sobbed. 'Truly it is you.'

Crinan began to speak and Amergyn translated his words. 'He will have the war trumpet sounded throughout his realm and summon the war bands to gather here under his banner. Together you will bring the wrath of Andraste down upon the Romans.'

'He will lead them himself?'

Amergyn shook his head. 'The king would tell you that he is too old for war, but the truth is that he has no appetite for battle these days.' His eyes drifted across the flame-haired women. 'His interests lie in other directions. Rurid, a great warrior in his own right, will lead his war bands.'

'Tell them they have my thanks. How many warriors can the Caledonian federation put in the field?'

Amergyn directed the question at Rurid and Cathal saw Gwlym's face freeze at the reply.

'Five thousand,' the blind druid whispered.

'Only five thousand? It is not enough.'

'It must be enough.'

XLIV

The column of Asturian cavalrymen picked their way across the heather-clad hillside, wary eyes constantly searching the heights above and the valley below. Barbarus had set flank guards, and a pair of riders patrolled ahead, but it wouldn't be the first time the Celts picked off an unwary auxiliary and that comforting silhouette on the horizon held an enemy spear rather than a friendly one.

The slope fell away gently on his left to where a narrow river wound through scattered groves of oak and ash. A tranquil, bucolic scene until you noticed the muddy scar and the deep ruts caused by fully laden two-wheeled carts. Those tracks marked the path of an army on the move. Not close, it was true. Barbarus had descended to the valley bottom to check those ruts and they'd been filled to overflowing with rainwater from the soft drizzle that coated his cloak with tiny droplets. That drizzle had been soaking them, on and off, for two full days and Barbarus reckoned it would have taken at least that long for the feeble fall to fill the ruts.

Still, the presence of all those warriors was enough to make a man like Barbarus wary. These hills were gentler by far than the rugged peaks of his home in northern Hispania, but he'd learned from experience that the people who inhabited them were equally tough and, if you pushed them, potentially even more savage.

Sixty troopers made up his command, two squadrons, and like him they were veterans of the wars in Siluria, Ordovicea and Brigantea. If Barbarus had his way there would be a second pair of squadrons on the far hillside for greater security. Better still, the entire wing with a couple of infantry cohorts marching behind them.

He'd never known a more frustrating campaign. Of course, an old soldier like him should never let something like that affect him. Keep the men in good trim, take to the saddle when the orders arrived, fight who you were told, when you were told, and then bed down wrapped in a damp blanket under a few stitched patches of leather. That was his life and he gave thanks for it, aching bones, rusty armour, and all the rest. A few more years and he'd have his citizenship, his diploma and his pension and he'd return to Hispania, never to take another order. But a unit took a lead from its officers, and the legionary commanders in charge of the Twentieth Valeria, the Second Adiutrix and the Ninth Hispana weren't happy.

Barbarus could understand why. By his reckoning this campaign should have been sewn up by this time last year. Yes, the Celts were dangerous, and, individually, brave warriors, but this force of shadows they'd been stalking was made up of half a dozen tribes and dozens more clans, many of them little more than extended families. They weren't an army, they were a rabble.

Mars' arse, the governor had *three* full legions. Just hit them one hard blow and the Celts would fall apart. He'd once seen a pack of lions sent out to hunt a herd of deer in the arena and it hadn't turned out well for the deer. Give the legions just one scent of blood . . . Certainly that was what the rumour mill said the Ninth's legate believed, and he had a lot of time for Gaius Valerius Verrens. No pampered patrician that one, but a proper soldier and with the scars to prove it. A commander who didn't mind getting his hands dirty, and there we't many of them.

The Ninth and the Second had crossed the great morass to discover the enemy vanished apart from a small blocking force that had, in turn, faded away like wisps of summer mist. Verrens had issued orders for an immediate advance and to harry the enemy at every turn, only to receive a command from Julius Agricola to hold his position and wait for the arrival of the Twentieth legion. They'd built a temporary camp on the first high ground at the end of the log roads, and used the time to construct a more permanent fort at the top of the largest rocky outcrop south of the river. Another month of perfect fighting weather passed and not a mile gained or a skirmish fought. He looked up at the sky, trying to gauge the position of the sun through the thick white cloud. How much further should they follow the trail before he turned back to make his report?

'Decurion?' One of the scouts rode up to rein in at Barbarus's side.

'What is it?'

'Something curious. Down in the valley half a mile to the front.'

'I don't like curious.' Barbarus frowned. 'It smells of month-old fish. Tell me?'

'Celts, but they're acting strangely. Best you see for yourself, sir.'

Barbarus halted the patrol and accompanied the scout. They left their horses in the lee of a hill and the man led him to where his comrade lay in the heather watching the valley. Barbarus joined them at the crest and the scout pointed to a clearing in a river bend surrounded by clumps of trees. The Asturian parted the heather and looked down at five Celts, that he could see, and one two-wheeled cart. Unfortunately for the Celts one of the wheels was axle deep in mud and hanging from its mount. Two of the men were stripped naked to the waist and apparently having some kind of wrestling match. The others lay back against a nearby tree, drinking from a skin and urging them to greater effort.

'They've been doing this since I found them,' the first scout said. 'They take turns and seem oblivious of anything around them.'

Barbarus studied the men. Harmless enough, or so it seemed. He was tempted to just bypass them, but the stack of spears leaning against the cart identified them as warriors, and that meant he had to do something. He sent the scouts to bring the patrol forward while he came up with a plan.

'Take ten men,' he told Septimus, his second in command. 'I want at least one prisoner. And see if the cart's repairable. At least we'll have something to show for this waste of time.'

'Why don't we wait until the bastards repair it for us?' the *duplicarius* grumbled.

'Because we haven't got all fornicating day,' Barbarus snapped. 'Get on with it. But be careful.'

He watched Septimus and his men use the contours of the valley to hide their approach. Only when they reached the valley floor and were within plain sight of the wrestling men did the *duplicarius* give the order to charge. With a whooping shout the ten men couched their spears and urged their mounts to a canter over the rough ground. The stream was shallow with low banks and no obstacle and they were across it before the first of the Celts reacted.

Barbarus saw them apparently freeze in horror at the sight of the advancing Asturian cavalry, but there was something that bothered him about the scene. Their first reaction should have been to look towards their spears. Instead they looked to each other. By now, inexperienced in battle or not, they should have been running. Still the little tableau hesitated as the auxiliary spears bore down on them. At last they were moving. So why did Barbarus's breath catch in his throat and the icy iron of a blade slide into his heart? 'No,' he croaked. 'Get out.'

Because instead of running directly away from the cavalry or towards their spears the Celts split like a sunburst, each taking a different direction. From here it was obvious, but all Septimus would see was his prey escaping. He must have called an order because the troopers split into twos, each pair hunting down a separate fugitive.

'To horse.' Barbarus ran to his mount and leapt into the saddle. He drew his sword and urged the horse directly down the slope, not waiting to see if his men heard his command.

To where Septimus's men were being slaughtered. Their killers rose out of the landscape like so many wraiths. They timed their appearance perfectly as each pair of Asturians bore down on the fleeing Celt who was luring him into a trap. Suddenly the hunters faced five or six enemies, their long spears reaching out for the men in the saddles. A horse reared, throwing its rider. The man rolled clear, drawing his long cavalry *spatha*, but before he could gain his feet his enemies closed in and the spears rose and fell until he went still.

Septimus's quarry had run for the far end of the clearing and he must have missed his course because Septimus was able to spear one of his ambushers and ram another aside to reach safety. He spun the horse and Barbarus willed his friend to climb the slope. But Septimus must have heard a call for help. Instead of riding towards safety he drew his sword and urged his horse back into the skirmish.

By now the thunder of hooves rumbled in Barbarus's ears as his men closed in behind him and he concentrated on the slope ahead. He knew this headlong rescue attempt contained an element of risk, but the Asturians still outnumbered their enemy by two to one and he would not abandon men he had fought beside for ten and twenty years. With Fortuna's favour the very sight of the new wave of attackers would drive the Celts away. If not, they would die.

Barbarus looked up to see two or three little groups still battling among the trees, proof that some at least were still alive. The man Septimus had tried to save must be dead, because the *duplicarius* was spurring his way across the clearing towards the slope, waving his sword. Barbarus could see his mouth opening and closing, but he could hear nothing. Suddenly the ground fell away and the air misted around him as he urged his horse across the stream. The Asturian battle cry was keening in his throat as he climbed the far bank, seeking out the closest target. Septimus's horse drove across his front and Barabus saw blood sheeting its flank from a gaping wound in the *duplicarius*'s thigh.

'Get out,' the other man screamed as he passed. 'Get out while you still can.'

Too late now, old friend, Barabus thought, driving his mount at a pair of Celts stabbing at a man on the ground. But Septimus's warning sent a knife point of alarm scoring across the inside of his skull. Why would he be urging flight when they outnumbered the enemy?

A great cry from all around gave him his answer as half-naked, tattooed Celts swarmed from the woods in their hundreds. The original trap had only been the bait for a greater prey.

And he was that prey.

Barbarus smashed his horse through a seething knot of the enemy, ignoring the spear points and the grasping hands, hacking down at exposed heads to expose bone and brain. He experienced a moment of fierce exhilaration before something hammered into his side and sent a great dagger of fire deep into his vitals. He shrieked with the agony of it and reeled in the saddle, vaguely aware of his command dying around him. A spear point tore his cheek and the vision of his left eye turned red. His half world spun, then shook, and he was looking up at the sky through a patchwork of branches and leaves.

Oddly, though his entire body had gone numb he could feel the soft drizzle on his skin and something that might have been a tear rolling down his cheek. A figure appeared in his line of vision and he was disappointed he could no longer see the sky. The man was massively built with fierce, hawkish features and a pair of rearing horses tattooed on his cheeks.

'Do we have them all?' Cathal asked Donacha, who had commanded the ambush.

Barbarus didn't understand the words, but he was experienced enough to know their import. Suddenly it seemed more important than ever to be able to see the sky.

'Yes, lord king.'

'Then finish them.' His attention turned to the body lying twitching at his feet. Barbarus's single eye saw the hammer raised and the glitter of gold as it fell. 'You know what must be done?' Donacha nodded.

Cathal registered the distaste in the young Venicones's face, but there was no help for it. This had been the entire reason for the deaths of these men. To flinch from it now would be to insult their memory.

'Then do it.'

*

309

'These people are beasts,' Gnaeus Julius Agricola spat in disgust.

Valerius studied the yellowing features of the head on the stake and tried to put a name to it, but the great dent in the forehead and other damage had altered the face so comprehensively it eluded him. Agricola had insisted on accompanying the cohort sent out to search for the overdue patrol.

'They're trying to provoke us.'

'And I am provoked,' the governor snapped, his face drawn and strained. 'What is it now? The heads, limbs and other parts of thirty of my men, staked out like meat on a butcher's counter.'

Valerius might have said he'd seen worse. That the Asturians might not be dead if Agricola had sent in much stronger patrols of cavalry backed by infantry as he'd suggested, but he kept his silence.

'We will continue,' Agricola said.

They followed the valley for another mile as it became narrower and deeper, picking up more remains along the way. Valerius saw the governor glancing at the surrounding peaks and the narrow gully ahead. In another man he would have suspected that what he saw in the grey eyes was fear. Eventually Agricola halted the column. 'They want to draw us in there. To destroy us.'

'Of course.' Valerius kept the frustration from his voice. 'But it means they're here. Not a mile ahead if the scouts are to be believed. Bring up a cavalry wing to flank them and another two cohorts to smash them. This is when we should show our courage and our power.'

Agricola flinched and Valerius knew he'd gone too far.

It had been like this ever since the governor had turned up with the Twentieth at the camp by the river crossing. Valerius had urged him to use every man they had to hound the retreating Celts like a pack of wolves.

'This is a coalition of barbarian tribes and the only thing that holds them together is their hatred and their fear of us. They do not have our strength, our discipline or our stamina, but most of all they do not have our supply lines. If they are running they can't forage and if they can't forage they can't eat.'

310

But Agricola looked at the jagged peaks on the far horizon and saw a hundred rat holes where the enemy could emerge to attack his rear or disrupt the supply route from the forts on the river estuaries. Before he would move every one of those rat holes must be stopped or at least checked. That meant cohort-sized forces moving warily into mountain passes where there was no sign any enemy had ever been. Watchtowers that never saw a warrior, and men spending their days digging when they should have been marching.

'Are you insinuating I am a coward, legate?' Fury made Agricola's voice quiver with emotion. 'Your insubordination in these last few months has gone beyond all restraint. You are not governor of Britannia yet, Gaius Valerius Verrens. You make too much of your friendship with the Emperor, but do not forget that Titus is soldier enough to allow a commander to administer his own discipline.'

'I make no such insinuation, proconsul.' So Agricola knew about Titus's offer. What else did he know? 'All I am suggesting is that we use the advantages we have to pursue the Celts into their heartland. They cannot run for ever. Eventually they must fight us and then we will crush them.'

'No,' Agricola snapped. 'Look at these valleys. You would have me become another Varus. You would destroy my name and my reputation. I will not lose my eagles.' His voice grew shriller and his eyes blazed fire. 'I knew it the moment you arrived in Britannia, Gaius Valerius Verrens. You were sent here to undermine me, like the disloyal worm you are.'

Valerius tensed, but someone laid a hand gently on his arm. 'Valerius!' Quintus Naso hissed.

Agricola looked from one man to the other and his anger faded, to be replaced by a look of calculation. 'You may thank your camp prefect for saving you, Valerius. Had you raised your hand against a proconsul of Rome your life would have been forfeit, legate or no. We will say no more of this for now. The Ninth,' he laced the title with contempt, 'will carry out punitive actions against every settlement and household within a day's march from this place. You will burn every house, confiscate all food stocks and animals, and take a single male from each as hostage.'

'These people have nothing to do with what happened here.' Valerius ignored Naso's warning look. 'They have already been plundered by Calgacus's warriors. They might be able to rebuild their homes before winter, but if we take their food they and their children will starve. They'll have a choice of begging outside our forts or joining the enemy.'

'You try my patience at your peril, Valerius, but for the sake of our former friendship I will explain. I *wish* to drive them to Calgacus, where they will help deplete what food he has and so quicken his army's disintegration. When their warriors begin to starve, the chiefs and kings who follow him will come to me on their knees begging to ally themselves to Rome.'

'But—'

'Enough of this,' the governor snarled. 'You will return to your legion or you will have no legion.'

XLV

Heat scorched Valerius's skin and he moved his horse a little further away from the flames. The scent of woodsmoke and burning thatch clogged his nostrils.

'I think he's gone mad,' Quintus Naso said. 'These people are not our enemy.'

Valerius looked past the camp prefect towards the huddle of women, children and elders standing in the mud staring in bewilderment as the sparks rose into the afternoon sky from their burning homes.

Against Agricola's instructions he'd allowed them to collect what treasures they could from the houses before the legionaries set their flickering torches to the dusty thatch. Their granaries and cattle remained untouched. Of course, they remained unaware of this potentially dangerous generosity and not all their attention was on the flames. Some of them directed their hatred towards the two officers as they sat unmoving, watching the scene unfold. Valerius had purposely dressed in his full ceremonial uniform: sculpted breastplate, scarlet cloak, legate's sash and all the other paraphernalia of his office. Gaius Valerius Verrens had given the orders for this and he wanted his men to know that he accepted his responsibility.

Normally, a legionary took great delight in burning things. Along with the scatological horseplay that substituted for humour, and the occasional illicit game of dice, it passed as entertainment in a world otherwise characterized by relentless marches, dull food, constant polishing and brutal discipline. But today, and all the many other days the Ninth had been allocated punishment patrols, there was none of the laughter and childish delight in how high the flames would soar and the way the sparks made strange patterns against the sky. Instead, they went about their tasks with slow, bovine reluctance that the centurions and decurions did little to counter. They knew that a few days before, the people whose lives they were destroying had been cheerfully trading and bartering with the legionary forage parties sent out to supplement their monotonous rations.

It was always the civilians who suffered, even when their aid for the enemy was reluctant, or in this case imaginary. The ambush that claimed Barbarus was the first of many. Small attacks and feints against Roman patrols became a constant feature of the march. Agricola's answer was to build forts to block the rat holes and more watchtowers to spot the rats, but every fort and every watchtower had to be manned and the legions' auxiliary support dwindled. And each loss must have its reprisal. Men wondered why they were being used to impoverish helpless civilians instead of attacking the enemy. Valerius asked himself the same question.

'Not mad,' he acknowledged eventually. 'Changed. His wife has never recovered from the birth of their son. Perhaps she never will. He receives weekly updates on her condition.' Valerius knew this because Tabitha sent him the same information by a different route. Domitia Decidiana's physical scars might have healed, but her mind was broken in some way. It might have been different if their son had been healthy, but he was a sickly baby who showed few signs of interest in the world. 'He feels betrayed by the gods and I believe he does not wish to give them the opportunity to betray him further. He fears Calgacus, perhaps rightly so, but he fears the ignominy of losing an eagle much more.'

'So we play dodge the shadow while the Celts laugh at us.' Naso shook his head in disgust.

'These Celts aren't laughing.' Valerius nodded towards the homeless families.

'No. The next Roman who passes this way won't be offered a cup of beer as I was last week. More likely he'll get a reaping knife in his throat. If only . . .'

'What?'

'That thing he said about you not being governor of Britannia yet.' Naso hesitated. 'Is it a possibility?'

Valerius took his time before replying. 'The Emperor has hinted at it,' he admitted.

'I think your fellow legates would welcome a change of leadership.' Naso held Valerius's gaze and his words contained an unspoken suggestion.

Valerius put out his left hand to grip the other man's arm. 'Let me tell you something, Quintus. Gnaeus Julius Agricola is my commander and the proconsul of Britannia. As long as he is physically capable of command I will follow his orders to the best of my ability and I will not tolerate any suggestion of mutiny. Do you understand?'

'Sir.' Naso slapped his fist to his chest in salute.

'Then let us march these men back to camp,' Valerius softened his words with a smile, 'wash the stink of this smoke from our throats with a cup of wine, and look forward to the day when we return to proper soldiering.'

XLVI

'The Emperor is dead.'

The words fluttered erratically around Valerius's head like a stricken butterfly, but their import was lost somewhere in the void that separated him from Gnaeus Julius Agricola. Yet he must have understood at some level because his heart seemed to stop and if he hadn't been seated he would have slipped to the floor because the power drained like water from his legs. A dream, surely? An echo of Agricola's announcement just two short years earlier that had heralded Titus Flavius Vespasian the younger to the throne of the Empire. But he had heard Ursus and Polio gasp, and there they sat on their couches with the same incredulous look of horror on their blunt features.

His head filled with that honest, handsome face, not, as he'd last seen Titus, filled out with the flesh of good living after years on the Palatine, but as it had been the first day they met. Hawkish and lean, the face of a commander of auxiliary cavalry, intelligent grey eyes and strong, angular features. Valerius had been burned black, eyes swollen almost shut and throat filled with sand, the result of two weeks under the Egyptian sun after a shipwreck. Only the most fortunate of coincidences had saved his life, and the man who saved him was Titus Flavius Vespasian.

They'd discovered they were of an age and they'd both served in Britannia, Valerius during Boudicca's rebellion and Titus during the bloody aftermath. Their fates should have diverged, never to come together again. Titus was the son of a general, one of Nero's favourites, and whatever rank Valerius held was only by the crazed emperor's sanction. Yet the bond they forged on the ride to Alexandria had endured and developed into a true friendship. Titus had saved his life again during the civil war they called the Year of the Four Emperors. Valerius had fought beside him in Judaea and helped pave the way for the destruction of Jerusalem. When Vespasian became Emperor that service had brought Valerius access, influence and riches, and he had served Vespasian as faithfully as he had the son.

Now Titus was gone. His friend. His emperor.

Agricola had called his generals together that morning after the arrival of an Imperial courier. They'd expected the summons to herald a change in policy. A directive from Rome to take the battle to the enemy after a long campaign season of frustrating delays and the pointless impoverishment of any civilian within reach. The instant he'd entered the tent Valerius had known something was wrong.

His mind registered more information. Titus had been taken ill during the rituals to celebrate his father's rise to divinity. Everything had been done, but his doctors had been unable to save him. He'd died on the Ides of September.

'Naturally, I must travel to Rome for the funeral and the mourning ceremonies,' Agricola went on. 'The Emperor's brother has declared a hundred days of mourning. We will suspend operations against the Celts immediately and resume the offensive in the spring. Twentieth Valeria and Second Adiutrix will withdraw and move into winter quarters south of the river. However, we must maintain a bridgehead and that,' he turned to Valerius, 'will be the task of the Ninth.'

Valerius nodded distractedly, but his mind was elsewhere. 'The Emperor had not named an heir.' The statement contained an obvious question.

'No.' A calculating look accompanied Agricola's answer. 'Titus Flavius

Domitianus has taken over his brother's responsibilities, but the courier would not speculate on whether he has the support of the Senate and the army. That is another reason I will be travelling to Rome. Depending on who emerges as Emperor, this could change everything. In the meantime, you, Valerius will return to Londinium to supervise the mourning rituals and take over my responsibilities as governor. You have the experience of Vespasian's ceremonies. A replication will do well enough. I know he was your friend, but that means nothing now. Can I depend on you?'

'Of course, governor.' Valerius wondered why Agricola should be treating him with such deference if he was aware of Domitian's enmity. A man could doubt the governor's generalship over the past campaign, but never his political acumen. Had there, after all, been some hint from the courier that a rival existed who would keep Domitian from the purple? It was possible. The younger brother was not half the man Titus had been. He had neither wealth nor the experience of high office; his father and brother had seen to that. His only qualification was his bloodline. Then again, could it be a ruse to separate Valerius from his legion? Much easier and more discreet for Domitian to rid himself of the man he hated in Londinium than at the centre of five thousand men who revered him.

For one thing was certain. The moment the Senate and people of Rome proclaimed Titus Flavius Domitianus Emperor, Gaius Valerius Verrens was a dead man. As dead as his old friend Titus.

At least in Londinium he would be in a position to protect his family and decide what was best for them. Whatever that was. With Titus on the throne Valerius's future had been assured, a province and the consulship within his grasp. Now all that had been snatched away. Only a few hours earlier he'd been worrying about Titus's plan to make Lucius his heir. Thank all the gods the Emperor had never made his wishes public. Domitian's first instinct would be to rid himself of any potential rival. Yet that might give Valerius a precious breathing space. Domitian hated him, but he was no threat to his power. Unless . . .

He stared at Agricola and a rush of possibilities galloped through his mind. The moment the governor stepped on board the ship that would carry him to Gesoriacum, Gaius Valerius Verrens would have command of Britannia's legions. Boundless opportunities were open to a man with three legions and effective control of the province. Such a man would face no centralized political opposition. Withdraw south and consolidate his strength close to the capital and he would have the beating heart of Britannia in his grip. All the power rested in the hands of the bureaucracy and the military. The pen must always bow before the sword. A new procurator. A subtle offer of limited devolved power for the tribal chiefs and an assurance that all their taxes would be spent in Britannia rather than funding armies on the Rhenus and Danuvius frontiers. Rome would take time to react. The new emperor would have to withdraw legions from Germania and Dacia, where the wild tribes of the east would certainly take the opportunity to make mischief. How long would he have before they came for him? A year? Two? Two years of life for Tabitha, Lucius and Olivia. And then?

He looked across to Polio, who gave him a nod of reassurance. Not so long ago the legate of the Second Adiutrix had advised Valerius to oust Agricola and take over the northern campaign. But that had been when his patron was on the throne. What Valerius was considering amounted to open rebellion against Rome.

If they wouldn't support him he would have to kill Polio and Ursus and replace them with ambitious young men from his own legion. Their faces ran through his mind. Whom could he trust? Did he have the iron it needed to plunge his sword into a friend's chest? It occurred to him that this was the dilemma Corbulo had faced after he lost Nero's confidence. The difference was that Corbulo's own officers had urged him to create an independent kingdom in the east. The general had fallen on his own sword rather than betray the code by which he'd lived his life. A *Corbulo does not have the luxury of choice – only duty.*

Valerius had tried to live his life by the same code, but now he was considering a path of disloyalty and rebellion against the Empire he'd served all his life.

Yet he couldn't discount it. He couldn't discount anything that would change the certain fate that awaited him when Domitian donned the purple.

And what was the alternative? Flight? Yes, there would be a short opportunity when he could use his power to charter a ship. Perhaps the means were already at hand. Tabitha had immediately recognized that the only place they would have any certainty of survival was in the east in Emesa, where her uncle, King Sohaemus, would offer a welcome and a place of sanctuary.

'Valerius?' The voice was Polio's.

'My apologies, legate. My mind was elsewhere.'

'I was suggesting to the governor that instead of withdrawing immediately, we use the last few weeks of the season to try to corner Calgacus and his forces and destroy them. One all-out effort with every man we have. I hope I have your support?'

Valerius looked at Agricola, but the stolid face gave him no clue to the governor's reaction to the suggestion. Polio's idea had merit. Even if they didn't succeed in forcing Calgacus to battle, the legionaries would be pleased to be on the attack again, especially given that they would soon be withdrawing and giving up hard-earned ground.

'No.' He shook his head and Polio exchanged a furious glance with Ursus, who must have endorsed the strategy. 'I believe it could be construed as a slur on the Emperor's memory. All Calgacus would do is continue to draw us into the passes as he has done all summer. We'd lose more men, and to what end?'

'Thank you, Valerius,' Agricola said. 'I think that will be all, gentlemen. Valerius, we should discuss the Emperor's mourning ceremonies.'

Polio and Ursus left the tent, Polio with a look that told Valerius he'd forfeited any chance of future cooperation. The governor picked up an odd-looking silver dice box Valerius recognized from an earlier encounter and rang the tiny silver bell, looking thoughtful.

'We have had our differences, Valerius. There is no denying it. I may have overstated things when I accused you of disloyalty, but despite that I believe I would have had every right to dismiss you. Now you no longer have Titus's support, that is doubly the case.'

Valerius stiffened at the slight, but he knew he had to be careful what he said and how he said it. 'I have always said that if you do not believe I can be of service to you I would be happy to return to my estates. It was never my intention to question your authority, but a senior officer has a duty to question a strategy he believes to be . . . misguided.'

'You believe me too careful, I remember. Yet you cautioned Polio for his over-enthusiasm only a few minutes ago. I do not believe he appreciated it, but I was grateful for your support. Why?'

'There isn't enough time to achieve what he plans and our forces are depleted by the garrisons we've been forced to leave behind. It makes more sense to advance in the spring with a full complement of auxiliaries. I suggest stripping the southern forts of all but their most essential soldiers and bringing them north next year. As I have said before, Calgacus can't keep running for ever.'

'Let us hope not,' Agricola said. 'But they always seem to have another rat hole to retire to. One of the reasons I hesitate is that I wonder just how many Celts they hide. Perhaps Calgacus is only showing us a fraction of his forces?'

Valerius had a thought. 'Let me send Rufus into the mountains to see if he can ease your fears.'

'The midget?'

'There's no one more capable. By the spring we'll know exactly what is hiding behind all those jagged peaks.'

'If he survives.'

'Rufus will survive.'

'And Calgacus will stop running.' The governor smiled. 'And next year we will crack him like a snail shell beneath a wagon wheel.'

XLVII

Rome

It had all gone perfectly.

Titus Flavius Domitianus lay back on the golden throne and allowed his gaze to drift over the crowd in the great marble-columned receiving room. Soldiers of his personal guard lined the walls, hands ready on sword hilts. Their presence made the waiting supplicants nervous and he enjoyed seeking out the individual signs of fear. A flickering eye, a nervous shuffle of feet, hands clenched tight to stop them shaking, droplets of sweat snaking down a fat man's cheek. This was power.

They said he had assumed the purple even before Titus was dead, but that wasn't true. He had watched his brother die; every agonized twitch and stifled groan. Heard the rasping final breath and waited till the hollow cheeks turned grey. Only then did he hurry to the Castra Praetoria carrying the usual gifts. He had already prepared the ground. The right officers had been bribed – none of them would survive the year; a man who could be bribed once could be bribed twice – and rumours had been spread that his father had made him joint heir, only for Titus to astutely rewrite the will. They had loved and revered his father and his brother. Not a man had hesitated to proclaim him Emperor.

'Advance, Gaius Tulius Glabro.'

A corpulent young man in an ill-fitting toga pushed his way through the crowd and stood in front of the dais, where two of Domitian's more savage-looking bodyguards awaited the Emperor's orders. Glabro eyed the men nervously and licked his plump lips.

'State your petition,' Domitian's scribe ordered.

Glabro cleared his throat. 'My uncle Julianus held the monopoly for the import of leather goods from Hispania until he was sadly lost at sea in the consulship of Paullus and Montianus. His wife's cousin, who had worked for him, took over the business. I seek to have the monopoly returned to my family.'

Domitian crooked a finger at his scribe and the man came to stand next to the throne.

'Does the wife's cousin have any influence, Abascantus?' the Emperor asked quietly.

The scribe shook his head.

'We are minded to grant your request,' Domitian said. 'Remembering that your father was a great support to my divine brother.' Glabro's eyes widened, making him look like a startled squirrel. The Emperor had just made him rich. In truth it had been the wife's cousin who had run the business while Glabro's uncle spent the profits. He barely noticed that Domitian was still speaking. 'But first I have a task for you to complete. Our games have grown dull and lacking in excitement. I lay upon you the burden of finding a new and exotic supply of animals for the arena.' Domitian smiled at the stupefied expression on the young man's face. Glabro was notoriously lazy as well as notoriously greedy. The idea of the fat barrel of lard sweating in some far-off desert or crawling through a snake-infested jungle in search of some mythical beast amused him. 'When you return in triumph we will discuss the Hispania monopoly more fully.'

He truly believed he had been born to be Emperor. All a man had to be was decisive. Make a decision and others would carry it out. The problem, of course, was deciding whom to trust.

The audience continued until he tired of it and passed a hidden signal to Abascantus. Guards cleared the room and left Domitian alone with his scribe.

'Bring me the parchment we were working on yesterday.'

Abascantus bowed as low as his great age would allow and backed out of the room with proper deference. He was a Greek freedman who had been in Domitian's household for years, and he knew all of his master's secrets. In time that might present an interesting dilemma, but for the moment he was too useful to discard. Naturally, Domitian couldn't allow him to know that and it suited him to keep Abascantus on edge.

The scribe returned a few minutes later carrying a large scroll and accompanied by two more servants, one with a portable writing desk and chair, and the other clutching writing materials. The men set out the desk with the styli and ink and the Greek handed Domitian the scroll.

'You have more names to add, Master and God?' *Dominus et Deus*. It had an almost poetic ring to it. So much more dignified than mere Caesar, or Augustus; men of great fame, true, but only men after all.

'Not for the moment, Abascantus. I merely wish to remind myself of the names already fixed.'

Abascantus unfurled the scroll and flattened the upper part on the desk using small metal weights designed for the purpose.

'You may withdraw. But summon the Augusta to join me.' Domitian saw a look that might have been alarm cross the scribe's bland features. Good to know he could still surprise a man whose life depended on his absolute discretion.

Domitian stepped down from the throne to study the list, putting a face to each name where possible and the reason for its inclusion.

The door opened and he looked up as Domitia Augusta walked across the marble floor. Slim and lithe, she moved with all the grace of a fawn. Even after ten years of marriage her beauty still moved him. He had wanted her from the moment he first laid eyes on her. Gaius Valerius Verrens had stood in his way. Domitian had won the contest, though the final act of that drama had still to be played. The fact that she hated him only added to his sense of power over her.

'You wished to talk to me, Caesar?'

He smiled. It was her conceit never to call him Master and God and his that he was pleased to allow her this one small victory.

'I have compiled a short list of those who have offended me or caused me hurt in some way,' he said. 'I thought you might look over it to see if you wished to add any further names.'

Domitia looked towards the scroll uncoiling from the table. 'It seems very extensive,' she replied with a tight smile. 'I am sure you won't have neglected anyone.'

'You don't seem surprised?'

'The only surprise is that you have taken so long. You are not a man to forget a slight.'

'No.' He laughed, instantly regretting the high-pitched squeak. 'Nevertheless, I insist you admire my handiwork.'

She stared at him. For a moment he thought she might refuse, but eventually she walked to the desk and looked down at the twin columns of names. He studied her closely to see her reaction when she found her own, but she disappointed him.

'It *is* very extensive.' Domitia's voice betrayed no emotion. She'd known her name would be there; the only surprise was that it didn't head the list. Another name had sent a shock through her, but of course he would be marked for retribution. 'The Senate will have difficulty conducting any business after all these losses. But what has poor old Arrecinius Clemens done to merit inclusion? Surely he is one of your favourites? What will you do without his tittle-tattle from the brothels?'

'He no longer amuses me, and he was heard to tell a scurrilous lie about me.'

'Poor Arrecinius. One story too many. What do you have planned for them?'

Again, no acknowledgement that she was included. He didn't know whether to be annoyed or impressed. 'Oh, I will think up suitable punishments to suit their crimes.' He held her gaze. 'But first I will let them believe they are safe and that I have no interest in them. Some, I will raise higher, so that their fall becomes even more painful. The fortunate will be exiled. The unfortunate . . .'

'Then we understand each other, Caesar.'

'I believe we always have, Augusta. You will come to my bed tonight.'

It was a command, not a suggestion, but she'd long understood he used their couplings as a form of punishment. She turned back to the list. 'Don't tell me you have already worn out the little Illyrian concubine you added to your stable only last week?'

Domitian moved in behind her, so she could feel the extent of his arousal against her buttocks. His hands moved to her breasts, squeezing and fondling, but she didn't respond.

'Selva is an accomplished bed wrestler, but her athletic antics pale into insignificance beside the pleasure I take from overcoming your reluctance. You feign unwillingness, but your base instincts betray you. Every squeal and every moan is a just reward for my efforts.'

It never occurred to him that every squeal and every moan was part of a performance designed to ensure her ordeal was kept as brief as possible. She stepped out of his grasp. 'I am your wife, Caesar. I know my duty.'

'Very well, you may leave me.' He turned back to the list and she left the room as Abascantus entered, exchanging a look that would have seen them in pieces on the Gemonian Stairs had Domitian observed it. The Emperor's eyes slipped down the list until he found the name he wanted. Domitia would have spotted it too, and for all her cool aloofness he understood the effect it would have had on her. Someone had to be first. Should he? It was so tempting. But would it be more satisfying to allow Gaius Valerius Verrens to live for a time in the knowledge that any moment could bring the sting of the knife and every sip of wine or bite of food herald agonizing death? It required some consideration.

'Summon Gnaeus Julius Agricola, proconsul of Britannia.'

Domitia went directly from her audience with the Emperor to the Palatine gardens. She found the cool shade of the cypress trees helped slow her heartbeat and calm her mind after such encounters. Soon she would have to find a new sanctuary, because Domitian had announced plans to double the size of the palace and these trees would be replaced by marble columns. A sturdy figure stepped out of the shadows to meet her.

'So you came?'

'How could one ignore such an intriguing missive from such a formidable lady?' Flavius Josephus took step beside her a few decorous paces away.

'You were discreet, I hope?'

'The only reason I am still alive is that I can conjure up the power of invisibility at will,' the Judaean said with mock gravity.

'Then a man with such powers would know that the Emperor has recently compiled a list of his enemies.'

'A man with such powers would be surprised if he had not.'

'And he would know that his name appeared on that list, along with a certain formidable lady's.'

Josephus stopped and bent to admire a flower, but she could see her information had shocked him.

'That would be most unfortunate.' He straightened, the swarthy features a little paler than before. 'I have come to be rather fond of Rome. And of life.' He studied her, waiting for more information, and as the silence lengthened he began to understand why he was here. 'Is it possible there is a way in which this mistake could be rectified?'

'You are a man who understands the value of information.' She ignored his question. 'I have certain information that might alter the make-up of the list. But information is not enough. It must be backed by irrefutable proof, and the subtlety and strength to use that proof in the most effective way. On the morning the Emperor Titus died, a servant failed to turn up for work. He has not been seen since.' For a moment Josephus thought his heart might stop. This was ground more dangerous than he'd ever trodden. Only the fact that his name on the list already condemned him kept him from walking away. He had heard the rumours; whispers of some extract of fish.

'It is likely this man is dead.'

'Then why would the Emperor's spies be seeking him in all his old haunts and questioning those who know him?'

'Because he does not wish to be found.'

'You will find him, Flavius Josephus.' Her voice took on an iron hardness. 'Because if you do not you will die. He is a Judaean and you have sources of information at every level of Judaean society in Rome.'

'And what do I do if . . . when I find him.'

'You may leave that to me.'

She turned and walked away, knowing that he would do her bidding. If any man could find the missing servant it was Joseph Ben Mahtityahu. Odd that a person of such obvious intelligence should be so steeped in intrigue and conspiracy that it never occurred to him that his name might not be on Domitian's list at all.

XLVIII

Londinium, April AD 82

Why was he still alive? The question dominated Valerius's thoughts as he waited impatiently in the anteroom for his audience with Gnaeus Julius Agricola. When Domitian had been confirmed Emperor Valerius had spent every waking moment anticipating the dread tramp of feet that would bring the executioners to his door. At times he would lie in bed drenched in a cold sweat as he imagined, not his own death, but those of Tabitha, Lucius and perhaps even little Olivia.

Yet gradually, with Tabitha's help, he'd found he was able to live with the shadow of impending death.

'Titus deserves your best,' she'd insisted with that strength which had sustained him so often. 'Give him it. Domitian would be insulting his brother's memory if he killed the man tasked with organizing his mourning ceremonies. This early in his reign he cannot afford to do anything that would alienate the army or the mob. We are safe for now.'

Everything was in place for their escape. He'd suggested that she take the children and flee east without him, but her reply had been the vow she'd made on their wedding day. '*Quando tu Gaius, ego Gaia.*

329

We were one from the moment we met, Gaius Valerius Verrens. We are one now. And we will be one the day we die.'

Seven months later the threat was little more than a dull ache at the base of his skull. Perhaps he was deluding himself and the Emperor had forgotten him. Domitian had certainly been busy in the early months of his reign. Agricola, who had only now arrived back from Rome, had waited months for a decision on the continuation of the northern campaign. His official letters reeked of frustration and suggested Domitian was more interested in Germania and Dacia than a province he apparently regarded as little more than a backwater.

Since his return three days earlier the governor had spent his entire time with his wife and son. Valerius felt sympathy for the man. Domitia's mental state had improved dramatically, but the baby's health continued to trouble the *medicus* who treated him. According to Tabitha he showed few of the natural signs of development for a child of his age.

'The governor will see you now, legate.' Valerius looked up into the mocking grey eyes of Agricola's aide, Metilius Aprilis. Their paths had crossed often in the time the governor had been detained in Rome. Valerius had sensed a change in the younger man's attitude since Titus's death. He'd been businesslike enough in their dealings, but nothing could disguise a hint of superiority on the thin lips. With his friend gone Valerius's authority was diminished and Aprilis was happy to let him know he knew it.

Valerius followed Aprilis into the governor's office, where Agricola waited at his desk. Agricola nodded a welcome and waved a hand to dismiss Aprilis. As Valerius took his seat on a couch by the window overlooking the Tamesa, Agricola studied a sheet of parchment. The dark hair was peppered with more grey than Valerius remembered and his flesh had a pallid, unhealthy appearance. When he looked up the Ninth's legate would have said the proconsul appeared a decade older than his forty-one years.

Agricola cleared his throat. 'The Emperor is pleased to allow us to continue our campaigns in the north,' he said. 'But he looks for a speedy and successful outcome. That should please you, Valerius. I know you had doubts about my strategy.'

'I'm happy that the campaign is to continue, sir. As always, whatever you propose will have the full support of the Ninth legion.'

Agricola's head came up. 'But not the full Ninth legion.'

Valerius froze. What was going on? 'I don't understand, governor.'

'No? I thought I'd made it clear in my letters that the Emperor intends a campaign to subdue the tribes of the Upper Rhenus and Danuvius. In fact, he told me he based those plans on a report prepared for his father by no less an authority than Gaius Valerius Verrens.'

Valerius frowned, remembering the discussions he'd had with officials in Augusta Raurica and Moguntiacum on the way to Britannia. Vespasian had asked him to check on the morale and discipline of the frontier legions. He'd found them in good condition, but the governor of the Upper Rhenus had championed an advance across the river to bring the local tribes under Roman control. Vespasian had carried out limited actions as a result of the information, but it seemed his surviving son would do more.

'I'm honoured.' He tried to inject some enthusiasm into the words.

'Don't be,' Agricola snapped. 'His intervention makes it all the more difficult for us to achieve victory. To ensure the success of the German campaign Emperor Domitian is stripping my legions of troops. He has ordered the transfer of most of my auxiliary infantry.'

'But—'

The governor held up a hand. 'That is not all. He commands that they be joined by vexillations from all four legions. Adiutrix, Augusta and the Twentieth Valeria will each supply two cohorts. The Ninth, in which he appears to take a special interest, will supply four cohorts.'

'That's almost half my legion,' Valerius protested.

Agricola's voice took on a mocking tone. 'The Emperor has graciously allowed us to make up the numbers by recruiting new auxiliary cohorts from within Britannia.'

'Untrained, ill-disciplined barbarians.' Valerius knew Agricola was perfectly aware of what he was saying. 'And when we do train them they'll be an even greater danger to the province. Has he forgotten what happened when Vitellius used our Batavians to garrison their homeland? Two years of rebellion and four legions consigned to oblivion.'

'I believe the Emperor is aware of that fact.' Irritation gave Agricola's voice a ragged edge. 'He did help put down the rebellion as part of his uncle Cerialis's command. I had thought to involve your scout, Rufus, in the selection process – he knows the tribes better than most – but I see from your distraught reaction that it would be an imposition too far. And, of course, he has a dog-like devotion to you. I seem to recall you planned to send him north when last we met?'

Valerius knew there was no point in further protest. He gave Agricola the details as Rufus had presented them in a report dictated to a clerk at the Ninth's winter camp on the north side of the marshes.

To Gaius Valerius Verrens, legate Ninth legion Hispana, from Gaius Rufus, scout. I followed the main force of Celts until they camped for the winter by the bank of a river on the flatlands between the mountains and the sea. Those from the north and west dispersed to their homes, but even so food seemed to be scarce and there will be empty bellies before spring. I have warned the camp prefect about the possibility of a raid on our supply lines if the weather holds and he has taken steps to increase security. You said your greatest concern was to find the location of the oppida or tribal capital of the northern federation. If such a place exists it was not within my powers to discover it. The mountains of the northlands are almost beyond my comprehension and entirely different from those of the Brigantes or even Ordovice country. A man could wander for a hundred years and still have no greater understanding of their geography. They are so steep as to render travel only possible through the valleys. These are narrow, sometimes only gullies, and often further constricted by lakes, which made it perilous to advance, even for a single rider. Their extent appears to be endless, their occupants barbarous far beyond the standards of the tribes we have encountered thus far. Each valley supports a single extended family, or small tribe, who may have congress with those in the neighbouring chasms, but otherwise seem to be entirely independent. They live in scattered huts, tending their fields and their cows, and their warlike activities appear limited to cattle-stealing from their neighbours or slave-taking from anyone they regard as an enemy. I could only penetrate a limited distance into the interior, but it seemed to me that the pattern of their existence was as I'd observed. I would conclude that there is no great mountain power, and that Calgacus has all the numbers available to him. I would also suggest there is no sanctuary for his army in these mountains. If he is forced to retreat there he will have no choice but to disperse them or starve.

Agricola considered the information with a frown of concentration. 'So Rufus concludes there is no threat from the mountains?'

'So it appears,' Valerius said. 'At least not in the kind of strength that should concern us. I would trust his judgement.'

'Oh, I do. It is just a question of what to do about it. If Calgacus has nowhere to hide that makes all the difference,' the governor mused. 'He must be pressed and continue to be pressed until either his army disintegrates or we can bring him to battle and destroy him.'

'Better the second, I think.'

'Yes, he is much too dangerous a man to leave free. Have word sent to your fellow legates to prepare to march the moment I join them.' Agricola laid a hand on Valerius's arm. 'Before the summer is out I will present Calgacus as a gift for the Emperor.' Without warning his mood changed. 'You may leave me now. I must sit with my son.'

XLIX

'He's split his force into three groups,' Gaius Rufus told the gathering of officers in the governor's tented pavilion. As always Agricola had ordered a sand table set up and the midget scout used his knife to outline the position.

'Like a trident. This river line is the base, along with the valley that cuts off to the east. The prongs are three awkward passes to the north. Here in the east, a rocky cut through the mountains. To the west a winding trackway across the hills and over open moorland. And in the centre,' he stabbed at the table with real venom, 'a proper bastard. A deep gully as tight as a virgin's crack, with steep wooded slopes and heights that would frighten a mountain goat.'

'You said he wouldn't go into the mountains.' Agricola didn't hide his frustration.

'I said if he sought sanctuary there he'd starve,' Rufus said evenly. 'Calgacus isn't running.'

'He wants us to follow him?'

'That's right, legate.' Rufus nodded to Valerius. 'But he can't tarry long. His warriors are carrying their rations on their backs. Everything he needs to keep his army together is out on the farmlands towards the coast.'

'We should burn the farmers out and starve the bastards,' Julius Ursus, legate of the Twentieth, grunted.

'And we will, in time,' Agricola said. 'But it does no good to take territory. We need to destroy this barbarian rabble once and for all. And this,' the governor pointed to the sand table, 'is where we will do it.'

His words and the confidence with which he spoke them brought a growl of approval from the gathered officers. Valerius had sailed from Londinium with Agricola and they'd reached the Boderiae estuary with a month of the campaigning season wasted and Naso already cursing at the delay. However, despite his assurance that he trusted Rufus's intuition, Agricola had quickly reverted to the cautious tactics that had previously hampered them. Every valley and potential rat hole on his left flank must be probed by a full cohort, followed by patrols deep into the interior.

He justified his care by sending engineers with the legionaries to map out positions for forts which, he said, would guarantee the security of the province after a final victory. Valerius and the other legates merely exchanged looks and shrugged. Calgacus and his army pulled back as they advanced over the same ground as the previous year. When he reached the river Tav he surprised everyone by following the line of the mighty stream north and west, away from his granaries and his herds. Agricola and his officers had puzzled over the change and the governor became even more cautious.

When Calgacus finally disappeared into the mountains the army halted and made camp a few miles downstream on a riverside plateau Agricola had marked down as a potential legionary fortress. Now, it seemed, he was ready to strike. Valerius was as jubilant as any of them.

'If he wants us to follow him that's exactly what we should do, but not the way he expects.' He studied the three prongs of the trident. 'He expects us to follow his main force up the centre. Instead . . .' The finger of his left hand trailed through the sand to the western pass Rufus had identified. 'Could you lead the army through these hills?'

The little man grinned. 'With my eyes shut.'

'Then Calgacus has destroyed himself.' He turned to Agricola with a smile. 'By dividing his forces he invites us to defeat them in detail.'

'You mistake me, legate.' Agricola was also smiling, but his was a smile of consternation. 'I do not intend to go anywhere near those mountains with my legions. No one will remember Gnaeus Julius Agricola because he lost three eagles in some northern bog.' The mantra that ruled his every decision. 'To force the passes is to invite not victory, but ambush. Anything could happen.'

'My apologies, governor.' Valerius bowed. 'I believed it was your intention to bring Calgacus to battle.'

'And so it is. But I intend that he comes to us. You say he is short of supplies?' He aimed the question at Rufus.

'Yes, lord.'

'And does he have an alternative route to the coastal flatlands?'

'Not that I've found, your honour.' Rufus didn't hide his puzzlement. 'He either goes through these mountains or over them.'

'So you were right, Valerius.' Agricola smiled. 'Calgacus has been the architect of his own defeat. He has trapped himself and his army. All we need to do is block his route back to his supplies and he must fight us or face starvation and the disintegration of his forces.'

Valerius said nothing. It was a credible enough strategy, even if it did depend on Calgacus compounding his error, which seemed doubtful.

'So where do we make camp while we wait for them to come to us?' Herenius Polio of the Second Adiutrix mused. 'I've been over this ground. There's a low ridge east of where the rivers meet, a place the locals call Pinnata. It would be large enough to accommodate all three legions and what's left of our auxiliaries and it's well placed for defence. Like a stopper in a wineskin.'

'That will be one of our camps,' Agricola agreed.

'One?'

'We cannot allow any of Calgacus's warriors to escape. He has split his force into three columns, therefore I will divide my legions. Not one stopper, Herenius, but three. Placed here, here and here.' The point of his finger made three small indents in the sand. 'Close enough for mutual support.'

Valerius waited for Polio or Ursus to speak out against what was clearly folly, but the two men only looked glumly at the table. Eventually he could stay silent no longer.

'Herenius is right,' he insisted. 'It makes more sense to concentrate the legions. If they are close enough to provide mutual support they're not in position to do the job you require of them. This rise dominates what is essentially a crossroads created by the junction of these two valleys. If we place scouts at the mouth of the northern valley to warn of Calgacus's approach and keep cavalry patrols in the hills we'll have time to deploy our troops to meet a threat from any direction.'

'Are you questioning my orders, legate?'

'It is my duty to point out . . .'

'No! It is your duty to obey.' He turned to the other commanders. 'Twentieth legion will defend the centre, Ninth legion the western valley and Second Adiutrix the heights to the east. Maintain extra vigilance. We must be able to respond to the first sign of a threat. You may leave us, gentlemen. Valerius, you will stay.'

Gaius Rufus gave Valerius a troubled look as he left the tent. 'Scout?' The little man hesitated in the doorway. 'Pass the governor's orders to the camp prefect,' Valerius went on. 'You will know better than I where the camp needs to be sited. Within signalling distance and close enough to the main axis of march and the Twentieth for mutual support, but tell him he must not compromise on defence. A wild beast is always at its most dangerous when it is cornered.'

'No compromise on defence, lord.' Rufus saluted. 'I'll see to it.'

When Rufus was gone Valerius and Agricola stared at each other for a moment before the governor spoke. 'You will stay with the Twentieth as part of my headquarters until battle is joined.'

'Are you arresting me?' A snort of disbelieving laughter accompanied Valerius's words. 'Am I being relieved of my command?'

'No,' Agricola admitted. 'But I cannot have you continually casting doubt upon my orders. You are no longer the Emperor's man, Valerius.

You do not have the same leeway. As it happens I am merely carrying out the Emperor's wishes. He seems to know you well. He suggested you were inclined to recklessness and acts of impulse. *In times of strain, I advise keeping him close.* His very words.'

'Then why do I still command the Ninth?'

'You would have to ask the Emperor for an answer to that question. For the moment you will attend my conferences and assist Ursus in preparing the Twentieth for battle.'

'And the Ninth? *My* legion?'

'Naso is perfectly capable of taking command for a few days. After all, you and Titus intended him to have the legion when Titus wanted you to replace me, is that not true? The Emperor showed me a letter.'

There had been no letter, but Valerius made no attempt to deny the accusation. It was true, after all, even if the agreement had been unspoken.

'If that is all, governor?'

'Do not take it badly, Valerius. As soldiers we must all accept the rise and the fall with equal equanimity. Within the week Calgacus will be forced to attack and I promise you will have your share of the triumph.'

L

'We will never have a better opportunity.'

Cathal looked at the others for agreement, but he understood all they really wanted was leadership. Colm and Emrys, the commanders of his sword brothers, and the Selgovae warriors who called him king. Donacha, ruler of the Venicones, and his druid brother Oenghus, who had left their people because they believed he could lead them to victory over the Romans. Vodenos, who led the survivors of the Brigantes' champions, and Rurid, war chief of the Caledonians. How he wished Olwyn could be here, but he knew she and the children would be safer with Donacha's family on the flatlands.

Gwlym stared at him with empty red-rimmed eye sockets that saw more than all the others combined. Only Gwlym knew the bitterness of the disappointment that burned like raw bile in his chest at the Roman failure to follow him into the gorge where he would have fallen on them like a swooping eagle and torn their vaunted legions to pieces. How he cursed the Roman commander's timidity. Yet he should have known, or at least guessed. Had he not puzzled over the caution that had left him to gather his strength for two whole years? Before he died a Roman prisoner had talked of the death of an emperor, but that did not explain the regular pattern of advance followed by retreat. Was it tactical astuteness or a sign of fear? Still, none of that mattered now.

The men who stared at him from their positions around the leather tent were all lean, honed fighters, but none of them, or the men who followed them, were hungry. They trusted Cathal to keep it that way. He urgently needed supplies, and now that they were in the mountains the only place he could appropriate them was from the Romans. When the legions hesitated at the mouth of the gorge it appeared his plans were in ruins, but that had changed overnight. By sheer necessity he'd needed to split his army into three to converge on the gorge by different routes. The gods favoured him. Why else would the Roman commander have followed his example and established camps at the head of three different passes?

'Two hours after dark our main force, the Selgovae and the Venicones, will fall on the weakest of the camps, that of the Ninth, here in the west. We will cross the walls, slaughter the garrison and take what supplies we need, firing the rest to deprive the Romans of them. You will take a Roman eagle, the eagle of the Ninth, and your names will be sung round the campfires of your people for ever.' He paused to allow them to digest his words. One or two pairs of eyes gleamed with anticipation of the glory to come, others frowned in fierce concentration, but some faces were blank and he couldn't be sure what lay behind the dark eyes glittering in the lamplight. 'The flames will draw reinforcements from the Twentieth legion in the central camp by the river. You, Rurid, will wait in ambush on the track between the two camps and destroy the replacement column.' The Caledonian war chief growled his approval. 'Once that is done we will combine to attack the remaining garrison of the central camp.' He turned to Vodenos. 'Your Brigantes will have the most difficult task. The eastern camp is too distant to interfere with the initial assault, but at all costs you must stop any reinforcements attempting to reach what remains of the Twentieth's garrison. It will mean waiting and sacrifice, but it is the key to the utter destruction of the Romans. We must have time to destroy the first two elements before we can move on the third.' Vodenos nodded agreement, but his swarthy features told a different story. 'You will have your chance for glory when we move south again, my friend,' Cathal assured him. 'And you will sup Roman wine with the rest come the morning.'

The morning. And victory.

Cathal had more than twenty thousand men at his command. Something like fourteen thousand would attack the temporary fort of the Ninth. He knew the defences would be formidable, but his numbers were so overwhelming they would simply swamp the defenders.

His scouts had been watching the Roman columns advance for weeks and they estimated their strength as much lower than the previous year. Perhaps the gods had brought some disease to strike them down, but whatever the reason it gave him a great advantage that might not last. Cathal reckoned the defenders of the western camp numbered fewer than four thousand men, and the entire Roman force fourteen thousand at best.

If he could smash the first Roman camp quickly and regather his forces to attack the second, Agricola was doomed. After his victory he would turn south, destroying the occupiers where he found them, and then . . .

He dashed the dream from his mind. 'We must be in position just after dusk.'

Of course, they weren't in position just after dusk, or anything like it. This was the first time Cathal had attempted a manoeuvre with so many warriors from different tribes in the darkness and in total silence, although he'd done what he could to ease their passage, sending scouts in advance to locate and identify the gathering points he'd chosen among the trees and scrub overlooking the western Roman outpost.

They'd positioned the camp where he'd predicted, on a piece of higher ground overlooking a river crossing. He'd slipped past the outlying cavalry defenders and watched with something like admiration as the soldiers transformed the rough slope into a formidable defensive position. A single ditch surrounded the perimeter, which was something like three or four hundred paces a side, with the spoil piled to create a mound in the rear before the earth was topped with sharpened wooden stakes. At one point the soldiers were forced to hack their way through a rocky outcrop to continue the ditch, and he studied this operation with particular care. While men excavated the ditch others marked out areas with coloured flags, raised lines of tents well away from the walls where they might be vulnerable to spears, built ovens and dug latrine pits. The frenzied activity, so meticulously regulated, fascinated and concerned him. He knew no gathering of tribesfolk could ever be persuaded to work with such precise coordination.

The only points of access and exit were four gates, one in each side, where a causeway crossed the ditch, guarded against a direct frontal attack by a raised mound of earth. Yet for all their efforts the Romans couldn't alter one natural flaw in their defensive position. A hillside dominated the north flank, and although it was being cleared by men with axes this too he studied with interest. When Cathal was satisfied he had identified every strength and weakness he withdrew and made his plans. Now he feared those plans would never come to fruition.

Time was his enemy, and it flowed through his fingers like water. Donacha's Venicones were late to start their march from the gorge. It turned out that, affable and loyal as he was, Donacha was a fussy, nervous commander who didn't have the confidence to hurry the disparate veterans who led his war bands. They, in turn, argued over who should have precedence, and the result was a delay of more than an hour. When they did get started, progress was slow over the rough ground. One chief lost his marker, leaving an entire tribe wandering around leaderless in the darkness. Another decided he'd found an easier route and ended up blocked from his destination by the force that had remained on the main track. Even Cathal's Selgovae weren't immune from the chaos and he spent hours sweating and cursing, harrying the sluggards and prodding the feckless into position. Every few moments his eyes would drift fearfully to the eastern mountains for evidence of the first glow of dawn that would signal the abandonment of the attack or discovery by the enemy. Yet gradually messengers appeared out of the darkness to announce that their commanders were in position. He allowed a short pause for rest before he gave the signal.

'Now,' he whispered to Colm.

The Selgovae put his hands to his mouth and the high pitched 'Ky-ick' of a circling buzzard echoed through the darkness. Cathal had originally suggested the cry of a hunting owl, but Colm pointed out there were so many of the real thing the chances of one precipitating a premature attack were too great. They could only hope that the Romans couldn't tell the one from the other.

All around him men began to move forward in the darkness.

LI

Quintus Naso completed his inspection of the Ninth's temporary camp by torchlight and, much as he expected, found everything to his satisfaction. The men carried out these duties every night with the same precision they conducted manoeuvres on the battlefield. If they showed any sign of complacency their centurions were quick to remind them of their duty.

It wasn't the perfect defensive position. Agricola's insistence on the necessity for mutual support dictated that the gap between each of the army's positions should be less than an hour's march. If not in line of sight, the sentries in each camp should be capable of seeing the pair of fire arrows that were the signal help was required.

This sloping, heather-clad hillside overlooking the river was the best the engineers could find within that narrow field of options. It was only after the camp had been laid out that they'd discovered that the west side of the position was a thin layer of earth overlaying solid rock. That had meant a slight but unfortunate constriction in the camp perimeter boundary, and much sweating and cursing from the soldiers forced to hack and chip their way through the rock to complete their portion of ditch.

His greatest concern lay on the north side of the camp where the palisade was overlooked by a steep hillside blanketed in scrubby oak and ash. If enemy spearmen managed to creep down the slope they'd be in a position to swamp the defenders on that wall with missiles and the Roman *pila* wouldn't have the range to reply. The *praefectus castro-rum* had countered the threat by placing one of the legion's artillery pieces, an *onager* catapult or a *scorpio* shield-splitter, every thirty paces. Naso ordered men to clear the slope of trees to provide a clearer field of fire and doubled the sentries.

'Who has the watch tonight?' he asked the *duplicarius* in charge of setting the guard.

'The First cohort of the Usipi have the initial three watches.'

Naso pursed his lips in distaste. The Usipi had been recruited from beyond the Rhenus during Vespasian's campaign to strengthen the frontier, though impressed was probably the better word. Fine warriors, every one a young man in his prime, they were unwilling soldiers with no love for Rome. Agricola had brought them on campaign only with the greatest reluctance. But the only alternative was an even more recently recruited cohort of Brigantes, still raw, wild and only half dis-ciplined. The last thing he wanted on his walls at night was an untrained Celt who'd probably have felt more at home with the enemy than in Roman armour.

'Make sure their officers keep a close eye on them,' he ordered. 'In fact, I want every eighth man to be a Roman officer.'

He knew the order would irritate the man and annoy the Usipi com-mander even more, but Rufus's message from Valerius rang in his ears. *No compromise on defence.* It still puzzled him why the governor had kept Valerius with him at the Twentieth's camp. Rufus, normally so loquacious, had gone strangely quiet when he'd asked the reason. Naso was happy enough to be in charge, but every man in the legion knew that a rift had occurred between Valerius and Agricola, and many spec-ulated on the reasons for it.

Naso had a feeling it had much to do with the governor's curious lethargy and his insistence on consolidating every piece of captured ground with forts that ate up the army's manpower. As a result of

Emperor Domitian's demands the Ninth was down to just over half its strength, with fewer than a hundred cavalry and auxiliary infantry cohorts of questionable quality.

He remembered the moment during the punishment raid on the Venicones. Naso had no regrets about suggesting Valerius would make a better governor than the current incumbent. In many ways Julius Agricola was a bureaucrat in a legate's armour. More happy with a stylus in his hand than a sword, caution was his watchword. It galled the men that they'd been campaigning for four years and seemed no closer to destroying the enemy's strength than in the beginning.

In Naso's opinion the job would have been done in half the time with Valerius in charge. He would have found a way to bring the Selgovae to battle with the might of all three legions and either killed or captured the legendary Calgacus. Without Calgacus the other northern tribes would have been forced to come to terms.

Perhaps he was wrong and Agricola's bid to lure Calgacus would succeed, but the giant Celt had never taken the bait in the past. The main thing that worried him was the governor's decision to split his force. If they were close enough to provide mutual support in an emergency why not just stay together? As far as Naso could see the Twentieth's camp was like the plug in an *amphora*. All it needed was a few watchtowers to ensure the Celts didn't slip past unseen and the result would be the same.

He stared out into the darkness. The likelihood was that they'd be here for some time. Tomorrow he would order the construction of a second ditch and bank, rocks or no rocks. For the moment one fact gave him a certain comfort. No Celt had ever dared attack a Roman fortress of this size and strength.

'Carry on,' he told the *duplicarius*, and walked back to the *praetorium* and his cot.

Two hours later he woke with the certainty his world was ending. Outside the *praetorium* tent the alarm bell clanged with deafening sound. He threw on his tunic and a servant helped him into his plate armour. Julius, one of the junior military tribunes, dashed into the tent. 'What's happening?' Naso demanded as he strapped on his sword.

'Celts outside the north wall, lord.'

'How many?'

'The decurion couldn't say for certain, but he estimates a substantial force.'

The servant completed the last straps and Naso rushed from the *praetorium* with his headquarters staff and his bodyguard section. They raced through the darkness to the baggage carts parked along the Via Sagularis inside the threatened wall. A messenger reported that the two reserve cohorts, including the double-strength First, were already in position on the parade square and ready to respond to an attack from any quarter. An archer ran up to join the group, followed by two slaves carrying an iron bucket full of hot coals.

Should he send the emergency signal?

Not yet. First he had to discover if this was a mere provocation. It could be a feint attack to get him to hold his position while the Celts hit the Twentieth with a larger force, or, more likely, made their escape from Agricola's trap. They paused thirty paces short of the palisade where two centuries of the Second cohort, the unit assigned to defend the position, waited in reserve.

'Careful, sir,' a centurion warned. 'They're sending over showers of spears every few minutes.'

'*Testudo*,' Naso ordered. With a rattle of overlapping wood his bodyguard instantly surrounded him with a protective carapace of shields. 'To the parapet.'

They advanced at a walk, ignoring the sharp clatter of spears and slingshots against the seasoned oak of the legionary *scuta*. The ground rose beneath Naso's feet as they arrived at the north wall. Crixus, the centurion commanding the palisade's defenders, was peering into the stygian darkness.

'What's happening?' Naso demanded.

'Beg to report a sentry heard movement during the first hour of the second watch.' Crixus's deep voice had an edge that betrayed his tension. 'He thought it might just be deer, but we manned the wall just in case. Next thing we knew there was a rush of screaming Celts from the

347

darkness. Thousands, it sounded like. By Fortuna's favour we were ready for them. A cast of *pila* and a volley from the shield-splitters stopped them dead and since then all they've been doing is making the odd feint to keep us honest,' he ducked down as a missile hissed out of the darkness, just missing his helmet, 'and annoying us with their spears and slingshots, but that's about it.'

'So they didn't press the attack?'

'No,' Crixus admitted. 'They just stood at the other side of the ditch screaming in that foul language of theirs, then retreated when we used the *onagri* and *scorpiones* on them.'

'A feint, then?'

'It didn't feel like it at the time,' the centurion said ruefully. 'But the more I think about it, yes.'

Before Naso could reply the strident blare of a horn split the night and a great roar erupted across the camp. 'The east gate.' He was already moving away and the *testudo* closed in around him. 'Hold this wall with your current strength at all costs,' he called. 'I may have to call on your reserves. Julius?' He called to his aide. 'As quickly as you can. My compliments to the First cohort. They should reinforce the defenders on the east wall.' His heart was racing, but his voice was calm. Twenty years of experience told him he was making the right decisions. There was just one more thing. This second attack was no feint. 'Signaller, loose your warning arrows.'

They waited while the archer dipped the first pitch-soaked arrow into the brazier and sent the flaming missile arcing high into the night sky, swiftly followed by another. Naso watched the second arrow fall in a glowing arc, knowing that reinforcements would soon be on their way from the Twentieth. He felt excitement, but, as yet, no concern. Twelve hundred of the best-trained, best-armed and best-disciplined troops in Britannia were now defending the east wall. He would back them to hold off any number of barbarians.

In the same moment Cathal launched his real attack.

He'd identified the weakness during his daylight study of the camp. The Romans assigned to cut the ditch through the rocky ground on the western flank had the most difficult task. Every foot they excavated took ten times the effort of their brothers digging in the relatively soft peat. When they piled the rocky spoil on top of the bank and placed their defensive stakes he noticed their frustration as they tried to secure the five-foot posts of the palisade. They were still working while every other unit in the fort ate and rested. Eventually they completed the task, but as he watched them clean their tools something became clear to him. As long as their section *looked* as strong as the adjoining walls the leaders of these men were satisfied. It had given him his idea.

The sword brothers of the Selgovae and their Venicones allies spent the day manufacturing two kinds of wooden hurdle. One was three paces long and two wide and constructed of tightly woven branches, the other smaller, but heavier, consisting of three or four timbers roped together. Eight thousand men silently worked their way into position while the guards were distracted by the two feint attacks. Cathal used the two fire arrows as his signal to advance. The Celtic warriors launched themselves towards the camp's defences, using the light hurdles to protect them from the Roman javelins that rained down as the guards reacted. When they reached the stone-cut ditch they used their burdens to bridge the gap in a hundred places. Warriors sprinted across the bridges and smashed the heavy hurdles into the palisade of stakes. Even firmly embedded, the frail walls might have succumbed to the battering rams, but these stakes were planted in thin soil laced with rocks and stones. As the wall disintegrated and thousands of Selgovae and Venicones warriors poured into the camp, the defenders, soldiers of the despised Usipi auxiliary unit, threw down their weapons and fled.

Standing amid the wreckage of the wall with the lifeless body of a Roman officer who'd been one of the few to stand and fight at his feet, Cathal felt a surge of exaltation. Howling warrior bands surged past him, hunting down the surviving defenders until all resistance on this side of the camp had been shattered. By now the men holding the north and east walls would know they'd been outflanked. If they stood and fought they'd be assailed on three sides. Their only hope was to join up with the other components of the beleaguered garrison. And that was what Cathal wanted.

He would kill them all.

'Come.' He led his bodyguard past supply wagons inside the wall and through the lines of tents, many already flattened, the flaps wide and the soldiers' belongings scattered around the entrances. One tent was in flames and in the flickering yellow light Cathal bent to pick up a small metal figure from the dirt. A woman in a long dress, with braided hair and one arm raised in a gesture that might be welcome or dismissal. A legionary's wife or lover? A goddess? A commotion among the tents to his left drew his attention. In the darkness dozens of warriors had stopped to seek plunder, squabbling noisily over the choicest pieces.

'Get those men moving,' he told Colm. 'They'll have plenty of time when the Romans are dead.'

The veteran warrior led Cathal's bodyguard into the mass of men, lashing out left and right with the flat of their swords. Cathal wondered how many more men had stopped to look for treasure or to avoid the fighting. To achieve a swift victory here and to move against the camp of the Twentieth legion before dawn he needed every available warrior.

As Cathal moved forward through the chaos he tried to gauge the ebb and flow of the battle from what he could hear. Shouts, screams and the clash of arms from right and left told him that at least a few defenders on this side of the camp continued to fight. Somewhere ahead of him a Roman trumpet blared and he wondered what it signified. A glint of metal in the darkness and the shadowy figure of a Roman soldier, helmet gone and head bleeding, charged from Cathal's left. He held a long spear aimed at the big Selgovae's chest.

Cathal turned towards his attacker and in one movement sidestepped the point and brought his hammer round in an arc that smashed the legionary's shoulder and threw him off his feet. Colm stepped out of the darkness and stilled the shuddering body with a thrust to the throat.

'Let's hope they are all so easy to kill.' Cathal's sword brother grinned.

'Let's hope not all of them are so brave,' the Selgovae king countered.

LII

'They've broken through in the west.'

Quintus Naso had to still a surge of panic at the aide's news as he watched the combined First and Third cohorts fend off the attack on the east gate. A few moments earlier it had all seemed so simple. Too simple. He cursed himself for falling for the same barbarian trick that had led to the butchery of the auxiliary patrol in the valley. A double feint. 'What about the other walls. Can they hold?'

'There are too many of them.' The aide's voice shook. 'Thousands. Those bastard Usipi fled without a fight. I've told the Second and Fourth cohorts to make a fighting retreat to the parade ground.'

'Good lad.' Naso hoped the praise would calm the boy. He'd done well. The south wall wasn't under direct attack and another officer might have ordered his men to try to escape by that route. Naso had no doubt the enemy would be waiting for them, and they'd have been cut to pieces as they tried to fight their way through the narrow gateway. The fort that had been their refuge had become a trap. He didn't even have to consider his options. There was only one thing to do.

'Have the signaller sound "recall". The legion will form a defensive square on the parade ground, First cohort to man the western flank.'

It was a complex manoeuvre that depended on the First's disengaging from the fighting on the east wall without the defences collapsing, and the five double-strength centuries making their way across the parade ground in time to halt the main enemy attack. The remaining cohorts would conform on their comrades in an operation they'd practised many hundred times under the watchful eye of Valerius and himself. He felt a momentary twinge of fear. Was it an ill omen that the commander had been kept away just when the enemy decided to attack?

Naso dismissed the thought. He still had no concern about the outcome of the fight. Once they were in square he had every confidence in his men's ability to hold off any number of barbarians until help could arrive. Armourers ran past carrying armloads of *pila* to stockpile in the centre of the square. The signaller's trumpet blared and he heard the shouted orders as the First cohort's centurions began the delicate task of unstitching their soldiers from the eastern defences. 'Eagle party to me,' he called, and led his command section and bodyguards to where the spears were piled.

It was only when Honoratus, the legion's *aquilifer*, moved into position beside him with the legion's eagle standard unveiled that the true immensity of his predicament and that of his legion dawned on Quintus Naso. The man who lost this gleaming, gold-covered piece of brass would be remembered throughout history with dishonour and disdain, his family reviled and their very future placed in jeopardy by his actions.

Honoratus's bodyguard took their places around the big eagle-bearer, each man a veteran and armed with a fearsome double-edged axe, but Naso took little comfort from them. If ever they were called upon to wield those axes to protect their charge it was finished. Brave men, they'd ensure the enemy paid dear for the taking, but it would be the Ninth legion's last stand. He heard a surging roar and the crack of snapping tent poles as a great ball of flame told him that someone had set the *praetorium* and its stock of lamp oil alight, and he knew the enemy would be on them in moments. Behind him the Third cohort was conducting a fighting retreat to make up the rear wall of the square. To his right and left he heard the shouts of command as centuries from the other cohorts filtered into their positions. Would they be in time?

'Make ready to receive the enemy.'

Thousands of Celts poured from the wreckage of what had been the perfectly aligned tent lines of the camp only to stumble to a halt at the sight of the wall of Roman shields that blocked their way. Almost two hundred legionaries, the elite of their command, made up the front rank of the defensive line facing them, with two more ranks at their back. Every man was fully armoured and stood behind the three layers of seasoned oak of a brightly painted *scutum*. The defensive wall bristled with spears and the men who confronted it understood how formidable it could be, though few if any had faced the Romans in battle. They looked to their chiefs for leadership, but they were as perplexed as the men they led.

Cathal and his bodyguard forced their way through the great mass of warriors until the king could see the Roman square.

'What are you waiting for?' he raged at Donacha. In the light of the burning pavilion he could see more and more Roman soldiers running to take their places in the square. 'They're still disorganized. Strike them now and make use of their confusion.'

He raised his great hammer and launched his men at the tight-packed legionary formation. A moment's hesitation before a great roar went up as the warriors advanced in a rush, the movement mirrored as the Selgovae and Venicones warriors on every side joined the attack. To Cathal, the Roman formation looked as solid and immovable as a rock, but these fighters were his bravest and his best and he believed the rock must crumble under their relentless attack.

When they were thirty paces from the square a trumpet blared and the walls of shields parted momentarily. A soft hissing filled the air for a few heartbeats to be replaced by the terrible shrieks of men in mortal agony as the first cast of *pila* scythed down the leading attackers like summer corn. Four feet of ash topped by a shank of iron as long as a man's forearm, tipped with a pyramid point honed to needle sharpness, the heavy spears, designed to punch through light armour, tore through flesh, muscle and viscera and cracked bone. Cathal winced at the death cries of his sword brethren and the charge stuttered as those behind negotiated the bodies of their fallen champions. A second cast and hundreds more fell, but now the great mass of warriors engulfed the square with a thunderous crash that rippled and bent the wall of shields.

For a moment it seemed the Romans must break, but somehow the square survived. Celts maddened by the loss of their comrades threw aside their spears and tore at the shields with their bare hands, only to reel back clutching at eyes or throat. Cathal, stalking the outer fringes of the attack with his bodyguard, noted how the second line of legionaries protected the heads of the first with raised shields, and a third rank stabbed at the closest attackers with long spears. Even if a Celtic sword or spear managed to pierce the wall of shields, the upper bodies and heads of the men who held them were protected by glittering iron. Only the most fortunate of strikes drew blood.

Cathal's casualties could already be counted in the hundreds, while the few wounded Romans were quickly replaced by the men behind them. He had a momentary vision of halting the attack and using what advantage he had to carry off the Roman supplies. Food for his army was a greater priority even than the broader aims of his plan.

Yet that plan could still work. By now the reinforcements from the main Roman camp would be marching into the arms of Rurid's Caledonians and a massacre between mountain and river. Cathal had always known that the numbers he brought to bear on this segment of the enemy force were his greatest asset. Victory must be won with blood. With sacrifice. The awful reality of that truth sickened him, but he must be as strong as the men fighting and dying in front of the shield wall. Sooner or later the Romans would tire. His heroes would burst through the shields and then it would be the long Celtic swords doing the killing.

His great height gave him a view across the heads of the attackers and the wall of shields. In the dying light of the flames he caught the glitter of gold.

The eagle of the Ninth.

Gwlym had told him of the mystical power the Romans invested in their golden baubles and the shock the loss of one would send through the Empire. He had thought to stand back and direct the fighting as the druid had advised, even though the heavy hammer itched in his hand. Now, with victory in the balance, he realized that would not be possible.

Already the front ranks of warriors had fought themselves to a standstill in places, but they wouldn't give way to those behind. The pause provided the Roman ranks with a respite Cathal couldn't afford. Once more he sought out a weakness. Occasionally a pair of warriors would survive long enough to tear one of the shields from the line causing a moment of confusion and a great cheer as the surrounding Celts butchered the fallen legionary. A man like Cathal might use that confusion to create a decisive breakthrough, but he had to be there to exploit it and that was down to luck. There had to be another way. He moved through the roaring mass of warriors shouting encouragement, but his eyes never left the Roman formation. At last it came to him.

'Find shields for your men,' he ordered Colm. 'And follow where I go.'

If you were breaking up an oak chest to reuse the wood where did you start? Not with the wood itself, but at the joints. The joints that held this Roman square together were the corners. All along the line his warriors faced sections of men who defended those to their left and right as well as themselves. But at the corners of the square the attention of those to the left and right of the pivotal soldier would be divided. Here an attacker would only face one man and those directly behind him in the formation. Kill those men and expose the legionaries on their flank. Kill those and you had an opening that could be used to create panic and confusion. An opening that led to an eagle.

Pride welled up in Quintus Naso's heart as he watched his depleted legion fight. After the first shock of the attack he'd never doubted his legionaries could hold the barbarians. How he loved these men. The Ninth contained as many rogues, shirkers and lifetime *milites* who couldn't be trusted to hold a hammer or use a saw as any other unit. But they were all ready to fight for each other and die for each other. The men of a legion shared tents, latrines, bad habits and bodily odours. They'd snarl at each other like dogs, beat each other to a pulp in a fair fight and grin bloodily at each other when it was over. A fool would be tolerated for a lifetime of service, but a coward or a thief wouldn't last a week.

Now these men stood shoulder to shoulder behind the big curved shields they cursed on the march, gripping the swords and spears that might be moulded to their hands. After an hour of hard fighting their shoulders would be aching, the sweat would be pouring into their eyes, the stink of torn bowels and new-shed blood thick in their nostrils, and the death cries of their enemies in their ears. But Quintus Naso knew they would stand for as long as it took.

An enemy cheer told him one of his men had fallen and he said a silent prayer to his memory. It was all the epitaph the man would ever get, because a legion on campaign had no time for funeral orations or the carving of grave markers. He could hear the centurions of the reserve centuries growling at their men to have patience and to be still; their turn would come soon enough. But in the interior of the square all was calm and disciplined.

A shouted order sent men dashing from the reserve ranks to replace the fallen. Headquarters clerks and slaves carried the wounded from the lines to the area set out by the *medici*, but the injured were mercifully few. It had been proved time and again that in straight combat no barbarian army was a match for a well-fought legion.

His mind strayed to the east, where help would be on its way. How many would Agricola send? Three cohorts at least, probably more. There would be no fanfare of trumpets when they came, no flaming arrows to warn of their progress. He only hoped whoever commanded them had the sense to cut off the Celts' escape route. If the reinforcements came over the west wall Naso and their commander would have the enemy between the hammer of the Ninth and the anvil of the Twentieth. Calgacus would be annihilated.

Would Agricola send Valerius? Of course he must, for all their personal enmity. Who was better equipped to lead a night attack? Not Ursus, who had a reputation as a cautious, even timid commander, or Polio, for all his attributes. Naso allowed himself a grim smile as he imagined their reunion in the midst of the carnage. *I return your legion, Valerius. You will find it is a little battered, but still intact.*

A burst of cheering drew his attention to the north-west corner of the square. His heart seemed to stop at an enormous crash that drowned the sound of battle, immediately followed by a second that brought a growl of dismay from the nearby legionaries. Instinct told him this was the crisis he had been waiting for. He turned, looking for someone to lead the counter-attack if one was needed, but his aides were all involved in the fighting. He gestured for a shield to one of his bodyguard and drew his sword. 'Second and third centuries to me,' he called.

'Sir . . .' Honoratus the standard-bearer stepped forward.

'Hold fast, *aquila*,' Naso told him. 'I will be back in a few moments. Keep your charge safe at all costs.'

'Of course, sir.'

Naso led the two centuries forward at the trot. The burning pavilion was little more than a distant red glow, but there was enough light from it and the stars to give him a sense of what was happening. As they approached the beleaguered angle the wall of men collapsed inward with soldiers falling back from a massive presence who dominated all around him.

Calgacus. The name entered Naso's head unbidden, but he didn't hesitate. A mixture of fear and exhilaration surged through him, but instinct told him this was his chance. 'First century,' he launched himself at the fighting. 'Kill that big bastard.'

Men from the outer wall turned to run and he screamed encouragement at them as he ran by. 'Hold. Hold fast for Rome.'

'For Rome!' They roared the automatic reply and the words must have steadied them because they turned back with their comrades. A barbarian shield reared into his face and he met it with his own, forcing the owner backwards and stabbing at his eyes with his *gladius*. The man shrieked and reeled away, to be replaced by another. Naso smashed his *scutum* into his body, only realizing as he did so that it was a Roman soldier, his iron helmet crushed into his skull and blood pouring down his face. All around him the legionaries of the first century manoeuvred to get a killing thrust at the giant figure in the gloom, exchanging blows with the Celts trying to protect him. A rushing sound was followed by a mixture of ringing metal and wet slap. Liquid splattered into Naso's face and he tasted blood on his lips. Despite the death of their comrade four or five men were managing to keep the roaring colossus at bay, like men baiting a bear in the arena. At last Naso saw his chance. Calgacus half turned to lash out at a legionary who'd got too close and the camp prefect darted in, *gladius* poised to plunge into his enemy's unprotected vitals. As he made to thrust he heard a warning shout and, with astonishing speed, Calgacus reversed his movement. Naso saw nothing, but he had a sensation of flying through the air, which turned out to be more than sensation when he landed on his back with a crash of armour.

The impact knocked all the air from him. A moment of confusion before he understood there was more to it than that. He couldn't move and he couldn't breathe. Men surrounded him and carefully picked him up. Glittering stars raced across the inky night sky as they moved him back into the centre of the camp and laid him gently on the flattened earth of the parade ground. He felt little pain, just a tightness in the chest that restricted his breathing to a hoarse whistle. Someone bent over him. Odd that he should have a wolf's mask. Of course, Honoratus, the standard-bearer, with his wolfskin cape. A familiar stolid face, the features twisted in emotion.

'What ha . . . ?' Naso tried to raise his head.

'You did it, sir,' the *aquilifer* choked. 'You saved us. We drove them back. The breach is filled.'

Naso lay back, aware of a new dampness on his cheeks. The eagle was safe. But where were Valerius and the reinforcements?

LIII

Valerius slipped the cowhide socket of his wooden fist over the oiled stump of his wrist.

'Tell me again,' he said, as Gaius Rufus helped him dress.

'All I know is that the sentries on the west wall saw a pair of fire arrows from the approximate position of the Ninth's camp.'

'The warning signal?' Valerius buckled his sword belt with his left hand.

'That's what it looked like.'

'Naso isn't one to panic.'

'No, lord,' the scout agreed. 'He must be certain Calgacus means business.'

'And he has fewer than three thousand legionaries, a few renegade Brigantes and a couple of auxiliary cohorts.' Valerius shook his head in frustration. 'Agricola should never have divided the command.'

Rufus shrugged. He left strategy to those who were paid to form it.

'How many men is Agricola sending in the relief column?'

'He didn't say, lord.' The little man frowned. Better for Valerius to discover for himself that the governor had merely looked into the western darkness for a few moments before returning to his tent with little sense of urgency.

Valerius strode out into the camp. Where were the troops for the relief column? They should be assembling on the parade ground, preparing for a forced night march. Yet there was no movement among the tents of the Twentieth legion. No centurions marching along the lines rousing their *contubernia*. In the torchlight the sentries went about their business as usual. The only troops assembled were Valerius's bodyguard, who waited, armed and ready, their horses fidgeting nervously in the torchlight outside the *praetorium*. Shabolz, the former Pannonian auxiliary, held the reins of Valerius's mount. 'Lord.' He nodded a welcome.

Valerius looked from the men to the curtained doorway of the headquarters tent, where two guards stood watching impassively.

'Have you had your orders?' he asked Cornelius Felix.

'No, lord.' Felix shifted uneasily in the saddle. 'We're still waiting.'

Valerius marched to where the guards stood. 'Valerius Verrens, legate Ninth legion, to see the governor.'

To his surprise the men moved aside without protest. 'We were told to expect you, sir. The governor is at his desk.'

Agricola, dressed in a simple woollen tunic and wrapped in a cloak against the chill night air, sat reading a scroll held to his portable campaign desk by four metal weights. He looked up as Valerius entered.

'The warning signal has been seen from the Ninth's camp. They may be under attack,' Valerius said without preamble.

'So I understand.'

Valerius felt a surge of anger at the governor's calm. 'I'd like to volunteer to lead the relief column.'

Agricola rose from his seat and walked to a painted marble bust of Titus that stood on a plinth in a corner of the room. He stared into the grey eyes for a long moment before turning back to Valerius.

'There will be no relief column.'

'What?' Valerius didn't hide his astonishment.

'At least not until daylight.'

'But my men, Roman soldiers, could be dying out there. You sited the camps for mutual support. Naso will be expecting reinforcements to come to his aid.'

'We've had word of enemy movement further up the valley.' Agricola was unmoved by Valerius's outrage. 'I will not send my soldiers on a night march that will lead them into almost certain ambush. No barbarian has broken the walls of a temporary camp since Caesar's time. Naso is perfectly capable of holding his lines against a few thousand Celts with the men under his command.'

'Calgacus is not just another barbarian.' Valerius struggled to maintain his temper. 'And Quintus has just six cohorts and a few unblooded auxiliaries. The Brigantes are worthless, you know that, and the Usipi not much better.'

'They can help hold a wall if their lives depend upon it,' the governor said dismissively.

'We cannot just sit here and do nothing,' Valerius persisted. 'Give me two cohorts of the Twentieth and two of the Gauls. If we march right away we can be there within the hour.'

'Cannot?' Agricola's head snapped up and his eyes glittered with fury in the lamplight. 'Do you presume to issue orders to a proconsul of Rome?'

'You gave me command of the Ninth legion. Those are my men—'

'And I can take it away from you,' the governor snapped. 'Have you not been listening? I have responsibility for every man in this army. Naso has three thousand men to defend a perfectly sound fort. You are asking me to send another two thousand into deadly peril.' His anger faded, and was replaced by weariness. 'Have patience, Valerius. We will march at dawn.'

He returned to his desk and waited for the other man to leave. Valerius bit back his fury and chanced one last throw of the dice.

'You are right that Naso is perfectly capable of holding the camp,' he said as calmly as he could. 'But this is Calgacus, who has proved himself not just a warrior and a leader, but a cunning and resourceful enemy. Have you considered that his aim may not be to destroy the camp, but to achieve a success that, though much less costly, would have the same effect on the army's morale?' Valerius allowed Agricola to think about it for a moment. 'An eagle stands proudly at the very heart of that camp, Julius. It is not just my eagle, or my legion's or even your eagle. It is Rome's. Calgacus knows that and he understands the damage he can do by taking it.' He saw the shadow of doubt creep into the other man's eyes. 'If you do not care to risk your infantry, give me a cohort of auxiliary cavalry. We could reach the camp in half the time and be through an enemy ambush before they even knew we were there. At best, our arrival will help Naso break the siege. At worst, a squadron can carry the eagle to safety.'

Agricola stared at the desk for a moment. He knew his reputation and all his great ambition rested on the success of the campaign in northern Britannia. But even if he triumphed, everything would be lost if it became known that he made no attempt to support one of his legions when their eagle was at risk. He made his decision.

'Very well. A single cohort. But if you get into trouble you must turn back.'

Valerius ignored the warning and ran from the tent. 'Wait here,' he called to his escort. 'Rufus, with me. Where are the tent lines of Aulus Atticus and his Ala Petriana?'

Cathal studied the eastern sky and knew he had one last opportunity to achieve victory. The Roman square was a square no longer, just a battered, bloody and all but exhausted mass that somehow still managed to retain its defensive integrity. After the failed attack that had left him with the ragged gash across his hip he'd launched his warriors again and again at the stolid lines of legionaries all through the long night. Their casualties must now be counted in their hundreds and the survivors could barely hold their shields or lift their swords. As much as their spirit, what kept them alive was the mound of Selgovae and Venicones dead that surrounded their position and hindered any Celts who still retained the energy to assault the ragged lines of painted shields. Many of them bled from open wounds inflicted by the vicious little swords that darted between the shields. They leaned on their spears or crouched down, finding what rest they could forty paces from the Romans they no longer had the strength to attack.

Not so many now. There would be wailing and tearing of hair in many a house and farmstead in the months to come. And he knew the cost would not be counted only in numbers, but also in the weakening of his authority and prestige. Yet all that would count for naught if he could only encourage them to one final assault that would smash the Roman square.

Cathal had long since abandoned the wider objectives of his strategy. The destruction of Agricola's army would have to wait for another day. He felt a flicker of unease that he'd heard nothing of Rurid's ambush. Would the Roman commander really abandon a third of his legionaries to face destruction? He moved among the tired spearmen calling encouragement, noting who would meet his eyes and who would not. King Donacha assured him that his Venicones were ready, but the men around him didn't show the same enthusiasm.

'One last effort and they will be ours for the slaughter,' he told them. 'Your names will be sung around the campfires of your people until the end of time. You are tired, but they are more tired. Everything they have will be yours for the taking. The man who brings me their eagle will have a sack of gold and a dozen cattle. Take away their eagle and you take away their pride and their honour. Take away their eagle and you spit in the face of Rome. This is your destiny. Just one last effort . . .'

Others passed on his words through the ring of massed warriors who still outnumbered their enemies by at least six to one. Gradually the men straightened or rose to their feet. It began as a whisper and rose to a murmur that grew in volume as they called encouragement to each other. Sword and spear crashed against shield and they waited for the command that would throw them forward for one final time. A soft glow appeared above the eastern hills. Dawn could only be moments away.

'Fresh spears.' Cathal heard the surprise in Donacha's voice. 'Truly the gods favour us.'

Fresh spears? The Selgovae chief looked to the east gate where warriors poured into the camp. Every man carried a sword and a shield and he recognized them with dismay as Rurid's Caledonians. He rushed

363

to the gateway as the war chief entered at the centre of a band of warriors.

'What are you doing here?'

The bearded man frowned. 'We waited where you said we should, but the Roman reinforcements never came. My men saw the glow in the sky and decided they had waited long enough. There is no plunder to be had crouched in the darkness under the trees.'

'Aaargh!' Cathal let out a roar of frustration that echoed across the fort. 'You fools.'

In the distance a trumpet blared out its strident call.

'When you said you needed a cavalry wing to help reinforce the Ninth I thought we'd be escorting at least a couple of cohorts of infantry.' Aulus Atticus nervously fingered the chin strap of his helmet.

'You understand your orders?'

'Of course, lord. We attack in squadrons and stay on the move. Any man of greater height and bulk than the normal to be singled out by every archer who sees him. I can assure you there won't be any tall men left alive when we leave the field.'

'Good enough. Nilus?' Valerius called to his signaller as he drew his heavy cavalry *spatha*. 'You may order the advance.'

LIV

Nilus put his trumpet to his lips and the braying blare echoed through the dawn. Rufus had guided them through the darkness, hesitating occasionally to check his surroundings, but there had been no sign of the ambush Agricola predicted.

When they'd reached the fort Valerius had been tempted to launch an immediate all-out charge to relieve the pressure on the defenders. Instead, he'd ordered Rufus to circle the walls out of earshot of the enemy.

Now, in the roseate bloom of the summer pre-dawn, Valerius and Atticus's thousand mounted archers and spearmen were ranged in two ranks along a shallow hillside to the west of the temporary fort. As one they moved forward at a walk which rapidly increased to a trot. 'Hold the line,' Atticus roared. 'If any of you bastards get in front of me I'll take a cane to your backs.'

Valerius's heart thundered so much with anticipation it felt as if it was coming out of his throat. He had no idea how this would end, only that it had to happen. Five hundred mounted archers was far too few to throw against this multitude of angry Celts, but he had no choice if the legion was to have the opportunity to recover. He could only pray Calgacus and his warriors were so occupied with Naso and the Ninth that they'd not thought to man the walls against the possibility of a new attack. He could see the west wall now and the gaps where Calgacus and his warriors had torn their way into the camp. He twitched the reins and lined up on one of them. Nilus rode at his right shoulder ready to take his orders, Felix on his left. Shabolz and the remainder of his bodyguard would not be far behind. 'Sound the charge.'

Another long blast increased the pace to a canter. He looked to his flanks and the long rippling lines of horsemen attempting to keep formation over the rough ground. The ditch and bank loomed before him. Now! The horse rose to fly the void, checked for an instant at the bank before lurching forward shoulder to shoulder with the mounts to right and left. Valerius shifted his weight to stay in the saddle and then they were through. Atticus must have issued a command, for the higher voice of a *lituus* cavalry trumpet shrieked out a message. A third of the Ala Petriana – ten squadrons – consisted of mounted archers. Like all cavalry their horses were trained to respond to pressure of the knees. Inside the camp the riders dropped their reins and unslung their curved bows, bringing them up and notching an arrow in a single movement. They crossed the outer road, swerving to avoid baggage carts, and were quickly among the wreckage of the tents. Valerius was fortunate that his route took him along one of the gaps between the lines, but others were forced to jump mounds of leather and equipment. The glowing embers of the burned-out *praetorium* appeared to his left. Until now he'd given little thought to what awaited them. If the Ninth had been overwhelmed the bones of every man in the charge would join them to be chewed on by the wolves and the foxes among the heather. But instinct told Valerius that Naso had managed to hold.

Then he saw the enemy. At first, from his elevated position, they appeared as a single great mass, but quickly his mind told him he was actually looking at an oval with an oblong of glittering iron helmets at their centre. He could even see the eagle party in the middle of the trapped ranks of Roman troops. Another look to his flanks and a surge of relief. He and Atticus had discussed their plan of attack, but it depended on the Celts pressing the Ninth hard. By Fortuna's favour the enemy had left a gap between their rear and the outer wall. A few baggage carts obstructed the passage, but he prayed that the skill of the Ala Petriana would allow the plan to work. Within a few strides the warrior mass became a sea of individual faces, mouths gaping and eyes wide in consternation. Forty paces and a new blare of the trumpet. Hundreds of arrows hissed from the bows of the front rank to be lost among the Celts. Their missiles in flight, the front rank split to left and right around the outer face of the barbarian rear. A heartbeat later the second line loosed an equally deadly shower of arrows and followed their comrades in an arcing turn. At first the volleys seemed to have no effect on the mass of tribesmen, but as Valerius followed Atticus he saw bodies crumple by the hundred. Almost every shaft had hit a mark.

The archers notched new arrows and began a relentless flaying of the outer ranks of attackers as they swept around the flanks, accompanied by a growing howl of frustration and alarm.

Valerius's eyes scanned the Celts for the giant figure he sought, but his attention was drawn by a new and deeper blast of a trumpet.

He knew what the familiar fanfare signified, but even so the effect came as a surprise. The remains of the Roman square seemed to pulse and throw back the attacking ranks of Celtic warriors, pressing them against those in their rear who were doing what they could to take cover from the arrow storm. Another pulse and the cries of consternation became shriller. Good Naso, to know just when to take advantage of the enemy's surprise to launch an attack of his own.

Valerius could visualize the exhausted Roman defenders' advance, one excruciating pace at a time, each step protected by the big *scuta* shields and accompanied by a stab of the *gladius* that harvested the men in front of them. There were still countless thousands of the enemy, but they were confused and tormented to the point of madness, attacked relentlessly at their front by men who should have been long since dead and at their rear by a force that rode infuriatingly out of their reach, stinging like deadly hornets with every stride.

Yet somewhere in that great crowd was a leader with the ability to change everything. Valerius searched the sea of heads, certain he would recognize his prey. Cathal, king of the Selgovae, the mortar that bound the northern alliance, would stand head and shoulders above any man in the thousands within view. The Cathal he remembered from the battle upon the ice would be in the place of the heaviest fighting, inspiring and encouraging, ready to take the battle against the enemy in a show of defiance that would draw his people along with him.

'There!' Shabolz's falcon's eye identified the giant figure among the crowd on the far side of the parade ground.

Valerius glanced at Atticus and the young man frowned. 'Too far,' he said, but he directed the closest archers to the area the Pannonian had pinpointed. The Gauls were riding along the flank of the attack, zipping arrow after arrow into the packed Celtic warriors. 'Save your shafts,' Atticus shouted the order to anyone who could hear. 'There. There is your man.'

They turned the angle of the inner road at a canter, Valerius and his men keeping the closest barbarians at bay with the edge of their long swords. Finally, Atticus turned to the man nearest him. 'Cuno, you have the longest range,' he called. 'The big man in the centre.' In a single smooth movement Cuno brought his bowstring to his lip, aimed and loosed.

Cathal felt the wind of the arrow passing his cheek and heard the smack as it pierced the skull of the man who had been protecting his left side. He looked round in surprise, only for Emrys to throw his shield in front of him. 'How can I conduct a battle if I can't see?' he snarled. Two sharp thuds answered him and his sword brother bared his teeth.

'You would do well to conduct it if you're dead.'

Suddenly the air was alive with arrows and Cathal's men closed about him with their shields. He tried to push them away, cursing, but the shafts fell like hail upon the fragile wooden barrier his sword brothers had erected.

'The attack,' he roared. 'We must keep up the attack.' But the men in front of him were bewildered by the renewed Roman defiance, and those behind cowed by the arrows that spitted the men next to them. Oenghus the druid attempted to rally them, only to go down with an arrow through his gaping mouth. They wavered, and Cathal knew he wouldn't get them to take a forward step again unless he led them himself.

'Lord king,' Emrys said urgently. 'Without you we are nothing. Without you this army will drift away like smoke on the wind. You must live.'

Cathal's mind denied it. He ground his teeth and cursed the gods for forsaking him and the Romans for their very existence. He knew Emrys was right and for a moment he allowed himself to be marched back, protected by a carapace of joined shields that shook and rattled from the arrows that sought him out. He could hear the cries of men dying all around and his mind filled with a red uncontrollable rage. Surely it couldn't end like this? He pushed the shields away and turned to rejoin the fight.

'No!' Emrys clutched at him, and Cathal actually felt the impact of the arrows that killed his sword brother even as the familiar, well-loved face twisted in its death agony. In the same heartbeat the shields were back around him and it was Colm's savage voice in his ear.

'Throw your life away and it is not just your family you are betraying, it is all of us. Emrys and every other man who fell here will die for nothing. Now, enough of this foolishness. Come, lord king.'

This time Cathal didn't resist the hands that pushed him down so his great height was lost among the throng of Selgovae and Venicones warriors. Seeing their leader being ushered to the rear they finally broke and rushed for safety through the ring of horsemen, who were powerless to stop them.

Valerius saw the archers home in on the giant figure and watched the warriors around him fall until his bodyguard closed their shields around him. Now he'd lost Calgacus in the chaos of retreating Celts.

Was he among the dead and injured being trampled into the dirt by his comrades? That no longer mattered. What did was that the Ninth had survived. The legionaries were too exhausted to push their attackers hard, and if they'd decided to fight it out Valerius doubted he had the strength to move them, but the Celts were demoralized and as tired as their enemies. They'd fought through the night and watched their bravest warriors die on Roman swords. That rock-like, unyielding wall of battered shields had sown doubt in their minds. They weren't defeated, but they believed they couldn't win, and the arrival of Atticus's bowmen had confirmed it.

'Let them go,' Valerius told Atticus. 'They still outnumber us and there's no point in provoking them into an unnecessary fight we might not win.'

Calgacus could have made the difference, but Valerius had drawn his teeth by taking away his greatest strength, his sheer size and presence, and ensuring that visibility meant death. Let them go. There would be other days. A lightning bolt of anger surged through him. If Agricola had given him the infantry he'd asked for the insurrection would have finished here and now and the conquest of the rest of the island become a virtual procession of Roman power.

He waited until the parade ground was cleared of all but the Celtic dead and the twitching bodies of the wounded and allowed his horse to pick its way through the bodies to the legionary square.

No one cheered. The men of the Ninth knew this was no victory, but an escape. They stood, gaunt-faced and bloody behind the big curved shields that had saved their lives, their arms red to the elbows with the blood of their enemies. Valerius met the red-rimmed eyes, but they were looking at something far beyond him, or perhaps something within themselves. They'd seen men eviscerated and skewered, blinded and maimed, felt muscles spasm on the iron of their swords and the warmth of their enemy's final breath on their faces. They'd heard the death cries of their comrades, and knew that, but for Fortuna's favour, it could have been any of them. Their walls had been breached and there would be a reckoning for that. They'd killed and they'd survived, but there was no glory in the outcome. He knew he should speak to them. Tell them they'd done well and none could have done better. But the words would have been hollow. He should have been here fighting beside them.

Men groaned, muscles aching as they lifted their shields to create a path into the centre of the square. As he rode inside Valerius saw the *medici* working frantically among hundreds of stricken bodies. A few centurions called to their men to hold their positions in case the Celts re-formed for another attack. No reserves. Every last man had been absorbed into the ranks to keep the countless enemy at bay. It was only then that he recognized Honoratus, the standard-bearer, by his wolf-skin cape, standing by a little huddle of men around one of the fallen.

Quintus Naso lay on his back with his eyes closed, his flesh so pale it was almost luminous, a line of watery blood running from the corner of his lip over his cheek. Hellenicus, the legion's chief doctor, crouched over him, hands clenching and unclenching, brow furrowed and bottom lip nipped between his teeth. He looked up and shook his head. 'There's nothing I can do. I wouldn't know where to start. I'm sorry.'

'He saved us,' Honoratus said. 'Calgacus had almost broken through when the camp prefect led the reserves to stop him. But . . .'

Valerius removed his helmet and knelt to pick up his friend's limp hand. Naso's plate armour had been hit so hard it had been forced deep into his chest. There was no blood, but plainly the damage was mortal. Naso opened his eyes and when he spoke his voice was the barest whisper. 'So you came at last.'

'I should have been with you.'

Naso's hand gripped Valerius's tight. 'The eagle?'

'Is safe, prefect. The enemy is defeated.'

Naso's eyes flickered wildly. 'I do believe my heart is split in two.'

The words were accompanied by a horrible choking sound. Blood welled up to pour from the dying man's mouth as his eyes dulled and the grip on Valerius's fingers went slack. Valerius felt a mix of sorrow and pride and rage he'd never experienced before. The rage was aimed at one man.

'Lord.' A hand shook his shoulder and he looked up into the eyes of Felix, his young escort commander. 'The governor is here.'

Valerius got to his feet. A legionary cohort was marching through the east gate with Agricola and his entourage of aides in their midst. On the hillside on the far side of the river he could see a mix of infantry and cavalry hounding the thousands of Celts still trying to flee south. He picked up his helmet and pushed through the survivors of the Ninth to meet the governor.

'So, Valerius,' Agricola greeted him with a complacent smile, 'it seems I have rescued your legion.'

'My legion did not need rescuing.' Valerius stared up at him in disbelief. 'It had already driven off the barbarians.'

'I disagree.' The governor turned to point to the men on the far hill. 'The enemy was regrouping for another attack when we arrived. Two cohorts of the Twentieth and my Asturian cavalry broke it up. Now they're running like frightened deer. I think we overestimated their fighting powers.'

'A hundred dead legionaries and a hundred and fifty wounded would disagree with you. If we had moved more quickly . . .'

Agricola's grey eyes narrowed dangerously. 'If we'd acted without thought we would have run into an ambush.'

'There was no ambush.'

'Oh, there was an ambush,' Agricola insisted. 'My scouts found signs of two thousand men waiting beside the trail. Perhaps they thought your handful of cavalry not worth the effort?' He turned back to the parade ground where legionaries and auxiliaries were carrying off the Roman dead for burial. The Celts would be left for the wolves and the ravens. 'A hundred dead, you say. I'm sorry. But not an excessive price to pay for what . . . two thousand enemy casualties?'

'One of them was Quintus Naso.'

'Then I'm doubly so. He was a good soldier and a good man. Of course, this means you must have your legion back. Now that we have them confused and on the run, we must keep them that way.'

Valerius knew Agricola expected thanks, but he couldn't bring himself to utter the words. Fortunately they were interrupted by the arrival of the Twentieth legion's commander. Valerius noticed that Tiberius Julius Ursus was accompanied by an Imperial messenger. Agricola turned away to meet them and Valerius tried to focus on the reorganization of his shattered unit.

He heard a sharp cry and turned in time to see the message the governor had just received fluttering from his hand to the trampled earth. As Valerius rushed towards him, Agricola slumped forward in the saddle and for a moment it looked as if he might fall. One of his aides put out a hand to steady him, but he pushed the man away and urged his horse towards the gate, his bodyguard following in his wake.

Valerius saw Ursus staring at the proconsul's retreating back in dismay. 'What's happened?' he asked. Ursus dismounted and picked up the courier's message. He handed it to Valerius.

'His son is dead.'

LV

Londinium

Tabitha hurried up the hill from the governor's palace where she'd spent the day sitting by Domitia Decidiana's bed. The cobbled pavements shimmered in the heat, but a Britannia summer was nothing to a woman brought up on the edge of the stifling Syrian desert. She was being followed again, she was certain, but Rufius Florus and three more of Valerius's escort troop accompanied her so she felt no concern. In any case, it had been happening so frequently since the death of Titus it had become almost a matter of course. She was fairly certain she knew who authorized it.

Domitia had almost fully recovered from Julius's birth. She had convinced herself the infant was normal, but, though he developed physically, there was a vacancy to the blue eyes and a lack of interest in his surroundings that made Tabitha and Ceris believe otherwise. For all the midwives' coddling, Julius had suffered constant coughs and colds during his first winter, and he proved a sickly child, prone to every passing malady. When he picked up a fever around the time of his first birthday it seemed like just another ailment. But the fever worsened in the heat and it had been accompanied by ceaseless diarrhoea. As the

374

weeks passed it became clear that even Ceris's ministrations couldn't save him and they'd been forced to watch the little boy fade away. All through his illness, his mother had refused to accept the seriousness of her son's condition. When he died she'd taken to her bed, and even the news that Agricola had abandoned his legions and was returning to join her didn't stir her.

Tabitha's route took them up past the forum and the basilica. As usual the steps were busy with lawyers and their clients making the most of the fine weather, and the gawpers who had the time and the leisure to watch them. Londinium had drawn in its breath when Titus died. The commitment of Vespasian and his elder son to the province of Britannia was never in question. Domitian was an unknown quantity who had never been expected to take the purple. Few of Londinium's inhabitants had survived Boudicca's rebellion against Rome, but the merchants and petty officials who were the foundation of the city's higher social classes knew well enough that Nero's withdrawal of support and Seneca's decision to call in his loans were among the causes of that terrible tragedy. Their fears seemed justified when long columns of legionaries, almost the equivalent of a full legion, marched through the north gate and down to the docks to take ship for Gesoriacum and the long march to the Rhenus and their eventual destination on the Danuvius frontier.

Yet in the months that followed Domitian ignored Britannia. In fact, he seemed to have forgotten the province's very existence. And for that, Tabitha Verrens was eternally grateful. She knew, who better, of the long history of enmity between the new emperor and her husband. Everything was in place if they had to run. A woman and her two children would act as decoys and give Tabitha, Lucius and Olivia time to make a fast ride to the south coast. There a boat awaited at Novus Portus to carry them across the sea to Germania and up the Rhenus river to Argentoratum. From there they would travel overland to Vesontio and the Sauconna River, which would carry them to the Rhodanus and the Mare Internum. Valerius had warned her to be extra vigilant, but they both understood that if Domitian wanted them dead no amount of vigilance, not even the fierce loyalty of Valerius's body-guard, would stop him. But Domitian was kept busy in Rome, where, if the whisperers had it right, he'd just had his cousin and fellow consul Flavius Sabinus executed. Jealousy appeared to be the only motive, since he'd moved the dead man's wife, his niece Julia, Titus's daughter, into his palace. Domitian's own wife, Domitia Augusta, had been forced out and was said to be marked for death, but something had happened that astounded the doom-sayers and she'd quickly returned to favour.

By the time they reached the villa it was mid-afternoon. Lucius would be with the legionary veteran Valerius had hired to teach him the *gladius*, and the cooks would be preparing the evening meal. The boy's absence would give Tabitha the opportunity to spend time with Olivia, who at four years old had developed into a precocious child with a personality that was a mix of her parents'. She was quick, fearless, adventurous and mischievous in equal measure, all of which served to disguise a deep-seated sensitivity and consideration for others. Between the ages of two and three the combination had made her moody and difficult to control, but now she relished her mother's company.

The sight of a familiar white horse in the stables off the courtyard swiftly banished Tabitha's optimism. Quintus, the *atriensis*, was waiting to greet her at the entrance with Ceris at his side, a scowl of distaste on her face. 'The governor's aide Metilius Aprilis awaits your pleasure inside,' the servant said.

'Very well,' Tabitha said. 'Tell him I will see him presently.'

When the *atriensis* was gone she exchanged a glance with Ceris. 'You know what to do?' The Corieltauvi girl nodded. 'Then see to it.'

A maid helped Tabitha change her shawl while she gathered her thoughts. She knew Valerius had his suspicions that Aprilis was the shadowy figure orchestrating her watchers, though whether it was on the instructions of Agricola neither of them could guess. There had been a time when she'd thought he'd been too close to Lucius for comfort, but the relationship, if that was the word for it, had come to a natural end. She met him frequently enough on her visits to the governor's palace and he'd always been polite and deferential. She'd detected a subtle change since Titus's death, but she reasoned that was natural enough in someone who regarded himself as a coming man. With Titus as his patron Valerius might soon have been in a position to help Aprilis achieve his ambitions. With Titus gone, Valerius was just another patrician who, at best, would be fighting for whatever crumbs Domitian allowed to fall outside his inner circle of friends. Yet just lately there had been another development. Twice she'd caught him staring at her in a way that might be described as calculating. What did it mean? She suspected she was about to find out.

When she walked through to the receiving room Rufius Florus and Hilario took station at her shoulder. It was unusual for them to accompany her in the house, but she felt the need to make an impression on her visitor and Hilario's fearsome scowl would certainly do that.

The man in the room turned as she entered, his eyes momentarily widening at the sight of her escort, but he recovered quickly and bent at the waist in a deep bow. She acknowledged the bow with a slight nod of the head and a smile. 'How nice it is to see you again, tribune. It's such a pity your duties have been so onerous lately that you've been unable to visit. Lucius misses your company.'

'With the governor away so often . . .' Aprilis returned her smile with a shrug. He was a handsome man, tall, with wide shoulders, a face that might be described as open and honest if you didn't appreciate the devious workings behind the blue eyes, and dark hair crimped into fashionable curls.

'To what do we owe the pleasure of this visit, Metilius?'

'The lady Domitia asked me to pass on her appreciation for your support during these recent difficult times. It is her wish that the governor should find some way to honour you as a token of her thanks.'

'I do what I do from friendship and my high regard for the lady,' Tabitha said quietly. 'Odd, though, that she did not tell me herself when I have just come from her side.'

The suggestion left Aprilis only slightly discomfited. 'You have me pinned, lady.' His words were accompanied by a disarming smile. 'The fact is that I came on my own initiative. Perhaps we could speak privately.'

Tabitha glanced at her bodyguard, Rufius Florus emotionless, Hilario glaring like a wolfhound on the brink of attack.

'We will walk in the garden,' she said. 'I will call you if I need you.' She led the way past the colonnaded walkway to the formal gardens with their paved pathways, shady fruit trees and beds filled with herbs and flowers. 'Now, Metilius.' She followed the path along the centre and he walked at her side. 'Let us get to the heart of this mysterious visit.'

Aprilis stopped abruptly and turned to her. 'I came to warn you that you are in grave danger, lady.' His voice lost all its lightness. 'And not only you, but Lucius and Olivia too.'

Tabitha gave him an appraising look. 'And what, precisely, does this danger entail?'

He held her gaze. 'I have a feeling you know only too well.'

She turned away and continued walking. 'My husband is commander of the Ninth legion Hispana and a member of the Senate. This house is protected by his personal bodyguard. No one would dare harm me or my children.'

'On the contrary,' Aprilis continued smoothly. 'Your husband is the source of the danger. I know for a fact that the governor carries a letter ordering his execution which only requires a single word of confirmation to be put into action.'

She stopped again. 'I think you underestimate Valerius, tribune.'

He shook his head. 'Gaius Valerius Verrens is a dead man, by order of the Emperor himself. The only question is the timing.' He moved a step closer and a familiar scent tickled her nostrils. The smell of male excitement mixed with something even more powerful. Fear. 'His name will be wiped from history. I have seen the reports the governor sends to Rome. The commanders of his legions might as well have never existed. I cannot save Valerius, but I will do what I can to save you and your family.'

Tabitha pretended she was considering his offer. 'One thing puzzles me.' She frowned. 'Why would you risk your career for the family of someone the Emperor believes is his enemy?'

'Because I've come to admire you, lady.' He moved forward, so close she was forced to endure his sour breath on her face. 'You are a very attractive woman, Tabitha. If I keep you and your children alive I expect you will find a suitable way to show your gratitude.' His hand slipped beneath her shawl to cup her breast, but she didn't flinch or push it away. He smiled. 'Don't call the guards. That would be unfortunate for the children.'

She almost laughed at his naivety. 'Why would you desire an old married lady like me?'

'A man tires of concubines with their practised wiles, and bovine slave girls, however willing.' His fingers worked at her flesh. 'I don't expect you to enjoy it, not at first, but your reluctance will give me even greater pleasure.'

She stared at him. She knew that for men like Aprilis the act was not about pleasure, but about power and manipulation.

A deep chesty growl from the far side of the garden made Aprilis half turn his head. In the same heartbeat Tabitha drew the little knife she'd been concealing beneath her shawl and placed the point very precisely against the large vein in his neck. He froze, his mouth half open to cry for help.

'Have you ever seen a man bleed to death, Metilius?' Her voice remained almost conversational. 'Just the slightest nick and there is no turning back. You feel the tiniest prick against your neck. It starts with little spurts that seem almost insignificant. You put your fingers against the wound and you can feel your heart pumping. You're certain you can get it to stop, but no matter how hard you press the blood just keeps coming and coming. You feel yourself fading away. That's the most wonderful thing about this death, Metilius: the person knows they are dying, but there is nothing they can do about it.' She used the pressure of the knife to turn his head so he couldn't avoid her dark, implacable eyes. 'And the person doing the killing can appreciate every moment of their agony. Not the agony of pain. The agony of knowing that all that awaits is darkness. I've seen it, Metilius. As their lifeblood drains away they are consumed by a kind of madness. They'll do anything to stop the bleeding. They'll use moss, or earth, push their fingers deep into their own body, but the heart keeps pumping and the blood keeps coming.' She turned his head a little more so he could see the corner of the garden where Ceris stood, her hand gripping the collar of a massive guard dog whose bulging shoulders and great shaggy head topped her waist. Aprilis quivered beneath the gaze of the beast's burning red eyes. 'Of course, then I would have to explain how you'd come to cut yourself and that might prove awkward. But that's not what I plan. Lysander here has been specially bred to react to the scent of blood. His previous owner spiked his walls with broken oyster shell so anyone climbing over would cut themselves, and then . . .' She shrugged. 'When I slice the vein Ceris will release him. You'll try to run, of course, but Lysander is very swift for his size – don't shake so much, Metilius, or I might cut you by mistake – and he'll knock you to the ground and then you'll feel his jaws working on your throat, that big head shaking as his teeth rip your flesh. Perhaps he'll tear your head from your shoulders; he's perfectly capable, as you can imagine. It will be quicker, of course, which I'll regret, but it can be passed off as an accident, especially with so many prepared to swear to it.'

'Please . . .'

She brought her face close to his. 'I do not need my husband's protection, Metilius, or that of my bodyguard. I am perfectly capable of eradicating vermin who threaten my family or myself. You will call off your watchdogs. You will never in future defile my house with your presence on any pretext. If you ever threaten my children again I will personally remove what are laughingly known as your manly parts and feed them to Lysander while you watch. Do you believe me, Metilius? You may nod.'

Aprilis moved his head slightly and winced at the sting of the point.

'Yes,' Tabitha said almost dreamily. 'You were that close.' She removed the knife point from his flesh. 'Now you may go.'

Without a word the young tribune stumbled towards the doorway to the courtyard, his hand clapped to his neck and his terrified eyes on the big mastiff. When he was gone, Tabitha sighed. 'Rufius,' she called. 'I know you've been listening. Tell Quintus to bring me parchment and stylus. I would write to my husband.'

Ceris ruffled Lysander's head and led him off to the kitchens. 'Come on, you useless old brute. Time for your dinner.'

LVI

'We will go north. Where else can we go?'

The answering murmur acknowledged the right of it, but contained no hint of enthusiasm. Ragged and filthy from days spent trying to stay ahead of the hunting Roman cohorts, the five men crouched around the glowing embers of a small fire set in a forest dell.

It had taken all of Cathal's energy to gather the remnants of his routed forces in the remote valley. He tried to ignore the accusing eyes and downcast faces in the firelight. Rurid the Caledonian, smug in the knowledge he'd suffered the fewest casualties of any of the tribes. If he'd been able to control his men they would have stayed in place to ambush the cavalry wing that had destroyed Cathal's hopes. King Donacha, a sword slash scarring his right cheek and eyes still dark with grief for the brother he'd lost to a Roman arrow. Torn by the knowledge that it might have all been so different if he hadn't hesitated while the legion was forming its defensive square. No reproach from Colm, Cathal's Selgovae sword brother, who would follow him to the last. It took him a moment to remember Emrys was dead, and he winced at the knowledge he, Cathal, had killed the man who among all the others could be called his friend. Vodenos and his contingent of

Brigantes were still missing, separated from the main force by the Romans who scoured the mountains and glens.

'You have nothing to say, priest?'

'What is there to say?' Gwlym shivered and pulled filthy blankets closer to his spare body. This had been the first time he'd felt cold in summer. Was it a sign of growing age or a symptom of defeat? 'The south has been grazed to the roots by your warriors,' he gave the word a mocking ring that had Colm's hand twitching over his sword hilt, 'and what little they didn't gorge themselves upon has been taken by the Romans. West? The hills might sustain a few dozen of Rurid's stinking mountain goats, but not an army. The sea lies to the east and I am not overly fond of fish. If we stay here we will end up eating each other. So where else but north, as our great leader points out.'

The words *great leader* held a bitter edge that wounded Cathal more than the reproachful looks of the others, yet the druid's contempt had a basis in fact. A true leader would have stayed aloof from the fighting and concentrated on what should have been his greatest priority: the Roman supplies that would feed his army through the winter. Cathal had trusted his subordinates to strip the Roman baggage carts of the staples that would fill their bellies when the snows came: sacks of grain and flour, dried and salted meats and fish, and the hard biscuits the legions carried in such abundance. Instead they'd become bewitched by the glitter of gold and silver ornaments and befuddled by wine. They'd carried off barely a tenth of what Cathal had expected. With enough supplies he would have been able to withdraw back into the mountains and lure the Romans to him. Now he had only one course of action.

'Prepare your warriors to march in two days. We will distribute what supplies we have among them. Any man who wastes a single grain of barley will have me to reckon with – make sure they know that.' He raised his hammer, still spattered with the blood and brains of the men he'd killed days earlier. 'Have the first warrior of any tribe who disregards my order brought to me and I will provide an example of what true discipline means.' His companions quailed before the intensity of the narrow eyes, and murmured their agreement. 'The Romans have built a fort to the north of the valley mouth. We must bypass it without being detected, but as far as possible we will stay close to the line of the mountains, sending foraging parties out among the farms towards the coast.'

'The Taexali will not like us taking their food,' Rurid warned.

'Then they should have supported us,' Colm spat. 'With another two thousand warriors we would have taken the camp and driven the Red Scourge out of their lands. Instead they were content to stay on their farms, sit on their hands and let us bleed in their stead. If they go hungry this winter it is their own doing.'

'We are an army,' Cathal agreed. 'We cannot fight on empty bellies. In time they will have reason to thank us.'

He knew that not a man there believed him, not even Colm, but that didn't matter because he didn't believe himself. How times had changed since he'd fought the Roman on the ice all those seasons ago. Cathal, king of the Selgovae, reduced to mealy-mouthed lies to hold together his fragile coalition of followers. The question was how long they would continue to follow him without a victory.

'What is our strategy?' Donacha might have read his mind. 'What is your plan now for defeating the Romans?'

It was a sensible enough question. Donacha and Rurid would have to try to convince the leaders of their war bands, just as Cathal had tried to convince them. Cathal would have preferred the question remained unasked. The truth was he had no answer. 'For the moment it is enough that we stay ahead of them and conserve our strength. The land between the mountains and the coast is fruitful, but it will not feed more than one army. While we eat, they will go hungry. When the time is right we will turn on them and destroy the weakest of the legions, the Ninth.'

'It was the Ninth who killed my brother,' Donacha pointed out. 'They may not be so easy to defeat.'

'Do you have a better plan, lord king?'

Donacha only stared at the flames, and Cathal wondered how long the courage and will of his closest and most valuable ally could be sustained. Eventually the younger man looked up and met his gaze. 'You are our leader, Cathal of the Selgovae. I only hope that when the time comes we will be worthy of that leadership.'

Cathal nodded. He rose and turned away lest they see the strength of his relief. Without Donacha and his Venicones it was over. Colm followed him, leading Gwlym by the arm. They wound their way through the trees to the rough shelter Cathal's men had built for him, where Olwyn waited with Dugald and Berta. He had sent for his family as soon as it became clear he had no option but retreat. It was they who had identified the small fort the Romans had built thinking to pen Cathal into the mountains. At first he'd been tempted to attack the auxiliary garrison, but his scouts had identified a second, much larger camp, less than three miles north. After the shambles of the night attack on the Ninth's camp it wasn't worth risking another blow to the morale of his shaken warriors. Better to slip by, using the river to protect his flank, and put a safe distance between himself and the Romans in the gently undulating countryside to the north.

He had reason for haste. Rurid, who knew his country well, warned of what he called a choke point a few days' march away where the western hills descended to within a few miles of the sea. If the Romans reached it first they would effectively trap Cathal's army in a small triangle, or force him back into the unforgiving mountains from which he doubted he would emerge with his forces intact.

Olwyn looked up in the lamplight as the three men entered, and the sight of her simultaneously raised his spirits and filled his heart with fear. The children were curled up in furs on the far side of the shelter. Colm led Gwlym to a makeshift bench and helped him sit before returning to the curtained doorway.

'I'll talk to Donacha and Rurid about the distribution of the provisions,' he whispered with a glance at the boy and girl. 'Like as not that Caledonian bast—' he saw Olwyn's look and grinned, 'he'll try to cheat us.'

'Make sure you keep some back in case Vodenos and his Brigantes find their way through the enemy patrols to us.'

Colm gave Cathal a look that told him what he thought the chances were and disappeared into the darkness.

'So it is decided, husband?' Olwyn said quietly.

He nodded. 'We go north in two days. We'll need to move fast once we get past the Roman camp, so be prepared to travel light.'

She smiled. 'I'm ready.'

He took a seat beside her on the scattered furs. 'Of course.' He returned the smile. 'I never doubted you.' He picked up the clay oil lamp from its shelf and studied the flame. 'Sometimes . . .'

She placed a finger on his lips. 'No regrets, Cathal of the Selgovae. You did what was right and no man could have done better. One day, when the Romans are defeated, we will return to our home beside the river and this will be nothing but a bad dream. Berta will marry a fine young warrior and we will find Dugald a princess, and we can grow old and fat together by the fire.'

He took her in his arms and held her to him, marvelling as always at the lightness of her frame. 'Aye,' he said. 'That will be the way of it.' He bent his head to breathe in the sweet, smoky scent of her hair. 'Donacha as much as said he doesn't believe we can win.'

'You must win.' Her voice took on the determination of a wildcat defending its kits. 'We cannot let these people turn us into slaves.'

A grunt of bitter laughter interrupted the conversation. Gwlym, all but forgotten in the shadows. 'Your Brigantes welcomed slavery. If Cartimandua had brought her warriors south to stand side by side with Caratacus the Romans would never have passed the Tamesa. If they had joined Boudicca the only Romans left on this island would be *our* slaves.'

'Cartimandua had her reasons,' Olwyn said defensively. 'As did my uncle. You must win.' She gripped Cathal's flesh so hard that he winced. 'You must win for Dugald and Berta and the future of every other child in this land. For every warrior who followed you and every widow the Romans have made. You must make sure that the name of Cathal rings out across all of Britannia as a beacon of freedom. Promise me.'

'I promise,' he said, not knowing how the vow would ever be fulfilled. How could he fail them?

LVII

The three men stood on the rampart of the temporary fort, cloaked against the rain, their gaze on the murky landscape to the north. To their left the mountains were a shadowy streak more sensed than seen. On their right hand, beyond a narrow river, lay a gently rolling landscape of farm, field and woodland that eventually ended three or four miles away where the waves lapped the beach. The commanders of three legions had gathered to vent their frustrations at yet another delay.

'We can't just sit here and do nothing.' Herenius Polio, legate of the Second Adiutrix, repeated the mantra they'd heard for the last hour and more. 'Move now and we have Calgacus like a mouse in the claws of a stooping hawk.'

'We have our orders.' Julius Ursus muttered the words as if they were a curse. 'We are not to attempt any further offensive operations until he returns. You do not know him as I do. Agricola will not countenance any disobedience.'

'Valerius, you are the senior among us.' Polio felt Ursus bridle at his side. 'I know you are the elder, Julius, but we all heard the governor: *If I fall the province shall be his.* His very words, Julius. Could it not be suggested that the governor has indeed *fallen*, that the impact of his son's death has rendered him incapable of carrying out his duties?'

'You are talking mutiny,' Ursus spluttered. 'If you were one of my centurions it would be my duty to strike you down.'

Polio's hand went to his sword hilt, but Valerius stilled it with a touch of his own. Time and circumstance had healed the division that had arisen between them at the time of Agricola's announcement of Titus's death. 'Enough, Julius,' he said to Ursus. Mutiny and its consequences were always a thorny subject, but never more than now. In the aftermath of the attack on the Ninth the entire Usipi auxiliary cohort had marched for the coast and commandeered three Liburnian transports to take them back to their native Germania. 'We are discussing strategy, not mutiny. Every man here must be free to express his thoughts. Are we agreed?'

'Very well.' Ursus bowed his head to his fellow legates. 'You have my apologies, legate. I spoke in the heat of the moment.'

'Then I will express mine,' Polio said. 'I believe that in the governor's absence due to his ill health, the man he designated as his successor should assume command. Agricola was distraught when he issued his edict against offensive action. You must do what you believe is right, Valerius. I for one will endorse in writing any orders you give. Julius?'

'I'm not certain.' The older officer shook his head. 'Agricola . . .'

In the long silence that followed, Valerius fought the conflicting emotions that tore him. He knew Polio was right: someone should take command. They'd been chasing shadows ever since they'd left Brigante country. Calgacus's forces were ripe for the plucking after their failure to destroy the Ninth. In the aftermath, Agricola had been so affected by his son's death it had blinded him to his duty. But did that give them leave to countermand the orders of a proconsul of Rome with the power of *imperium*? Any emperor might see it as an act of mutiny. Mutiny meant death. If Valerius, in particular, accepted the command he might as well send Domitian his head on a silver plate. He still couldn't understand why the Emperor who hated him so deeply allowed him to live. Sometimes he woke in the night feeling like a mouse being watched by a cat. Perhaps that was the reason? Domitian intended to prolong his suffering. No matter. He had made his decision.

'You need not concern yourself, legate.' Valerius brushed droplets of water from the lanolin-coated surface of his cloak. 'I have no wish to take over the command of the expedition.' He ignored Polio's astonished stare. 'In my opinion the governor's indisposition is temporary. He has every right to order a halt until we can advance again under his guidance. Whether I think those orders are correct or not, we have a duty to follow them.'

'So the legions should hold their positions?' Polio didn't hide his disgust.

Valerius nodded. 'That's my assessment of the situation.' Ursus murmured agreement. 'But to return to your original point,' he continued, addressing Polio, 'I don't believe we should simply sit here and do nothing.'

'What?' both men said simultaneously.

Valerius smiled. 'Agricola's orders are that the legions shouldn't conduct offensive operations during his absence. That means maintaining this camp. Are we agreed?' Ursus and Polio nodded. 'But they don't preclude us from carrying out patrols, and the size and composition of those patrols is entirely up to the judgement of the individual commander.'

Ursus saw it first. 'So if I sent out, for instance, my First cohort and a cavalry wing to carry out a sweep of the farmland five or six miles north in search of enemy activity . . .'

'And I did the same,' Polio chimed in, with a look of enquiry at Valerius.

'Precisely,' he said.

'If the *patrols* of all three legions happened to meet up,' Polio said admiringly, 'that's a force of four thousand fighting men, foot and horse. More than enough to give Calgacus pause.'

'True.' Ursus's acknowledgement was tentative. 'Enough to give him pause, but not enough for an outright confrontation. At least not without an unacceptable risk?' He looked to Valerius.

'You're correct, legate. But I wasn't thinking of an outright confrontation.' He swept his wooden fist over the vista to the north. 'What lies out there?'

'Calgacus?' Ursus suggested.

'The people who sustain Calgacus,' Valerius corrected him. 'We know from the prisoners and deserters we've captured that some of his men are already going hungry. Our foraging patrols report the farmers and tribal chieftains complaining that Calgacus's army have already stripped them clean. If we can stop his war bands supplying themselves . . .'

'Search and destroy,' Polio suggested. 'One big sweep through the country he hasn't touched yet. Everything we don't take we burn. He can't operate in a desert.'

'Every farm we burn adds another few spears to Calgacus's army,' Valerius said. 'And drives those currently beyond our reach into his arms. We want him weakened, not strengthened.'

'Then what?'

'Rufus?' Valerius called. 'Get yourself up here.'

They waited while the scout ran up the earthen bank from where he'd been waiting among the baggage carts and saluted breathlessly. 'At your orders, legate.'

'Tell these gentlemen what you told me.'

Rufus stood before the three legates. 'I've been talking to the farmers in the country we've passed through and watching Calgacus's foraging patrols at work among those to the north.' He paused, considering his next words. 'It seems to me they're asking for trouble. They work to a set pattern. They'll choose a nice juicy area between the mountains and the coast, appear at dawn and work their way from farm to farm taking what they can find and leaving the farmers and their families very little. They always give themselves plenty of time to get back before dusk, because by now they're heavily laden or slowed down by the farm carts they've looted.'

'That's all very well,' Ursus said, 'but of little use unless we know where they're going to strike next.'

'As I said,' Rufus continued, undaunted, 'they work to a pattern. By looking at where they've been and having an idea of how the land lies further north, I reckon I can pretty much tell where they'll turn up next. All we have to do is get there first, lie up for the night and hit them before they reach the farms.'

The plan clearly appealed to Polio, but he had a suggestion. 'Why not wait?' he argued. 'Let them strip the farms and hit them on the way back to their camp. That way we get the grain and Calgacus gets nothing but the blame.' He saw Valerius frown and shrugged. 'If you're feeling generous we can dole out grain to the farmers a few days later as an act of kindness – without telling them it's their own food.'

'Perfect.' Even lugubrious Ursus couldn't hide his enthusiasm. 'We can hit Calgacus where it hurts most, but it's just a patrol, not an offensive action by any one legion, so we're obeying the governor's orders.'

'But if Agricola doesn't return before the start of the next campaigning season,' Polio persisted, 'I want your pledge that you will either take command and lead us north or endorse my letter to the Emperor asking that we be pulled back. My centurions report that the men are at the end of their tether. After five years on campaign rations, without a roof over their heads or a warm bath, it won't take much more to make them join the Usipi.'

Valerius felt their eyes on him. 'Very well,' he agreed. 'If Agricola doesn't return by the spring I will take command and lead us north. We will finish it next year or not at all.'

LVIII

'You have been busy, I hear?' Julius Agricola didn't invite his three commanders to sit. The governor had arrived at the legions' winter camp five days before Polio's deadline expired. Agricola looked pale and drawn and his whole manner was oddly lethargic, as if the very act of existence was a trial to him. Valerius had been surprised to see Metilius Aprilis among his retinue. The governor's question and its implication that he'd been receiving regular reports of their activities drew a splutter of outrage from Julius Ursus.

'You will find that your orders were obeyed to the last detail, proconsul,' he snapped. 'My legion has not advanced a single inch since you left with a month of the campaigning season still available to us.' Now it was Agricola who reacted, the grey eyes narrowing dangerously. But Ursus wouldn't be deflected. 'Men in camp need to be worked if they are not to become stale, and that is what we did. Work them hard. Constant patrols, and if one of those patrols came across a barbarian foraging party what were they to do? Ignore them?'

'Hundreds of enemy dead and more taken captive. Enough grain seized to feed an entire legion over the winter with some to spare to be returned to help sustain its original owners.' Valerius suppressed a grim smile. With this level of detail the clerks of three legions would face some harsh questioning in the morning. 'I do not remember any of that being included in my orders?'

'A fortunate consequence of the expedition's patrolling activities,' Polio assured him. 'Surely something to be applauded, not censured?'

Agricola studied the three men, his gaze settling on Valerius, who had remained silent. Eventually he decided he had nothing more to gain. 'Where is Calgacus now?'

'He wintered three days' march north of here,' Valerius replied. 'His scouts watch us from the mountains for any sign of a general movement.'

'Will he stand and fight?'

Valerius shook his head. 'He never has in the past. It's more likely he'll try to get us to divide our forces again' – he ignored Agricola's glare – 'then turn on the weakest element. His people are going hungry thanks to the success of our patrols. Our granaries will be very tempting.'

The governor took a moment to gather his thoughts. 'Then prepare your legions, gentlemen. There will be no division of forces. With all the rains we've had the grazing will be sufficient to support our cavalry in another week. We will march as a single unit with the Twentieth in the van and the Ninth bringing up the rear. Calgacus will retreat north again. Our cavalry will harry his forces every step of the way and we will hound him until he has nowhere else to run or no option but to turn against us. To the very end of the earth if that is what it takes. You will receive my orders through my aide, Aprilis. He will be joining the Ninth legion as a replacement for the late *praefectus castrorum* Quintus Naso.'

Valerius had to bite his tongue to stifle a protest. The appointment should have been his to make and Metilius Aprilis was the last man he would have chosen. He was too aware of the fate of his predecessor as the Ninth's legate to feel comfortable working in close proximity to the man who'd probably given him the fatal push.

Agricola seemed oblivious of the anger he'd caused, because his thin lips twisted into a semblance of a smile. 'He has shown a sudden enthusiasm for campaigning. It seems Londinium is stifling his military talents. Now, if you would leave me, I am weary after my journey.'

Valerius bowed with the rest, and together they hurried from the headquarters tent. Ursus was wrapped up in his own thoughts, but Valerius exchanged a glance with Polio.

'I wish you good fortune with your new camp prefect, legate,' the other man said. 'But I wouldn't be turning my back on him too often.'

'It seems our commander is even less trusting than I'd thought,' Valerius agreed with a bitter smile. 'He seems to know about every last spear and every grain of barley we captured.'

'Yes, there will be a reckoning for that. One of my clerks is going to spend the rest of his enlistment digging latrines. Still,' the Second's commander half-turned to look northwards, 'he has us on the move at last. This time we will finish it.' He shook his head wearily. 'We must finish it. Will we, do you think, or . . .'

'Yes,' Valerius said. 'I think we'll finish it.'

When he returned to his tent he received an odd look from the guards. It was only when he entered that he discovered why. A hulking figure in a hooded cloak sat on a bench in the corner. Valerius recognized his visitor even before he stood up and threw back the hood.

'Hilario? Shouldn't you be with the mistress?'

Hilario scowled at the implied rebuke. 'The lady sent me,' he said. 'She said it was time I was back with the legion. I didn't do anything wrong,' he added, reaching beneath bis cloak.

'You have a letter for me?'

'Yes, lord.' The big fist emerged with a battered scroll case.

Valerius took it and placed it on his campaign desk. Tabitha had taken the trouble to double-seal it, which told him it was no normal missive. He held the leather cylinder down with his wooden fist and worked at the straps with the fingers of his left hand. When he broke the seals and pulled back the flap he discovered it was not one letter, but two. His heart quickened as he recognized the form of the larger, but he unwrapped the smaller, little more than a scrap of parchment, first. He smiled as he saw the familiar flowing lines of writing.

'You've done well,' he said to Hilario. 'You can go and join your tent-mates. They'll be pleased to see you again. But be ready to march at dawn tomorrow.'

'Yes, lord,' Hilario replied with a salute that would have broken a lesser man's ribs.

Valerius read: *Husband, I write this in haste because I suspect the enclosed is of some importance, so I will forgo the normal endearments. I fear Hilario may have misunderstood my urgings to be inconspicuous, but Rufius and Ceris are out and there is no other I can trust. If the gods are kind he will leave with the governor tomorrow. Agricola is . . . no, I must not digress. The enclosed letter was delivered by what I can only describe as a man of mystery. At first I feared he was an assassin when I found him in the gardens teaching Lucius the rudiments of some game soldiers play, having somehow evaded the guard. He would not tell me his name, but he showed me a piece of jewellery he said you would recog-nize, a gold ring with a large green stone set in a coiled snake.* Valerius caught his breath at the description which confirmed his hopes and his fears. *He could not carry the letter further because he had encountered some merchants of his acquaintance in Londinium and feared they might divine, and possibly reveal, his purpose. He begged me to forward the letter to you by the fastest possible means and to convey the kindest thoughts of the sender. His manner and deportment convinced me of his good faith. I make no judgement, Valerius, I only hope this finds you in good health and good spirits. Your loving wife, Tabitha.* She had added a single line as an addendum. *Aprilis is with Agricola. Do not trust him if you value your life.*

When he read the penultimate sentence Valerius felt a twinge of guilt that he immediately dismissed. Tabitha would hear the truth about Domitia Longina Corbulo when he returned to Londinium, but a shiver accompanied the thought. What did the Emperor's wife have to tell him that was important enough to risk discovery and death even when carried by someone she trusted with her life?

There was only one way to find out. He broke the seal on the second scroll and unrolled it. It came as no surprise to discover it was in a code he instantly recognized. At first glance it was an impenetrable block of numbers which could mean nothing. Look again and a structure could be discerned. His eye sought out the symbol that would allow him to unlock the code he and Domitia Longina Corbulo had contrived between them a decade and more earlier. It gave him the letter for which the number 1 had been substituted. Discard the first two long sentences, which were meaningless and designed to discourage and dismay. The rest was simply a matter of transcribing. He reached for his stylus.

My dearest Valerius, I give thanks that you are reading this for it means you live and I have acted in time. It is no secret between us that the Emperor wishes you dead. Orders have already been issued to that end which require only official confirmation. The man I remember will have taken steps to combat this, but you should know that you still have friends in Rome, and those friends have been able to put in place certain safeguards that avoid the requirement for immediate action. These safeguards relate to the circumstances of the recent death of our mutual friend and certain information about the causes. Should this information come to light it would cause embarrassment and possibly more serious consequences even for the most powerful. Valerius reread the last two sentences with a frown of concentration. *Our mutual friend* undoubtedly referred to Titus; was Domitia hinting his death was suspicious? Yes, that must be it. Why else would it cause *serious consequences even for the most powerful?* Who was more powerful than the Emperor himself? He felt a pang of grief for his old friend and a fierce rage welled up inside him. The official statement suggested he'd died as a result of a long illness. Instead it appeared he'd been murdered in the most obscene fashion by his own brother. He picked up the stylus again and continued to decipher the code. *Multiple copies of this information have been compiled and are held by people I trust. Those they concern have been made aware of this fact, and will undoubtedly be seeking the identity of the holders. Steps have been taken to ensure that in the event of any unfortunate accidents the documents be passed to senators of irreproachable character who will be outraged by their contents and take the appropriate action. Still, there can be no certainties with a man such as he. Should you hear of my demise, or that of those close to me, take your family and seek refuge where you can. D.*

Valerius read the letter through again, imprinting the words on his mind. When he was satisfied he could recite it at will he put the parchment to the flame of the oil lamp and watched it shrivel and blacken, dropping it before the flames reached his fingers. More reluctantly, he destroyed Tabitha's letter in the same fashion.

As the flames died he turned his thoughts back to the letter's contents. Did Domitia really think her husband's hand would be stayed by the threat of accusations based on something that might not even exist? That their ultimate survival – for that final line proved she too was under threat – would be somehow guaranteed? It seemed she did, and Valerius, dredging up his memories of a younger Domitian, could perhaps understand why. Who understood that complex, murderous and mercurial character better than she? Three different elements ruled his life and dictated his moods, like three horses straining in different directions: vanity, insecurity and the need to feel loved.

To be accused in the Senate of the vile crime of fratricide would rock him to his very foundations. Titus had been loved by many, but respected by all. Even the suggestion he'd been murdered would inflame the mob. Worst of all for Domitian, the legions Titus commanded had worshipped him. An emperor might lose the mob and the Senate, as Nero had, and somehow limp on, but without the army he was doomed. Domitian would scour the Empire to hunt down the incriminating documents, but he would never know if he'd found them all. Still, there were no guarantees. He would continue to watch his back for the assassin's knife, but Domitia's letter at least raised the hope that he might live to see his family again.

But first he had to overcome Calgacus.

LIX

The Romans were on the move and he did not know what to do. 'It is finished.' Cathal struggled to keep the emotion from his voice. 'I have failed you.'

'It is not finished as long as you are alive, husband.' Olwyn's ferocious assurance was an attempt to restore his courage and he knew it. But her pink cheeks were sunken, the bones of her face showing like knife edges and the blue eyes dull and tired. She knew the reality as well as he. 'The sword brothers of the Selgovae will never desert you.'

'Even if you are right, what use are my loyal Selgovae without the Venicones and the Caledonians? Donacha says the chiefs of his war bands will desert if we move another mile further north. They pine for their own lands and they are sick of running. They have had enough of watching their wives try to make a meal with half a cup of flour and a handful of grass and their children crying with the pain of their empty bellies.'

They had wintered at a place the locals called Devana on the estuary of the river Dan, where the ground never froze and fish and wildfowl supplemented their meagre diet until they inevitably ran out. He'd sent out emissaries to the tribes in the north and the scattered communities of the western mountains urging them to unite with him against the invader. The only result was a trickle of untried young men determined to prove themselves, but a further drain on his supplies.

The warrior kings of the north had heard of the Romans, but no Roman had set foot on their land or burned one of their homesteads. Their warriors owned swords and spears, but at heart they were farmers. What incentive did they have to leave their families and their fields to fight with a man who had no great victory to boast of? His foraging parties had been forced to search far afield for provisions as the farmers grew wise to their ravages and took greater care in hiding their stores. More and more of the foragers fell victim to Roman ambush, some disappearing as entirely as if they had been swallowed up by the earth itself. Warriors became reluctant to volunteer, even though every raid gave a man a chance to put away something, however little, for his own family. That was when the complaints had grown into anger and then threat.

'And what of Rurid and his Caledonians?'

'All they want to do is fight. If they did not fear me they would fight each other.'

'Then fight.' The words were accompanied by a hacking cough. Gwlym had spent the winter in virtual hibernation, barely stirring from his blankets unless it was to take a bowl of broth, spooned into his mouth by Olwyn or Berta. At times it had been difficult to tell whether he was alive or dead. 'Fight the Romans.'

'Fight three legions with fifteen thousand men? Fifteen thousand men weakened by hunger and camp fever? The Romans have at least as many, fit and well fed. The one thing I learned in the attack on the Ninth's camp is that we cannot defeat them man to man when they hide behind their wall of shields and iron and we have nothing but swords and spears and willing flesh.'

'I didn't say defeat them,' the druid croaked. 'I said fight them. Sometimes defeat is only a different kind of victory.'

'You talk in riddles, old man,' Olwyn snapped. 'Do not listen to him, Cathal.'

'See,' Gwlym chortled. 'For all her fine words she does not want you to fight. She wants you safe, with your great ugly head on your shoulders, so you can warm her bed, which is where you will die, Cathal, king of the Selgovae, forgotten and embittered – if you do not fight.'

'What do you mean, priest?'

'If you do not fight your army will melt away like the snow in springtime,' Gwlym said with infinite patience. 'You will have a choice of surrendering to the Romans and being carried away in chains, or returning to the hills of your homeland defeated and reviled as the man who created so many widows to no purpose. Perhaps, if you are fortunate, King Crinan will make you his court entertainer, or Bruda will let you clean out his cattle pens.' He ignored Cathal's growl of fury. 'But if you choose to make a stand your warriors will follow, your warriors will fight, and, if necessary, your warriors will die for the privilege of saying they stood beside Cathal of the Selgovae and went sword to sword and spear to spear with the Romans. It does not matter, even, that you may be outnumbered. The more legionaries Agricola throws against you the greater the honour, the further the myth will travel. For that is your fate, lord king, win or lose, dead or alive: to be remembered. To become a beacon for your people. In generations to come the name Cathal will be a rallying cry for the inhabitants of this island. A legend.'

'Or just another body to make a meal for the crows and the foxes,' Olwyn whispered.

'No,' Gwlym cried. 'Don't you understand? That is what must not happen. Alive or dead, the great King Cathal, the mighty hammer of Rome, must vanish in the mountain mists. As a man, however great your prowess, your story ends with your death. As a ghost your name will live for ever.' Still, he sensed doubt. 'Would Boudicca's name still be revered if her corpse had been found among the countless dead of her last battle? No, she would just be another commander who underestimated the Romans and led her army to the slaughter. But she was not found. Twenty years later Catuvellauni men still huddle around campfires and whisper that she is alive. In Iceni country women swear they have seen the queen, and her daughters Banna and Rosmerta, walking among the trees or by the river. Her fame will be eternal.'

Cathal felt his wife's hand settle on his, the slim fingers light as a butterfly's wings. He turned to look into Olwyn's eyes and saw tears there, but also a fierce, almost hawkish pride. A message passed between them and Cathal nodded.

'We will fight.'

But where?

He cast his mind to his surroundings. They could take up position on the high ground beyond the river and draw the Romans on to them. His Selgovae would hold the centre, of course, with Rurid and the Caledonians in the place of honour on his right, and Donacha's Venicones defending the much more important left with their flank covered by the coastal marshes. The only drawback was that the river here was relatively narrow. After witnessing the ingenuity of the Romans at Brynmochdar and watching them build their defensive camps, he had little doubt that they would swiftly find a way to cross. Cathal had a momentary vision of a Roman legion falling on his flank like wolves. No, it would not do. It was not sufficient just to fight the Romans; enough of his army must survive to spread Gwlym's myth. Wherever he fought, the ability to conduct a fighting withdrawal was as important as his dispositions for battle. He had the image in his head. All he had to do was find it.

'We cannot go north . . .'

'Then go west,' Gwlym said. 'Follow the river and the gods will give you what you seek.'

'I no longer trust in the gods.'

'You have a better plan?'

Roman patrols had already been seen south of the river by the time they were ready, but the enemy cavalry were happy to watch the straggling column rather than harass it. For the first three days the going was easy on the flat riverside plain, but on the fourth the country became more hilly and Cathal's army of ragged skeletons struggled to keep pace with their horseborne chieftains. It was on the morning of the fourth day that he saw the mountain in the distance, like a standing stone silhouetted against the western horizon. It drew him like a honey bee to a flower, and he ordered a change of direction. As the sun rose to its height, he saw it more clearly: a conical hilltop set upon a great raised plateau.

'I must know the name of that mountain,' he called to Colm.

The farms they passed had all been abandoned at the first sighting of the column of ragged warriors, but Colm found an ancient abandoned by his family.

'It is called Bein a Ciche, the Hill of the Beast. A great monster once lived there, but it was slain and the Old People built their stone walls on its height and ruled all they surveyed.'

Colm laughed. 'They must be old if they are older than you.'

'Their bones were dust before I was weaned.' The old man frowned. 'But their mark is all around you, in the stones, and the earthen mounds where they lay with their treasure.'

'Enough,' Cathal said. 'Take him back to where you found him and give him some bread and cheese.'

It was another hour before he saw it. The head of the column had reached a long, shallow slope that reached out towards the foothills of the mountain. It was perfect.

'Here,' he said, almost to himself. 'Here is where we will fight.'

LX

'Another one?'

'He was hiding among the bushes on the far side of the river,' Gaius Rufus confirmed.

Valerius studied the shaking, emaciated figure held upright by two auxiliaries. His thick beard and dark, straggling hair were matted and dust-caked, and the Roman could see the bones of his ribs through the rents in his ragged plaid tunic. Yet the hooded, glittering eyes held no hint of defeat and Valerius sensed the claw-like fingers itching for a knife to plunge into his throat.

'A scout?'

Rufus shook his head. 'He can hardly stand. A straggler or a deserter.'

'Ask him how far ahead Calgacus's army is.'

The little scout spat out a burst of Celtic and the prisoner's lips twitched into a sneer before he replied.

Rufus grinned. 'He says he knows of no Calgacus, but you will find the army of King Cathal when he wants you to find them. They will fall on you like wolves and like wolves they will tear your flesh and send your army running like sheep over the precipice.'

'We have captured a poet.'

'He says Cathal will take your golden breastplate as a trophy to hang in his house for others to admire. Your fine helmet will be a pot for his children to piss in and your wooden hand will be cast into a river so your soul will wander helpless for all eternity.'

'Cut his throat for his insolence.' Metilius Aprilis studied the prisoner with cold-eyed contempt.

'No, put him with the rest,' Valerius ordered. 'And make sure he's fed.'

'With respect, you're too soft with the prisoners, legate.' Aprilis's tone held anything but respect. 'We should make an example of them to deter the others and save ourselves the trouble of keeping them.'

Valerius met his new camp prefect's stare. He didn't like or trust Aprilis, but Agricola's former aide had proved a competent administrator and a strict disciplinarian, the ideal combination for the position he held. He knew Aprilis would be reporting his every word and deed back to his master, but he suspected that had been happening anyway. So what was the true purpose of the appointment? It was a question he couldn't yet answer, but he could feel an ominous twitching in the centre of his back that hinted no good would come of it.

'Once he's fed properly he'll fetch a decent price as a slave. When this is over he might even be persuaded to enlist in the native auxiliary cohorts. The Brigantes are shaping up well.'

'But how will they react when they discover Calgacus has his own contingent of Brigantes? When they face their tribesfolk on the battlefield will they run off to join them or will they fight?'

'We'll just have to make sure they don't face them,' Valerius said wryly, but the truth was he'd been asking himself the same question. If it came to a battle, how would their newly trained British auxiliaries react to facing their own countrymen? As he'd warned Agricola, the Batavian rebellion set a terrible precedent for disaster. If a cohort of auxiliaries changed sides at the crucial point of a battle it could end in slaughter.

Once they'd crossed the river, Agricola had altered his dispositions to place the Ninth in the van of the endless column of legionaries and auxiliaries. It had been a surprise to discover that the signs showed Calgacus didn't continue north, but instead had followed the river west. They'd marched in his wake over the wide swathe of trampled grass and bushes, avoiding the surprisingly numerous black splatters of involuntarily ejected ordure that gave some suggestion of the poor health of the enemy, picking up sickly prisoners along the way. Cavalry rode ahead and on the flanks, and beyond them roved Rufus and his scouts, returning with the news that they were drawing ever closer to their enemy.

Was there a change in Calgacus's behaviour? As they closed, Valerius would have expected to discover a new sense of urgency in his opponent, but Rufus detected none. They discussed the possibility of ambush, despite the open country to their front and flanks. Their path carried them through empty fields where the legionary *caligae* crushed whatever spring plants the Celts had left whole, pasture bare of cattle, sheep or goats, and abandoned houses. Standing stones, man-made mounds and stone circles flanked their route, but Valerius knew they were the creations of men long dead and meant little to the people who worked the fields, apart from fear of the spirits that might lurk there. The marching legionaries sweated in the afternoon heat, but they were in good spirits. It was as if every man had a sense of inevitability. As if, at last, the long campaign was coming to a close.

On the afternoon of the third day they breasted a rise and Valerius had his first view of a mountain that dominated the western horizon. For some reason the sight made him feel very close to the enormous warrior he'd fought on the ice all those years earlier. He looked at the terrain around him. There was a broad platform of high ground on the far side of the river.

'No point in advancing any further today,' he told Aprilis. 'Have the engineers find a place to cross and we'll start building the camp on that ridge. Send messages to Ursus and Polio to let them know, and,' he pre-empted the camp prefect's protest, 'of course, the governor.'

He called forward Rufus, who had just returned from one of his forays.

'I want to know what they call that mountain,' he told the little man. 'See if you can find out.'

They were interrupted by a trumpet blast as the signaller relayed the order for the day's halt.

Rufus laughed. 'I do not have to. The local people say it is the beginning of the Graupius mountains, the great wilderness that spreads from here to the western sea. It is sacred to them. There is a fort there, but it is long abandoned, and in any case, Calgacus is too wily to cage himself in a fort.'

'So Mons Graupius?' Valerius suggested.

'If you like,' Rufus agreed.

'The governor likes to know these things for his map.'

Rufus gave him a knowing look. 'But . . . ?'

'I'm curious to get a closer view.' Valerius removed his helmet and wiped sweat slick hair from his brow. 'How far ahead is Calgacus's rearguard?'

'Less than an hour's ride. A few outriders to cover their back. They were just short of the mountain when I turned back.'

'Then we can be there and back before dark. Cornelius?' he called to his escort commander. 'Bring the lads up. We have more work to do before they can pitch their tents.'

Rufus led them across the river at a shallows on one of the winding bends and they rode up the far bank. Ahead of them lay a rolling fertile landscape crossed by tracks and chequered with fields and pasture. Rufus avoided the paths and kept to the higher ground.

'Safer this way,' he said. 'The river sweeps in a great half circle to the north. By riding directly west we cut off the base and save time and the horses' strength.'

'This is good land.' Shabolz ventured a rare opinion. 'I wonder where all the farmers and their families have gone? They must be terrified of us.'

Rufus bit off the words *Maybe with good reason*. He'd seen the way some of the Ala Petriana acted with the women they found. He shrugged. 'The tracks say west, but they're staying away from Calgacus as well, for the moment. Into the hills. Maybe the old fort is an ancient sanctuary, like the one at Trimontium.'

'For the moment?' Valerius had caught the emphasis on the phrase.

'If they think he can beat us you won't be able to move for sickles and skinning knives trying to cut your balls off. It's always been the way.'

Every time Valerius raised his head the mountain was closer. They were through the hills now and approaching the river again. Beyond it the country appeared uniformly flat with the mountain on the far horizon. There were other summits to the north and south, but he only had eyes for the conical peak to his front. They recrossed at a ford and Valerius noticed that Rufus slowed the pace. He asked why.

'This is as far as I've come in the past. I have no idea what's in the woods or in the dead ground. So we go a bit more carefully and we keep our eyes open.' He looked up at the position of the sun. 'Maybe we should turn back soon? One mountain's not much different from another.'

'But why has Calgacus chosen to come to the mountains at all?' Valerius said, thoughtfully. 'We know he needs supplies, but all the corn and fodder available to him is in the untouched lands to the north or our own granaries. Those mountains can't sustain an army. Unless he wants to lose it, he must turn north or south, yet he does neither. All he has accomplished is allow us to force him closer to the mountains where he has no room for manoeuvre. Something isn't right.' He could feel the escort's doubt and their nervousness at being so close to an overwhelming enemy in such small numbers. 'One more rise,' he conceded. 'We will see what is over that ridge and then go back.'

Their horses plodded doggedly up the slope, with Rufus in the lead, but it was Hilario, twice his height, who reacted first, hauling at the midget's bridle. 'By all the gods, stay off the skyline.' He looked frantically back to Valerius. 'Stay where you are, lord, if you value your life.'

'What is it?' Valerius demanded.

'Calgacus,' the big man replied. 'And he's got his whole army with him.'

'Cornelius, you and Shabolz with me.' He dropped from the saddle and ran up the bank. 'Tell the others to be ready to move at my order.'

'Well, Agricola wanted a fight.' Rufus led his own and Hilario's horse past Valerius. 'It looks as though he's got one.'

Valerius reached the top of the rise and squirmed forward to a clump of bushes where Hilario lay prone. Shabolz and Felix moved in beside them. 'There, lord.' The big cavalryman parted a pair of branches.

Valerius had seen barbarian hordes before, and more numerous ones – Boudicca's rebels and the army of the Parthian King of Kings dwarfed these numbers – but what he saw still took his breath away. The mountain peak that had drawn him here was off to his right. Calgacus had formed up his army on a hill to his immediate front. Perhaps a thousand paces away, across a shallow dip, what seemed like every Celtic warrior in the north was arrayed in ranks across the horseshoe of the lower slopes. Thousands upon thousands of them in three distinct divisions, their banners waving in the breeze and their spear points glittering in the sunlight. Calgacus's horse, including the remaining cavalry animals he'd stolen from Valerius, grazed on the tender shoots of the plain or drank from a small stream in the bottom of the dip, their riders at their sides. 'What's that?' he asked Shabolz, who had the best eyes of any of them.

The Pannonian squinted into the sun. 'I think they must be chariots, lord, maybe ten of them gathered in a bunch on the right flank. Have you ever fought chariots, lord?'

'No,' Valerius admitted. 'But I've seen them from a distance.' He remembered the little two-wheeled carts darting about the slope opposite Colonia carrying Boudicca's war chiefs. But this was different. 'I don't think we need to be frightened of them on this ground. That looks like marsh at the bottom of the dip. Too many obstacles to allow them to manoeuvre properly. In any case, there aren't enough of them to make a difference.'

'Looks like plenty to me,' Hilario growled, making the others laugh.

'Plenty for all,' Valerius agreed. He wriggled backwards and the others followed. When they were out of sight of the hill he stood and tried to gather his thoughts as his men waited patiently. 'Cornelius,' he called to the escort commander. 'You'll go back with five men and tell the governor what you've seen. We have Calgacus at bay. Tell him to make his best speed with the legions.'

'And you, lord?' the decurion said with a frown.

Valerius exchanged a glance with Shabolz and Rufus. 'We'll be staying here.'

LXI

Cathal and Olwyn watched hand in hand from the top of the hill as dusk fell, the sky gradually softening into astonishing bands of colour: crimson, gold, silver and turquoise, the deeper blue of a winter sea, and finally the black of night. He felt her shiver and he knew she too was wondering if this was the last time they would look upon this marvel of the gods together. He wanted to pick her up, feel the lightness of that slim girlish form in his arms, and the firmness of her against his body, but he understood it could not be. Hard enough for her to face what was to come without prolonging or intensifying the pain.

'It is time,' he said.

'You know I would rather stay and share your fate, whatever it is?'

'I know,' Cathal assured her. 'But it cannot be. You must go, for the sake of Berta and Dugald, and all the others who will not leave without your example. Rurid's guides will lead you back to King Crinan. He has agreed to take you in and treat you with honour and respect. I will join you if I can.'

She turned to him and pressed against him, her head barely reaching his chest. Her body heaved with emotion and he knew she was trying not to weep. He stroked her hair, marvelling, as ever, that his massive hands forged by sword and axe and hammer could be so gentle. It had always been that way with them. Cathal so huge and so strong, treating her like a precious jewel, until Olwyn's inner fire lit their mutual passion.

'Forgive me. My pride brought us here.' The catch in her voice almost choked off the words at their source. 'I encouraged you to leave Mairos and take your warriors to the hills. When the Argento Rìgh refused to aid you, it was I who urged you not to turn back. When you faltered, who else but Olwyn could put the fire back in your belly and the sword in your hand? And all for what? Gwlym . . .'

He placed a finger on her lips. 'Of course Gwlym used you as a weapon to keep me on the course he set. Just as he is using my name as a weapon for those who come after us to oppose the Romans. It has always been the trial of kings and queens to be manipulated by clever priests. There is nothing to forgive.'

After a moment, Olwyn pushed herself away, drawing herself up to her full height and meeting his eyes. 'Then I will prepare the children.' She took a deep breath and turned to walk down the rear crest of the hill. What was in that last look? Despair? Fear? Reassurance? His eyes had been too blurred to see. 'We will meet again, lord king.'

He moved to follow her, then stopped himself. Let them go. Sending the women and children away, all those who'd somehow found their way to their men after that first season amid the growing knowledge they wouldn't be returning, had been the hardest decision he'd ever had to make. Yet Gwlym's description of the aftermath of Boudicca's last battle left him no choice. The Romans had butchered the aged, the injured and the helpless until their arms were red to the shoulder and could barely lift a sword. Even then, their officers had urged them on to even greater slaughter. Men, women and children. None had been spared.

It had to be done in the dark, and by ways invisible to the Romans who would be watching him even now. He had deliberately chosen this hill, rather than the higher slopes where the old fort stood, because it offered the potential for a tactical withdrawal. From the front, the distinctive contours concealed the river protecting his left flank and the

412

smaller stream on his right. Both streams coursed through hidden valleys and the southernmost provided a ready-made escape route in case of need. The first two hours of the march would be shielded from the invaders by a lesser range of hills to the south. From there, the escapers could go where they willed.

King Crinan had offered the women and children shelter until they decided to move on or stay. He had no fear that the Romans would come after them, since they'd shown no previous inclination to penetrate the narrow mountain valleys.

Reluctantly, Cathal tore himself away from the image of Olwyn's retreating back and turned his gaze east. On the slope below, campfires had begun to spring up like fireflies as his men gathered together for warmth and companionship in the growing gloom. Cathal did nothing to prevent them. He wanted the Roman scouts to know they were here. Because they were out there, and by now they would have reported his position to Julius Agricola.

And tomorrow they would come.

Valerius had posted the remainder of his escort in groups of four along the crest of the hill with orders to alert him to any movement in the enemy lines. He knew it would be impossible to tell for certain in the dark; even the hundreds of fires could be a ruse to mask a withdrawal, but he was reassured by the occasional sign of men moving among them. One group seemed to be having a celebration because he could hear the sound of a whistle and raucous drunken shouts.

He lay among the bushes wrapped in his cloak, accompanied by Shabolz, Rufus and Hilario. By now Agricola would have alerted his generals. They wouldn't travel by night, but he'd have them on the move by first light. A brisk march would bring the legions to Mons Graupius at around the third hour, as long as the governor accepted Valerius's assurance that the route was safe from ambush. The cavalry might be here hours earlier if he was prepared to risk unleashing them.

Valerius listed the forces that would face Calgacus's thousands in the

413

morning and he concluded for the hundredth time that, one way or the other, tomorrow would bring Agricola victory. Whether it would be the conclusive victory that would bring him his return to Rome and the triumph he craved was another matter.

'You seem troubled, lord,' Rufus whispered.

'I still can't understand why Calgacus has decided to fight. There's no reason why he couldn't keep retreating. Even if he chose to retreat into the mountains he'd have the option of emerging where it suited him and we might be fifty miles away. Every day he keeps his army intact is a victory for him. Even if he was forced to disperse them he could wage a war of raid and ambush against us that would keep Agricola occupied for years.'

'Why does any soldier or warrior fight when he has the option to walk away?' Valerius could hear the scout's mental shrug. 'Honour, pride, duty, even vanity. Perhaps Calgacus is as sick of running as we are of chasing him. He's been on the move for four or five years. Maybe he wants it over and done with?'

'Perhaps,' Valerius acknowledged. 'But even if he fights tomorrow and loses, he can continue the fight for years if he survives with any part of his army intact.'

'Then let's—'

Rufus froze in mid-sentence and Valerius heard the hiss of a sword being drawn. The little man moved his mouth close to Valerius's ear. 'We have company,' he breathed.

'Where?'

But Rufus was already on the move, and he must have touched Hilario on the way because a giant shadow blocked the stars then disappeared down the rear slope in the scout's wake. Shabolz moved in closer to Valerius. 'They're on the slope below us,' he whispered.

Valerius drew his sword with his left hand and lay with it at his side. 'How many?'

'Four or five that I can hear, but there could be more.'

'We stay here.' Valerius had already ruled out returning to the horses. If Rufus thought he needed more help he would have taken Shabolz.

They waited, nerves tingling, for what seemed an age, ready for the inevitable howl and rush of swords.

What came was Hilario, unnervingly silent for a man so large, appearing out of the darkness like a ghost. He carried a large bundle over his shoulders and he stooped to lay it beside Valerius. Valerius ran his hand over the body. Blood stuck to his fingers and the distinctive smell of excrement told him the corpse's bowels had been pierced. 'A scout?' he asked the big man.

'More like a deserter.' Valerius hadn't even heard Rufus return. 'He was carrying a bag full of loot he'd taken from the local farms.'

'The others?'

'The same. They were travelling independently, staying well clear of each other. This one walked into us.'

'All right.' Valerius sheathed his sword. 'You and Hilario get some sleep. But first take this carrion somewhere else. He stinks.'

'Not as much as he will tomorrow,' Hilario snorted. 'And he'll have plenty of company.'

Valerius must have dozed, because he was woken by Shabolz's nudge and when he opened his eyes the first ash-grey light of the pre-dawn painted the sky. He heard the sound of metal clinking and his hand instinctively went to his sword. Shabolz laid a hand on his arm and shook his head. Rufus and Hilario were already on the alert, but their eyes were fixed on the east. Valerius's ears picked up a sort of muted, distant thunder. A Roman cavalry trumpet brayed its familiar tune.

Agricola was here.

LXII

Half a mile to his left Valerius watched the first of Agricola's troops march over the ridge in column. From their loose formation, uniforms and shields he could tell they were a cohort of auxiliaries, probably the Brigantes recruited barely a year earlier when Domitian had withdrawn so many experienced troops to Germania and Dacia.

Their arrival was greeted with a mighty roar by the massed ranks on the hill opposite. Trumpets blared defiance and banners waved. Valerius expected the new arrivals to turn and take up a position on the left wing as was the normal disposition. Instead, they advanced another two hundred paces and turned to march across the enemy's front and form a cohort square opposite Calgacus's left flank. This would normally be the position of honour occupied by the elite First cohort of a legion. He could only guess the legionary troops would be ordered to form up in front of the auxiliaries. Yet there seemed little room between them and the Celtic cavalry who trotted back and forth across their front.

Roman auxiliary cavalry troopers who'd taken up station on the flanks two hours earlier watched Calgacus's horsemen warily but made no move to stop their enthusiastic but innocuous manoeuvring. The chariots seemed to be operating independently, as was the fashion of the north Britons, and he noted that they kept to the far side of the broad green swathe of marshy ground.

A unit of Batavians followed the Brigantes and took up station on their flank. Where were the legionaries? Valerius half turned in the saddle and noticed a command group a short distance away observing the units marching into position. He trotted towards them and was surprised to see Metilius Aprilis, his camp prefect, where he would have expected the governor, at the centre of a group of aides.

'Legate.' The younger man greeted him with a perfunctory salute.

'Metilius,' Valerius acknowledged. 'It's good to see you and our auxiliaries, but where is the Ninth? Where are the legions?'

'The legions will form the second line.'

'What?'

'It is not my doing.' Aprilis shrugged. 'This is the governor's express order.'

'He must have misheard the estimate of the enemy numbers I sent. There are fifteen thousand of them on that hill, not fifteen hundred. This is not a detachment – it is Calgacus's entire army.'

Aprilis sniffed. 'I believe he is aware of that.'

'We need heavy infantry to storm that hill. Not lightly armed auxiliaries.'

'Perhaps you'd like to advise the governor that you think his tactics are wrong?'

'Perhaps I will. Where is he?'

'He set up his headquarters on the level ground a mile back.' Aprilis smirked. 'He was quite out of sorts until your news arrived, but it cheered him immensely. I doubt he'll thank you for your advice.'

'Nevertheless . . .' Valerius turned his horse and called for his escort. They rode past columns of Nervians, Tungrians and Varduli from northern Hispania. A regiment of Gauls attached to the Ninth gave a great cheer when they recognized their legate and Valerius stopped to salute them as they marched past grinning with pride.

A few minutes later he approached a group of tents with the governor's pavilion at the centre. Guards surrounded the compound and a thousand-strong cavalry wing was watering their horses in a nearby river. Valerius recognized their commander as the young Gaulish officer Aulus Atticus. 'Is the governor giving your lads a rest, prefect?' Valerius called as he rode up.

Atticus rose to his feet and saluted, but Valerius waved him back to his seat on a felled tree by the river bank. 'He is, legate.' The officer smiled. 'But he promised we will have our opportunity to cross swords with the enemy.'

'Then may your deeds today and that of the Ala Petriana ring down through history.'

The young man's grin widened and Valerius would swear the hardened cavalryman blushed.

Valerius approached the centurion in charge of the guard. 'Gaius Valerius Verrens, legate Ninth legion Hispana, seeks an audience with the governor.'

The centurion nodded recognition. 'If you'll just wait here, legate.'

Valerius turned to watch the marching units as he waited. Still no sign of the legions. What did Agricola think he was doing?

'If you'll come with me, legate.' The centurion had emerged accompanied by one of Agricola's soldier clerks, who led Valerius to the pavilion tent and pulled back the curtained doorway.

'Valerius.' Agricola rose from his desk with a disconcertingly broad smile of welcome. If Valerius was expecting anything it wasn't this. 'So you found him for me?'

'I'm not sure whether we found him or he found us.' He tried to match the governor's mood.

'Will he attack us, do you think?'

Valerius had pondered the question through the night. 'No. If he was going to leave the mountain he would have done it while our auxiliaries were deploying.'

Agricola caught the emphasis on the word 'auxiliaries' and raised an eyebrow. 'An innovation. One you don't approve of, I gather? Yet this is the man who used gladiators to break the Twenty-first's line at Bedriacum?'

'More out of necessity than part of any plan.' Valerius remembered the idea had been Serpentius's, and every man who took part had died. 'The day didn't end well for us, as you'll remember.'

Agricola laughed dismissively. 'You were fighting legions, not barbarians.'

'I'm sure you have your reasons for using the auxiliaries.'

'Indeed.' The governor sobered. 'Your description of the terrain gave me the idea.'

'But you haven't seen the ground,' Valerius said quickly.

'No.' Agricola ushered him to the inevitable sand table. 'But your young man gave me a great deal of detail. A clever one, that; he has great potential.' The contours of the sand model were exactly as Valerius visualized the hill in his memory. 'We know that with his armour and shield a legionary weighs at least a tenth more than an auxiliary. When they reach this bog at the bottom of the dip it would have the same effect as a river. They would slow, and the momentum of the attack would be lost. Calgacus would have his chance to fall on us as we flounder in the swamp. You see?'

Valerius studied the model. 'Yes.' Perhaps it made sense after all. He realized the experiences of the past two years had led him to underestimate Agricola's abilities as a general. 'I should have seen it. With the swamp and the hill the situation is perfect for light infantry. I shouldn't have doubted you, Julius. You have my apologies.'

Agricola stared at him, discomfited for a moment. 'Nor I you. Let us not forget that we wouldn't be here if you hadn't disobeyed my orders and continued to hound the Celts last summer and starve them of their supplies.' The two men stared at each other and a wry smile flickered across Agricola's lips. 'We will never be friends, Valerius. But I hope we can be trusted comrades.'

'Of course, proconsul.'

'So no legionaries floundering in the mud.' The governor's voice quickened as he continued. 'Instead the auxiliaries will skip across it, more or less, and take the attack to the enemy. While Calgacus is pinned, the legions in the second line will swing round the flank of the

419

auxiliaries, here and here, to smash into his outlying units, and once they are engaged the cavalry will make a wider flanking movement to hit the rear enemy ranks. What is his army's condition?'

'Many of them are hungry and their morale is low,' Valerius admitted. 'But I believe the core of Calgacus's force is capable of causing us heavy casualties.' He watched for Agricola's reaction, but the governor only nodded. 'He has also chosen his position with care. If he faces defeat he has the option to withdraw north or south, or even conceivably fade away into the mountains.' Agricola grimaced with distaste. 'If he does that it might take years of campaigning to finally hunt him down.'

'We must finish it here and now.' The governor's sudden anger betrayed the pressure being imposed on him from Rome. 'I have moved Polio and his Second legion north of Calgacus's position. There is no escape for him by that route.'

'Calgacus is the key.' Valerius saw his opportunity. 'We know from our prisoners that without him his allies won't continue the fight.'

'Yes?'

'Let me try to negotiate his surrender.' He waited for the inevitable explosion, but it never came. 'He and his warriors have been fighting us for four long years. His harvests have gone uncollected and his people starve. It is the same with the Venicones and the Caledonians. They have been fighting for so long they have forgotten why they are fighting. They are tired of war. Offer them an honourable way out and they will take it. I have met Calgacus; I believe he would accept their decision. If I succeed you will have destroyed the power of the northern tribes for ever and brought them under Rome's control without losing another man. Even if I fail, the very fact of the offer will widen the cracks between the allies.'

Agricola stared at him. 'You could be signing your own death warrant.'

Now it was Valerius's turn to smile. 'From what I understand it is you who holds my life in your hands.'

Agricola's expression didn't alter, but the long silence that followed told Valerius that Domitian's execution order was a reality. 'I must have Calgacus,' the governor said eventually. 'And the tribes must accept Roman rule.'

'Of course.' Valerius head spun at this unlikely victory.

'Then I agree. I will give you an hour before I leave for the field. If you have not persuaded him by the time I arrive, we will attack. Do you understand, Valerius? You have an hour. No more.'

'I understand.'

'Leave a good man to act as a messenger in case I need to contact you.'

'Shabolz is the best I have.'

'The Pannonian? Excellent. And take the Ala Petriana with you. Atticus has his instructions.' Agricola rose to his feet and grasped Valerius by the wooden hand. 'May Fortuna favour your efforts, legate.'

Valerius could only nod his thanks. He strode out, calling for his escort.

Julius Agricola settled back into his chair. He tapped his stylus on his desk, contemplating the conversation that had just occurred. Had he made the right decision? In a way it didn't matter. He had nothing to lose except the life of Gaius Valerius Verrens.

LXIII

From his place on the hill, Cathal watched the Roman cohorts moving into position. The sun had risen on a fine morning. He could smell the faint scent of crushed grass on the breeze and the song of plover, lark and curlew welcomed the day on the moorland to his rear. Outwardly, he appeared untroubled, but his heart thundered in his chest at the sight of his enemies and part of his mind was with Olwyn and the children making their long journey south.

He forced himself back to the present. He knew he had chosen his position well. His army occupied a half circle of hillside overlooking the plain where the Romans marched in their frighteningly disciplined squares. Donacha, Rurid and the recently returned Vodenos were with their tribes, the Caledonians and the Brigantes on the left of Cathal's Selgovae, and the Venicones and Taexali to the right, where the ground fell away to the river. In the early stages of the coming battle they had one order and one only.

To hold.

He would let the Romans come to him. The role of his mounted warriors and the petty chiefs in their fragile chariots was to cause chaos and confusion when the enemy attacked.

He had an image of the battle in his mind. The compact squares changing into more vulnerable line as they advanced, as Gwlym had assured him they would. They would hold their cohesion until they reached the marsh, then the lines would falter depending on the ground conditions. There would be gaps and angles the cavalry and the chariots could exploit when the infantry emerged. Those gaps and angles would be exaggerated when they began to climb the rocky slope towards the great mass of Cathal's warriors waiting above. Only when the Roman line was ragged enough would he throw his champions at the enemy shields, where the sheer physical weight and overwhelming numbers would smash them backwards.

Only one thing puzzled him. The long years of fighting these hardy, disciplined soldiers had given him not only an understanding of the qualities that bound them and made them so difficult to fight, but the differences that divided them. There were two separate types of Roman infantry and, in general, they could be differentiated by their armour and the shape of their shields. The men forming up below carried curved shields and wore chain armour, which meant they were what Gwlym called, disparagingly, mercenaries. Men from different tribal cultures who fought for money rather than loyalty, though that made them no easier to kill. He'd learned from the few deserters who had joined him that some were even native Britons. Agricola had recruited Brigantes and warriors from the southern tribes who had become bored with the dullness of domestic life under Roman rule, where no man could carry a sword without permission. But where were the legions?

Cathal knew for certain that three legions had marched in his wake, the Twentieth, the Ninth and the Second. All three had been depleted by one means or another, but they still represented a more powerful military threat than the auxiliary units presently arrayed against him. He'd sent out mounted scouts to discover their whereabouts, but the enemy cavalry was too numerous and they'd returned empty-handed.

'What is happening now?' Gwlym demanded. The blind druid wore a fresh white robe and his matted white hair and beard had been washed and combed after a fashion.

'Still no sign of the legions.'

'Then you must prepare for whatever trick they are about to play against you.'

'Do you still think it was right to fight here?'

'You had no choice.' Cathal felt a chill run through him at the resignation in Gwlym's voice. The last few weeks had been like watching a fire gradually fade and die for want of fuel. 'Your alliance would have fragmented, your army faded into oblivion and your name been forgotten in a week. Remember. Defeat can still be another kind of victory.'

'Colm and my sword brothers have orders to carry away my body—'

'What is it?'

'Riders. Coming from the Roman lines.'

The small group of mounted men had passed through the front ranks of Roman soldiers and were making their way at a trot towards the bog in the bottom of the dip.

'Kill them before they come any closer,' the druid advised, but for once his voice contained no real malice.

As Cathal watched, a more numerous group of his own cavalry rode to intercept the approaching riders. 'Tell them to put up their spears,' he ordered one of his bodyguard. He noticed a flash of green and realized that whoever it was wanted to talk, not fight. Eight of them if he counted correctly. 'The Romans carry the branch of truce,' he told Gwlym.

'All the more reason to kill them.'

The riders crossed the bog and Cathal noted that they included one senior officer and another figure he recognized. 'And it appears that our friend the midget is included in their number.'

'More still, then. But you have ever been overly loquacious, Cathal of the Selgovae. Let us hope it will not be the death of you.'

'We will hear what they have to say.' Cathal waved at the warrior in charge of the cavalry to escort the enemy riders forward.

'Keep a good hold on that branch, Hilario.' Valerius curbed his horse as they waited on the Roman side of the marsh. Most of it was just heavy ground, but there were broad patches of proper bog where the mud glistened black and pools of rainbow-hued stagnant water promised a proper soaking for the unwary. He'd seldom felt so isolated as he did here in the middle of two great armies. Vulnerable, too. Calgacus's Celtic warriors filled the heights above in their thousands. The bearded or moustached faces looked much more threatening from here, glaring their hatred for the uniform he wore and cradling sword or spear with a seasoned warrior's ease. These were the best of them, he realized, Calgacus's bravest and most wily, whittled down to a hardened iron core by years of campaigning and unity. One word from their leader would launch fifty of them to slaughter the impudent little band of Romans unwise enough to get too close.

'If you think a few leaves are going to save us, you're more foolish than I thought, lord,' Hilario muttered, proving that Valerius wasn't the only member of the party who felt exposed. They'd left their swords behind, not that they'd have done much good anyway. Rufus, who sat to Valerius's left with his lips pursed, had accepted the order to accompany them with his usual equanimity. Valerius supposed that between the two of them they could have said what needed to be said, but the members of his escort had insisted that a minimum of six bodyguards – even unarmed ones – was the requirement of his rank. He'd chosen four by ballot, but Hilario would have accompanied him even if he'd ordered him not to and Felix had invoked the privilege of rank.

A group of Celtic riders approached the other side of the bog and Valerius was pleased to see that their spears were at rest. One of them called out.

'He says we can cross,' Rufus said quietly. 'But he must enquire whether his king wishes to speak to us.'

'A warmer welcome than I expected.' Felix eyed the field of glistening spear points above.

'Still plenty of time for things to heat up,' the little man said. 'I hope you'll be keeping your words sweet, lord,' he said to Valerius. 'I wouldn't want to be among these wolves when they're angry.'

They waited for what seemed an eternity before a well-built young man wearing a gold neck torc appeared and gestured for them to follow him.

Valerius urged his horse up the boulder-strewn slope with Rufus at his side and the others in pairs following behind. They covered a good sixty or seventy paces before they reached the great mass of warriors and Valerius pictured a cohort of the attacking auxiliaries marching up here in his stead, every step under a hail of spears and slingshot pellets and hampered by rolling boulders. He kept his gaze to the front, ignoring the curled lips and hate-filled eyes. At the very last moment the great horde parted in front of their guide. In their midst the only assault was on the nostrils. It wasn't just the usual army stink of sweat-stained wool and leather, dried piss and the misplaced ejected shit of sick men who'd occupied the same ground for twenty-four hours and more. This was a much deeper scent of men who'd retained the odours of everything they'd experienced over the last five years. Years of constant movement and hard stony beds, of sleeping in rain and snow beneath the stars, of bad food and the threat of illness, churning guts and an arse that felt on fire. But there was more. An aura seemed to hang over them like a cloud. It contained a mix of savage hatred and an almost sexual excitement. The fear of death and mutilation, but also fear of failure, and an intense, visceral fury at the enemy who had forced this life upon them. They were lean and feral, an enormous wolf pack in human form. What few clothes they wore were ragged, but their spear points were polished to a killing sharpness. It came to him in that moment that he had been wrong. These warriors would never surrender to Roman rule. Yet he must try.

Valerius looked up and was surprised at the warmth he felt for the man who waited for them upon a rocky knoll, a head and a half taller than any around him. Beneath the mail vest he wore, Calgacus too was leaner than he remembered, the price of his years of defiance written plain across his swarthy features. A nose honed to an axe edge by hunger, cheeks hollow behind the beard, and narrow eyes sunk deep into his skull. Older, too. Deep lines that might have been cut by a knife point scored his broad forehead below the rim of his richly decorated Roman helm.

Still fearsome enough, though, with another great sword strapped to his back and a massive smith's hammer hanging in a sling from a leather belt on his waist. He stood, surrounded by his sword brother bodyguards, dwarfing the white-clad figure beside him. Valerius shivered as he finally set eyes on the druid who had kidnapped his wife and child and would have burned them if he hadn't been thwarted. Oddly, he sensed Gwlym's mind was elsewhere. The weeping red pits of the priest's eye sockets seemed to be looking beyond the battlefield, where the Roman forces continued to gather, to a place only he could see. Cathal's eyes widened a little when he recognized the identity of the Roman emissary, but it was to Rufus he spoke when the delegation reined in before the knoll.

'I am glad to see you alive, Arafa,' he said in his sing-song Latin.

'And you, lord king,' the scout replied as he and Valerius dismounted.

'It is always good to meet old friends, but I fear you have picked a poor day for it.'

'What better day could there be, lord king,' Valerius asked, 'if our meeting avoids the spilling of more blood?'

'You are not wearing your fine sword.' Calgacus might not have heard him. 'It is not right for a warrior to be unarmed. It demeans his status. You should all have worn your swords. It would not have made you any less welcome. Of course,' he turned to Valerius with a half smile, 'you will still have your little knife. But now, I think, you must go.'

'Would you not hear what I have to say, Calgacus?'

'Calgacus?' The Celtic giant shook his head. 'That name again. Once it made me smile, but I fear we must dispense with it.' His voice grew in power. 'I am Cathal, king of the Selgovae, and war leader of the Caledonian federation of free tribes, and I am ready to do battle.'

The men around him didn't understand the words, but they heard the defiance in his tone and a great roar went up from those within hearing distance.

'Perhaps there need be no battle,' Valerius persisted. 'Your warriors have fought and marched for five long years, and to what end? They are dying on their feet from camp sickness. You can barely feed them. Their wives go hungry as they wait in their huts for men who may never

427

come home, and their children cry in the night for their fathers.' He ignored Cathal's dangerous glare. 'The only reason you would fight today is that you are too weak to run any further. You cannot win. Yet apart from a few chosen hostages the governor has decreed that every man here can walk away from this hill with his sword or his spear in his hand and return to his family. If you are willing to surrender yourself there will be no more killing. Ask yourself, King Cathal, why so many must die for the sake of one man's vanity.'

The men of Valerius's escort tensed for the expected violent reaction, but Cathal only uttered a bark of bitter laughter and it was Gwlym who replied.

'Forty years since you Romans first polluted the soil of this island and still you understand so little of its people. Everything must be seen through Roman eyes, even if that leaves you blind to what is happening in front of your nose.'

'The priest is right,' Cathal growled. 'You see sick and tired men who are barely capable of holding a sword. You talk of one man's vanity. But I see fifteen thousand warriors ready and willing to lay down their lives for a cause. And it is not *vanity* that drives me to lead these men into battle, but duty. There are no slaves here, Roman, and there will be no slaves, even if you place us all in chains. In our minds we are free and that is why we will always be free whatever happens to us. Look at you. You already have everything you need. Why would any man want more? Olwyn talks of great palaces of stone and homes created only for the gods that have pillars like forest oaks. Yet still you would drive us from our wooden huts and our poor fields, trample our crops underfoot and take away our children to bend them to your will. You call us barbarians and offer us something called civilization, but all you truly bring us is robbery, slaughter and plunder. You see our courage and call it dissent and rebellion. You see our willing sacrifice and call it stupidity. If I do not fight today your roads will bind us like a prisoner's ropes, your taxes will impoverish us, and your demands for tribute will starve us. If you were in my place, Gaius Valerius Verrens, you would not shrink from facing the enemy. Why, if circumstances were only

a little different you might be standing at my side and I would welcome your sword. Open your eyes. You are no tyrant. Can you not see
what I see?'

Valerius stared at him, struggling to find words that would equal the
other man's eloquence, passion and honesty. What could he say in
reply to a statement in which every single word hit home like a *ballista*
bolt with the authentic ring of truth. Cathal was right. He had been
blind. If he thought of his enemies at all it was as a mindless mob. A
threat that must be defeated, disarmed or destroyed. It had never
occurred to him that they might be fighting for a higher cause. That
the sacrifices they endured were not the result of an all-consuming hatred for Rome or a warrior's need to prove himself, but to protect their
freedom and that of their families. Olwyn had tried to tell him as much,
but, of course, he hadn't listened. He saw one of Cathal's bodyguard
staring at him with a look of shrewd expectation. He'd thought of
Cathal's sword brothers as dumb animals who followed their brutish
king because they had no other choice, rather than individual human
beings. It had never occurred to him that the warriors the Selgovae led
might be intelligent men with minds and talents of their own. He wondered if that was how he treated everyone who was not of his race or
class. He remembered his contempt for Petronius, the *quaestor* of
Colonia, for the way he treated Lucullus, the father of Maeve, the
Trinovante girl who had loved and betrayed him. Perhaps he had been
too long a soldier. In the end, for all his good intentions, an officer
wasn't expected to treat his men as individuals, but as coins to be spent
when their lives would bring the most value. A good officer would try
to make their deaths worthwhile, but did that make him any better
than a bad one?

'I . . .' He tried to speak, but the words died in his throat. All the time
Cathal had been talking he'd sensed unease in the Celts around him,
and now he saw why. Agricola's legions had arrived, a great snaking
column of glittering armour and brightly coloured shields breasting
the hill to form a second line behind the auxiliaries. Time was running out.

Before he could gather his thoughts a blare of trumpets erupted from the Roman lines. The hill was shaped like a crescent moon and the thousands of warriors on the far left reacted to the provocation by surging forward until their chiefs brought them under control.

'Tell them they must hold their positions until my signal,' Calgacus snapped to one of his bodyguard. He turned back to Valerius. And froze. Because the Roman army was on the move.

Metilius Aprilis watched the little group of riders cross the dip and disappear into the great mass of enemy on the hill. How he despised hypocrites like Valerius Verrens, a small-minded *new man* who was conceited enough to believe he could shape events put into motion by true patricians. Did he truly think he could persuade the mighty Calgacus to surrender? Of course not, but people like Verrens always had to be at the centre of the stage where their deeds would be magnified out of all proportion to their true nature.

He had heard the stories. When the name Verrens had first been mentioned as a potential usurper of Agricola's position he had made a point of finding out as much information about Valerius as he could. It helped that he had friends in the Palatine archives with access to reports from the time of previous emperors. What emerged was a tale of boundless ambition dressed up as duty, cowardly spying disguised as diplomacy, downright treason, betrayal, side-switching, murder – or more correctly assassination – all clouded by an ill-deserved helping of Fortuna's favour without which he'd have gone to the executioner's axe a dozen times over. Aprilis had been ordered by Agricola to watch Verrens's wife in Londinium, but a cousin on the staff of Titus Flavius Domitianus, then merely the Emperor's impoverished and more or less powerless younger son, had revealed Domitian's pathological hatred for Verrens. Aprilis prided himself on having a nose for a coming man, and, powerless or not, a member of the Imperial family was worth cultivating. It had been simple enough to offer himself as a conduit for Domitian's wrath – he'd done similar work for Agricola in the case of the odious Fronto, Verrens's predecessor as legate of the Ninth.

When Domitian declared himself Emperor after his brother's early and unlikely death, Aprilis had been certain the order to terminate his enemy would arrive swiftly. Indeed, it had been suggested an accident might be arranged, but before he could put anything in place the suggestion had been mysteriously rescinded.

Still, Metilius Aprilis was not a man to shrink from responsibility. He had played on Agricola's increasing paranoia and the disturbing effects of his personal tragedy, and the governor had agreed to his suggestion that he might be placed in Verrens's headquarters to report on his movements. Part of him knew the transfer from Londinium was as much to do with Verrens's dangerous shrew of a wife as with his duty to Domitian, but the battlefield was not the place to concern oneself with such minor details.

What mattered was that Verrens was now on that far slope at the heart of fifteen thousand barbarian warriors and Metilius Aprilis knew the Emperor wanted him dead.

The question was what to do about it? Agricola had placed him in overall command until the governor's own arrival, so Valerius had gone off on his diplomatic mission while Aprilis still retained control of the entire army. He heard the sound of marching feet to his rear and turned to see the legionaries of the Ninth and the Twentieth moving into position. The governor's dispositions puzzled him as much as they had Verrens, but that wasn't his main concern. If the legions were up Agricola wouldn't be far behind, so he had to act quickly.

He watched the enemy for any sign of threat, but apart from a cheer close to where Verrens and his escort had disappeared nothing untoward occurred. Of course, the cheer might mean his victim was already choking in his own blood, but Aprilis was nothing if not thorough.

He thought he'd run out of time when a trumpet blast announced the governor's impending arrival. Then, entirely unexpectedly, came his opportunity. The mass of warriors on the left of Calgacus's line had been shifting and twitching all morning. At the sound of the trumpet they surged forward, only to stop a moment later.

'Look, on the left,' he shouted. 'They're breaking the truce. Sound the attack.'

'But . . .' His signaller looked towards the now static enemy.

'Do not question my orders. They're going to attack us. We must move first.'

The signaller's trumpet blared, to be echoed by his counterparts in the auxiliary cohorts. For a moment it seemed nothing would happen . . . then they hefted their shields and, as one, lurched into motion towards the hill.

LXIV

'Get them out, Colm,' Cathal told his sword brother. 'And keep them safe.'

The order given, he forced Valerius and his delegation from his mind and concentrated on the coming battle. A cacophony of sound enveloped the hill, rising and falling like thunder as the Selgovae, Venicones, Caledonian and Brigante warriors invited the attackers to march to their deaths or roared their defiance against Rome.

A Roman auxiliary cohort consisted of close to five hundred men, and Cathal counted sixteen squares on the plain between the hill and the high ground, where the legions waited, still motionless. As the eight thousand auxiliaries advanced they performed an almost elegant manoeuvre that made the formations flow from square into line. Now the line was four ranks deep and the wall of oval shields spread across the dip so far it looked as if the flanks might overlap his own. Three regiments of cavalry walked their horses on each flank of the attack, but it seemed they were content for the infantry to take the initiative because for now they made no independent movement. Soon they were crossing the bog, and as Cathal had hoped the lines faltered and buckled as the auxiliaries were slowed by mud that varied from ankle to knee deep.

'Now,' he shouted above the noise, 'signal the cavalry to attack.'

One of his warriors waved a green banner from the top of the knoll and Cathal's horse and chariots burst into movement from the bottom of the slope. They had no discernible formation because they operated as individuals, or in small groups that mirrored their tribal loyalties. The horsemen rode to within spear range and launched their missiles at the struggling Roman infantry, causing more consternation than casualties. Cathal knew this was no ground for a two-horsed chariot, but the war chiefs who owned them insisted they be part of the attack. Now they lurched forward in the cavalry's wake, leaping and bucking over the uneven ground until they too were within range, where the chariot stopped and the spearman leapt out to make his throw. By now Cathal's cavalry had replenished their spears and returned for a second cast as the chariots retreated, with similar results to the first.

A horn blared on the Roman left and now the auxiliary cavalry showed their worth. Every man born to the saddle, they moved from a walk to a canter over a dozen paces and rode in a smooth arc to take Cathal's now disorganized horse in the flank. Cathal winced as they struck. They carried ten-foot spears that swept the Celtic horse warriors away in a blizzard of iron points before they could even draw their swords from their scabbards. The slow-moving chariots were similarly overwhelmed, each surrounded by five or six auxiliary troopers who pinned driver and spearman while they stood helpless on the chariot bed. It was over in minutes. The Romans circled away and Cathal saw the grassy turf strewn with the bodies of his warriors, their mounts standing head down over their former masters, limping broken-legged from the fray, or lying shuddering on their sides. A single chariot had escaped the massacre and only a few dozen horsemen managed to return to the ranks on the hill.

And the infantry kept coming.

By now the long lines were past the bog and had regained their integrity while they tramped their way across the bloodstained grass. As he watched, the front ranks started climbing the slope, heads down behind their shields for protection, but trudging upwards with an unhurried calm that was chilling to witness. Again, the terrain affected their formation, but not to the extent he'd hoped. Still, Cathal had chosen this hill for a reason. The height advantage his warriors had over their attackers also gave them a much greater range for their throwing spears, and now the deadly missiles arced out to plunge down into the advancing auxiliaries. Slingers added their lead or stone shot to the hail and at every point along the line men heaved stockpiled boulders down the slope to cut the legs from the attackers and send them tumbling backwards. At last gaps appeared in the ranks, but they were instantly filled by those behind, who stepped over the writhing bodies of their comrades without a downward glance.

And still the legions remained in position.

Cathal felt his first flutter of real concern, but he thrust it aside. This was no time for panic. The slaughter of the cavalry apart, the battle was developing just as he planned it. The only thing to trouble him was the implacable advance of the Roman infantrymen. He looked out across the hill. He still had double their strength and the advantage of the slope. His warriors must prevail by sheer weight of numbers alone. But the doubt remained.

'I have to know when the front rank reaches the mark,' he snapped. He'd ordered marker stones placed across the hill at the point where he believed the Roman attackers would be most off balance, but he couldn't see see them from where he stood.

'You will know by the first trumpet of the *carnyx*, lord king,' a bodyguard assured him.

Cathal waited for what seemed an eternity as the clamour grew in intensity and his warriors demanded to be allowed to charge the enemy. He ground his teeth as a thunderous roar from the far side of the line announced that some tribe or portion of a tribe had not waited for his order.

'Wait,' he cried, lest a general attack be triggered by the premature engagement. 'Wait for the call.' At last it came, a long blast of the *carnyx* that echoed across the hillside. 'Now,' he roared.

Like a wave tumbling on to a beach, the massed ranks of Celtic warriors fell on the vulnerable lines of attackers struggling up the slope.

Cathal ran in their wake, desperate to witness the outcome of his strategy and heedless of the cries of the bodyguards who called him back. His heart sank as he saw the confusion on the left of the line where the slope was shallower and Vodenos and his Brigantes had triggered the premature attack in their enthusiasm. Here in the centre, the Selgovae smashed into the Romans in a single solid mass with a crash that sounded like thunder as individual warriors threw their bodies into the wall of hated wooden shields. Cathal held his breath as the auxiliary lines rippled and buckled as the soldiers dug their feet into the earth and dust, gritted their teeth and bunched their shoulders against the inside of their shields. And held.

They could never have done it without the help of those in the ranks behind, who threw their weight against their comrades' backs. For a long moment it was as if the battle paused, an interval filled with grunting and cursing as the sides heaved against each other. Then the killing began.

The traditional role of an auxiliary unit was as light infantry who acted as vanguard and rearguard for the legion and carried out patrols. In battle they were normally used to follow up a victory and hunt down Rome's defeated enemies. But Agricola had always insisted that his auxiliaries could substitute for his heavy infantry when required. Some of the attacking units, the Batavians and Tungrians, wore plate armour rather than chain, and every man was armed with a *gladius* rather than a *spatha*. And a *gladius* was an unrivalled weapon for close-quarter killing.

The men wielding the *gladii* wore armour, brass or iron helmets with cheek- and neck-guards, and fought from behind shields. Their enemies above them were armed mainly with spears, but the auxiliaries' heads were protected by the shields of those in the ranks behind. Once the line stabilized they were able to force the shields forward and create the narrow gap required for a lunge with the *gladius*. Every man in the auxiliary line was trained to make the same sequence of movements. The warriors they faced wore tunics at best, or more often fought naked to the waist.

'Now!' A decurion shouted the order.

The lethal triangular point of the short sword pierced the flesh of the enemy warrior's belly a hand's breadth before being withdrawn with a vicious twist of the wrist that left a gaping wound and as often as not the victim's entrails dangling. Soon the air was filled with the shrieks of men condemned to a lingering, agonizing death, shocked by the damage done to their bodies. They dropped to the ground, holding their guts in their hands, and tried to crawl back up the hill through a sea of legs as the men coming down behind them were forced against the shields by the weight of their following comrades.

'Now!'

Cathal heard his warriors die. Watched the Roman ranks remain intact. His instinct was to rush to join them. To add his long sword and his hammer to the attack and break the line. But that was how he'd reacted during the attack on the Roman camp and all he'd done was add to the chaos and kill Emrys. Reluctantly he remained in position and tried to take a measure of the battle line. Away to his right the Venicones had attacked in their tribal groups, because Donacha had no authority over his war chiefs and little interest in the campaign since the death of his brother. The result was that the Romans were making ground there as they were on the left. A roar of a different tone drew his attention to a gully where the auxiliaries had actually made a breakthrough and a fierce struggle was taking place as his warriors fought to stem the Roman tide.

As he watched in horrified fascination, Gwlym walked past him in the direction of the fighting with his hands outstretched. 'Where are you going?' Cathal demanded.

'My time is over,' Gwlym said calmly, without breaking stride. 'The time of the druids is past. In truth, it was past the moment the Romans took Mona.' Cathal watched the blind priest go, making no attempt to stop him. The last he saw of Gwlym was a figure in white surrounded by Roman swords, a pair of scrawny, clutching hands, and a violent splash of scarlet as he disappeared from view.

'Lord king?'

437

He looked round to find the men of his bodyguard staring at him.

'What is it?'

'You said we must make the decision.' Cathal remembered his instructions and Gwlym's insistence that he must never be found, dead or alive.

'Colm. I meant Colm should make the decision. Where is Colm?'

LXV

'Get off your horses and walk behind me,' Colm ordered. 'Stay between your animals. Cover up your armour as best you can. Keep your heads down and don't make eye contact with anybody. Your lives depend on it.'

Valerius knew they had no choice but to trust the commander of Cathal's bodyguard. He and the others complied as best they could, staying in pairs protected by the flanks of their mounts and as well hidden from the roaring bands of warriors as possible. Colm led them diagonally downhill by a worn path that took the easiest course. He carried a natural authority and even chieftains weighed down by torcs of gold made way at his barked orders in his own tongue.

Valerius was so absorbed by their predicament it was minutes before he realized the Selgovae had spoken decent Latin, though with an accent that reminded him of someone.

'Just like old times, eh?' Gaius Rufus flashed him a grin. 'In the shit right up to our necks again.'

'In those clothes you could pass as one of them.' Valerius nodded at the homespun tunic and trews the scout wore. 'At least as a Brigante. Maybe you'd be better off on your own.'

Rufus's lip twisted scornfully and Valerius realized with a twinge of shame that he'd offended the little man. 'Gaius Rufus doesn't leave his friends just because things get a little rough. Besides, who'd look after Hilario?'

An unintelligible mutter from behind might have signalled agreement or protest and Felix hissed at Hilario to keep his mouth shut.

It was their good fortune that every eye on the hill was concentrated on the approaching auxiliaries and nobody thought to stop them or question Colm's authority. But the men they passed recognized the Roman horses and the uniforms between them. Grunts of puzzlement became growls of anger and soon Valerius was aware of a crowd following them.

'Don't look back,' Colm hissed. 'Keep following. They won't do anything while you're with me.'

But Valerius's covert glances had registered a change in the men around them, a different pattern of facial hair, tunics of an inferior quality and weapons fashioned in a different style. That and a brittle edge in Colm's voice told him they'd moved from the Selgovae lines into those of another tribe, probably the Venicones. Above the roars he heard the unmistakable sound of a clash of arms and the noise rose in a new crescendo.

'What's happening?' he called to Colm, certain no one else would hear him.

'Shut up,' the Selgovae said through clenched teeth. He relented a moment later. 'Our cavalry and chariots attacked the Roman line. Now they're getting a lesson from your cavalry.'

The news should have cheered Valerius, but all he could think of was staying alive. He had to fight the temptation to order his men to mount and try to cut their way through to safety. This slow procession allowed the mind to conjure up ever more painful and brutal ends. Certainly there would be no mercy from these men for the hated Romans. They'd been exiled and hunted for four years. All they wanted was a chance to fight for their revenge.

The growls had turned to jeers and what sounded like threats. Valerius heard a high-pitched voice muttering a prayer to Jupiter a few feet back. He recognized the voice of Capito, the youngest member of the escort. They'd moved off the path and here the ground was rougher and more uneven.

A scuffle and a yelp. Someone called out Capito's name and Valerius half turned to see the boy sprawled on the rocky ground with a dozen snarling Celts standing over him. Capito tried to get to his feet, but someone kicked his legs from under him. Colm shouted a protest and the young trooper tried to rise again. Valerius saw a flash of bright metal and Capito screamed. It happened so quickly no one had time to react. Valerius had once seen a feeding frenzy as a pack of sharks turned on one of their injured. This was the same. The knives and swords rose and fell until Capito was nothing but a mess of blood, bone, rags and gore-stained metal.

'Mount up,' Colm screamed. 'Mount up and ride. There's nothing I can do for you now.' Valerius hauled himself into the saddle. Rufus was already moving ahead. 'Make for the river,' the Selgovae shouted. Valerius could hear Felix and Hilario and the three surviving troopers urging their horses on. Soon Hilario was riding at his side, his face set in a scowl of concentration.

No question of stealth now and no thought for the uneven ground. They could hear the feral howl of the men chasing them as if they were a pack of hunting dogs. They barged through the warriors in front to barks of protest, and soon every eye was on them. Valerius tried to choose the least crowded path, but all he could see was a wall of spears. He was aware of a Roman *pilum* whirring past his head and a slingshot smacked into his back with enough force to have broken bone if the impact hadn't been dulled by his cloak and leather breastplate.

'Wheel right,' he cried, hoping the men behind could hear him. A gap, but it led into a short gully, and they emerged into an even more congested area. Valerius wheeled again and it was a moment before he realized he was riding uphill and veered immediately left. The movement brought him in behind Hilario and Rufus and the sound of clattering hooves at his back told him Felix and the rest had stayed with him. Rufus shouted something over his shoulder and urged his horse further ahead. Hilario matched his movement. Their course would take them into a packed bunch of warriors where the hill steepened. Valerius saw immediately what they intended. If they could smash through the Venicones they'd be in the clear, even if it would take Pegasus to keep them safe on the descent. Yet every stride took them deeper into danger. Men threw themselves bodily in front of the horses and spears and swords slashed at the Roman mounts' flanks. As if time slowed Valerius saw Hilario reel in the saddle and a heartbeat later horse and rider were down, smashing the enemy aside as they tumbled down the slope. Yet his sacrifice had given them a chance. If they could only reach the gap . . .

But Gaius Rufus, brave, loyal Gaius Rufus, was a warrior of a different mettle. The little man hauled on the reins and before Valerius could draw breath he was out of the saddle and standing over Hilario's prone body like a terrier defending its master. A knife appeared in his hand, but a knife was no match for the swords and spear points that sought him out. A pair of warriors laughed as they lunged at the midget and Valerius heard a terrible scream as they lifted the struggling body on their points like a trophy.

A scream of his own erupted from his throat and he turned his horse towards them, driven beyond sanity by despair and the need to avenge his friend. Men thrust and cut at him, but he ignored the blades and points. No Celt would kill Gaius Valerius Verrens until he was ready. Two strides later some unseen warrior thrust a spear shaft between Valerius's mount's legs and the horse stumbled and went over on its shoulder. For a moment Valerius had an image of them tumbling side by side, his mind whirling as his body went through a full circle which ended with a sickening crash that turned his world red and tore the helmet from his head. Blinded, but aware of what was going on around him, he heard scuffles and snarls as men fought over his body. Then a familiar voice. Colm had somehow tracked them across the hillside.

Valerius must have absorbed more of the Celtic language than he realized. He was certain he heard the Selgovae claiming his body, armour and any plunder for King Cathal of the Selgovae, and pointing out his helmet, which would be worth twelve cattle and was ample reward for their valour.

'On your life, stay still.' Colm's lips were close to his ear. 'Your leg is trapped under your horse and you scraped your scalp on a rock when your helmet came off. The skin has fallen over your eyes and it looks as if the top of your skull has been ripped off. You look more like a corpse than most dead men I've seen. Stay completely still and I might yet get you out of this. The others are all gone.' He had answered Valerius's unspoken question and despite his condition the Roman noticed an odd catch in his voice.

Time stood still. Or perhaps it flew past on wings of fire. Valerius was aware of Colm's reassuring presence and he heard the Celt speak but could make nothing of the words any longer. He made a mental inventory of his injuries. His leg was surely broken and his scalp felt as if it was on fire. He had a feeling he'd also broken his nose and his tongue told him he'd lost at least one tooth, which vexed him more than all the rest because he was vain about his teeth. At one point Colm covered his head with a cloak and the mildewed scent told him it had belonged to Gaius Rufus.

'Arafa was my friend,' the Celt said in a tone that spoke of more than friendship. 'We were seldom apart that winter and he taught me how to speak your tongue. He said you were the very best of Romans. I will do what I can to save you. For him.'

All the while Valerius sensed the battle ebb and flow like waves lapping on a beach. Eventually Colm said: 'Things are going badly for us. King Cathal needs me. I must go.' He lifted the cloak to pour water over Valerius's lips and thrust a half-full skin into his hands. 'I will return when I can.'

Valerius wanted to plead with him to stay, but the only thing that emerged was a faint croak. Instead he lay back and bathed in his agony, listening to the sound of the battle and praying no one discovered he still lived. He must have fallen asleep because he dreamed of the dead. Dead emperors and dead friends. He had been touched by the shadow of great men, but most had been great only by virtue of their rank. Nero, who had frittered away an empire in debauchery and depravity, and whose last breath Valerius had felt on his cheek. Galba, whom he'd watched butchered in the forum along with his heir, and Otho who took his own life so others might live. Poor Vitellius, unsuited to the purple, who didn't deserve to end up in pieces on the Gemonian Stairs. Vespasian, best of them all, and Titus, murdered by his own brother, who might have been greater still. And friends, the faces clear in his mind, but too many to list after so many wars. Of them all, Serpentius – slave, gladiator, prince – was the best, but Arafa, the little giant who'd shared his ordeal in the Temple of Claudius, had touched his heart in a way he could never have foreseen.

He heard the tramp of hundreds of feet. Someone was singing a rousing battle song and Valerius risked pulling back the cloak and lifting the flap of skin from his eyes. A river of warriors flowed down the mountainside towards the south-east and he realized from his position that they'd be hidden by the hill's contours from the watching Romans. A flanking movement if he'd ever witnessed one. If he wasn't careful Agricola was about to get his arse well and truly kicked. Valerius guessed they were men Cathal had kept out of the battle for precisely this purpose, but his instinct told him the attack was also his last throw of the dice. An explosion of sound announced the completion of the assault, but a little later the few survivors stumbled back up the hill, bloodied and shocked and carrying their wounded. Cathal had failed. Worse, Agricola must have thrown his cavalry reserves against them because soon the cries of the maimed were drowned by the rattle of hooves as the mounted spearmen and archers scoured the hill. Some of them passed so close Valerius could have called for help, but somehow it seemed too much effort. He waited for silence and lay back and closed his eyes.

A few hundred paces away Colm was trying to find his bearings so he could return to the stricken Roman. Cathal had asked him to lead the Selgovae contingent in what they knew was little more than a diversionary attack to allow the king to withdraw with what was left of his

444

shattered army. They'd barely left the slopes of the hill when what seemed an entire legion fell on them like swooping eagles. He'd been avoiding their cavalry ever since, but he was too preoccupied to hear the trooper who swept out of a gully and severed his spine with a swing of his *spatha*. He dropped like a stone and was dead before he hit the ground.

Valerius woke to find the blanket had disappeared. He was cold, cold to the very centre of his being, so cold that a block of ice might have been set near his heart. He could feel himself fading, but suddenly a jolt of energy surged through him and he remembered why he must stay alive. He could feel Tabitha's loving caress and the focus of Lucius's adoring eyes, hear the lilt of Olivia's voice as she sang a childish rhyme. He clung to the memory. He couldn't leave them. Not yet.

The top of his skull was an inferno, making all the other pain seem inconsequential. It was still leaking blood; he could feel it running down his cheeks. Somehow he managed to push the flap of skin and hair back into place and untie his legate's sash. He wrapped the scarlet cloth around his head and bound his scalp into position. The effort drove him to the brink of exhaustion and he had to fight for breath. His last memory was of Tabitha's voice murmuring words he couldn't understand. Or perhaps it was Domitia's.

Shabolz worked his way methodically up the hillside as the sun rose, checking the Roman dead. He'd already found the body of Aulus Atticus surrounded by a dozen enemy with a gaping spear wound in his groin and an expression of outraged dignity on his young face. It was an odd place to be, far in front of his unit's position, and the Pannonian wondered if he'd been killed in some reckless charge to save Valerius and his men.

He didn't expect to find them alive. There was little hope unless they'd been kept as hostages. But he owed it to his brothers of Mithras to give them a proper burial, and Valerius and Arafa were brothers of the soul if not the fact. He saw a little cluster of dead horses and moved towards them. Hilario lay on his back with a look of serene contentment on his normally savage features, his neck broken by his fall. Arafa had been less fortunate. The little scout had died hard and Shabolz prayed his friend had found peace and rest among whatever gods he followed. He marked their positions with discarded spears and continued up the mountain in search of Gaius Valerius Verrens.

It seemed impossible that such a man could be gone. A giant, not in stature, but in character. A warrior who had taken a legion's eagle, but who'd think nothing of risking his life to rescue a stranded child. A true aristocrat, but one with no patrician airs. A commander who would share a cup of rough wine with his men without first wiping the lip. A man his soldiers would follow to the gates of Hades and beyond. A hero of Rome.

He picked his way methodically upwards and his eye was drawn by a roan cavalry horse lying among a group of large boulders away to his left. As he walked towards it he recognized the legate's familiar scarlet sash fluttering like a banner in the soft breeze.

Epilogue

ROME, AD 96

The door from the gardens was open, as he'd been told to expect, and he slipped inside. It was a warm, still September night, but he wore a thick hooded cloak. Since the fire that took most of his flesh in Antioch all those years ago he'd never felt truly warm. Moving swiftly despite the limp in his left leg, he made his way through the empty marble corridors to the room where he'd been told he'd find the man he sought.

He froze at the sight of two guards outside the chamber. They must have seen him, but they might have been statues for all the attention they paid. Despite the danger he moved warily towards them, eyes never leaving the sword hand of the closest sentry. Big, solid men in ornate breastplates, their faces masks of stone in the flicker of the oil lamps. When he moved between them into the doorway he could almost feel the grate of the sword point in his spine.

The room was in darkness and he waited while his eyes acclimatized to the gloom. A large room, sumptuously furnished, the air heavy with the scent of jasmine and the evening's spilled wine. The sound of heavy, nasal breathing drew him towards the far end. One man. Abed and asleep, but that wouldn't do.

He found an oil lamp and reached into his cloak for flint and iron. Light flared to fill the room.

'What . . .' A long, drawn-out groan as the figure on the bed stirred. He waited.

'What's going on?' More ill-tempered mutters. 'I didn't ask to be wakened.' A harsh intake of breath and a growing realization. A head appeared above the blanket, hair standing up like a hedgepig's spikes and eyes blinking. 'Who are you?' Eager hands searched frantically beneath the heaped pillows.

'The sword isn't there.' The voice of a talking crow. Fire and the smoke had destroyed his voice.

'Guards! Guards!'

'You're wasting your time.'

'Who are you?'

His victim's appearance was more shocking than he'd expected. The years had turned him into the image of his father, a man the intruder had loved. No outright fear yet. Power had given him a dangerous sense of invincibility. In any case, who would be frightened of a ragged, crook-backed beggar? He pulled back the hood.

'By all the gods, you're an ugly old bastard.' The beady, piggish eyes he remembered flickered to the doorway, but the intruder took a step to his right to close the avenue of escape. 'You look like a piece of over-done pork. Guards!'

'You came close to Antioch, but not close enough.' He twitched the cloak away to reveal his wooden hand.

'No. No, it can't be.' Astonishment mixed with terror in the familiar high-pitched voice. 'You're long dead.'

'No,' Gaius Valerius Verrens said. 'You are.'

With his left hand he felt for the little metal button on the inside of the right wrist. A gleaming four-inch blade appeared with a sharp snap.

Titus Flavius Caesar Domitianus Augustus, Master and God, screamed and flew from the bed towards the doorway. Valerius was there to meet him, working the blade deep into his body as the screams became shriller, until he could feel the point scrape on bone.

He stepped back and allowed Domitian to slump to the floor, bloody hands frantically clawing at his midriff. Other men entered the room. More knives gleamed in the lamplight. Valerius replaced his hood and retraced his steps to the garden with the dying emperor's shrieks echoing in his ears.

She was waiting by the door to the garden. The years had changed her, of course, but not as much as they had him. She was handsome now, rather than outrightly beautiful, but the girl he remembered was still there in the middle-aged woman's face.

'It's done,' he said.

'I never doubted it. He caused you so much pain.'

'And you.' Their love had once been an all-consuming passion. All he felt for her now was sympathy.

'I have to see your face.'

She reached up to move the cowl, but he gently pushed the hand away. 'Better to remember me as I was.'

A tall young man appeared from the darkness and Domitia Augusta stifled a cry as she recognized the handsome features she'd known so well.

'Tell your mother and Olivia to meet me by the Ostia gate, Lucius,' Valerius said. 'We must move quickly if we're to be at Portus by dawn.'

'We'll be waiting, Father.' Lucius walked past Domitia with a slight nod of acknowledgement and a look of mild curiosity as if she reminded him of someone.

'You don't have to go,' Domitia insisted. 'You will be safe now. Honour and wealth await you for your part in what happened tonight. You could go back to your estate and take your seat in the Senate again.'

He knew the offer was sincere, but he didn't even consider it. 'I think I'd prefer to be forgotten.'

She heard something of the old humour in that broken voice.

The sound of approaching footsteps distracted them and Domitia swivelled to face whoever was approaching.

When she turned back she was alone.

The End

Historical note

As I suspect many historians would concur, following in the footsteps of Julius Agricola, as recorded by his son-in-law, the historian Tacitus, can be a frustrating and sometimes infuriating business. Tacitus's eulogy to his wife's father, the governor of Britain between AD 77–78 and AD 84, is a panegyric of its time, written in a certain style for a certain audience, with one eye on the political hierarchy of which Tacitus was part. It is at heart an adventure story, with Agricola as its stainless if rather dull hero, but it pays little heed to either geography or chronology. *Hammer of Rome* deals primarily with events between AD 78, after Agricola had consolidated his conquest of Wales, and the summer of AD 83 when he is believed to have fought the battle of Mons Graupius and defeated the mighty Caledonian federation. The first question that occurred to me as I began my campaign with Valerius and the Ninth legion Hispana was why Agricola took so long. Marching at a leisurely twelve miles a day – a legion in a hurry could manage twenty – the Ninth could have covered the three hundred and fifty miles or so between its base at York and Bennachie, in Aberdeenshire, where I've chosen to site the hitherto undiscovered battlefield, in thirty days. According to Tacitus, his father-in-law took five years. Yes, Tacitus says there was political, social and military consolidation, but that in itself is puzzling. Agricola would have been under pressure to complete his task in as short a time as possible. Rome preferred that governors, especially those with four legions at their disposal, didn't spend too long in their provinces, lest their ambition get the better of them. In the latter part of the *Agricola* it becomes clear that the destruction of Caledonian military power is the priority. Why waste time building forts, roads and townships in the early part of the campaign?

Then there is the geographical progression, which is confusing at best. At one moment we have him campaigning beyond the Forth, as far as the Tay. The next he is supposedly crossing the Solway, a hundred and thirty miles south, and gazing out with covetous eyes towards the island of Hibernia. Given the dearth of vantage points where it's possible to see Ireland from the Scottish coast, even on a clear day, I think it's much more likely he crossed from the Ayrshire coast to the Mull of Kintyre as part of his reconnaissance of the western route.

We can follow the progress of Agricola's twin spearheads through southern Scotland by the siting of his legionary marching camps. Conveniently for British historians, a legion, or whichever portion of it was on campaign, built a defensive camp at the end of every day's march. The two columns advanced more or less up the line of the M74 in the west and the A68 in the east, eventually converging on the Forth somewhere near Edinburgh. It is beyond the Forth, which Agricola probably crossed close to Stirling, that things begin to heat up. We have a suggestion that the Celtic forces may now outnumber Agricola's troops, a night ambush where the governor, who has unwisely split his forces, rides to the rescue of the beleaguered Ninth, and then Mons Graupius where the Caledonian army, led by a war chief called Calgacus, inexplicably decide to fight in the open.

Where did this great horde of warriors come from? The Caledonians are generally associated with the Grampian Mountains, to which the battle gave their name, and the Highland massif. Yet if you overlay a map of Agricola's camps with the Atlas of British Hill Forts, the Caledonians might as well not exist. There is little sign of occupation in an area that has lain largely undisturbed by the plough for two thousand years, and no evidence of any great tribal capital or settlement. As late as 1746, an army largely recruited from the Highlands could barely amass five thousand men at Culloden, and the most powerful clan chief led only five hundred soldiers, many of them reluctant conscripts. It's clear to me Agricola made no attempt to force the central Highlands, not because he feared any threat, but because he believed no threat existed. There's every likelihood that the people Agricola encountered in what is now Scotland were a peaceful, largely pastoral society, which only turned to tribal warfare as a last resort. The great hill forts like Woden Law and the Mither Tap of Bennachie, which seem to project Iron Age power, influence and military might, had been long abandoned by AD 80 (the 'fort' at Eildon Hill North, also abandoned, was much more of a sanctuary) and the people lived on scattered farmsteads, not in the mountains, but in valleys and on the coastal flatlands. The historian Tom Stanier, in his treatise 'The Brigantes and the Ninth legion', makes a convincing case for a substantial element of the tribe's decamping en masse and fleeing north as refugees rather than accepting Roman rule. This mass migration before the advancing legions and the gradual assembling and hardening of opposition seems to me to make more military sense than the sudden appearance of a mystical tribal federation and a leader who miraculously summoned every warrior in the north of the country. Far from neutralizing any threat from the northern tribes, I think Agricola created one where none had previously existed.

Why Bennachie, out of so many candidates? I believe the geography fits better than any other potential site, but the main reason is the location of the nearby marching camps. Kintore and Logie Durno are perfectly positioned for the legions to converge on Bennachie, and Logie Durno is the largest camp in the north of Scotland, capable of comfortably accommodating three legions. In my imagination it becomes the location for the celebration after the battle, when Agricola gathered his troops to hand out *phalerae* and reward bravery in a great ceremonial parade. It also helped that I stumbled on a field just west of Blairdaff and Finnlairg Farm, near Kemnay, that perfectly fits the topography of Agricola's battle. Tacitus tells us that the 'Caledonians' numbered thirty thousand and the Romans barely half that, with eventual casualties of a suspiciously rounded ten thousand and three hundred and sixty respectively.

So just what can we believe? Some historians doubt Mons Graupius ever happened, but I think the name Aulus Atticus proves otherwise. Tacitus cites him as the only Roman casualty of the battle – apparently auxiliaries didn't count – and his relatives or descendants would still have been alive when the *Agricola* was published. Apart from Atticus no other Roman is mentioned. It appears the commanders of Agricola's legions were not to be allowed to take any of the shine from his victory. Historian Birgitta Hoffman, who has spent years studying the archaeology of the Gask Ridge frontier, which Agricola may have created, probably puts it best. Comparing Tacitus's *Agricola* and his *Commentaries*, she says: 'Both start off with a double blitzkrieg, Caesar against the Helvetii and Ariovist, Agricola with the Ordovices and Anglesey. Both consider invading an island at roughly the same time in their career and both describe a night attack on a legion, where the general saves the situation at the last moment. And lastly both culminate in a final battle preceded by great speeches about civilization and freedom. One recurring event may have been coincidence, but the pattern here is too persistent.'

Whatever the answer, and for all its faults, Tacitus's *Agricola* provided me with a wonderful foundation for Valerius's ninth, and sadly final, adventure.

And what of Valerius's Ninth legion? Did it or didn't it disappear into the Scottish mists along with its coveted eagle? The truth is that unless some lucky metal detectorist unearths an unusually shaped piece of bronze in a Perthshire glen we'll never know for sure. The Ninth may or may not have had a reputation for ill-fortune. It was certainly one of the legions that threatened to mutiny at Gesoriacum (Boulogne) during Claudius's invasion of Britannia in AD 43 because the soldiers resented being asked to campaign beyond the edge of the 'known world'. In AD 60 it lost half its strength in an ambush by a contingent of

Boudicca's army. And, according to Tacitus, Agricola had to ride to the legion's rescue during Calgacus's night attack, which I've depicted in this book. The last physical evidence of the legion's presence in Britain is a building inscription in York dated to AD 108. A legend has grown up – propagated by Rosemary Sutcliff's wonderful *Eagle of the Ninth* – that the legion was annihilated in the early second century during a period of violent upheaval that led to the construction of Hadrian's Wall. Yet records exist of officers serving with the unit as much as ten years later and an inscription mentioning the Ninth legion and dated to the 120s has been discovered in Nijmegen in Holland. Some historians believe the Ninth was destroyed in Judaea in the Bar Kokhba revolt of AD 132, or simply disbanded in disgrace a little later. Others continue to argue for the Scottish scenario. There's no real evidence for or against either and it's even possible both could be true. It was common for battle groups or *vexillationes* to be split from legions to fight in other war zones. Substantial elements of the Ninth could have been fighting on two fronts, perhaps for decades. The only thing we know for certain is that the Ninth disappears from the records by the time of Marcus Aurelius.

*

Author's note: Gaius Valerius Verrens came to life for me after a telephone call from my then editor, Simon Thorogood, sometime in 2008, when he suggested that my Caligula series should become the only two-book trilogy in literary history. He asked me to consider abandoning my character, Rufus, keeper of the Emperor's elephant, and come up with a more mainstream hero. As a slave, he felt Rufus was reactive rather than proactive: things happened to him, but he had little power to direct events. When I put my mind to the problem I remembered a character who made a minor appearance during the Boudiccan rebellion in what was to be the third of the Rufus books. I'd read a line in Tacitus that mentioned how, in response to pleas from the people of Colchester for reinforcements, Catus Decianus, procurator of Britannia, sent a tiny force of two hundred men – an assortment of military odds and sods – to face the might of Boudicca's horde. Their commander's name in the original book was Crispinus, but I decided Valerius had a more martial ring to it. As for a title, when I asked for some guidance I was told 'anything with Rome is selling well at the moment'. And so *Hero of Rome* was born. At that point I only had a single book in mind, based on events I'd already researched about the last stand in the Temple of Claudius. Simon was interested in a trilogy, so I gave him two more titles, *Defender of Rome* and *Avenger of Rome*, with not the slightest idea what the storylines would be. I never believed in my wildest dreams there would eventually be nine books. It was my great good fortune, and by pure chance, that the Valerius I created existed in a time of turmoil, battles and political strife that both suited and shaped his character. His career and his class allowed him to move fairly seamlessly between rank and file legionaries and the great men of his time. He has done the bidding of seven emperors, only two of whom died in their beds, and one of those in suspicious circumstances, fought Britons, Dacians, Batavians, Romans, Parthians and Judaeans, and been hunted to the very ends of the Empire. I hope you've enjoyed reading his adventures as much as I've enjoyed writing them.

Glossary

Abhainn dubh – The River Forth.

Ala milliaria – A reinforced auxiliary cavalry wing, normally between 700 and 1,000 strong.

Ala quingenaria – Auxiliary cavalry wing normally composed of 500 auxiliary horsemen.

Alauna river – The River Allan.

Amici – A Roman emperor's inner circle.

Aquilifer – The standard-bearer who carried the eagle of the legion.

As – A small copper coin worth approx. a fifth of a **sestertius**.

Asturian – Native of the mountains of northern Hispania.

Aureus (pl. Aurei) – Valuable gold coin worth twenty-five **denarii**.

Auxiliary – Non-citizen soldiers recruited from the provinces as light infantry or for specialist tasks, e.g. cavalry, slingers, archers.

Ballista – Portable catapult capable of hurling heavy stones four or five hundred paces.

Beltane – Ancient Celtic festival marking the beginning of summer.

Beneficiarius – A legion's record keeper or scribe.

Caligae – Sturdily constructed, reinforced leather sandals worn by Roman soldiers. Normally with iron-studded sole.

Campi Flegrei – The Phlegraean Fields, a broad area of volcanic activity on the north side of the Bay of Naples close to Puzzuoli.

Carnyx – A Celtic trumpet.

Century – Smallest tactical unit of the legion, numbering eighty men.

Classis Misenensis – The Misenum fleet, Rome's largest and most powerful naval force, based in the Bay of Naples.

Cohort – Tactical fighting unit of the legion, normally containing six centuries, apart from the elite First cohort, which had five double-strength centuries (800 men).

Colonia – A colony of retired legionaries set up and given special rights and dispensations on the orders of the Emperor.

Consul – One of two annually elected chief magistrates of Rome, normally appointed by the people and ratified by the Senate.

Contubernium – Unit of eight soldiers who shared a tent or barracks.

Cornicen – Legionary signal trumpeter who used an instrument called a *cornu*.

Decurion – A junior officer in a century, or a troop commander in a cavalry unit.

Denarius (pl. Denarii) – A silver coin.

Domus – The house of a wealthy Roman, e.g. Nero's Domus Aurea (Golden House).

Duplicarius – Literally 'double pay man'. A senior legionary with a trade or an NCO.

Equestrian – Roman knightly class.

Fortuna – The goddess of luck and good fortune.

Gladius (pl. Gladii) – The short sword of the legionary. A lethal killing weapon at close quarters.

Governor – Citizen of senatorial rank given charge of a province. Would normally have a military background (see **Proconsul**).

Groma – Measuring staff with cross piece and plumb lines used by Roman engineers to lay out roads, camps and any other major building projects.

Imaginifer – The standard-bearer who carried the *imago*, the Emperor's image, when the legion was on the march.

Jupiter – Most powerful of the Roman gods, often referred to as **Optimus Maximus** (Greatest and Best).

Kerse – Old Scots word identifying an area of fertile alluvial land in a river valley.

Lectica – A sedan chair carried by slaves.

Legate – The general in charge of a legion. A man of senatorial rank.

Legatus iuridicus – Legal official of senatorial rank appointed to aid the governor of a province.

Legion – Unit of approximately 5,000 men, all of whom would be Roman citizens.

Lictor – Bodyguard of a Roman magistrate. There were strict limits on the numbers of lictors associated with different ranks.

Lituus – Curved trumpet used to transmit cavalry commands.

Manumission – The act of freeing a slave.

Mars – The Roman god of war.

Milites – Lowest ranking legionary. Soldier with no specialist duties.

Mithras – An Eastern god popular among Roman soldiers.

Mule – Self-deprecating title Roman legionaries gave themselves, after Marius's Mules, the soldiers of the Roman general Gaius Marius, who formed what became the Imperial legions.

Ordo – The council of a hundred leading citizens responsible for running a Roman town.

Ordovices – Celtic tribe which inhabited the mountainous area of north Wales.

Pannonians – Members of a powerful Balkan tribe which lived in what is now Hungary. Provided auxiliary units for the Roman Empire in return for relief from tribute and taxes.

Phalera (pl. Phalerae) – Awards won in battle worn on a legionary's chest harness.

Pilum (pl. Pila) – Heavy spear carried by a Roman legionary.

Praefectus Castrorum – Literally camp prefect, the third most senior officer in a Roman legion, often a soldier who had risen through the ranks.

Praetorian Guard – Powerful military force stationed in Rome. Accompanied the Emperor on campaign, but could be of dubious loyalty and were responsible for the overthrow of several Roman rulers.

Prefect – Auxiliary cavalry commander.

Primus Pilus – 'First File'. The senior centurion of a legion.

Princeps – Chief man of the state, an unofficial title conferred upon the Emperor.

Principia – Legionary headquarters building.

Proconsul – Governor of a Roman province, such as Britannia or Syria, and of consular rank.

Procurator – Civilian administrator subordinate to a governor.

Quaestor – Civilian administrator in charge of finance.

Salve – Latin word for welcome.

Samhain – Ancient Celtic festival held at the end of October to mark the end of the harvest season and the onset of winter.

Scutum (pl. Scuta) – The big, richly decorated curved shield carried by a legionary.

Selgovae – Celtic tribe who occupied the western Borders during the 1st century AD. The Eildon Hills may have been their spiritual capital and gathering place.

Senator – Patrician member of the Senate, the key political institution which administered the Roman Empire. Had to meet strict financial and property rules and be at least thirty years of age.

Sestertius (pl. Sestertii) – Roman brass coin worth a quarter of a **denarius**.

Sicarii – violent Judaean sect related to the Zealots, who opposed Roman rule.

Signifer – Standard-bearer who carried the emblem of a cohort or century.

Spatha – Sword wielded by Roman cavalry. Longer and heavier than the **gladius**.

Testudo – Literally 'tortoise'. A unit of soldiers with shields interlocked for protection.

Thuaidh river – The River Tweed.

Tribune – One of six senior officers acting as aides to a legate. Often, but not always, on short commissions of six months upwards.

Tribunus laticlavius – Literally 'broad stripe tribune'. The most senior of a legion's military tribunes.

Tuessis river – The River Tay.

Valetudinarium – a hospital, in this case a Roman military hospital.

Venicones – Celtic tribe who inhabited the lands between the Forth and the Tay in Scotland during the 1st century AD.

Vexillatio – A detachment of a legion used as a temporary task force on independent duty.

Victimarius – Servant who delivers and attends to the victim of a sacrifice.

Victory – Roman goddess equivalent to the Greek Nike.

Votadini – Celtic tribe who occupied what is now East Lothian and the eastern Borders and are believed to have made an accommodation with the advancing Romans in the 1st century AD.

Acknowledgements

Once again I'm indebted to my editor, Simon Taylor, and the production team at Transworld, with a special mention for my wonderful copy-editor Nancy Webber, for helping make this book what it is, and my agent, Stan, of the North Literary Agency, for his constant support and encouragement. Even after fifteen books and ten years of ups and downs, I wouldn't be a writer without the support of my wife Alison and that of my children, Kara, Nikki and Gregor, for which I will be for ever grateful. The advice of Dr Murray Cook, Stirling Council's archaeologist, gave me a unique insight into ancient life in the area around Bennachie, which he has dug so extensively and with so much success. Amongst the numerous books that have helped me create an image of the life and times of Roman soldiers in Britain and the native Celts who opposed, and, in the occasional case, abetted them, I should single out Peter Salway's *A History of Roman Britain*; *An Imperial Possession: Britain in the Roman Empire* by David Mattingly; *Before Scotland* by Alistair Moffat; *Roman Scotland* by David Breeze; *The Last Frontier: The Roman Invasions of Scotland* by Antony Kamm; also, although the fort probably wasn't built until after the events depicted in *Hammer of Rome*, a special mention for *Garrison Life at Vindolanda: A Band of Brothers* by Anthony Birley, which provides an unrivalled glimpse into the minds of the men who garrisoned Roman Britain. As on previous occasions, *Roman Military Equipment* by M. C. Bishop and J. C. N. Coulston was invaluable for recreating an authentic Roman military, along with *Roman Battle Tactics* by Ross Cowan and *Exploring the World of the Celts* by Simon James; and Miranda J. Green's *The Druids* performed a similar function for my depiction of the rites and religious traditions of the native inhabitants.

ABOUT THE AUTHOR

A journalist by profession, **Douglas Jackson** transformed a lifelong fascination for Rome and the Romans into his first two highly praised novels, *Caligula* and *Claudius*. His third novel, *Hero of Rome*, introduced readers to a new series hero, Gaius Valerius Verrens. Eight more novels recounting the adventures of this determined and dedicated servant of Rome have followed, earning critical acclaim and confirming Douglas as one of the UK's foremost historical novelists. An active member of the Historical Writers' Association and the Historical Novel Society, Douglas Jackson lives near Stirling in Scotland.